NOW
THE HELL
WILL START

NOW
THE HELL
WILL START

ONE SOLDIER'S FLIGHT FROM
THE GREATEST MANHUNT
OF WORLD WAR II

BRENDAN I. KOERNER

THE PENGUIN PRESS

New York

2008

THE PENGUIN PRESS
Published by the Penguin Group
Penguin Group (USA) Inc., 375 Hudson Street, New York, New York 10014, U.S.A. • Penguin Group
(Canada), 90 Eglinton Avenue East, Suite 700, Toronto, Ontario, Canada M4P 2Y3 (a division of Pearson
Penguin Canada Inc.) • Penguin Books Ltd, 80 Strand, London WC2R 0RL, England •
Penguin Ireland, 25 St. Stephen's Green, Dublin 2, Ireland (a division of Penguin Books Ltd) •
Penguin Books Australia Ltd, 250 Camberwell Road, Camberwell, Victoria 3124, Australia (a division of
Pearson Australia Group Pty Ltd) • Penguin Books India Pvt Ltd, 11 Community Centre,
Panchsheel Park, New Delhi – 110 017, India • Penguin Group (NZ), 67 Apollo Drive, Rosedale,
North Shore 0632, New Zealand (a division of Pearson New Zealand Ltd) • Penguin Books
(South Africa) (Pty) Ltd, 24 Sturdee Avenue, Rosebank, Johannesburg 2196, South Africa

Penguin Books Ltd, Registered Offices: 80 Strand, London WC2R 0RL, England

First published in 2008 by The Penguin Press,
a member of Penguin Group (USA) Inc.

Photograph credits
Pages vii, 21, 60, 331: Private collection of Edna Wilson
27, 260, 274, 295, 299: Private collection of Kathryn Cullum Lee
93, 105, 111, 121, 269: U.S. Army Military History Institute
168: Pitt Rivers Museum, University of Oxford (PRM 1998.221.47.2)
180: Pitt Rivers Museum, University of Oxford (PRM 1998.327.3.447)
323: Rafael DeSoto, courtesy of Rafael DeSoto, Jr.

LIBRARY OF CONGRESS CATALOGING IN PUBLICATION DATA
Koerner, Brendan I.
Now the hell will start : one soldier's flight from the greatest manhunt of
World War II / Brendan I. Koerner.
p. cm.
Includes bibliographical references and index.
ISBN 978-1-59420-173-8
1. Perry, Herman, 1922– 2. World War, 1939–1945—African Americans—Biography.   3. United States.
Army—African Americans—Biography.   4. African American soldiers—Biography.   5. Stilwell Road
(Burma and India)   6. Military deserters—United States—Biography.   7. Escapes—Burma—History—
20th century.   I. Title.
D810.N4P4756 2008
940.54'8—dc22
2007043078

Printed in the United States of America

1   3   5   7   9   10   8   6   4   2

DESIGNED BY NICOLE LAROCHE

Who was the slum-dweller now, and who looked down from commanding heights? There is nothing like a War for the reinvention of lives . . .

—SALMAN RUSHDIE, *Midnight's Children*

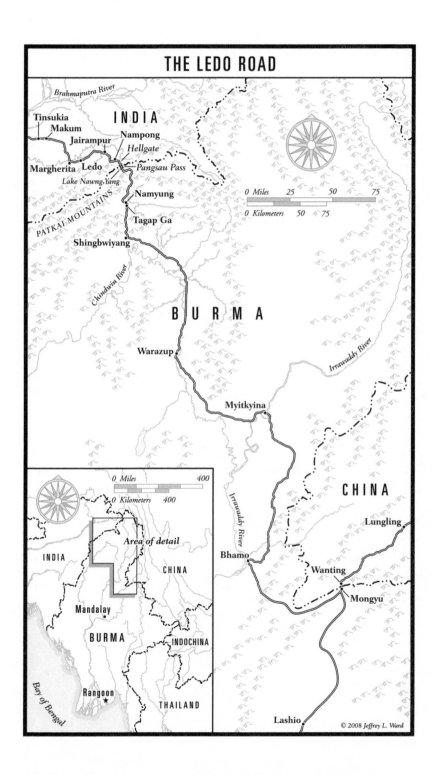

THE LEDO ROAD

Brahmaputra River

INDIA

Tinsukia
Makum
Jairampur
Nampong
Hellgate
Margherita
Ledo
Pangsau Pass
Lake Nawng Yang

Namyung

PATKAI MOUNTAINS

Tagap Ga

Chindwin River

Shingbwiyang

BURMA

0 Miles   25   50   75

0 Kilometers   50   75

Warazup

Irrawaddy River

Myitkyina

Irrawaddy River

0 Miles   400

0 Kilometers   400

Area of detail

INDIA

CHINA

CHINA

Lungling

Bhamo

Wanting

Mandalay

Mongyu

BURMA

INDOCHINA

Bay of Bengal

Rangoon ★

THAILAND

Lashio

© 2008 Jeffrey L. Ward

ONE

It is best to use discretion when confronting an emotionally shattered man, especially if he's holding a semiautomatic rifle.

Lieutenant Harold Cady should have heeded that common-sense advice on the morning of March 5, 1944. But several fellow soldiers were watching as he drew near Private Herman Perry, a sobbing, trembling GI armed with a .30-caliber M1. Cady couldn't have the spectators thinking he was soft, or his hard-ass reputation would be ruined. He'd show them he could quell this bad egg Perry, loaded rifle be damned.

Perry was walking toward the muddy roadside, a few dozen yards from Cady's parked jeep. He glanced over his shoulder and spied the onrushing lieutenant. "Get back!" Perry yelled. "Get back!"

Cady had left his pistol at the battalion's camp, near the Burmese village of Tagap Ga. But he didn't appear fazed by his lack of firepower: he advanced to within four feet of the quivering Perry.

Perry spun and faced his pursuer. He nervously pressed the M1's stock against his right hip and trained the muzzle on Cady's chest. Tears spilled down his gaunt, dark cheeks.

"Lieutenant, don't come up on me," Perry sputtered.

Cady froze. The dank and toxic Burmese jungle, its chaotic flora tinted a hallucinogenic green, towered over the two Americans. To the west loomed the Patkais, the mountain range that lines the northern border between India and Burma. Their thickly forested slopes, teeming with monkeys, tigers, and ornately tattooed headhunters, peeked through wisps of haze.

Courage recouped after a moment's pause, Cady now crept forward. Perry repeated his six-word warning, this time in a frantic shriek: "Lieutenant, don't come up on me!"

Cady took another step. He crouched low, like a wrestler set to grapple, then placed his outstretched arms on either side of the M1's barrel, as if preparing to clap his hands around the rifle and wrest it away. It was a risky move, but Cady couldn't imagine this kid actually being dumb enough to shoot. That would be straight-up suicide: the Army wasn't shy about using the noose, particularly on black GIs like Perry. The slangy repeated warnings, the rifle pointed at his heart? Cady figured it was all part of a childish tantrum, and that this wayward Negro just needed a little correction.

But Perry was far too broken to care. He'd been working sixteen-hour shifts crushing rocks along the Ledo Road, the rugged Army highway on which he and Cady now stood. His limbs rife with leeches, his bowels tattered by disease, Perry had come to loathe not just the jungle's hardships, but also the officers who treated him like chattel. He'd found solace in furtive puffs of opium and ganja, but the narcotic veil was always too fleeting. Stress and rage had slowly corroded Perry's will.

Now Cady wanted to haul him off to jail. Perry knew the next stop after that: the Ledo Stockade, an Army prison known for its brutality. Perry had served time there once before, enduring three grim months of taunts, parasites, and broiling confinement in "the

Box." He'd sworn that he'd sooner die and go to hell than spend another day behind barbed wire.

Hell or the stockade? That terrible choice, rather than a vision of the gallows, was foremost in Herman Perry's addled mind on the morning of March 5, 1944. Soon enough he'd visit both those dreaded places. But he'd also discover paradise.

The 465-mile Ledo Road—or at least what's left of it—stretches from the Indian province of Assam to the Chinese border, with much of the route swooping through Burma's northern plains. In the darkest days of World War II, when Japan seemed poised to conquer all of Asia, the road was devised to keep wobbly China flush with supplies. Instead it became a mammoth relic of twentieth-century hubris—a mud-caked Ozymandias jutting from the Indo-Burmese wilderness.

The jungle began reclaiming the Ledo Road as soon as the war ended. The highway's thin gravel layer quickly sluiced away in the drenching monsoon rains, as did many of the bridges that spanned the route's abundant streams. In the fall of 1946, a reporter named David Richardson, who'd covered the Allied military campaign in northern Burma, returned to check on the road's condition. He was stunned by the swiftness of the jungle's reconquest:

> The jungle, like a selfish woman, was stretching its green fingers out
> to take back The Road that had once been part of it. Creepers and
> weeds were already ankle-high across sections of the highway. In
> other places, the vegetation came drooping down from overhead.
> Where The Road had been graded, the rains had washed so much
> of the earth away that there were large bites in The Road, looking
> as if they had been made by some giant dinosaur. Erosion had set

in, deeply rutting miles of the highway, splitting it open like an earthquake.

Herman Perry toiled along the road's first eighty miles, which today wind through some of the world's dodgiest territory. The route starts just outside the town of Ledo, located in the crook of India to the east of Bangladesh. Once a hub of the American war effort, Ledo is now a dismal collection of tin-roofed shacks abutting an ancient rail station. The road's "Mile Zero" is marked with a commemorative billboard, erected by an Indian politician who yearns for greater trade with Burma (rechristened Myanmar by its sinister junta). REJUVENATE OUR LIFE LINE, the faded sign proclaims, REVITALIZE OUR RELATION-SHIP. Narrow train tracks, over which thousands of American GIs once traveled, lie deserted behind the billboard, overgrown with de-cades' worth of brush. Frayed ropes tether listless, emaciated cows to the rail joints.

The first several miles of road are paved with modern asphalt, and frequented by trucks piled high with tea leaves or lumps of coal. At Jagun, the road veers right at a red-domed temple adorned with swastikas, the classic Hindu symbol co-opted by the Nazis. The town is patrolled by mysterious men in pleather jackets, AK-47s slung over their shoulders, who glower at the vegetable peddlers squatting in the dust. Trucks and buses are often forced to stop here due to *bandhs*, road blockades orchestrated by drunken, rock-throwing teenagers.

The Patkais come into view at the town of Jairampur. Few if any Westerners make it this far—a hard-to-obtain permit is required to visit the Indian province of Arunachal Pradesh (formerly the North-East Frontier Agency), of which Jairampur is one of the remotest gateways. A few yards past the Indian Army checkpoint is a clue as to why access to Arunachal is so tightly controlled: a sign decorated with a skull-and-crossbones graphic, accompanied by alarming, all-caps text:

IT'S TIME TO ACCEPT THE REALITY!!!

MILITANTS ARE FIGHTING FOR A WORTHLESS
CAUSE. THE AVERAGE LIFE OF A MILITANT IS
THREE TO FOUR YEARS. WHY SHORTEN
YOUR LIFE FOR A LOST CAUSE?

The road soon curves upward, its surface deteriorating throughout the climb; the asphalt turns worn, then cracked, then finally to dirt. Hovels built of woven bamboo mats alternate with hillside tea gardens, their bushes studding the slopes like emerald-colored sheep. Leathery, hunched-over women pick the tea leaves by hand, tossing them in papoose-like baskets strapped to their heads.

Above the village of Nampong, a wooden archway marks the formal entrance to the Patkais. FRIENDS OF THE HILL PEOPLE is posted on its crossbeam, a message from the Indian Army to the impoverished, ethnically distinct "tribals" who inhabit the jungle. The locals chuckle at this slogan, for the military and the tribals are anything but close.

Beyond the Nampong archway, the road disintegrates into reddish goop. Reed-thin men in dhotis crouch along the roadside, breaking rocks with chisels or eating fistfuls of yellow-stained rice. A mile or two on, any vehicle short of a bulldozer can no longer navigate the sludge; anyone wishing to proceed farther must do so on foot.

The road's bogginess makes for a grueling hike. Each step emits a scatological squish as boots sink into rivulets of mud. Walls of trees and vines, sprouting atop cliffs created by American dynamite, keep the path cast in shadows. The only travelers here are barefoot tribals, lugging sacks of food or cloth; bored, greasy-haired soldiers hassle them for bribes.

Finally, the border: a crooked limestone plaque with one arrow pointing toward India, the other to Burma. The terrain morphs as the road snakes down the Patkais' eastern slopes: the mud dissipates, replaced by boulders embedded in scarlet clay. Small settlements, reeking of pig dung, chili paste, and cheap cigarettes, crop up along the road's periphery. Peering down at the plains below, one can glimpse the placid beauty of Lake Nawng Yang; the Americans called it the Lake of No Return, on account of all the crashed planes concealed in its depths. Skeletons of U.S. Army trucks occasionally protrude from the chest-high elephant grass, headlamps dangling free like popped eyeballs.

Though the road beyond the lake seems drivable, working vehicles are rarely seen. The Burmese instead travel on foot: schoolchildren in billowing *longyis*, wispy women with cheeks painted a creamy white, paranoid military thugs in high-cuffed pants and knockoff Members Only jackets. It is not only poverty that keeps the motor traffic to a minimum, but also the road's dilapidation; the rocks are murder on tires, and many streams are only passable via bamboo ferries. It is hard to believe this hardscrabble trail was once considered an engineering triumph for the ages.

The Ledo Road's decrepit fate would have come as no surprise to its American builders, who knew firsthand the jungle's malice. They suffered heavy casualties due to accidents, disease, snipers, booby traps, and ravenous animals, all for the sake of a road that ultimately contributed precious little to the Allied cause. The GIs grimly dubbed it the Man-a-Mile Road, though based on the official death toll, a more accurate nickname would have been the Two-Man-a-Mile Road. The British, meanwhile, used the moniker White Elephant

pervasiveness of African Americans along the road was no
t. Influenced by the pseudoscience of the day, the U.S. Army
d blacks innately dim and gutless, and plotted to keep them
e front lines. "The average Negro is naturally cowardly," one
colonel wrote when asked if blacks were fit for combat. "Every
try combat soldier should possess sufficient mentality, initia-
, and individual courage; all of these are, generally speaking, lack-
in the Negro."

Home-front politics compelled the Army to form a few black
ombat units, but the vast majority of African American draftees
vere shunted into menial jobs: construction, cooking, trucking,
laundering. The Army viewed the Ledo Road as an opportunity to
create a distant wartime ghetto, where thousands of black conscripts
could be quietly dumped and used as manual laborers.

As a bastion of Jim Crowism, the Army required black GIs to be
commanded by white officers, an arrangement that inevitably led to
strife. Generations of segregation had ensured that men of differing
skin color regarded one another as virtually alien species. As a result,
racial animosities flared in the stateside training camps, where blacks
and whites were forced to cross paths. Those divisions only deepened in the Indo-Burmese jungle, exacerbated by the traumas of
daily life: rotting clothes, voracious insects, unpalatable food, excruciating loneliness. Many black troops came to despise their white
superiors as vicious dolts; many whites, in turn, reviled their black
charges as lazy or inept.

The acrimony often caused soldiers to tumble into madness and
despair. Among the most seriously afflicted was Herman Perry, considered an irredeemable "fuckup" by his commanders. Perry shirked
duties, back-talked, and smoked ganja and opium whenever he
could; he seemed destined to spend the war in the Ledo Stockade
alongside other GIs who couldn't toe the Army line. Instead he be-

Road, after a breed of sacred pachy⌐
expensive to feed and care for.

The American leadership could hav
by owning up to reality. The lethality of
ness, with its lashing monsoons and ender.
no secret. And everyone could see that Chin
shek, was an extortionate rogue, keen on sque⌐
rather than battling the Axis. The journalist Eri
ered the war in Asia for CBS Radio, offered tl
Chiang's brutal, kleptocratic regime:

> I had some familiarity with dictatorships which used
> apparatus of propaganda, censorship, and secret-police te⌐
> what they were really doing; but this was the first one I had⌐
> used the machinery to hide the fact that they were really doin⌐
> ing. Worse: they had no *intention* of doing anything. They wer⌐
> ply sitting out the war, making a gesture here and there for
> benefit of their allies. No one was fooled.

Yet the Americans still built the road for Chiang, squanderi⌐
blood and treasure on a duplicitous tyrant. The military brass, af⌐
flicted by egoism, myopia, or indifference, never could bring themselves to alter plans. The men in the field paid the price.

The bulk of those star-crossed soldiers were, like Perry, African
American. Of the roughly fifteen thousand American troops assigned
to build the Ledo Road, at least two-thirds or more were black—the
highest concentration of African American troops in all of World
War II. They were so prevalent in the Patkais, piloting bulldozers
and dynamiting hilltops, that some tribals claim they didn't realize
until years later that white Americans existed, too.

The
accide⌐
deem⌐
off tl
Arm
infa
tiv⌐
in

came a folk hero to comrades and natives alike, lionized for his near-magical ability to dodge bullets, tigers, and the military police as he trekked through the jungles of Burma and Assam. Again and again, Perry's exotic journey appeared on the verge of coming to an ignoble end; again and again, he'd slip behind the tree line, salve his wounds with a patch of moss, and vanish back into the tribal realms, surviving to run another day.

Perry found more than refuge in the Indo-Burmese wilds. Like an opium-scented version of Mr. Kurtz, the deranged ivory trader in Joseph Conrad's *Heart of Darkness*, Perry was bewitched by jungle society. He charmed his way into the hearts of the Nagas, a fearsome, head-hunting people who'd inhabited the Patkais for untold centuries. By the summer of 1944, Perry had started anew in an isolated Naga village—not as a guest, but as honored royalty. Like several madcap Brits before him, Perry reveled in the primitive joys of Naga culture: the communal spirit, the simple rituals of love and celebration, the loose sexual mores. To a young man accustomed to a cramped, segregated corner of Washington, D.C., and before that to the deprivations of the Jim Crow South, the Nagas' protohippie lifestyle must have seemed a splendid, tranquil dream.

As Perry's legend flourished, his Army superiors grew to respect his genius for survival. A lesser man, they realized, wouldn't have lasted a week in the hostile Patkais. In their more gracious moments, some officers called Perry by his well-known nickname: the Jungle King. Others, however, couldn't let go of the fear and hatred they'd been raised on: they referred to Perry as a hunted rodent, rather than a man.

For one military policeman in particular, a stoic Texan named Earl Owen Cullum, Perry's saga would become the yarn he'd tell a thousand times, the defining event of his long, accomplished life. Wracked by insomnia in his final years, Cullum would creep downstairs to record memories of his days traversing the Brahmaputra Plains, hot on Perry's trail. And he would contemplate the role he'd played in sealing Perry's fate.

But it is Perry, not his adversaries, at the soul of this tale. And his story begins along a highway worlds apart from the one that slashes through the Indo-Burmese jungle: a thoroughfare known to Tar Heels as Morgan Mill Road.

TWO

There was a clear pecking order among the three Perry boys, at least in terms of pugilistic talent. Aaron was the prodigy, blessed with the lithe body and agile feet of a classic welterweight mauler. Nicknamed both the Anvil and Bad News, Aaron's trademark punch was a crushing right jab. "A body of bronze with a mule-kick in his gloves," gushed *The Washington Post*'s Walter Haight, after watching the youngest Perry brother flatten a palooka from New York. "One of the best fistic prospects in District boxing history."

Roscoe's gifts paled in comparison, though he still scratched out a brief professional career. The eldest of the trio, Roscoe was a bear to lay on the canvas, and might have been a real contender if not for his lumbering speed. His big shot came in 1942 at Griffith Stadium, home to baseball's Washington Senators, against a diminutive brawler named Lew Hanbury; a few months prior to the bout, Hanbury had literally pummeled an opponent to death. Roscoe showed tons of heart, taking the killer the distance, but he ultimately lost on points. The defeat spoiled Roscoe's hopes for boxing stardom, though he'd keep fighting for small purses here and there.

Last on the totem pole was Herman, the middle brother. He was a smidgen too stocky to jackrabbit around a ring, and his disproportionately large feet made him slightly awkward, like an adolescent adjusting to a growth spurt. Aside from his physical shortcomings, Herman was also skittish about absorbing punishment; he worried that a right hook or an uppercut might damage his pretty face. So although he'd sometimes fool around at Washington's Twelfth Street YMCA, Herman preferred pastimes of a gentler nature.

Chief among those was the wooing of young ladies. The proverbial lover, not a fighter, Herman enjoyed strolling about D.C.'s stately parks arm in arm with his sweetheart of the moment. Girls found it difficult to resist Herman's charming patter, as well as his soulful eyes and slender cheekbones. His good looks are evident in a 1941 photograph, in which he gazes serenely at the lens, the faintest of smiles curling on his lips—an oddly alluring pose for a mug shot.

Herman claimed to be twenty-two years old when that photo was taken, but he was actually still a teen. According to the Perrys' family Bible, Herman was born on May 16, 1922, on the rural outskirts of Monroe, North Carolina. His mother, Flonnie Perry, was eighteen and unwed; his father, a man by the name of Fraudus Allsbrooks, vanished soon after the birth. Flonnie already had one son, two-year-old Roscoe, by a boyfriend named Otis Mac. She'd soon bear Mac two more children—Edna in 1924, then Aaron in 1926—but they'd never tie the knot.

Though their fathers were largely absent, the Perry children never lacked for love or attention. The whole family lived with Flonnie's parents, Edward and Henrietta, in a shack off Morgan Mill Road, which connects Monroe to South Carolina's Lancaster County, where the Perrys had once resided. Rounding out the packed household were Flonnie's two younger siblings, Flossie and Vander.

Everyone picked cotton alongside the aging Edward, a grueling profession that paid next to nothing: the average daily wage for a North Carolina farmhand was a measly nine cents.* The Perrys earned extra cash by doing laundry for well-off folks, but the family still struggled: their roadside hovel lacked electricity, to say nothing of indoor plumbing.

Shortly after Aaron was born, Flonnie decided she'd had enough of Morgan Mill Road and its dead-end prospects. She found herself a husband named John Henry Johnson and moved north with him to Durham, where the textile mills and tobacco factories were hiring. Her four out-of-wedlock kids, meanwhile, remained in Monroe. Henrietta took charge of their upbringing.

Growing up along Morgan Mill Road was not without its small joys. On Saturdays, everyone donned their sharpest clothes and rode wagons into Monroe's center, as part of a countrified see-and-be-seen ritual. Whites and blacks mingled freely at these informal weekly pageants, united in their fondness for scoping out potential mates and admiring each other's finery.

But this was still the Jim Crow South. The routine indignities of segregation were an inescapable part of Tar Heel life, as was the Ku Klux Klan and its vitriolic rallies. Monroe was run by an old-school sheriff named Jesse Alexander Helms, whose son would later become the five-term Republican senator known for opposing Martin Luther King Jr. Day and waxing nostalgic about the days of "Whites Only" drinking fountains. The archetypal southern lawman, Big Jesse reveled in humiliating Monroe's black citizens. Civil rights pioneer Robert F. Williams, born and raised in Monroe, was forever changed after witnessing one of the sheriff's rampages in 1936. On the town's Main Street, Williams saw Big Jesse slug a young black woman accused of a petty crime; Helms then "dragged her off to the

---

*For comparison's sake, an unskilled highway laborer made twenty cents an hour, though the *Charlotte News & Observer* denounced even that wage as well below the level of subsistence.

nearby jailhouse, her dress up over her head, the same way that a caveman would club and drag his sexual prey." Williams never forgot the sound of the woman's flesh tearing on the pavement as Big Jesse yanked her along.

Roscoe, Herman, Edna, and Aaron all attended the segregated Winchester Avenue School, the quality of which was hampered by government policy: black teachers in North Carolina earned 44 percent less than their white counterparts, and the state spent 73 percent less per black student than per white. But the illiterate Henrietta insisted that her grandkids learn the three R's. Getting an education, even one marred by fraying textbooks and underpaid teachers, seemed the children's only chance of avoiding the fields.

Even before the Great Depression, North Carolina's agriculture industry had been spiraling downward: cotton prices tumbled 80 percent during the 1920s, and abusive farming methods ravaged the state's soil. But the Depression administered the coup de grâce: by 1931, Tar Heel farmers were actually losing money on each pound of cotton they produced.

Hunger soon followed. Emaciated men foraged for greens and blackberries, their faces wan with malnutrition; a reporter bemoaned the "consistently hollow, blotched eyes" he encountered among the state's starving farmers. Durham tried distributing free flour to the needy, but the giveaway went awry; the throng lined up at the city market's "Negro entrance" ended up stampeding through plate-glass windows. To alleviate the food shortage, state officials advised black families to raise their own crops and livestock. They didn't seem to realize that this was a legal impossibility for many such families, who didn't own the land on which they lived. White landlords often denied their black tenants permission to plant simple gardens, let alone keep cows or goats.

Yet for all its ghastliness, the Depression helped create a promised land for poor African Americans from the Carolinas and elsewhere in the South: Washington, D.C. The New Deal, President Franklin D. Roosevelt's economic salvage plan, established dozens of federal entities, from the Farm Security Administration to the Civilian Conservation Corps, each of which required hundreds or thousands of staffers. Job seekers flocked to Washington, eager to hop on Uncle Sam's payroll—filling out bureaucratic forms in triplicate, however dull, still beat the sorry prospects elsewhere. By the end of the 1930s, over two hundred thousand federal employees would be living and working in the District of Columbia, adding nearly 50 percent to the city's population in less than a decade. The overcrowding got so bad that in 1942, forty thousand of those workers were ordered out of the capital; a large number of them were reassigned to office buildings in New York, a city that actually seemed spacious by comparison.

Virtually all government jobs, however, were reserved for whites. Despite his reputation as a model progressive, burnished by his wife Eleanor's outspoken support for civil rights, President Roosevelt was rather meek when it came to confronting segregation. Afraid to alienate the white southern Democrats who formed a vital part of his electoral coalition, Roosevelt never raised a public stink about federal hiring practices, which excluded blacks from all but a handful of symbolic posts. A lucky few African Americans found work running letters between government buildings, or mopping the floors of the Treasury Department. But for the most part, those in charge of handing out the New Deal's jobs deemed excess melanin an unpardonable shortcoming.

Blacks had to settle for the trickle-down effect: the influx of white, decently paid civil servants into Washington created thousands of unskilled service jobs. Busing tables or cleaning white folks' homes hardly qualified as plum assignments, but they were still less back-breaking and better paying than picking cotton in the Carolinas.

Flonnie was the first to head north. Things had turned sour for her in Durham: after bearing a fifth child, Henry, in 1931, she and her husband had separated. Flonnie and the toddler moved to Washington, where she found work as a domestic servant—a choicer gig than toiling in a Durham factory. Once settled in D.C., Flonnie got word down to her offspring: forget about Big Jesse's Monroe, come join the Great Migration.

HERMAN DROPPED OUT of junior high and bolted for the nation's capital in 1937 or 1938, along with Roscoe. This is likely the point at which he added a few years to his age, to make himself eligible for the sorts of jobs that a business owner might not give a fifteen-year-old. Herman was hardly alone in fudging his credentials or taking other drastic steps to land a job, as the competition for employment was fierce among black migrants to Washington. Young arrivals from the South were often so destitute that they'd take almost any paying gig, no matter the risk or status.

One revealing anecdote about the city's tight labor market involves Thurgood Marshall, the future Supreme Court justice. While attending law school, Marshall got a job clearing dining-car tables at Union Station. He was unusually tall for the era, at a shade over six feet, yet was issued a normal-size uniform; the pants' inseams barely passed his calves. When he asked his supervisor for a longer pair, the man refused. "It's more trouble to find a new pair of pants," he told Marshall, "than it is to find a new nigger."

But smooth-talking Herman beat the odds. He landed a meat-cutting job at a grocery store on Benning Road NE, close to the

National Arboretum and Gallaudet University. Roscoe, meanwhile, bused tables near Capitol Hill. The two boys helped out Flonnie and young Henry when they could.

Herman also tried attending the ninth grade at Dunbar High School. But he found the education no better than in Monroe: blacks-only Dunbar was woefully overcrowded and underfunded, as the District's Board of Education spent its budget building gleaming new facilities for white students. When he wasn't working, then, Herman took to hanging on the streets and engaging in juvenile malfeasance: smoking, loitering, bullying. These habits brought him to the attention of truant officers, who were always keen to nab potential ruffians. On more than one occasion, they briefly detained Herman at a boys' reformatory near the Maryland border.

After flitting among dingy boardinghouses upon first arriving in Washington, Herman eventually found suitable accommodations on Florida Avenue NW, in a small redbrick row house around the corner from Meridian Hill Park. Despite the park's elegant cascade fountain and sprawling lawn, the neighborhood was crowded and dirty, teeming with migrant families who huddled into windowless back-alley dwellings originally built for horses. Wooden barrels served as toilets and communal taps spurted warm, parasite-ridden water. Disease was endemic: the sound of tubercular residents hacking up clumps of blood permeated the urban night.

As is often the case in a boomtown, the demand for these decrepit dwellings was absurdly high. A two-room abode without even a scrap of ventilation went for $12.50 per month, half a busboy's monthly wage. Aghast that such slums could exist a stone's throw from the White House, Eleanor Roosevelt helped push though a 1934 law banning alley residences. But the prohibition's enforcement was halfhearted at best; the police knew that poor blacks had nowhere else to go. Some families pulled up stakes and built themselves shanties on D.C.'s eastern edge, but there was always a newly arrived family from the Carolinas or southern Virginia willing to chance the alleys.

The housing crunch was partly engineered by a ruling class as virulently racist as Big Jesse and his redneck crew. Its privileged members often expressed their pro-segregation views before the Senate District Committee, the congressional body that ran Washington in the days before home rule. Alfred Calvert, head of the Lincoln Park Citizens' Association, offered such testimony in June 1941, at a committee hearing on housing policy. The blacks who tried to defy convention and move into white neighborhoods, Calvert claimed, only wanted to see their names in the newspapers. He went on to blame these alleged attention-seekers for decreasing property values, thereby punishing hardworking whites like himself. "Mixing of the races," Calvert declared, "is not wise or according to God's plan."*

Whites of Calvert's ilk concocted several effective methods of enforcing segregation, the most basic of which was a legal clause included in most home-buying contracts. The clause forbade the new owner from ever selling or renting to an African American; some of the more selective neighborhoods added Jews to the verboten list, too.

In those rare instances when legal ploys failed to keep the races apart, a few Washingtonians turned to terrorism. In 1940, when a black schoolteacher named Edna Holland moved into a home at 1324 Harvard Street NW, in a white enclave near Sixteenth Street, her neighbors tried to void the sale. When their legal challenge failed, someone placed a bomb in Holland's vestibule, obliterating her home's facade while she and her children slept. No arrests were ever

---

*The next speaker at the meeting, Geneva Valentine, began her testimony with a devastating rejoinder to Calvert's words: "My first reaction was to ask that [his] testimony be stricken from the record. Now I want it to stand as an indictment of people of his character."

made in the bombing, and the Federal Bureau of Investigation declined to pursue the case.

African Americans were thus forced to cluster around the neighborhood they called either Shaw or U Street, Washington's answer to New York's Harlem and home to the "Black Harvard," Howard University. Also known as "Colored Boulevard," U Street had been no-go territory for whites since the "Red Summer" of 1919, when race riots swept across the country. Washington's riot was sparked by bogus rumors of a "Negro fiend" raping white women. A mob of unemployed whites, many of them veterans of World War I, gathered to seek revenge, rampaging through D.C. for two straight nights. After several African Americans had been lynched or severely beaten, the black residents of Shaw decided to make a stand. They built barricades on U Street and placed riflemen atop the Howard Theatre. White streetcar passengers were thrashed to bloody pulps, and white pedestrians were picked off by sniper fire.

Since that violent clash, U Street and its environs had developed into a mecca of black culture, not just for Washington, but for the entire United States. It was where a young Duke Ellington jerked sodas as a teenager and honed his piano skills at Jack's Place and the Poodledog Cabaret; where the Tommy Myles Orchestra kept things hopping at the Lincoln Colonnade; where a young Langston Hughes worked as a gofer at the *Journal of Negro History*; and where black intellectuals gathered in storefronts to debate the issues of the day.

Yet in a bitter racist twist, the upper echelons of Washington's black culture were largely off-limits to migrants like the Perrys. The capital's longtime African American residents, many of whom could trace their D.C. roots to the 1860s or earlier, disdained the new arrivals as filthy and uncouth—an attitude reminiscent of a big-city sophisticate embarrassed by his country cousin. The black aristocracy was made up of professionals who catered to their fellow African Americans, as well as service employees of a higher caste: not busboys in grubby cafeterias, but men like Ellington's father, James, who served canapés and rye whiskey at White House cocktail parties. These blacks were the ones who danced at the Colonnade in stiff, high-collared suits, attended concerts at the Washington Conservatory of Music, and worshipped in the front pews of Shaw's most regal churches. The women spent their days planning formal teas and bridge games as members of myriad genteel clubs: the Merry Maids Art Club, the Personality Girls Club, the Lucky Twelve Social Club, the Tillie Club. They looked forward to seeing their daughters' coming-out balls highlighted in the society pages of *The Washington Tribune*, and to their sons' acceptance into the right fraternity at Howard—preferably one of the mannerly brotherhoods that restricted membership to students with skin lighter than a brown paper bag.

Migrants such as Herman Perry, barred from Washington's black elite, filled their fleeting leisure time with more proletarian pursuits. Gambling parlors concealed in row-house basements were one of the strongest draws. Their games of chance were often marred by violence: drunken quarrels over dice had a way of escalating into stabbings. But the parlors were seldom raided, as the cops were busy with more pressing matters: by the mid-1930s, Washington's murder rate had risen to two-and-a-half times that of New York.

The other worrying pastime was drugs, particularly the fifty-cent marijuana cigarettes known on the street as "muggles." New York gangsters used Washington as a key transshipment point, a gateway to markets as far afield as Georgia and Florida. The Treasury Department's Narcotics Bureau was responsible for spearheading investigations into the capital's drugs trade, and scored the occasional success. The most celebrated of these was the Twelfth Street raid of 1936, in which Treasury agents shut down an apartment described as "the worst den of vice in the city," where addicts smoked opium and reefer among silken drapes and tapestries.*

Herman's preferred vice was neither gambling nor drugs, but girls. He fancied himself a budding playboy, perhaps even an aspiring member of Washington's black aristocracy. To that end, he developed an affinity for pinstriped, single-breasted suits and classical music. Ladies swooned over Herman's debonair persona, not to mention his boyishly handsome face.

Alma Talbot, Herman Perry's girlfriend.

It didn't take long for Herman's Don Juanism to get him in trouble. He knocked up a girl named Elizabeth Hall, who bore him a daughter, Portia. In keeping with the familial example set by Flonnie, Herman didn't marry Hall. He moved on instead to a new lover, a skinny-limbed teen named Alma Talbot, with whom he was smitten. The two quickly became inseparable, picnicking and promenading in Meridian Hill Park.

---

*Days before the raid, a numbers runner named Gorman Wright had been shot to death on the premises, and his sidekick, "Toots," gravely wounded.

Roscoe, meanwhile, was channeling his postadolescent energy into a more lucrative endeavor: boxing. Like so many young African American men in Washington, Roscoe donned the gloves at the blacks-only Twelfth Street Y. The gym brimmed with fighters who dreamed of headlining the two-thousand-seat Turner's Arena at Fourteenth and W streets NW—or, better yet, the larger Uline Ice Arena further downtown. A boxer could earn over $1,000 for appearing on the main card at Uline's, enough dough for almost any black man to forgive the fact that the arena barred African Americans from attending its ice-skating exhibitions and hockey games.*

Roscoe briefly lived the dream. He won his professional debut in 1941, knocking out a chump named Tommy Hoover in the first round. It was all downhill from there, but at least Roscoe earned a little cash while getting his brains scrambled.

Aaron, who moved up to Washington in 1940, would earn far more. Sinewy and somewhat cocky, Aaron enrolled at the Garnet-Patterson School, a junior high at Tenth and U streets NW. But it became obvious early on that his future lay in the ring, not the classroom. Flonnie signed him up for after-school boxing at the Police Boys Club No. 2, where Aaron handily beat all comers with his graceful, destructive jab. He made D.C.'s American Amateur Union (AAU) team and was sent to a national tournament in Boston, where he was knocked out in the first round by a more experienced boy from Tennessee. But anyone with an iota of boxing sense could see that, with the right guidance, Aaron was destined for the sport's national stage. Indeed, he'd soon inspire a bidding war among some monied Washington bigwigs, as boxing promoters, shady restaurateurs, and outright charlatans all vied to own a piece of Aaron's greatness.

---

*The Uline Ice Arena would later become the site of the Beatles' first American concert, on February 11, 1964.

The close-knit Perrys knew that Aaron would spread the wealth: once the money started rolling in, he'd surely take care of Flonnie, his siblings, and even his relatives down South. But for the moment, at least, Herman was content to watch his little brother slug through the amateur ranks. He'd sit ringside as Aaron trounced overmatched teen after overmatched teen, grinning ear to ear whenever the referee raised the Anvil's arm in triumph.

Herman had more to smile about than just Aaron's nascent career. Only a few years earlier, he'd been living in a shack in rural North Carolina, with few prospects beyond picking cotton. Now he had a steady job, a girlfriend he adored, and even an infant daughter. Washington, for all its squalor and caustic racism, had still turned out to be a promised land—just as Flonnie had foretold.

As LIFE WAS falling into place for Herman Perry, the situation across the Atlantic turned grave. The Nazis invaded France on May 10, 1940, and their grim-faced troops marched through Paris just thirty-six days later. Astonished by the blitzkrieg's might, Roosevelt and Congress finally accepted the idea of a peacetime draft, which they'd long resisted as politically untenable. The Burke-Wadsworth Act, also known as the Selective Training and Service Act of 1940, was brought before Congress just six days after the fall of France. The bill required all men between the ages of twenty-one and thirty-five to register with their local draft boards, and then serve for one year if selected by lottery.

The politicians knew that many voters feared a repeat of World War I, in which Americans had died for Europe's sake—or, in light of what had happened since, for no good reason at all. To assuage these isolationists, the new act clearly stipulated that draftees could only be stationed in the Western Hemisphere or in U.S. possessions, for the sole purpose of defending American territory. And the number of men training at any given time was capped at nine hundred thousand.

To the surprise of many journalists who predicted widespread draft evasion, young men registered in droves. On the first day that registration cards were accepted by Washington, D.C.'s Draft Board Area No. 13, police had to be called in to prevent a stampede of 8,581 aspiring soldiers. Tens of thousands of male Washingtonians complied with the act, among them Herman Perry, who delivered his draft questionnaire to Frank Norton, chairman of Local Board No. 10, on November 28, 1940.

Had Perry not fudged his age in order to work, he could have escaped registration—he was just eighteen when he received his questionnaire, though he'd been masquerading as a twenty-two-year-old. But Perry decided to see the lie through and visit the draft board. Perhaps he feared losing his job should his true age come to light: in a competitive labor market like Washington's, there were always a dozen unemployed youngsters from the Carolinas who would love to chop meat on Benning Road.

Perry was scheduled to take the draft board's physical examination on February 5, 1941. But for reasons that can only be guessed at, he failed to show for the appointment. He may have been busy at work and his boss wouldn't give him the afternoon off. Maybe he simply forgot the date. Or perhaps he'd been swayed by the black press, which was questioning the morality of fighting on behalf of a segregated country. Newspapers like the *Chicago Defender*, the Baltimore-based *Afro-American*, and *The Washington Tribune* had spent the past few years making unflattering comparisons between the United States and Nazi Germany, bitterly lampooning the two nations' embrace of racist ideologies. The black press also gleefully reported the musings of antiwar black intellectuals like Dr. Eric

Williams, a Howard political scientist who insisted that "the war in Europe means nothing to the Negro."

Black opponents of the draft were particularly incensed by the Army's policy of segregating its units. In January 1941, the *Defender* published an editorial lauding the Conscientious Objectors Against Jim-Crow, a Chicago organization that was encouraging black men to refuse military service. The newspaper heartily agreed with the group's main principle: that no African American should be compelled to serve "in an army that segregates him and his fellow black conscripts as though they were lepers." The *Defender's* editorial board pointed out that only blacks were singled out for such treatment: "This inexcusable Jim-Crowism is the more revolting when one realizes that it is practiced only against American Negroes. There are no separate units for American Chinese, Filipinos, Hungarians, Poles, Swedes, Italians, etc."

The editorial infuriated FBI director J. Edgar Hoover, who yearned to imprison the whole lot of black publishers as subversives. Federal agents would soon start harassing John Sengstacke, the *Defender's* publisher, and his journalistic allies, threatening them with arrest if they continued (in Hoover's estimation) to place black interests above those of the nation at large.

Whatever Perry's reasons for ditching his physical, the punishment was swift. On the morning of February 24, a military policeman named George Wilson showed up at Perry's door and placed him under arrest for violating the Selective Training and Service Act of 1940. It was not the first time that a Washington resident had been nicked for this offense, though actual prosecutions were still rare. Several black men, for example, had been arrested within hours of the draft's opening, for providing false addresses on their questionnaires. They were released after explaining that they'd been in the process of moving when the questionnaires were distributed.

The arrests were as much about lowering Washington's crime rate as they were about ensuring the draft's integrity. "Crime control, as regards both prevention and repression, should be improved by the Selective Service Act," declared Dr. James Nolan, director of the Washington Criminal Justice Association, as the draft kicked into high gear in late 1940. His hope, shared by the city's police force, was that petty draft offenses could be used as pretexts to round up thugs—or, as happened in practice, to jail young black men from Shaw.

Among the first to be so ensnared, Perry was hauled downtown to the Bank of Commerce and Savings Building, at Seventh and E streets NW. Wilson marched the dazed butcher upstairs to the office of Needham Coy Turnage, a crotchety federal magistrate. Turnage, who was also grand master of D.C.'s Masonic lodge, listened to Wilson swear out a complaint. The MP asked that Perry be charged with lying on his questionnaire in addition to missing the physical: as the grand jury would later assert in its indictment, "Herman Perry falsely, knowingly, willfully, unlawfully and feloniously did state that he had not been convicted of treason or felony, whereas in truth and in fact he had been convicted of a felony."

The nature of that felony is never mentioned in the case file, and there is no record of Perry ever having been detained on charges graver than juvenile delinquency; it is not unreasonable to believe that the felony charge was simply trumped up to make the case stronger. But Wilson's word was enough for Turnage, who ordered that Perry be "committed to the jail of Washington, D.C., there to remain until discharged by due process of law."

Perry was transported to Washington's dungeonlike jail. Before being cast into his cell, the clean-shaven Perry was propped against a wall and photographed. Perry's pupils are enormous in the black-and-white mug shot, and the camera's flash fills his eyes with starry twinkles. His bushy hair looks as if he'd been sporting a hat just

Mug shot of Herman Perry.

moments earlier, and he's wearing a stiff-collared white shirt. A broad, fleshy nose flares atop loosely pressed lips.

Nothing about Perry's expression hints at the depth of his misfortune: his bail had been set at $1,000, which might as well have been $1 billion considering his family's modest means. Given the languid pace of justice in Washington, Perry knew he'd be locked up for a long stretch, in a facility that made the boys' reformatory seem like a holiday retreat.

Perry would end up spending two months in Washington's fetid nineteenth-century jailhouse, amid killers and dope fiends. The second-rate attorney his family hired, Edward Berger, took his sweet time preparing a defense, a task made all the more difficult by the fact that his client had allegedly confessed to the magistrate. Perry finally entered a plea of "not guilty" on April 4, at which time the case was handed over to the U.S. Attorney's office. Twenty-four days later, for reasons never cited in the paperwork, the federal prosecutor assigned to the case of *United States v. Herman Perry* decided that pursuing the matter any further would be a waste of time. He entered a declaration of nolle prosequi—"we decline to prosecute."

Released forthwith, Perry tried to stay upbeat. Down two months wages plus legal fees, he returned to the meat counter and to his girlfriend, Alma. But he knew he'd have to show for his next Army physical, or he'd surely spend another, even longer spell in jail.

Even if he passed the physical and his draft lottery number came up, the optimistic Perry figured he'd pull through okay. Service was only for twelve months, after all, and the law required that he be stationed on friendly soil—maybe even close enough to Washington that he could keep things cooking with Alma, and catch a few of Aaron's bouts.

THREE

In its prime, the Imperial Japanese Army was a juggernaut for the ages, as savagely efficient as the Mongol hordes or Roman legions. Its troops first stunned the world in 1931 when they easily overran the frigid Chinese province of Manchuria. A *Time* reporter who witnessed the fall of Chinchow, a key Manchurian stronghold, couldn't help but admire the invaders' prowess: "It was fun to see the Chinese populace, yellow if ever a populace was, waving Japanese flags hastily home-made during the night to appease the Japanese conquerors, men who still fight for the word and substance of 'Glory.'"

The speedy capture of Manchuria was just a prelude. The Imperial Japanese Army next rolled down eastern China, bombing Shanghai into submission and viciously sacking Nanjing, the nation's capital. By 1940, Japanese troops occupied virtually all of China's Yellow Sea coastline, plus large chunks of its eastern provinces. The humiliated Chinese were reduced to sabotaging dams and levees as they fled into the hinterlands.

Trained to view their Chinese foes as less than fully human, the victorious Japanese dutifully obeyed their commanders' "Three Alls Policy": kill all, burn all, loot all. In Nanjing, Japanese soldiers raped upward of twenty thousand women, many of whom were subsequently disemboweled, decapitated, or nailed to walls and left to suffocate. "Perhaps when we were raping her, we looked at her as a woman," one of the participants recalled. "But when we killed her, we just thought of her as something like a pig." Tens of thousands of men were similarly massacred, often buried alive in mass graves. Some were spared at first, only to be later used for bayonet practice.

With eastern China secured, Japan moved on to the second phase of its imperial design. The nation's Far Right leaders believed they were divinely ordained to lord over Asia and its racially inferior peoples—a Japanese spin on Manifest Destiny. The latter-day samurais in Tokyo dreamed of leading the "Greater East Asia Co-Prosperity Sphere," a network of puppet states stretching from India to the South Pacific. They vowed to create this Sphere "no matter what obstacles may be encountered. . . . We will not be deterred by the possibility of being involved in a war with England and America."

Japan didn't dawdle. In September 1940, its army invaded French Indochina, quickly seizing the vital port city of Haiphong. Days later, Japan signed the Tripartite Pact and entered into a military alliance with Nazi Germany and Fascist Italy. The treaty recognized "the leadership of Japan in the establishment of a new order in Greater East Asia."

But making that order a reality would require plentiful ores and petroleum, prerequisites for warfare that Japan's home islands sorely lacked. So in drawing up their plans for Asian domination, Japan's generals prioritized the invasion of lands awash in oil or metals— among them the unruly British colony of Burma.

The Japanese figured Burma for a cakewalk. Wedged between

Thailand, China, and India, the colony had always been a nightmare to govern, owing primarily to its ethnic jumble. Over 130 ethnic groups and subgroups called Burma home, and their rivalries ran deep. The majority Burmans, who accounted for roughly two-thirds of the population, were envied by the Karens, Shans, and Chins, who were in turn distrusted by the Was, Kachins, Palaungs, and Tavoyans. Each group jealously guarded its ancestral territory, particularly the hill tribes of Burma's isolated north.

Whiskey-soaked British administrators made matters worse, wasting their days in prissy, whites-only social clubs while Burma's provinces went to seed. The colony's army, meanwhile, was laughably feeble, beset by low morale and antiquated equipment. Reinforcements from the colonial motherland would not be forthcoming, since Britain was preoccupied on the war's European front.

Many Burmese actually yearned for a Japanese invasion. The British were cruel and condescending masters, convinced as they were of the natives' innate stupidity. Colonial officials assumed the Burmese only understood the rod: the Whipping Act mandated a minimum of thirty lashes even for petty offenses, and British policemen—among them a young George Orwell—never hesitated to use their fists or clubs. Burma's young were thus receptive to Japanese propaganda, which extolled the anti-Western notion of "Asia for the Asiatics." Many idealists even pledged to fight for Japan, as part of the clandestine Burma Independence Army (BIA) that was forming in Thailand.

Japan coveted Burma for more than just its natural resources. Conquering the British colony would also tighten the noose around China's besieged Nationalist government, led by Generalissimo Chiang Kai-shek. After fleeing eastern China in 1937, the Nationalists had established a temporary capital in Chongqing, an arid city in the central province of Sichuan. It was a miserable place from which to rule, a dust bowl that reeked of bus exhaust and rat droppings. Japanese bombs constantly rained from the skies, forcing residents to huddle in caves. Years of drought had caused a terrible famine; women and children risked arrest to eat the bark off decorative trees. Addicts vaporized their sorrows in the city's 1,300-plus opium dens.

Chiang's government-in-exile controlled a large but desolate swath of China's interior, extending from the Indochina border in the south to a few hundred miles north of Chongqing. The Nationalists' territory abutted not only the Japanese-occupied east, but also a blob-shaped northern region held by the Chinese Communist Party, led by Mao Zedong. Chiang and the Communists had been embroiled in a nasty civil war before the Japanese invasion. Despite a fragile truce, both sides ached to renew their internecine feud.

The question for Chiang was whether his government would survive long enough to resume its fight with Mao or would wither for lack of supplies. The Nationalists' traditional ports were all in Japanese hands, and Chongqing was more than two hundred miles from the nearest major railway. To keep itself flush with goods, then, Chiang's regime had built a land route in 1938: the Burma Road.

The 715-mile road connected the Burmese town of Lashio to Kunming, a Chinese city controlled by Long Yun, a one-eyed, opium-addicted warlord whose allegiance the Nationalists had gained through bribery. The road had been built by hundreds of thousands of peasant conscripts, a significant percentage of whom died due to disease, accidents, and starvation. These workers—whose ranks included children—cleared the way with trowels, bamboo sticks, or their bare hands: as a U.S. Army lieutenant named Ronald Reagan later remarked in a newsreel, the Burma Road had literally been "scratched out of the mountains with fingernails."

If and when Burma was conquered, Japan would surely blockade the road near Lashio, thereby halting the flow of food and materials to Chongqing. The Japanese hoped this stratagem would destroy the Nationalists once and for all, and lead to the creation of a puppet state in China's heartland.

The Burma Road was hardly the Nationalists' only means of receiving supplies. A trickle of cargo was also coming by air, as the China National Aviation Corporation (CNAC) shuttled planes to and from British-controlled India. And underground commerce abounded: for those who could afford to shop, Chongqing's stores brimmed with goods produced in Shanghai, Hong Kong, even Tokyo. "The trade across the 'fighting lines' was not a matter of spasmodic, illegal smuggling," observed the American newsman Eric Sevareid. "It was an established, tolerated industry by which tens of thousands made their living."

But this wasn't enough for Chiang: he wanted a steady, aboveboard stream of lorries rolling into Chongqing, too. So if the Burma Road was doomed to close, a substitute would have to be built from scratch.

The job of planning that replacement road was given to the mellifluously named Dr. Tseng Yang-fu, a Chinese railway official. Starting in the spring of 1941, Tseng dispatched surveyors to inspect several proposed routes. The results were discouraging, to say the least: inclement weather and diplomatic hurdles combined to prevent virtually every survey team from completing its mission. One group, for example, tried reaching Sadiya, India, via Tibet, only to discover that the Tibetans were loath to let foreigners disrupt their nation's Buddhist tranquility. Rather than kill the trespassers, Tibetan officials frustrated them with endless stalling; after weeks of fruitless negotiation for passage, the surveyors gave up.

The only surveyor to finish his assignment was Yuen Mung-hung, a minor functionary from the Ministry of Communications. He was sent to map a nine-hundred-mile tract of wilderness that ran through Fort Hertz, a British garrison in northern Burma, to the town of Ledo near the Indo-Burmese border. Disparaged by the British as "the end of the world," Ledo was a remote and ugly nowhere. Its chief industries were tea planting and coal mining, the latter of which had turned the Burhi Dihing River a sickly gray. Western visitors were rare, given North-East India's penchant for tribal violence. There had been an infamous 1891 incident in Imphal, two hundred miles south of Ledo, in which the chief commissioner of Assam province had been beheaded, along with his bugler and three others, while trying to quell a separatist coup. The executions, much publicized in the British press, had badly tarnished the region's reputation.

Ledo had one thing going for it: a rail link to Calcutta, that notorious hive of scum and villainy situated on the Bay of Bengal. Goods unloaded at Calcutta's port could thus be transported by train to Ledo, though the journey was an eight-hundred-mile slog; the rail gauge narrowed en route, so that everything had to be transferred from one set of trains to another before completing the trek. On the skinnier set of tracks, the cars moved at a tortoise pace, lurching side to side at every bend. With great luck, a carton of supplies could make it from a docked ship in Calcutta to Ledo's train station in ninety-six hours.

The route surveyed by Yuen crossed some of Asia's cruelest terrain: malarial jungles, the uncharted Patkais, elephant-grass valleys deluged by two hundred inches of rain per year.* The Patkais and their foothills were especially treacherous, and natives of the adjoining lowlands avoided them if possible. "It is said that numbers of persons who leave [Burma] for Assam never arrive here," noted the British explorer Henry Lionel Jenkins. "They lose the path, and,

---

* For comparison's sake, Seattle gets about thirty-six inches of rainfall per year.

wandering about in the jungles, starve to death, or are killed by wild animals."

The only people to flourish in the Patkais were headhunting Naga tribesmen, who booby-trapped the forests with razor-sharp *panji* sticks and still sacrificed captives to their gods. E. T. D. Lambert, a gung-ho British political officer who'd traversed the Patkais in 1936, called the Nagas "the most primitive and warlike people in India."

But Yuen dismissed the region's hazards as easily surmountable, assuming that 104,000 laborers could be recruited—or, more accurately, rounded up by Nationalist press gangs. These gangs ensnared workers like cattle, draping ropes around the waists of able-bodied peasants and dragging them from their villages. Yuen noted that the Burma Road had been completed in just one year, using conscripts paid (sporadically) with fistfuls of uncooked rice. As long as Chiang Kai-shek didn't mind several thousand peasants dropping dead from overwork or disease—and there was no reason to believe he would—Yuen predicted the new road would take twelve months to complete.

Dr. Tseng Yang-fu, Yuen's boss, liked the idea of a road originating in Ledo. But he suggested altering the route so that it veered in a more southerly direction. Tseng wanted to track the road along an existing mule-and-oxen trail in Burma's Hukaung Valley, a tiger-ridden basin east of the Patkais. From there the road would snake down to Myitkyina, a city on the banks of the yawning Irrawaddy River. The final stretch would then curve northward and eventually spill into the portion of the Burma Road that lay inside China. Tseng's plan would halve the road's distance, from 900 miles to a more manageable 465.

By January 1942, Chiang Kai-shek was keen to get this so-called Ledo Road built. And he knew just the ally to pay for its construction: the United States.

———

THE AMERICANS HAD BEEN supporting Chiang's regime for years, providing him with fighter planes and nine-figure loans. But after formally entering the war in December 1941, the United States had upped the ante, showering Chiang with a staggering $1.13 billion worth of loans, supplies, and outright gifts. President Roosevelt feared that if China wasn't adequately funded, Chiang might lose heart and sue for peace, thereby freeing up hundreds of thousands of Japanese troops to fight in the Pacific.

China's capitulation would also put a crimp in Roosevelt's vision for a postwar international order. The president envisaged China as the anchor of a democratic Asia, and Chiang as a committed defender of the "Four Freedoms": freedom of speech, freedom of worship, freedom from want, and freedom from fear.

Yet Chiang believed in none of these ideals, nor did he have the slightest interest in establishing an Asian beachhead for democracy. He was, at heart, a thug, whose true loves were those of a corrupt strongman: unchecked power, self-enrichment, and well-tailored uniforms bedecked with medals. Chiang's Nationalist government closely resembled a Fascist dictatorship, albeit a sloppy one.

The Generalissimo had first made a name for himself in the waning days of the Qing Dynasty, when he assassinated a fellow member of the anti-imperial Revolutionary Alliance. Hitching his star to Sun Yat-sen, founder of the Kuomintang political party and China's first president, Chiang rapidly ascended the political ladder. Along the way, he reinvented himself as a strident anti-Communist, despite having once studied in Moscow.

Like any tyrant worth his salt, Chiang had taken advantage of internal strife (in his case, a 1927 trade-union uprising in Shanghai) to seize political power, proclaiming himself the only man capable of quashing the Communist menace. From that point on, Chiang pursued Mao Zedong's scrappy Red Army to the ends of China. These military expeditions were in part financed by extortion: Chiang would hold wealthy families' children hostage until their parents coughed up thousands of yuan for the anti-Communist cause. Meanwhile, enemies of the state—that is, anyone who voiced a whit of public criticism—were jailed or gunned down in the streets.

Despite having once led the Whampoa Military Academy, China's answer to West Point, Chiang was a bungling general, unable to differentiate between lost causes and advantageous positions. He was also a terrible judge of subordinates. In 1937, for example, he placed warlord-turned-Buddhist-mystic Tang Shengzhi in charge of protecting Nanjing. After promising to defend the Nationalists' capital to the death, Tang fled without bothering to inform the city's residents, leaving them to be raped and massacred by the Japanese.

Blackmail on an epic scale was Chiang's real talent. The Generalissimo knew he could squeeze huge sums from the Americans by simply hinting that maybe, just maybe, he was considering peace with Japan. When Secretary of the Treasury Henry Morgenthau dared mention that the United States would like to see one $500 million loan repaid in the distant future, Chiang countered that such onerous financial obligations might nudge China closer to surrender. Aware that China's withdrawal from the war was an anathema to his boss in the White House, Morgenthau didn't press the issue.

Chiang lavished these riches on himself and his cronies, while doing nothing for the rural masses—kleptocratic behavior that turned millions of Chinese into Communist sympathizers. The peasants, noted Eric Sevareid, "saw their generals and political leaders grown dyspeptic with overeating while famine was striking again and again and thousands were dying by the roadsides." Oblivious to this suffering, Chiang ordered his troops to seize the peasants' crops, allegedly for the good of the nation. Villagers who protested were bombed by China's air force.

Given all the evidence to the contrary, why did Roosevelt mistake Chiang for a great statesman? His judgment may been clouded by his family's historical ties to China: Warren Delano Jr., the president's maternal grandfather, had earned a fortune in Canton in the 1830s and 1840s, largely from the opium trade. China was thus a magical place in Roosevelt lore, and the president may have credited himself with a deeper understanding of the so-called Middle Kingdom than he actually possessed.

Or perhaps the blame lies with the cabal of American officials who'd fallen under Chiang's sybaritic spell. After years of being wined, dined, and otherwise pampered in Chiang's court, veteran diplomats were willfully blind to the Generalissimo's sins. In February 1942, one such State Department official filed a report describing Nationalist China as "a mass movement of people led by a great leader . . . [Chiang's] determination, persistence and on the whole broad gauge outlook constitute perhaps the most important element in China as a fighting ally." Roosevelt could scarcely have received more erroneous intelligence on the Chongqing regime.

Whatever the reason for the president's credulity, the upshot was that the United States jumped at the chance to fund Chiang's road. The War Department tentatively approved the project on February 22, 1942: China and Burma would supply the manpower, while the United States would contribute all the necessary machinery. Chiang said the road could be completed in a little over five months; Dr. Tseng Yang-fu was even more optimistic, knocking two months off his boss's estimate.

In a rare moment of prudence when it came to dealing with Chiang, the U.S. Army requested a more impartial estimate of the road's construction time. An American officer with an engineering background,

Major John Ausland, was sent to travel the dirt caravan path that connected the northern Burmese plains to the Patkais.

Ausland was dismayed by what he found. His jeep bogged down in muddy ruts and the trail was interrupted by dozens of streams, passable only via rickety bamboo rafts. The trek got really treacherous north of Shingbwiyang, a Burmese village 103 miles short of Ledo: the trail disappeared into a lime green thicket, forcing Ausland to leave his jeep and walk. A torturous mile later, having macheted his way through knots of shrubs and weeds, he realized that his body was covered with blood-fattened leeches. The dense foliage made it nearly impossible to see more than a few feet in any direction.

Ausland turned back, his mission incomplete. Upon returning to China, he filed a glum report: contrary to Chiang and Tseng's sunny predictions, Ausland estimated that the road would take a minimum of two and a half years to build.

Shortly after Ausland departed Shingbwiyang, a Naga raiding party seized 150 heads from the Kachins, a rival ethnic group in the Burmese lowlands. Ausland hadn't even seen the jungle at its worst.

AUSLAND'S PESSIMISTIC REPORT was lost amidst grimmer news from Burma: as predicted, the Imperial Japanese Army easily captured the capital, Rangoon, in March 1942. Japan's three hundred thousand soldiers were greeted as liberators, as was the twelve-thousand-strong Burma Independence Army that had fought alongside the invaders. The BIA celebrated Burma's supposed emancipation by slaughtering an untold number of Indian immigrants, who were widely despised for having run the colony's banks and moneylending operations.

Like the Chinese Nationalists in the late 1930s, the British could do little but adopt scorched-earth tactics, burning their own oil fields as they retreated north. But the Imperial Japanese Army could not be slowed. After seizing Myitkyina, through which the Ledo Road was slated to run, the Japanese bayoneted wounded British soldiers and beheaded most of the town's surviving males. Six hundred thousand people fled to India, most on foot with all their worldly possessions balanced atop their heads. Of these refugees, 10 to 15 percent died en route, primarily from disease and exhaustion, although the strafing of Japanese warplanes exacted its own awful toll. Bloated cadavers and charred skeletons littered the roads to India; the refugees filed by with kerchiefs over their noses, too rushed to bury the dead.

Ursula Graham Bower, a British anthropologist who lived among the Naga tribes of the Indo-Burmese hills, visited an Assamese convent soon after the evacuation had ended. There she met an eight-year-old Anglo Burman girl whose tale of survival was both harrowing and all too common. Abandoned by her brother as they fled, the orphaned girl had relied on the kindness of male protectors, most of whom perished from cholera and malaria before reaching India. Two British soldiers took her under their wings in the Hukaung Valley, until the pair were bayoneted by a Japanese patrol right in front of her eyes.

"They then deliberately smashed her spectacles so that she was virtually blind," Bower wrote. "Since she could not see to walk, she then crawled. Conditions on the route were appalling and she not infrequently found herself crawling over corpses."

AMONG THOSE FORCED to escape Burma was Lieutenant General Joseph Warren Stilwell, a caustic American known to his detractors as Vinegar Joe. After serving as an intelligence officer in World War I, Stilwell had been sent to Beijing to learn Mandarin and keep

an eye on the nascent Chinese republic as it wobbled into modernity. Stilwell's fluency, honed through years of study at the Army's
finest language schools, was a rare skill among American officers.

Initially tabbed to lead an invasion of North Africa, Stilwell had
instead been sent to Chongqing to serve as commander of America's
China-Burma-India (CBI) theater of operations. On paper, at least,
Stilwell's role was the South Asian equivalent of Dwight D. Eisen-
hower's in Europe, or Douglas MacArthur's in the Southwest Pacific.
Yet the CBI would always play second fiddle to those more illustrious
commands. Fixated on Berlin and Tokyo, the War Department
treated Stilwell's theater as an afterthought, a place to keep Japanese
forces tied down while the war's pivotal battles occurred thousands
of miles away. Starved for attention, supplies, and even a clear sense
of purpose, the men of the CBI would spin the theater's acronym
into an acerbic nickname: Confusion Beyond Imagination.

Roosevelt asked just one thing of Stilwell: keep China in the war.
This meant catering to Chiang Kai-shek's whims, a duty that made
Vinegar Joe's stomach churn. Unlike the president, Stilwell immediately recognized Chiang as an extortionate goon, not to mention a
shoddy general. In his diary and communiqués, Stilwell referred to
China's despot as Peanut, a derisive code name inspired by Chiang's
short stature, bald pate, and (in Stilwell's estimation) tiny brain.

The antipathy was mutual. Chiang was outwardly cordial toward
Stilwell, but secretly apoplectic over Vinegar Joe's appointment to
run the CBI. The Generalissimo, like all Chinese leaders since time
immemorial, was a diehard xenophobe; after a Western official left
Chiang's presence, his first order of business was to have the windows flung open, to air out the beeflike stink of the *laowai* (a pejora-
tive term for "foreigner"). When Chiang first learned that the
Americans were dead set on sending a commander for the theater,
he specifically asked for a general with no knowledge of China or the

Far East, surmising that such a neophyte would be easy to cheat and bully. The Chinese-speaking, pigheaded Stilwell was Chiang's nightmare of a colleague.

The two men first dined together in March 1942, at the dictator's opulent residence outside Chongqing. Stilwell hoped to confront the Japanese in Burma, yet had virtually no combat troops of his own. He asked Chiang to loan him China's Fifth and Sixth armies, but the Generalissimo balked; those were his best troops, and he didn't want to risk them defending a British colony. Chiang's top priority was keeping his military intact, in preparation for a postwar showdown with Mao. As far as the Generalissimo was concerned, World War II was a matter for the foreign barbarians to settle on their own.

"What a sucker I am," an exasperated Stilwell wrote in his diary after the banquet, having realized that China's commander in chief wanted no part of the war.

Under pressure from Washington, Chiang relented a few days later. But he secretly told his officers that Stilwell was a mere adviser whose orders needn't be followed. Stilwell led the Chinese deep into Burma before Peanut's deception became apparent. Greatly outnumbered by the approaching Japanese, the Chinese units melted away, selling their gas and rice on the black market before hightailing it for home. Others turned to banditry, robbing and killing the refugees headed for Assam.

One Chinese general, whose division Stilwell was counting on to mount a counterattack in Burma's southeast, simply vanished along with his troops. Another hijacked a locomotive, in a desperate attempt to avoid combat. Vinegar Joe agonized over what to do about such mutinous officers: "I can't shoot them, I can't relieve them, and just talking to them does no good." The few worthwhile Chinese commanders were harassed by constant telephone calls from Chiang, who, whether out of spite or stupidity, told them to do the exact opposite of whatever Stilwell ordered. Betrayed in his darkest hour, Stilwell half joked to his aides that he'd rather fight alongside Mao's Communists.

The last straw for Stilwell was the infamous "watermelon incident," in which Chiang decreed that every four Chinese soldiers in Burma should be given one watermelon. Vinegar Joe viewed the order as an overt symbol of Chiang's treachery—the Generalissimo had no right to reward these troops, especially given their dreadful performance. Stilwell's contempt for Peanut was sealed.

When the inevitability of the Japanese rout finally sank in that May, Stilwell made a beeline for Assam with over one hundred soldiers, nurses, cooks, porters, and missionaries in tow. Among the marchers was Jack Belden, a *Time* magazine correspondent who would spin the retreat as a triumph and turn Stilwell into a paragon of Yankee grit. The adulation was deserved: the fifty-nine-year-old general led the painful trudge across the worst of Burma's northern landscape, never once hopping on a vehicle or resting a minute longer than the lowest enlisted man. Several of his party succumbed to heatstroke, others buckled from leg infections caused by leeches and insect bites, but Stilwell never fell off the pace.

Covering more than fifteen miles a day on foot, Stilwell's ragtag bunch reached the safety of North-East India on May 20, 1942. Stilwell himself had lost twenty pounds and was suffering from jaundice, yet still flew to Delhi on May 24 to confer with the humbled British. At a press conference at Delhi's Imperial Hotel, Stilwell was candid about what had gone down in Burma: "I claim we got a hell of a beating. We got run out of Burma and it is humiliating as hell." After weeks of being deluged with War Department lies about the campaign, including absurd pronouncements of imminent victory while Stilwell was retreating through the muck, reporters gorged on Vinegar Joe's bluntness.

The Burma defeat gnawed at Stilwell, who couldn't stand the thought of being remembered for losing his first wartime command. Retaking the country thus became Stilwell's singular obsession, as surely as Chiang's was clobbering Mao Zedong. The big question was how: American combat troops would be scarce, given the CBI's low priority in Washington, and the British were busy fretting over how to defend India against a likely Japanese invasion.

Stilwell's solution was to take Chinese conscripts and whip them into fighting shape at a base in Ramgarh, India, far from Chiang's insidious grasp. These soldiers would then lead the charge into Burma, supported by elite American and British units. The Generalissimo was predictably unhappy with the plan; he lived under the delusion that peasant conscripts, who mere weeks before might have been raising scallions in the Sichuan sticks, were innately able to drive tanks and fire mortars like veterans. "With the U.S. on his side and backing him, the stupid little ass fails to grasp the big opportunity of his life," Stilwell despaired.

But Vinegar Joe and the Generalissimo were on the same page about one thing: the Ledo Road, which Stilwell considered crucial to his strategy. He planned on using it to keep his assault troops supplied as they cleared the Japanese out of northern Burma. But the road was also a perfect pretext for invasion: as of mid-1942, 80 percent of its proposed route was controlled by the Imperial Japanese Army. By this circular logic, Stilwell needed to invade Burma to build the Ledo Road, and he needed to build the Ledo Road to invade Burma.

Avenging the thrashing he'd received was only the beginning of Vinegar Joe's ambitious plans. "Stilwell was almost alone in his faith that, not only could the road be built, but that it would be the most potent winning factor in the war against Japan," the British general

William Slim would write in his memoirs. Stilwell envisioned leading thirty divisions of American-trained Chinese troops all the way to Kunming, then pushing back against the Japanese occupying force in eastern China. Stilwell's army, continued Slim, "would drive through China to the sea, and then with the American Navy strike at Japan itself."

Stilwell refrained from sharing these pie-in-the-sky designs with his admirers in the media. When pressed on his reasons for wanting the road, Stilwell instead offered a pithy sound bite: "I walked and crawled out of Burma, but I mean to ride when I go back."

ALL WAS GOING according to plan for Stilwell until an unlikely rival emerged: Claire Lee Chennault. A debonair American aviator, Chennault would help turn the Ledo Road into a macho pissing match between himself and Stilwell, one that Vinegar Joe couldn't bear to lose. At times, it would seem like Stilwell stuck with the road solely to avoid giving Chennault the satisfaction of being right.

The Texas-born, Louisiana-bred Chennault started flying during World War I, eventually working his way up to captain in the Army Air Corps. Never in doubt of his own brilliance—a trait he shared with Chiang—he quit the military in 1937, bitter over his superiors' failure to acknowledge the supremacy of his preferred fighter tactics. Rather than retire to his hometown of Waterproof, Louisiana, Chennault moved to China, where he became an adviser to Chiang's scraggly air force. Following his patron as the Nationalists retreated to Chongqing, he established the American Volunteer Group (AVG), a band of mercenary pilots better known as the Flying Tigers. The AVG's hard-drinking, gung-ho fliers were paid up to $750 a month, plus a $500 bonus for every Japanese plane they downed. They fought valiantly in the skies above Burma, in one instance preventing Japan's dreaded Red Dragon Armored Division from crossing the Salween River Gorge and invading China proper.

The AVG disbanded in July 1942, and Chennault became a full-time commander in the Army Air Forces*; he would soon become a brigadier general in charge of the Fourteenth Air Force, based in China. As a lifelong prophet of air power, Chennault scoffed at the Ledo Road as a strategic dinosaur. He insisted that China could be supplied far more efficiently through the air, by making better use of the trans-Himalayan route known as the Hump. The China National Aviation Corporation had been flying the Hump since the 1930s, at one point ferrying supplies to the Flying Tigers' base in Kunming. In October 1942, the U.S. Army's Air Transport Command took over the Hump flights from CNAC.

There was just one problem with the Hump: it was extraordinarily lethal. The route cut through the eastern Himalayas, a region where blinding storms and violent turbulence were the norm. Gusts of snow and ice dashed C-46 and C-47 cargo planes against the mountainsides, and in the days before widespread radar, a midflight loss of visibility meant almost certain death. C-46s and C-47s that survived the rough passage had to contend with Japanese fighter planes that darted forth from Myitkyina. On average, more than a dozen aircraft—nicknamed "flying coffins"—were lost each month; pilots who survived their crashes usually perished in even crueler fashion, starved in the mountains or beheaded by the Japanese.

Still, Chennault's whole career was staked on advancing the cause of aviation, and he tirelessly sold Chiang on the idea that the Hump, not the Ledo Road, would get China through the war. Chiang listened to Chennault because the American, though stub-

*The Army Air Corps had been transformed into a component of the newly created Army Air Forces in June 1941.

born to a fault, could be genial and diplomatic when called for. Most important, Chennault realized the way to the Generalissimo's heart was through his wife, the conniving Madame Chiang. Born Soong Meiling to a prominent Christian family, Madame Chiang was a sucker for Chennault's rugged good looks, genteel manners, and southern drawl. (Curiously, the Wellesley-educated Madame Chiang had learned to speak near-flawless English with an Alabama accent.)

Stilwell's tell-it-like-it-is persona played well with *Time* and *Life* magazines, but it did him no favors in coaxing help from Chiang, a product of the culture that invented kowtowing. In late June 1942, Chiang sent Washington the "Three Demands," an ultimatum actually authored by Chennault. The demands were onerous and tilted heavily toward air power: Chiang wanted three divisions of American troops, five hundred combat planes, and at least five thousand tons of supplies per month over the Hump. If the United States failed to comply, Chiang warned, then he'd be forced to make "other arrangements"—a euphemism for surrender.

The Three Demands made no mention of the Ledo Road. Chennault had persuaded the Generalissimo to commit the bulk of his labor resources to building airstrips in southern China, the better to accommodate Hump flights—and, once aviation technology inevitably improved, to serve as bases for the long-range bombing of Tokyo. Like a child who drops an old toy for a new one, Chiang instantly lost interest in the road he'd been raring to build just six months earlier. Though Chiang professed to still welcome the road's construction, and even promised to commit some engineers to the project, the 104,000 Chinese laborers that Yuen Mung-hung had recommended would not be forthcoming.

Yet Stilwell wouldn't be cowed, least of all by a backstabbing flyboy working in concert with that "stupid little ass" Chiang. He insisted that the United States build the Ledo Road itself, providing the manpower as well as the machinery. Stilwell okayed final plans for the road on November 10, 1942; President Roosevelt offered his personal approval twenty-eight days later, with assurances that the project would be a top War Department priority.

The job of building the Ledo Road was assigned to the Services of Supply (SOS), an Army branch responsible for such mundane chores as unloading ships, laying pipes, and mixing concrete. The SOS was also a convenient dumping ground for black soldiers, whom the Army generally considered too feebleminded and cowardly to serve in combat; in World War I, about 80 percent of the nation's African American troops had been "SOS'd," spending 1917 and 1918 unloading freighters at French ports.

The Americans were to be assisted by tens of thousands of indentured laborers, known as "coolies" in the politically incorrect lingo of the day. These workers, whose lot in life was one notch better than outright slavery, were to be obtained largely through the Assam Tea Planters' Association. The coolies were mostly natives of Bihar and Orissa, impoverished states west of Bengal, and came to Assam on three-year contracts, earning roughly sixteen cents a day; the average daily pay for a GI, by contrast, was around two dollars.

Familiar as they were with the hostility of the Indo-Burmese wilderness, the British couldn't believe that Vinegar Joe wanted to involve American troops in such a potential debacle. Among the skeptics was Winston Churchill, the prime minister, who summed up his opinion of the Ledo Road in a single, damning clause: "An immense, laborious task, unlikely to be finished before the need for it has passed."

Disregarding the British, however, was one of Stilwell's favorite pastimes, as he considered them to be treacherous pantywaists who'd rather keep their dinner jackets spiffy than actually kill anybody.* Their reticence about the Ledo Road, Stilwell believed, was because they were averse to sacrifice and hard work. Besides, he'd worked on rural highways before, supervising the construction of two such projects during his 1920s stint in China. Both, however, had ended badly. One eighty-two-mile road from Fenchow to the Yellow River decayed into nothingness soon after its completion; another near Sian was aborted after the Chinese government seized Stilwell's equipment for use in a military campaign against a local warlord.

This time, though, American GIs would be the ones crushing rocks and clearing timber. And if anyone could withstand the hardships of jungle labor, it was black Americans—at least according to the era's conventional wisdom. Blacks were reputed to be more resistant to malaria than their white counterparts, as well as stronger pound for pound. The most dubious claim was that African Americans could actually see in the dark, which would therefore make it easier for them to toil in jungles that turned pitch-black by 4:00 P.M.

The first two SOS units to arrive in Ledo that December, the 45th Engineer General Service Regiment and the 823rd Engineer Aviation Battalion, had landed in Karachi five months earlier, unsure of their mission in the CBI. The theater's head of SOS, Lieutenant General Raymond A. Wheeler, was cool to the road plan, but lacked the gumption to challenge Stilwell, his former West Point professor. He put Colonel John Arrowsmith, the 45th's commander, in charge of the project.

On December 16, 1942, the 823rd broke ground on the Ledo Road, and the 45th trailed behind with layers of gravel. The units started with just six bulldozers between them, and vintage ones at

---

*The distaste was more than mutual, as the British chortled at Stilwell's calculated folksiness as a cover for base incompetence. "Except for the fact that he was a stout-hearted fighter suitable to lead a brigade of Chinese scallywags, I could see no qualities in him," sniffed Field Marshal Alan Brooke, chief of the Imperial General Staff, who deemed Stilwell an inferior tactician.

that. But Stilwell nonetheless expected that the road's first hundred miles would be completed before the spring monsoons hit.

Come the spring of 1943, however, Vinegar Joe would be sorely disappointed with the state of the Ledo Road. The job was every bit as tough and perilous as the British had warned, and vastly more men would be needed to forge ahead. The call went out for fresh bodies unravaged by malaria and exhaustion. And the War Department, in turn, tapped the 849th Engineer Aviation Battalion, an African American unit that counted Private Herman Perry of Washington, D.C., among its ranks.

FOUR

After the Selective Service misadventure that landed him in jail, Herman Perry knew he was likely fated to wear an Army uniform. But months, then seasons passed without a peep from the draft board. Pearl Harbor went up in flames, Roscoe boxed twice at Turner's Arena, and young Aaron honed his jab at the Twelfth Street Y. Through it all, Herman remained a civilian butcher.

The middle Perry brother wasn't alone in wondering what the holdup was. Black men nationwide were puzzled by the draft's lethargic pace, unaware that the logjam was by design. Reluctant to darken its collective pigmentation too much, the Army was using a byzantine quota system that capped its share of black manpower at between 9 and 10 percent. But the Army couldn't even hit that modest target, due to a shortage of segregated training facilities: African Americans couldn't be absorbed in large numbers until more blacks-only barracks and mess halls were built. Under clandestine pressure from the War Department, local draft boards used this pretext to stymie or rebuff thousands of qualified black registrants.

As a result, by early 1943 over three hundred thousand black men would be caught in draft limbo, tapped for service but unsure of when—or even if—they'd begin active duty. Tens of thousands more were flat-out rejected, often for no good reason other than a prejudiced draft official's whim.

The bottleneck secretly pleased the military, whose leaders assumed that blacks, despite their reputed muscularity and night vision, lacked the biological talents necessary to become effective combat troops. Their belief was rooted in racial science, one of twentieth-century academia's most ignominious fads. Looking for evidence to confirm the a priori assumption of black inferiority, physiologists of the 1920s and 1930s had examined countless human cadavers. They'd concluded that blacks suffered from a variety of anatomical quirks—elongated heel bones, shallow chest cavities, one-piece nose cartilage—that made them ill suited to tasks requiring stamina rather than brute strength. War planners thus worried that African American soldiers couldn't march long distances, or grind out days of battle on little food.

The scientists also maintained that men of African descent possessed smaller cranial capacities than their European counterparts, a deficiency said to be caused by irreversible "premature ossification" of the skull.*

This anatomical flaw, they contended, meant that blacks were innately less intelligent than whites, as well as predisposed to cowardice, sloth, alcoholism, and sexual licentiousness. The military saw no reason to doubt these pseudoscientific claims, which implied that African Americans were psychologically too weak for the war's front lines.

The military's prejudice, while nothing new, hadn't always been

---

*A turn-of-the-century edition of the *Encyclopaedia Britannica* listed average cranial capacities as follows: European, 45 ounces; Negro, 35 ounces; highest gorilla, 20 ounces.

so virulent. In the aftermath of World War I, the Army had even briefly considered expanding its use of black troops. General John J. Pershing, head of the American Expeditionary Force (AEF), had been impressed by the performance of the 369th Infantry Regiment, or "Harlem Hellfighters," who fought heroically at the battle of Argonne Forest. "Under capable white officers and with sufficient training, Negro soldiers have always acquitted themselves credibly," observed Pershing, a veritable progressive by the standards of the day.

The Army asked its officers to evaluate the performance of the two hundred thousand black soldiers in the AEF, of whom only a minuscule number—under 3 percent—had seen combat. The officers, predominately southern patricians, responded with near universal outrage that a looser racial policy would even be considered. Major Albert Brown, an officer with the African American 183rd Infantry Brigade in France, offered a typically damning appraisal, singling out his unit's supposedly deleterious effect on civilian hearts and minds: "[The black soldier's] craving for sexual intercourse is at times uncontrollable, making him a menace to the female population of any neighborhood in which he is quartered."

African Americans assigned to labor battalions received similarly poor reviews from their white superiors. "The enlisted men are negroes [sic] and have all the vices peculiar to the Ethiopian race," wrote one colonel from a Services of Supply unit based in Britain. "Their average mentality is that of a child of ten and they have a controlled enthusiasm for work. . . . Their most common offenses are sneaking away from their work, going absent without leave, drunkenness, and peculation."

Such blatant bigotry, combined with the growing vogue for racial science, persuaded the Army to cleanse its ranks. Blacks were discouraged from joining the peacetime military after World War I, and they were forbidden from enlisting in the nascent Air Corps. Long-standing black regiments—some of them dating back to the years immediately following the Civil War—were quietly disbanded, their members denied the right to reenlist. By 1935, the Army had a grand total of four African American officers, and three of them were chaplains. By June 1940, blacks made up just 1.5 percent of the Army's manpower; virtually all were employed as cooks, cleaners, or manual laborers.

But as the United States drifted toward World War II, the National Association for the Advancement of Colored People pressed President Roosevelt to end this whitewashing. *Crisis*, the NAACP's official journal, took up the cause in a 1939 manifesto: "The *Crisis* wants Negroes all through the Army and the Navy, and other defense services. There is no reason why we should not have Negro aviators, or generals or admirals." Meanwhile, a group called the Committee for the Participation of Negroes in the National Defense Program, headed by a Howard University history professor named Rayford Logan, lobbied Congress to add a nondiscrimination clause to any draft legislation it might pass.

Politics compelled Roosevelt to pay attention to the NAACP and its proxies. The president would be seeking an unprecedented third term in the fall of 1940, and he needed black votes to fend off the challenge of Republican businessman Wendell Willkie. Yet Roosevelt couldn't afford to appear too progressive on race, lest he ruin his electoral prospects among white southerners. So the White House crafted a clever hedge, one aimed at burnishing Roosevelt's civil rights credentials while slyly preserving the status quo.

To the delight of black leaders, the Selective Training and Service Act, which Roosevelt signed into law on September 16, 1940, included a seemingly revolutionary clause: "In the selection and training of men under this act, and in the interpretation and execution of the provisions of this act, there shall be no discrimination against any person on account of race or color." Anyone who read that snippet alone might conclude that the Army would no longer reflexively spurn blacks, or relegate those who slipped through to menial jobs. Optimists dared hope that integrated units were in the offing.

But a few sentences later, the act's legalese turned evasive: "No man shall be inducted for training and service under this act unless and until he is acceptable to the land or naval forces for such training and service and his physical and mental fitness for such training and service has been satisfactorily determined . . . as may be determined by the Secretary of War or the Secretary of the Navy." In other words, the military would have final say over who possessed the necessary qualities to fill its glamour jobs, who was fit solely for labor, and who couldn't serve at all. The clause made it easy for the Army to keep on discriminating, as long as it was careful to cite a black draftee's alleged lack of smarts or stamina, rather than his skin color. This technique of bigotry took its cue from the Deep South, where rigged literacy tests had long been used to justify the exclusion of blacks from juries and voting booths.

As for the faint dream that units might be integrated, the War Department quickly scotched that notion. Secretary of War Henry L. Stimson may have come from a prominent family of northern abolitionists, but he harbored some very southern ideas about the competency of black soldiers. "Colored troops do very well under white officers but every time we try to lift them a little bit beyond where they can go, disaster and confusion follow," he wrote in his diary on September 27, 1940. "I hope to Heaven's sake they won't mix the white and the colored troops together in the same units for then we shall certainly have trouble."

This justification of Jim Crowism on pragmatic grounds would become a hallmark of the military's rhetoric throughout the war. Generals and admirals would always insist that, although they harbored no prejudices themselves, the uneducated white masses weren't ready for progress. In a confidential memo outlining the Navy's view of segregation as a necessary evil, Rear Admiral Walton R. Sexton reprinted a letter of support he claimed to have received from an anonymous southern congressman:

> It is much more important that we have the full-hearted cooperation of the thirty million white southern Americans than that we satisfy the National Association for the Advancement of Colored People. I realize that you have never lived in the South. I have lived there all my life. You know that our people have volunteered for military service more readily than the people of any other section of the Nation. If they be forced to serve with Negroes, they will cease to volunteer; and when drafted they will not serve with that enthusiasm and high morale that has always characterized the soldiers and sailors of the southern states. . . . I do most earnestly plead with you to see that there is a complete segregation of the races. To assign a Negro doctor to treat some southern white boy would be a crushing insult and in my opinion, an outrage against the patriotism of our southern people.

On October 8, 1940, Assistant Secretary of War Robert Patterson sent President Roosevelt a draft of the military's plan on integration—which, in a nutshell, said that there would be none:

> The policy of the War Department is not to intermingle colored and white enlisted personnel in the same regimental organizations. This policy has been proven satisfactory over a long period of years, and to make changes now would produce situations destructive to morale and detrimental to the preparation for national defense. . . .

It is the opinion of the War Department that no experiments should be tried with the organizational setup of these units at this critical time.

At the top of Patterson's memo, Roosevelt jotted two letters: "O.K."*

FIFTEEN MONTHS AFTER his release from jail, Herman Perry finally got the call: he was inducted into the Army on July 29, 1942. After receiving his uniforms and inoculations at a reception center in Washington, D.C., Perry, like millions of his fellow draftees, was given the Army General Classification Test (AGCT). The exam's 150 questions covered vocabulary, math, and "block counting" (visualizing hidden sections in geometric figures). The AGCT ostensibly measured "general learning ability," and was used to determine which draftees were officer material and which should spend the war building latrines. Scores ranged from Category I ("very superior") to Category V ("very inferior"). Whites who scored in the lowest quintile were usually trained as infantrymen, on the assumption that scant brainpower was required to squeeze a trigger; blacks who bombed on the test were assigned to labor and supply units.

Blacks tended to score lower on the AGCT than whites: between March 1941 and December 1942, 49.2 percent of blacks who took the test scored in the bottom quintile, versus 8.5 percent of whites. Segregationists used these results to defend the relegation of blacks to noncombat roles. "It so happens that a relatively large percentage of the Negroes inducted into the army have fallen within the lower edu-

*Roosevelt's political fears also caused him to shy away from endorsing a federal antilynching law. He justified his do-nothingness to Walter White, head of the NAACP, by pointing out that southerners chaired the most important congressional committees. "If I come out for the antilynching bill now," the president told White, "they will block every bill I ask Congress to pass to keep America from collapsing."

cational classifications," Stimson wrote to Representative Hamilton Fish III, a Republican congressman from New York. "Many of the Negro troops have accordingly been unable to master efficiently the techniques of modern weapons."

As is usually the case with intelligence tests, however, the raw numbers could be manipulated to fit a variety of narratives. Stimson neglected to mention that northern blacks generally outscored southern whites on the AGCT—an indictment of the effects of rural poverty, rather than race. Nor did Stimson reveal that one of the AGCT's chief architects, a Columbia University psychologist named Henry Edward Garrett, was also a rabid segregationist obsessed with proving white intellectual supremacy. In later years, Garrett would rail against the Supreme Court's decision in *Brown v. Board of Education*, cofound the International Association for the Advancement of Ethnology and Eugenics, and characterize the goal of the civil rights movement as the "mongrelization" of the white race. "I think racial mixing is undesirable in this country and could be catastrophic," he once opined. "Racial amalgamation would mean a general lowering of the cultural and intellectual level of the American people."

Garrett was a key member of the Committee on Classification of Military Personnel, as well as a trusted War Department consultant. The AGCT was based on Garrett's risible assertion that "you can only measure ability to learn by finding what a person has already learned." Such an axiom assumes equal access to educational opportunities, an ideal that has never existed anywhere, let alone in the United States before *Brown* overturned the separate-but-equal doctrine. Garrett was surely too smart to have missed this flaw in his logic, but he conveniently ignored it in the service of proving his dodgy racial theories.

Perry's AGCT category isn't noted in what remains of his personnel file, though his lack of a formal education beyond the ninth grade suggests that he probably fared as poorly as Garrett intended. The fact that Perry was assigned to the 849th Engineer Aviation Battalion, a labor unit, suggests that his score languished in the fourth or fifth quintile. But even African Americans who placed in Category I frequently ended up with shovels in their hands. To mollify the NAACP and its allies, the Army had created a few black combat units, including such high-profile organizations as the 761st Tank Battalion (aka the Black Panthers) and the 332nd Fighter Group (the Tuskegee Airmen). But there weren't nearly enough of these showpiece units to accommodate every high-scoring black draftee. So African American college graduates were often lumped into battalions alongside illiterates: the War Department prized the principle of segregation over the efficient use of talent.

This waste of brainpower rankled the black press, which, despite its initial misgivings, now urged readers to support the war. In January 1942, the *Pittsburgh Courier* had published a letter by a man named John Thomson, who advocated a war on two fronts: one against the Axis, the other against racism and segregation. The *Courier* dubbed this strategy the "Double V" campaign, for victory at home and abroad; by demonstrating their patriotism and valor on foreign battlefields, African Americans would prove they deserved legal equality in the United States.

To bolster the Double V, black newspapers like the *Courier* and the *Chicago Defender* were filled with three types of stories: those hailing the gumption of black draftees ("Frail Tennessee Youth Eats His Way Into Navy"), those decrying racism's effects on the war effort ("Soldier, Oppressed by Jim Crow in Our Dual Democracy, Tries Suicide"), and those hailing the achievements of dark-skinned foreign troops ("Colored Russian Paratroop Officer is Idol of His Men").

Editorial cartoons depicted rednecks as Hitler and Tōjō's unwitting friends, or noted the grim irony of Americans decrying Japanese atrocities while lynchings at home went unpunished.

Yet the black press was preaching to the choir, as few whites knew the *Courier* and *Defender* even existed. The newspapers' earnest pleadings certainly fell on deaf ears among the Army brass, as Perry would soon discover.

Herman Perry in dress uniform.

WITH BASIC TRAINING beckoning, Perry bid good-bye to his family, his infant daughter, Portia, and his girlfriend, Alma Talbot. He commemorated his final hours in Washington by posing for a formal portrait, clad in his Army dress uniform. The photograph was snapped in front of a backdrop depicting Capitol Hill, with a family of two-dimensional swans swimming underneath. Perry posed with his legs splayed, his head coyly tilted, and a cigarette dangling from his left hand. He cut a dashing figure.

Perry joined the 849th Engineer Aviation Battalion at the Myrtle Beach General Bombing and Gunnery Range in South Carolina. The base was also being used to train B-26 pilots, but the black GIs were expressly forbidden from mingling with the flyboys, as well as with any other whites apart from their immediate superiors. The Army realized that the universality of the draft had made the training camps combustible; in the era before TV and cheap air travel, an Ozarks hillbilly and a black Detroiter were aliens to each other, and tolerance had not been part of their respective school curriculums. White feared black as some unknowable, unclean Other, and vice versa. To suggest that interracial dialogue might reveal each group's basic humanity was an idea too bizarre to consider.

Even highly educated, self-styled liberals couldn't quite fathom the concept of blacks and whites eating together, or shopping in the same stores. A segregated America had blossomed into perhaps the wealthiest nation the world had ever known, and whites saw no reason why the military, that most conservative of institutions, should become a social laboratory. In May 1942, the War Department commissioned a survey entitled *Attitude of White Enlisted Men Toward Sharing Facilities With Negro Troops*. To no one's surprise, white soldiers from the South were loath to socialize with blacks. But so, too, were Yankees; when asked whether they favored fully integrated movie houses at training camps, for example, just 11 percent of white northerners said yes. More than half wanted blacks to sit in their own sections, while nearly a third demanded whites-only showings.

The Army had every intention of heeding the majority's wishes. "The Army accepts no doctrine of racial superiority or inferiority," stated a War Department pamphlet entitled *Command of Negro Troops*. "It may seem inconsistent, therefore, that there is nevertheless a general separation of colored and white troops on duty. It is important to understand that separate organization is a matter of practical military expediency." The pamphlet added that even 38 percent of blacks thought segregated units were a good idea.

Just as Perry was warned not to fraternize with Myrtle Beach's white trainees, the base's white soldiers were given similar instructions to avoid consorting with their black counterparts. This advice was part of the standard orientation at training camps located south of the Mason-Dixon Line. At Camp Hood, Texas, for example, arriving whites were greeted with a warning tacked to the barracks' bulletin boards: "All men are cautioned to treat [black soldiers] with respect but not to cultivate friendship with them. For the best interests of everyone stay completely away from them. 'Ya'll remembah, Sirs, dis is de Souf!'"

Perry and the rest of the 849th seemed fortunate to have a commanding officer who was smarter and more compassionate than most: Lieutenant Colonel Wright Hiatt. An Indiana native and West Point graduate, Hiatt was just twenty-seven years old when he took over the battalion, though with his neatly parted blond locks and boyish visage he actually looked closer to twenty. A brilliant hydraulics engineer, Hiatt had spent the first part of the war stationed in Newfoundland, returning home in November 1942 after his young wife died of a cerebral hemorrhage. The heartbroken Hiatt was given command of the 849th three days before the new year.

Hiatt was, by all accounts, a kind and temperate man who genuinely cared for his men, regardless of race. But he wasn't quite cut out for running the 849th—he was more of an egghead than a disciplinarian, and he was still grieving over his wife. Feeling overwhelmed, Hiatt delegated a great deal of authority to the unit's commissioned officers, all of them white. Most were newly minted lieutenants who'd been rushed through Officer Candidate School (OCS)—"90 Day Wonders," in Army slang. Among the Wonders was Lieutenant Harold Cady, originally from rural Chemung County, New York. Raised by his aunt and uncle in the town of Big Flats, Cady had voluntarily enlisted in the Army in June 1940. Assigned to the Coast Artillery Corps, Cady survived the bombing of Pearl Harbor before entering OCS. He had a wife and young daughter back in Woodhull, New York, a sleepy farm town near the Pennsylvania border.

Mindful that the 90 Day Wonders had little interracial experience, the Army did its best to instruct them in the proper handling of black subordinates. *Command of Negro Troops* was part of this effort. "There is no place in this Army for the attitude, 'These men are so limited in ability that there is no use trying to make good soldiers of them,'" the pamphlet's authors declared. They went on to caution against cracking jokes "which are dependent on the traditional ideas of the white man concerning Negro characteristics," as well as the wanton use of such epithets as "boy," "darky," and "uncle."

Nevertheless, the relationship between the 90 Day Wonders and the 849th's rank and file was toxic from the start. Perry and the battalion's other GIs—euphemistically called "engineers"—were supposed to be learning the nuances of airstrip construction. Instead, they were chiefly used to clear brush, mop floors, and otherwise act as the base's unpaid janitors. The enlisted men repeatedly complained about the utter lack of black recreational facilities, and about the favoritism shown to suspected Uncle Toms. They envied the officers as well, cruelly deriding them as "peckawoods" who'd be digging ditches if they'd been born with darker skin.

The hostile situation that Perry endured at the Myrtle Beach

Bombing Range was the norm nationwide. Though outwardly committed to quelling racism, the Army allowed many of its training camps to be run like antebellum plantations. Rather than learning how best to kill or outwit Nazis, black draftees instead found themselves peeling potatoes and scrubbing toilets. They were housed in the shabbiest barracks and fed cold or putrid food—scraps deemed unfit for white consumption. Anyone who dared complain or protested their lot with a wisecrack was quickly punished, either tossed in jail or slapped around.

At camps that doubled as prisons for captured Germans, blacks were appalled to discover how their treatment compared to that accorded the prisoners of war. At Mississippi's Camp McCain, for example, African American GIs fumed over the fact that the base's 7,700 German prisoners were allowed to use the superior whites-only latrines and drinking fountains, and were served relatively high-quality meals of roast pork and potato salad.*

The letters pages of black newspapers filled with anecdotes of training-camp woe. The authors, often writing under pseudonyms such as "Fellow American" and "Unknown Soldier of the Race," detailed their disillusionment with Army life, often in language that revealed the shortcomings of their educations. "They got us here washing diches [sic], working around the office houses and waiting on them, instead of trying to win this war they got us in ditches," one private stationed at Randolph Field, Texas, informed the *Pittsburgh Courier* in 1942. "Please report this to the NAACP and tell them to do something about this slavery place, where a colored soldier haven't got a chance."

---

*At Camp Wheeler, Georgia, meanwhile, blacks had to awaken at 5:30 A.M.—an hour earlier than everyone else—and clean toilets in the white barracks. At Camp Forest, Tennessee, MPs wielding Tommy guns forcibly removed blacks from the base's whites-only movie theater. And in Arizona, farmers struck a deal with the War Department to use members of the African American 93rd Division as unpaid cotton pickers.

Neither Perry nor his comrades in the 849th appear to have written any pained missives to the *Courier* or the *Chicago Defender*, perhaps because they feared retribution. The battalion's 90 Day Wonders were overly keen on court-martialing soldiers who committed minor acts of rebellion. This was a common tactic employed against black troops, who called it "railroading." The officers' targets were usually men who, like Perry, preferred to use their mouths instead of their fists. Evelio Grillo, a sergeant with the African American 823rd Engineer Aviation Battalion, said that while thuggery was rarely punished, verbal challenges to authority were dealt with harshly: "Threats of courts-martial were reserved for 'smart niggers' like me, who became involved in discussions with officers about injustices and discrimination."

The Army's justice system made railroading easy enough. Summary or special courts-martial, in which one to three officers determined a soldier's guilt in a matter of minutes, were easy to organize, and defendants were often tried without legal counsel. Acquittals were exceedingly rare.*

In just its first year of existence, the 849th conducted 103 summary and special courts-martial, an astronomical figure for a unit with fewer than 750 enlisted men. Even the Army's Office of Inspector General, not prone to overstatement, termed the battalion's justice "excessive." The Myrtle Beach Bombing Range's guardhouse filled with black GIs serving time; their resentments only deepened after weeks of bread-and-water diets and arduous punishment chores. Their buddies on the outside, meanwhile, went AWOL at alarming rates, disappearing for days at a time.

---

*Among the thousands of African Americans court-martialed was Jackie Robinson, the Hall of Fame second baseman who broke baseball's color line in 1947. Robinson was charged in 1944 with disobeying an MP's orders; among the transgressions listed in the court documents was "giving several sloppy salutes" to a captain. Already famous for his athletic exploits at UCLA, Robinson lucked out: he was acquitted and given an honorable discharge.

Perry and his beleaguered unit were finally ordered overseas in May 1943. Their destination was a mystery: to prevent Axis spies from learning of a ship's intended route, soldiers were never informed of where they'd be sailing. The engineers were told only that they'd be embarking from New York, after a short stay at Camp Kilmer, New Jersey.

Taking advantage of his last days in the Carolinas, Perry used a weekend pass to visit his remaining family in Monroe. He strutted around town in his dress uniform, aware of its aphrodisiac effect on girls, and posed for blurry pictures atop the hoods of fancy automobiles. The relentlessly upbeat Perry never mentioned the hardships of training camp, but instead gushed over the 849th's impending adventure. Most likely they'd be off to the Pacific, to build airstrips on captured islands. Or perhaps they were bound for Europe, where American bombers had just started pockmarking the German landscape.

"He was happy, he was all elated," recalls Edna Wilson, his only sister, who was living in Monroe during Herman's farewell visit. "It seemed like he was loving the Army. He wasn't sad about it or anything."

As PERRY SETTLED into his temporary quarters in northern New Jersey that May, racial strife was spreading throughout the nation's training camps. Despite the Army's diligent efforts to separate black from white, lethal fights had begun to flare with regularity; many black soldiers would later half joke that they saw more combat at basic training than overseas. "I remember one night it looked like a small Battle of the Bulge," said one soldier assigned to an artillery battalion at Camp Stewart, Georgia. "Instead of Germans against Americans it was black Americans versus white Americans on an army post that perpetuated segregation and prejudice. There were three soldiers killed, two or three MPs killed."

The enmity came to a head at Camp Van Dorn near Centreville, Mississippi. The black 364th Infantry Regiment was transferred to the camp on May 25, after a violent stay in Phoenix, Arizona. The unit's soldiers had gone berserk after one of their comrades was shot for resisting arrest, leading to an all-night gunfight. The GIs had holed up in Phoenix's southeast section, forcing the MPs to strafe civilian residences with machine-gun fire. At least three people were killed, and nearly two hundred soldiers were arrested.

Camp Van Dorn was located deep in the boonies, making it an ideal place to exile the rowdy 364th—if the unit acted up again, at least the MPs wouldn't have to shoot up any urban neighborhoods. The camp was also notorious for its prisonlike conditions; one black regiment was forced to toil on a politician's nearby farm, like common convicts. Bivouacked at opposite ends of the post, blacks and whites patrolled their respective turf, armed either with rifles (the whites) or broomsticks (the blacks, who weren't permitted to keep weapons).

Just five days after the 364th's arrival, a black soldier from Chicago, Private William Walker, was gunned down at Camp Van Dorn's entry gate. The killer, a local sheriff named Richard Whittaker, said he'd witnessed Walker tussling with an MP. Whittaker stated that he only fired after an enraged Walker lunged for the sheriff's pistol.

Eyewitnesses told a different story to the *Chicago Defender*. They claimed that the MP had been clubbing a defenseless Walker over the head as punishment for losing a sleeve button. When Walker raised his hands to deflect the blows, a white sergeant ordered the MP to shoot. The black private turned to flee just as Whittaker arrived; the sheriff then pumped three rounds into Walker.

A melee ensued that night, as members of the 364th jumped and pummeled any whites they could find. "The black wears many masks which conceal his true feelings," said an African American private who witnessed the bloodshed. "But that night at Van Dorn the black mask was dropped and I saw stark black hatred."

The white GIs, in turn, plotted to hijack some tanks and roll through the black section of camp, a scheme they dropped after hearing rumors that the 364th had stolen several rocket launchers. A number of soldiers died when the MPs suppressed the riot, and the 364th was exiled to a place even more inhospitable than southern Mississippi: the Aleutian Islands, where the regiment helped build the Alaska-Canadian Highway.

The Camp Van Dorn imbroglio kicked off a bloody summer, as black soldiers felt emboldened to respond to racial slights with guns and cudgels. Training camps from California to Georgia were marred by black-versus-white shoot-outs, usually sparked by minor dustups over perceived mistreatment or disrespect. In a two-week span that June, five training-camp riots below the Mason-Dixon Line resulted in at least twenty casualties.

The weirdest incident took place near Mississippi's Camp McCain. On the night of July 5, 1943, thirteen black soldiers from the camp sprayed the nearby town of Duck Hill with gunfire. The GIs were avenging rough treatment they'd received the day before, at a Fourth of July festival in Starkville, some sixty miles to the east. Unable to reach distant Starkville on foot, the avengers settled for Duck Hill, a town they also reviled: it had been declared off-limits to Camp McCain's black trainees, on account of local rumors that a "Negro fiend" was raping white women. The GIs also knew Duck Hill as the site of an infamous 1937 lynching, in which two African American murder suspects had been mutilated with blowtorches.

The Duck Hill raid ended in a semicomical whimper: no one was killed or wounded, and the raiders were easily apprehended. The

Army tried to hush up the incident, but the Memphis *Commercial Appeal* got hold of the court-martial transcripts and exposed the affair. The story was in turn picked up by *Time*, which predicted more racially charged violence to come: "There were no casualties at the battle of Duck Hill. But the Army could not underestimate its significance, for there are many Duck Hills around the big Southern camps."

The training-camp violence coincided with racial clashes in the civilian world, most notably in Detroit, where southern blacks had arrived en masse to work in the wartime factories. A Packard employee echoed the prevailing white opinion of this migration when he declared, "I'd rather see Hitler and Hirohito win than work beside a nigger on the assembly line." On June 20, small clashes at a Detroit park escalated into an orgy of arson and murder, aggravated by preposterous rumors of kidnapped babies, interracial rapes, and Ku Klux Klan caravans. Thirty-four people were killed in a day and a half of violence, twenty-five of them black. "It is blood upon your hands, Mrs. Roosevelt," editorialized the *Daily News* of Jackson, Mississippi, blaming the violence on the First Lady's crusade for racial equality.

Perry and his pals in the 849th spent hours discussing and debating the Detroit riots, as well as the earlier "zoot suit riots" in Los Angeles.* Some men considered protesting the violence by refusing deployment, reviving a tactic once advocated by the Conscientious Objectors Against Jim-Crow. Others went AWOL to Harlem, where they split time between carousing and listening to subversive preachers rant about the futility of the Double V campaign. During the 849th's two-month stay at Camp Kilmer, up to 8 percent of the battalion was missing on any given day; tired of court-martialing the

---

*This was a series of clashes in early June 1943 that pitted white soldiers and sailors against minority Angelenos, particularly Mexican Americans. The disturbance was named after the baggy, heavily pleated suits favored by the city's young gangsters.

scofflaws to no avail, several officers begged for transfers to less troublesome units.

The 849th was scheduled to travel to its port of embarkation at Staten Island, New York, on July 9, 1943. The men would have to march a mile or so to the rail station, then board trains bound for New York. Given the unit's defiant streak, Hiatt feared chaos once the battalion hit the road. He ordered that armed guards be placed in each train car, as well as around the camp's perimeter. He considered lining the marching route with black policemen, but decided against it "due to the animosity between M.P.s (colored) and the E.M."; the enlisted men detested like-complexioned MPs as the worst sorts of Uncle Toms.

The morning of their departure, several members of the 849th's Company C* stole two kegs of beer from the Camp Kilmer store. They drank throughout the day, and were pretty well lit by the time the march began at 6:00 P.M. Ten minutes into the procession, a fight broke out toward the rear of the column, where Company C was marching; two soldiers who'd been arguing over cigarettes were swinging at each other, and their comrades had circled around to egg them on. A few spectators jumped into the fray, among them Private Frank Goodwin, one of the battalion's biggest troublemakers—"a poor soldier, very difficult to control, and an alleged marihuana addict," according to his company commander.

What had begun as a one-on-one fight quickly escalated into a full-blown riot, as white MPs and officers arrived on scene to break things up. Months of frustration came pouring out in the ensuing free-for-all. "Rifles were being swung, bayonets were flashing and one man had a piece of timber and was using it as a club," stated Lieutenant Jesse Coker, a witness to the fracas.

---

*The 849th was divided into four companies: A, B, C, and H&S (for Headquarters and Service). Perry belonged to Company A.

Hiatt, who'd gone ahead to the train station, didn't realize something was amiss until Company C failed to arrive. He drove back along the route and came upon the skirmish. "It appeared to me that the M.P. officer and his men were particularly ineffectual, seeming to aggravate the disorder rather than stop it," Hiatt wrote in his report. "Colonel Landon and I had the four worst acting colored soldiers parted and dispersed the crowd." The stragglers were escorted to the trains, and the 849th proceeded to New York without further incident.

Hiatt tried to keep the embarrassing episode under wraps. But word spread and rumors swirled, until the half-hour riot had taken on epic proportions. "We have received a report that the 849th Engr. Bn (Av) mutinied on board ship en route here," a Delhi-based colonel would write in a confidential memo that September. A full investigation ensued, in which Hiatt characterized the disturbance as the engineers' last-ditch effort to avoid deployment. His final report invoked the stereotype of black troops as congenital cowards: "Men were trying every possible means to avoid shipment overseas, including voluntary exposure to venereal disease."

ON THE OPPRESSIVELY muggy night of July 10, 1943, donning wool uniforms and forty-pound packs, the 849th walked the gangplanks onto the USS *West Point*, a former luxury liner turned overcrowded troop transport. A brass band played onshore as Herman Perry and thousands of other soldiers waved good-bye to America. As Staten Island receded, then disappeared into the distance, the 849th was ushered to its quarters below deck. Perry surely would have lingered topside longer had he known what awaited in the *West Point*'s squalid bowels.

FIVE

The USS *West Point* was on its second incarnation when Herman Perry stepped aboard. The mammoth ship had been christened the SS *America* on August 31, 1939, with Eleanor Roosevelt smashing the customary champagne bottle across the bow as thirty thousand Virginians cheered. Having cost a then exorbitant $17.6 million, the *America* was meant to ferry passengers from New York to England in supreme luxury. United States Lines, the vessel's owner, spared no expense on amenities: guests enjoyed an ornately tiled swimming pool, an art deco cocktail bar, a circular smoking lounge lined with ebonized beechwood, and suites as posh as Fifth Avenue's finest. The *America*'s centerpiece, though, was a balconied first-class restaurant, where turtle soup was served beneath Pierre Bourdelle's lacquered murals.

United States Lines publicized the *America* as a rival to Britain's *Queen Mary* and *Queen Elizabeth*, and President Roosevelt lauded the ship as symbolizing "an early return of the merchant fleet of the United States to a dominant position on the oceans of the world." But the day after the *America*'s raucous christening, the Nazi blitz-

krieg hit Poland; U-boats began prowling the North Atlantic soon
thereafter, decimating the tourist trade. So the *America*'s maiden
voyage in August 1940 was not to Liverpool or Southampton, but to
less perilous San Juan, Puerto Rico. Ten months later she was commandeered by the U.S. Navy and recommissioned as the *West Point*.
Her magnificent trappings were stripped away—the windows covered with metal plates, open decks buried beneath anti-aircraft
guns, the hull's classic red-and-black color scheme replaced with
blue-gray camouflage. Bunks were crammed into every vacant nook,
nearly quintupling the ship's capacity to more than eight thousand
passengers.

The *West Point* was put to work transporting British and Canadian reinforcements to South Asia. The ship was two days out of
Cape Town, headed for Bombay, when the radio blared news of Pearl
Harbor. Its flag no longer that of a neutral nation, the *West Point*
delivered its troops to India, then helped evacuate civilians from
imperiled Singapore.* She'd rarely rest in port for the remainder of
the war, constantly plying the oceans laden with young men bound
for Casablanca, Guadalcanal, or New Caledonia. On its trips back
home, the *West Point* carried Axis prisoners, beginning with the remnants of Erwin "the Desert Fox" Rommel's *Deutsches Afrikakorps* in
April 1943. The POWs were billeted near the ship's boilers, secured
behind thickly barred doors and starved for air and light.

It was in these same dank, sweltering quarters that Herman Perry
would spend his time at sea. Though the 849th's officers were still
reeling from the Camp Kilmer riot, the battalion's GIs weren't con-
signed to the *West Point*'s worst digs as punishment. Enlisted men
were always stashed below deck on transport ships, with the dingiest

---

*Singapore fell to the Japanese on February 15, 1942, in the largest-ever surrender of British-led forces.
Japan renamed the new addition to the Greater East Asia Co-Prosperity Sphere *Syonan-to* ("light of the
south island"), and began the systematic extermination of its Chinese residents.

accommodations reserved for blacks. On a vessel that had been celebrated for its opulence just two years earlier, hailed by the president
himself as a floating symbol of American greatness, Perry would be
treated like minor cargo.

The Navy segregated its ships for the same pragmatic reasons
that the Army isolated blacks at training camps: to prevent violence
and to mollify soldiers whose fighting resolve might slip should they
be forced to mix with the detested Other. Rear Admiral Walton R.
Sexton elucidated the Navy's position in a 1942 memo, the same one
in which he quoted a congressman's view of integration as a potentially "crushing insult" to southern patriots:

> Men on board ship live in particularly close association; in their
> messes, one man sits beside another; their hammocks or bunks are
> close together; in their common tasks they work side by side. . . . How
> many white men would choose, of their own accord, that their clos-
> est associates in sleeping quarters, at mess, and in a gun's crew
> should be another race? How many would accept such conditions,
> if required to do so, without resentment and just as a matter of
> course? The General Board believes that the answer is "Few, if any,"
> and further believes that if the issue were forced, there would be a
> lowering of contentment, teamwork and discipline in the service.

In addition to segregating Army units aboard its transports, the
Navy balked at allowing black recruits to serve on ships, except as
cooks; many African Americans drafted into the Navy thus ended up
as Seabees, building docks and warehouses instead of manning destroyers. Sexton acknowledged the injustice of this policy in his
memo, but pled that such discrimination "is but part and parcel of
similar discrimination throughout the United States not only against
the negro [sic], but in the Pacific States and in Hawaii against citi-

zens of Asiatic descent. . . . These concepts may not be truly democratic, but it is doubted if the most ardent lovers of democracy will
dispute them, particularly in regards to inter-marriage."

The practical case for segregation wasn't foremost in Perry's mind
as he first surveyed his *West Point* quarters, a spartan room with hundreds of cots slung from pipes or bolted to the walls. These canvas
beds, stacked four high, were crammed so close together that there
was barely room to walk. Sergeant Frank Lowry, an infantryman who
later sailed the *West Point* to Marseilles, recalled the claustrophobia:

> The tiers of bunks and narrow aisles took up every square foot of
> available space, consequently each man had to keep his gear on the
> bunk with him. There was barely enough vertical clearance between
> bunks for a man to squeeze in. To keep one's bunk from sagging and
> crowding the man below, it was frequently necessary to tighten the
> ropes that held the canvas to the steel frame. From any bunk, a man
> could reach out and easily touch half a dozen of his buddies in
> nearby bunks.

A steel trough sloshing with seawater served as a communal toilet.
The whiff of the prior occupants' sweat and shit lingered in the air,
a stench made worse by an utter lack of ventilation. Heat radiating
from the *West Point*'s steam valves cooked the room, and Perry
quickly broiled in his fatigues and combat boots.

Nine stories above this human coop, Lieutenant Colonel Wright
Hiatt and the 849th's officers were ushered into suites once reserved
for United States Lines' well-heeled clientele. The expensive furni-
ture and decorations had been removed, but topside life aboard the
West Point wasn't half bad. *The Pointer*, an onboard newsletter published by the aspiring journalists among the crew, made the ship
sound like a floating college dorm:

Considerable areas of the ship are air conditioned with the latest designed machinery. An extensive ventilating system adds to the comfort of the personnel. A spacious Sports Deck on the topside, a splendidly appointed swimming pool, a fine gymnasium, an adequate library, soda fountain, and the latest facilities for motion pictures all add to the recreation and enjoyment of those on board. In the expansive galleys and the best ice boxes anywhere to be found the food for the ship's complement is stored and prepared.

In photographs taken in one of the *West Point*'s best mess halls, a converted lounge ringed by paintings of Columbus discovering the New World, junior officers beam over plates of bacon and eggs. There is never a black face among them.

A NEWCOMER TO MARITIME TRAVEL is likely to suffer from crippling *mal de mer* his first time at sea. This was doubly true for soldiers before the advent of Dramamine, when the most common remedy was a gruff command to toughen up.* But self-discipline is no defense against seasickness, and thousands of passengers succumbed once the *West Point* left New York's harbor. Troops above deck hugged the ship's railings and heaved their ham-on-white sandwiches into the Atlantic foam. The 849th's afflicted members, confined as they were to the belly of the hull, crawled to the elongated latrine and thrust their heads inside.

The epidemic was exacerbated by the *West Point*'s nonstop zigzagging, a standard antisubmarine tactic. With a top speed of twenty-

---

*Dramamine, announced to the world on Valentine's Day 1949, was originally tested on American soldiers traveling to occupied Germany aboard the USS *General C. C. Ballou*. Prior to this antihistamine's invention, the "cures" for seasickness ranged from aspirin to toast to hydrocyanic acid. One slightly effective remedy, used by some soldiers of the American Expeditionary Force during World War I, was cocaine dissolved in wine or water.

five knots or better, the *West Point* was fast enough to outrun any U-boat, and thus traveled alone rather than in a convoy. But Captain Robert Dyer, the ship's commander, knew that German subs were apt to lie in wait should an Allied ship steer too predictable a route. So he abruptly shifted the *West Point*'s course every few miles, a precaution loathed by GIs whose tummies were already roiling.

Seasick or not, an enlisted man's routine aboard the *West Point* was drab and never-changing. The better part of Perry's day was spent queuing for chow in the GIs' canteen, formerly a third-class dining room. Whites were served first, of course, and members of the 849th stood in line until their fairer-skinned comrades had finished up. Bare-chested mess-men ladled out lukewarm, gelatinous chili con carne for both breakfast and dinner. (Lunch wasn't served.) Perry and hundreds of others ate standing at long tables, sliding down toward the exit as new diners squeezed in. At the tables' ends, trash cans stood ready to accommodate those who couldn't stomach the acrid stew. The entire process, from queue to cleaned plate, took hours.

His hunger barely sated, Perry's next stop was a room filled with drums of boiling, soapy seawater, in which soldiers washed and sterilized their mess kits. Failure to perform this sanitary ritual inevitably led to a case of "the GIs," an Army euphemism for acute diarrhea. It was imperative to clean one's bowl as quickly as possible, since the room's briny odor wreaked further havoc on the queasy. "The steel deck was always wet and slippery with spilled food and lost meals," wrote Lowry. "Frequently men were unable to retain their meals long enough to get out of the hold, consequently most did not linger while they were eating or washing their mess gear."

Fresh air and a few puffs of a Chesterfield might have helped alleviate the misery, but above-deck breaks were a privilege denied the 849th, save for the nights when all 7,928 passengers practiced abandoning ship. Perry had no choice but to return to the labyrinth of bunks, where the absence of sunlight warped everyone's sense of time. Guards were stationed just outside the unlocked doors, to ensure there was no repeat of the Camp Kilmer unpleasantness. Soldiers begged for turns at the drinking fountains reserved for whites, but were ordered back to their berths. All Perry could do to fend off boredom was chat, play cards, or stare at the outline of the man in the cot above. Sleep, already difficult due to the ship's violent motion, became virtually impossible as the room's loudspeakers screeched constant admonitions against smoking below deck.

The *West Point* crossed the equator roughly six days into the voyage, an event that crew members commemorated with a round of friendly hazing: passengers who'd never before sailed into the Southern Hemisphere were dunked in tubs of water, forced to crawl through garbage, zapped with cattle prods, and otherwise degraded by naval officers dressed as "Davy Jones" or "Neptunus Rex." The playful torment continued until the neophytes were judged to have evolved from "pollywogs" into "shellbacks." Excluded from this collegial fun were the ship's African American GIs, who continued roasting in their cots as the *West Point* sailed toward its first port of call.

Though he could see nothing from his bunk except hundreds of his seasick friends, Perry sensed that the *West Point* had entered calmer waters on the morning of July 22, 1943. Soon enough the engines hushed and the vessel's side-to-side list mellowed into a gentle rock. Perry deduced that the *West Point* had arrived in port, but where? Judging by the number of meals the 849th had queued for, his best guess was that they'd been traveling for twelve days— was that long enough to get them to Europe? The 849th wasn't blessed with any globe-trotters, so wild speculation had to suffice.

Whether by officer or stairwell guard, word finally arrived: the ship had docked at Rio de Janeiro to pick up supplies. No one would be allowed ashore, as the *West Point* was scheduled to shove off in less than twenty-four hours. It's unknown whether Perry was afforded time above deck while docked at Rio, to gaze at the bustling Brazilian port and enjoy the cigarettes that were forbidden down below.

Next came another nine days at sea, a rough passage across the South Atlantic. The heat and congestion of the 849th's quarters, combined with the miserable diet, began to take its toll, especially on the men's nostrils; a high-school locker room smelled of roses by comparison. Showering was done with seawater, in combination with a coarse black soap that supposedly lathered well in brine. Woe to the man who, using his mess bowl as a mirror, nicked his face while shaving, then rubbed salty water in the wound.

Just as back in Myrtle Beach, the men of the 849th were offered no recreation, no way to break the monotony of *West Point* life. They weren't invited to the promenade deck for Variety Night or the jitterbug contest, and they certainly weren't welcome in the ship's gymnasium. About the only fun the engineers had was floating flaming wads of paper down the toilet trough, to singe the butts of unsuspecting pals. It was a poor substitute for actual leisure, but it was better than lying in one's bunk morning, noon, and night.

The next stop was Cape Town on July 31. This time the 849th's officers were allowed ashore, but Perry and the enlisted men were confined to quarters—South Africa's government didn't want any more blacks in their racially stratified country, and American officers worried that GIs would go AWOL and blend into the slums. So while Hiatt and his underlings enjoyed a day in the city, dining at Afrikaner restaurants and taking in views of Table Mountain, Perry languished on the *West Point*. Thus began the schism between how white officers and black GIs would come to view their respective times in the China-Burma-India theater of operations: for the former group it was a grand adventure, for the latter a dismal trial.

The trip's final stretch lasted twelve more days, as the ship chugged north past Madagascar and into the western expanse of the Indian Ocean. The only event of note occurred as the *West Point* veered around the Cape of Good Hope and slammed into a gargantuan black fish, reputedly forty feet from head to tail. After that, the hull dwellers felt nothing except the constant chop of water against the vessel's port and starboard. No great student of geography to begin with, Perry was utterly baffled as to where they could be heading. He only knew that he wanted off the *West Point* fast, so he could write home and inquire about Aaron's boxing fortunes: despite having lost his first professional bout to the improbably named Tiger Nelson, young Aaron was on a winning streak that summer, and primed to fulfill his promise as a world-class fighter.

On the *West Point*'s thirty-second day out of New York, having covered 14,202 miles, the ship docked once more. This time, however, the 849th was told to grab its packs and come topside—they'd arrived. Wobbly-legged and weak from poor nutrition, yet delighted to escape the *West Point*'s stinking innards, Perry lugged his duffel up the stairs, emerging into the clammy monsoon-season air of western India's great port: Bombay.

UPON BEING INFORMED that they'd arrived in India, the undereducated and untraveled GIs aboard the *West Point* scratched their heads in puzzlement—would they soon be surrounded by men in feathered headdresses smoking peace pipes? Perry was among the bemused, having never before seen an Indian man with his loins wrapped in a dhoti, or an Indian woman draped in a vivid sari. Nor was he prepared for the alien sights and smells of Bombay's fringe: the wandering cows gorging on garbage, the statuettes of elephant-headed and six-armed gods, the throngs of scabby beggars, the pungent scent of sewage wafting through the air. Perry couldn't have felt any more disoriented had he landed on the moon.

Adding to the soldiers' bewilderment was the mystery of why they'd been dispatched to India. Why hadn't they been sent someplace they'd heard of, someplace with an obvious connection to the fight against those evil Japs and Nazis? Try as they might, the engineers of the 849th couldn't figure out how this distant British colony played into the Allies' plans.

Hiatt and his lieutenants revealed little while debriefing the men. They were mum about the unit's mission, offering only basic advice such as how to obtain local currency (officers would change everyone's dollars into rupees) and warning the men to rebuke the entreaties of whores. Perry and his fellow GIs were also ordered to avoid discussing racial prejudice with the Indians. The fear was that spies or turncoats would learn the true extent of America's racial polarization, and use that information to the Axis's advantage. Byron Price, head of the Office of Censorship, had put his training as an Associated Press editor to work in explaining this policy to the NAACP: "Here at home we understand the situation and there is no barrier for free expression. The enemy not only does not understand it but finds it prime ammunition for promotion of his 'divide and conquer' propaganda."

The 849th wasn't given a chance to explore Bombay proper. The battalion was hustled from the *West Point* to waiting trains, which whisked them 125 miles northeast to Deolali, a British rest camp. Deolali was where the raj's soldiers, having finished their tours of duty, were sent to await ships back home to Liverpool or Cardiff.

Many of these men had been driven mad by sunstroke or disease, giving birth to a term inspired by the camp's singsong name: doolally, slang for "crazy." During World War II, the United States used Deolali to acclimate its troops to India's saunalike conditions.*

Just beyond the camp's perimeter was a high-walled yard that smelled worse than the *West Point* after mealtime. It was perpetually ringed by vultures, who always seemed to have blackened scraps of carrion dangling from their beaks. The soldiers wondered what this creepy place might be, until an Indian informed them that it was a pyre ground for cremating corpses. The stink didn't bother the Americans so much as the vultures, who frequently swooped down and tried to relieve unalert soldiers of their food. Those who fought back by pounding the scavengers atop their heads were reprimanded by superstitious Indians, who considered the giant birds sacred.

Perry spent two weeks at Deolali, marching through monsoon downpours as part of what Hiatt referred to as the "toughening up process." Each day, though, the unit's ranks grew thinner; dysentery was pervasive, as the engineers grew ill from eating goat meat cooked in muddy pits, or apples washed in fetid water. Anyone who's ever suffered from dysentery can attest to the disease's severity. "If I had to ever go through that again, I'd sooner be dead," said John Leber, a native of Wrightsville, Pennsylvania, who served in the CBI with the 317th Troop Carrier Group. "It's painful. It's a parasite that gets into your digestive tract, and it eats into the tissue of your intestines, and you bleed. I mean, I was bleeding out my rectum like somebody having a period, a lady having a period or something. . . . I survived it, but I never got my weight back after that." Though sulfa drugs

---

*Deolali was also one of several camps where the British tested chemical weapons during World War II, ostensibly to develop countermeasures against Japan's stockpiles of mustard gas. According to the Organisation for the Prohibition of Chemical Weapons, "live human volunteer subjects were exposed to high doses of mustard agents, with anywhere from adequate protection to no protection at all."

had recently been invented, they were not yet part of the Medical Corps's standard armamentarium; for the most part, victims of dysentery could only drink boiled water and pray.

To give the men some sense of what to expect, the officers handed out copies of the War Department's *Pocket Guide to India*. Literate men like Perry read the contents to their less erudite brethren, sharing such salient facts as "No Hindu would dream of killing a cow" and "One should tip for everything." The booklet also drew an implicit analogy between the anticolonial Indian nationalists, led by Mohandas Karamchand Gandhi, and African Americans. The not-so-subtle comparison was meant to discourage GIs from discussing the "Negro question":

> Indians want democracy to win. Some of the bitterest antitotalitarians in the world are among the leaders of the Indian Nationalist movement. But Indian politics have been bitter and complicated. Sometimes political interests overshadow matters of national defense. That has been true in the other countries.
>
> India is threatened as we are threatened. Your very presence in India may help draw all Indians together in the common cause if you win their confidence and friendship. American democracy has been a source of inspiration to many Indian leaders. Our ideals, our way of living, give them hope for the future. It is up to you to live up to that idea they have of us.

The 849th's enlisted men still had no idea where they were headed, or what India had to do with the war; the *Pocket Guide* mentioned something about "driving the Japanese back to Tokyo," but was vague as to how the Army's presence on the subcontinent might further that goal. So on the morning of August 27, upon being ordered to march to the Deolali train station, Perry had to wonder what was next. There was gossip, for sure—rumors of a secret project in Assam, wherever that was. But Hiatt and his lieutenants were tight-lipped about the mission's particulars; it's possible that even the 849th's officers were in the dark, their telegraphed orders from Delhi consisting of nothing more than broad instructions to move the unit east.

If Perry expected that the *West Point* would be his worst Army transit experience, he discovered otherwise aboard the train out of Deolali. While the officers lounged in comfortable berths, dining on scrambled eggs and pork chops, Perry was crammed into the train's version of steerage: a boxcar with no adornments except for slatted wooden benches. The train spent days passing through India's central provinces, chugging past the likes of Nagpur, Raipur, and Sambalpur. Twice daily it paused at one dusty village or another to take on coal; as the train slowed, lame and leprous beggars ran to the windows of Perry's car, stretched out their arms, and cried, "No mama, no papa! *Baksheesh, sahib!*" The officers would disembark to dine at the station's restaurant, but the enlisted men stayed on the train. They'd amuse themselves by peering at the snake charmers and sword swallowers who performed alongside the tracks, risking their lives or esophageal linings for the sake of a few rupees.

Bread was picked up at these stops, too—flat and doughy naan that became the black soldiers' primary means of sustenance, supplemented by a smattering of C rations.* The trick to eating the stuff, as an African American sergeant named Mose J. Davie later recalled, was timing your meals just right: "When the train stopped for you to eat, you got some hardtack full of bugs and weevils out of the boxcar. You couldn't eat it in the daytime. You waited until night

---

*A C ration, or C rat, typically consisted of tinned meat accompanied by crackers and a dessert (usually a pudding). For GIs, the unappetizing meal kit's highlight was the accessory packet, which contained four cigarettes.

so you couldn't see what you were eating." Worse than the troughs
of the *West Point*, the trains' toilets consisted of nothing more advanced than holes drilled into the floors; embarrassed to use these
crude facilities, many men chose to delay nature's call, to their intestines' painful chagrin.

There was a one-night layover on Calcutta's outskirts, as the
849th waited to switch to northbound trains. The battalion camped
out along a stagnant pool, black with sludge. Across the way was a
clutter of hovels, and the sex-starved soldiers gawked at the Indian
girls hanging clothes to dry. The girls in turn beckoned with come-
hither fingers; they were not professional prostitutes like those in the
city's famous brothels, but their impoverished families could use the
extra income. The MPs, always vigilant of the black man's supposed
predilection for "Ethiopian vices," made sure no one from the battalion went AWOL in search of female companionship.

The frustrated 849th boarded trains on the Bengal-Assam Railway the next morning. Perry ate and slept atop his bench for three
days straight as the ancient engine dragged them across the Ganges,
bound for Darjeeling. At the village of Parbatipur they switched to a
narrow-gauge train, which took them east across Bengal to the banks
of the mighty, scythe-shaped Brahmaputra River, Assam's defining
waterway. At Dhubri they switched from train to barge, one with a
turbaned Charon at the bow continually shouting out the river's
shifting depths. At Pandu it was back to trains even more rickety
than the last, and Perry stared out at the green and endless tea
gardens—Assam's answer to the cotton fields of his North Carolina
youth. Somewhere along the line he began to feel the first pangs of
illness; records don't mention his exact diagnosis, but all signs point
to dysentery.

The journey ended on September 7, and Perry spilled out into the haze of Margherita, a market town less than five miles from Ledo. Ringed by towering rain forest, Margherita reverberated with the polyglot tones of soldiers, coolies, and Burmese refugees. The bazaar was lined with tin-roofed stalls where vendors hawked rice and bamboo baskets; in the shadows of the trees, toothless merchants furtively beckoned with more alluring goods, like cigarettes or tins of soup stolen from Army depots.

Along the train tracks at the market's edge, small and leathery men squatted in the dirt, smoking strangely fragrant cigarettes and chattering in a catlike tongue. Nearly naked from the waist down, they carried square-bladed swords across their chests or backs, and fixed death stares on Americans who snapped their pictures without offering recompense. These were the Nagas, the ornery and paranoid hill people who'd long raided the surrounding tea gardens in search of coolies to behead; their animist religion held that captured skulls were powerful talismans. But the Nagas had learned to profit from the Allied forces' presence in their homeland, selling knives as souvenirs and lopping off the heads of cobras for GIs craving a vicarious thrill. Some Nagas even carried around sacks of human skulls they'd seized, offering Americans a peek at the grisly trophies in exchange for coins or trinkets.

At last, at an Army outpost known as Headquarters Base Section III, Perry and the 849th learned why they'd been transported to the other side of the globe. Hiatt told his men that, contrary to the training they'd received in South Carolina, they wouldn't be building any airstrips. Instead they'd be working on a road meant to keep America's Chinese allies flush with supplies. The Army Air Forces, said Hiatt, had loaned the battalion to the Services of Supply, and they'd henceforth be operating heavy machinery—particularly bulldozers and rock crushers. The soldiers scratched their heads or grumbled, wondering if they were being punished with exile to a wartime back-water—much like the 364th Infantry Regiment, which had ended up in Alaska after the Camp Van Dorn fiasco.

Perry was deathly ill by now. And as the battalion rode lorries through the town of Ledo, the forested peaks of the Patkais looming in the distance, he took a turn for the worse. While his comrades proceeded toward the Burmese border to set up camp, Perry was left to convalesce at the Army's Twentieth General Hospital. Built atop a mass grave for casualties of the 1942 Burma evacuation, the hospital was chaotic and filthy; mud floors were the norm, and cows and jackals roamed the hallways. There was a separate wing for Chinese patients, who contributed to the unhygienic conditions by bringing live chickens into their ward.*

On September 13, Perry was judged well enough to rejoin his unit in the Patkais, where the 849th had started work on the Ledo Road. As Perry's truck began its slow ascent up the mountains, he noticed a white sign posted by a gated, dirt-strewn bridge—the last bridge in Assam. The sign read only: HELLGATE.

It would have been up to Perry's driver to explain this milestone's meaning: once a man passed the Hellgate, it was said that his odds of coming back alive were fifty-fifty.

SOON AFTER ARRIVING at the 849th's rustic camp, a cluster of wood huts clinging to a hillside clearing, Perry sat down to write letters home. Above all, he wanted to check on Aaron's pugilistic progress; surely the family's boxing prodigy had fought several times since Herman's departure over two months earlier. Yet he also wanted to

---

*The Twentieth General Hospital was staffed by doctors from the University of Pennsylvania, who spent their leisure time practicing thoracic surgery on dogs. The knowledge gleaned from these experiments later contributed to the development of the first heart-lung machines, which made modern bypass surgery possible.

reassure his family that everything was fine, all things considered, and that he'd arrived at the Pangsau Pass none the worse for wear. In his letter to Edna, he couldn't reveal much—officers censored all outgoing mail, to make sure that no sensitive information was betrayed. But the upbeat charmer from Florida Avenue was still much in evidence in Perry's upright cursive, as was an inkling of the ordeal soon to come:

Hello Edna,

Just a line to let you hear from me. So far every thing is o.k. hope you can say the same. I got your letter a couple of days ago it came in time.

there is not much I can say except hello and goodby my time for writing is very short So Ill say how is Lewis and the family. if you have never tried living the hard way then you wont understand whats its all about.

Ill be looking for an answer soon its about time for you to send a Xmas pkg. I cant tell you what to send you will have to figure that out yourself I can say this don't send anything that will spoil before it gets here. it will take almost two months to reach me. its very hot here hotter than you have ever seen it.

So far I have made out o.k. I hope Ill be able to say this in the next letter. guess Ill close my address is at the bottom of this page.

Love, Herman

SIX

Though decimated by disease, the Army's engineers had zoomed up the Patkais in early 1943. They flattened clumps of white-barked trees with "Cats," as they called their rusty bulldozers, then graveled the upturned earth with stone. When rocky outcroppings blocked their path, daredevil members of the 823rd Engineer Aviation Battalion scaled thirty-foot cliffs and stuffed crevices with TNT; dynamite boomed nonstop across the hills. Hunched and calloused coolies lugged off the postexplosion debris, as well as the maggoty corpses of refugees who'd died while fleeing Burma.

On February 28, the road builders reached the Burmese border, a foggy, wildflower-covered highland thirty-eight miles east of Ledo. They posted a sign declaring THIS WAY TO TOKYO, a nod to Lieutenant General Joseph Warren Stilwell's grand designs.

Then came the St. Patrick's Day deluge. A portent of the hellacious monsoon season to come, the storm turned miles of finished road into swampland overnight. Mudslides flipped Cats into vine-strewn gullies as the Americans huddled in their tents, awestruck by the viscous sheets of rain. When the weather finally broke, the Chinese conscripts that Stilwell had been training in Ramgarh, India, came trampling through, headed east to confront the Japanese—the first phase of Vinegar Joe's plan to avenge his Burma defeat. Unfortunately for the engineers, the Chinese soldiers' pack mules and horses wreaked havoc on the road's moist gravel, leaving hoof-shaped pockmarks every few inches. Months' worth of labor was undone in less than a week.

Rather than completing the road's first hundred miles by May, as Stilwell had demanded, the engineers bogged down along the Indo-Burmese border. They'd struggle to clear and grade a patch of jungle, then watch helplessly as monsoons erased their gains. The downpours were accompanied by heat so dire that it inspired a ghoulish ditty: "Long may you live / And when you die / You'll find hell / Cooler than CBI." Triple-digit temperatures combined with rain to create a constant haze of steam; soldiers' fatigues literally rotted away in the humidity.

Asked by a *Time* reporter to assess the engineers' progress after a typically dismal, waterlogged few weeks, one colonel sarcastically replied: "Doing great. Only lost a half mile this month." A high-ranking medical officer, meanwhile, offered a franker assessment in his diary that August: "An obvious failure . . . The road is not progressing worth a damn."

The road had barely budged for months when Herman Perry left the Twentieth General Hospital on September 13. He reunited with the 849th near the Pangsau Pass, which the troops had dubbed Hell Pass—a fitting nickname for such a wretched locale. When first informed that he'd be stationed in the jungle, Perry likely envisioned a happy scene from one of Johnny Weissmuller's *Tarzan* films, with monkeys frolicking in sunny treetop homes. But the Patkais' shadowy forests were anything but inviting. An Army public relations man, evidently possessed of literary ambitions, neatly captured the jungle's malice in a 1945 pamphlet: "Venture a few hundred feet from the highway and you enter a dim, matted world possessed by natures [*sic*] most vicious beasts, birds, insects and pests. . . . The jungle, in reality, is tall and dark and silent as death."

A work camp near the Pangsau Pass, aka Hell Pass.

The engineers at Hell Pass lived in log-and-canvas huts that regularly flooded with reddish, knee-deep goop. The huts' wooden floors were designed to repel the venomous snakes that slithered through the hillside brush and coiled in empty boots. Yet the floors didn't deter red ants, which swarmed in the thousands and chewed men's flesh to pulp. Officers avoided the ants by lodging in more civilized quarters, elevated on bamboo poles and serviced by Indian valets who laundered clothes and shined shoes.

After spreading gravel and clearing boulders for sixteen hours a day, Perry's nightly reward was a meal of tinned corned beef ("corned willy") and rice, with bacterial water to slake his thirst. Some of the engineers supplemented this lackluster diet with fresh-caught frogs, which they blinded with flashlights, then speared with bayonets. They roasted the critters over open flames, as curious gibbons crouched along the tree line; the long-limbed apes screeched from dusk until dawn, making sleep elusive for the exhausted GIs.

Leeches, rather than shrieking gibbons, were the menace most reviled by Perry and his fellow engineers. Red or green or chocolate brown in color, these slimy annelids drooped from trees or clustered on blades of neck-high grass, waiting to gorge on the blood of passersby. The only reliable way to separate leech from skin was with a lit cigarette. Painful as this method was, it was better than allowing the three- to five-inch parasites to feast until sated; the circular wounds the leeches left behind usually became infected, oozing gooey pus for days or weeks. The GIs called these lesions "Naga sores," since the limbs of Naga tribesmen often bore such gory scars.

The leeches had a particular affinity for the body's most sensitive areas: eyelids, nostrils, and especially the privates. A man defecating in the jungle might later discover that a leech had crawled from grass to buttock during the process, and made itself at home deep within a particularly vulnerable orifice. An Army captain wrote of one comrade's wince-inducing encounter with a sneaky bloodsucker:

> One night while he was sleeping one of these leeches had gotten into the tube of Red's penis. When he awakened it was swollen to

the point where he could not urinate. It was becoming extremely painful and there seemed to be nothing they could do to remove the leech. When the pain became most excruciating, he was actually thinking of gouging it out with a knife. Lieutenant Quinn finally suggested making a forceps-shaped tool out of bamboo. It worked fine and they were able to get hold of the leech and pull it out.

Lice attacked with similar aggression, nesting in the soldiers' hair, beards, and pubic regions; the nurses at the Twentieth General Hospital were stunned by how many of the speck-sized insects they found when prepping patients for surgery. Sergeant Smith Dawless, an Army journalist who became the Ledo Road's unofficial poet laureate, bore lyrical witness to the malevolence of lice:

Oh, give me cobras, give me mice.
But do not give me bamboo lice.
They revel in your blankets,
Cavort among your clothes,
And sixty times a minute
They drop upon your nose.
They shinny up your shoulder
And swarm around your face.
For each one you extinguish
A dozen takes its place.

Anopheles mosquitoes might have been less grotesque in their methods, but they were also far deadlier. The malaria rate along the Ledo Road was astronomical: 955 cases per every 1,000 men. It was perfectly normal for a soldier to experience a dozen or more episodes of malarial fever during his stay in the jungle. In other exotic war locales where malaria was endemic, infection-control teams doused mosquito breeding grounds with pesticides. But due to a lack of chemicals, as well as simple negligence, the Ledo Road was seldom sprayed.

The malaria situation was aggravated by the fact that Japan had conquered the Dutch East Indies so early in the war. The island of Java, invaded by the Japanese in February 1942, was the world's only source of cinchona trees, the bark of which is used to make the antimalarial drug quinine.* Deprived of this vital pharmaceutical resource, the Allies had to rely on Atabrine, an antimalarial synthesized from coal tars. Though mildly effective if taken regularly, soldiers disliked swallowing their recommended five grains of Atabrine a day; the drug turned their skin a deep, repulsive yellow, and it was rumored to cause both psychosis (true) and impotence (false). Some concerned sergeants manually forced the pills down privates' throats before mealtimes. Yet as evidenced by the hordes of feverish men who crammed Ledo's hospital wards, the compulsory Atabrine regimens were hardly panaceas.

The hospitals also teemed with victims of typhus, a mite-borne illness with symptoms akin to dengue fever. David Richardson, a correspondent for *Yank: The Army Weekly*, witnessed the ailment's toll on combat troops in northern Burma:

> Scrub typhus was tough. One day a man would be okay, slogging along through the jungles, cussing Stilwell and offering to trade his fruit bar and powdered coffee for a cheese and a powdered chocolate. And the next he would suddenly collapse with a 104 fever and go blind and start turning black. When a man got it, we gave him pills, tried to keep him warm and started digging another hole.

---

*The cinchona tree is actually native to the Andes, and its image graces the modern Peruvian flag. In the nineteenth century, the Dutch smuggled cinchona seeds to Java, where quinine could be produced far cheaper than in South America. The Andean quinine industry collapsed as a result.

Usually he died quickly and we would leave him under a little
rustic cross.

Many soldiers were given an experimental typhus vaccine before
entering the Indo-Burmese wilderness. The vaccine, alas, hadn't
been engineered to protect against a particularly aggressive species
of mite that inhabited Burma's Hukaung Valley, just to the east of
the Patkais. Scores of men thus succumbed to typhus, bewildered
to their dying breaths as to how Burmese bugs could have bested
Western medicine.

Then there were the Bengal tigers, thickly muscled cats that
preferred the taste of pigs and oxen, but would settle for humans in
a pinch. When heavy rains forced the tigers to flee their saturated
jungle abodes, a series of maulings inevitably followed. The tea
planters of Assam were quite familiar with this cycle; missing limbs
and missing coolies were usually the work of displaced tigers.* Attacks on American soldiers were frequent enough that officers noted
them with dispassion. "Tiger killed soldier in Warazup," a colonel
with the Forty-fifth Engineer General Service Regiment wrote in
his diary one June day. "Next night badly mauled another soldier
and next night killed native—animal apparently forced to dry ground
a/c the flood." Officers struck back in their leisure time, hunting
the maneaters with dum-dums†; the striped pelts made for sumptuous rugs.

The same rains that rousted tigers from their homes also caused
numerous fatal accidents. Men were crushed by boulders that

---

*Peter Gray, one of the most successful tea planters in Assam, was among those who lost an arm—as well
as a trusted servant—to a tiger. The animal dragged a sleeping Gray off his veranda, letting go of the Brit
only after four servants intervened. Aside from having his arm severed, Gray's hair turned white from shock;
it remained that color for the rest of his life.

†A bullet that has been modified to expand upon impact, usually by shaving the tip. The Hague Convention
of 1899 outlawed dum-dums for use in combat, though this prohibition has frequently been violated, particularly during World War I.

cracked off cliffs, buried alive beneath torrents of mud, or smashed by falling trees. Flash floods, meanwhile, were the special bane of bridge builders. One minute a group of soldiers would be lashing together bamboo poles atop a Burmese river, wondering why a clique of half-naked Nagas were pointing and clucking at their rickety creation; moments later the GIs would be swept off by a wall of water, never to be seen again.

Two-and-a-half-ton supply trucks, nicknamed 6x6s, were prone to skidding off the road's tortuous switchbacks; in one seven-mile stretch leading up to Hell Pass, there were more than two hundred such hairpin curves. When the gravel finish had been eroded by rains or Chinese mules, the road's lethality soared. Errant stones or misjudged turns caused trucks to plunge from road to ravine, a drop as far as two hundred feet. The drivers, many of them untrained on 6x6s before arriving in the CBI, also had to be careful when shifting gears on steep grades; the aging trucks were liable to catch fire if their axles were overstressed.

The elements and animals may have been the 849th's toughest foes, but enemy snipers added to the terror. The Imperial Japanese Army never conquered the Patkais; its troops were bedeviled by the same obstacles that made the Ledo Road such a Sisyphean endeavor for the Americans. Yet Japanese scouts still roamed the hills, taking potshots at construction crews.* Cat drivers were required to have armed escorts riding shotgun, and their vehicles were fitted with makeshift armor cobbled from scrap. The armor came in handy not just in repelling sniper fire, but also when the bulldozers ran over unexploded shells buried in the jungle muck.

Japanese planes buzzed over the engineers, too. Some broadcast

---

*Japanese scouts were masters of stoking terror among combat units, too. One of their favorite tactics was sneaking into an Allied camp in the dead of night, slitting a few throats at random, and then vanishing into the bush. This obviously had a deleterious effect on the ability of American GIs to get a good night's rest.

English-language taunts over Army radio frequencies, or dropped leaflets urging GIs to desert; others dropped bombs. Sergeant Mahon East of the Forty-fifth was among those gravely wounded by Japanese bombers, as he was gassing up his unit's Cats one morning. The blast scorched half the skin off his face, turning it an ashen white that contrasted sharply with his usual complexion. Upon returning from a two-month convalescence, his colleagues dubbed him Sergeant Two-Tone.

East remembers a curious friend who wasn't so lucky. During a later bombing raid, this young man peeked his head over the embankment behind which he and East had taken cover. "He wanted to see what [a Japanese plane] looked like," says East. "He's standing up and looking, and a sniper just cut his head right off, just like you took a knife to it. So, we lost him."

THOUGH PRESIDENT ROOSEVELT had promised to make the Ledo Road a top priority, the reality ended up being just the opposite. Washington rapidly came to view the project—and the China-Burma-India theater as a whole—as a sideshow, unworthy of more than token support. War planners had been content to set the road in motion, for it seemed so clever in theory. But once they realized how much money and manpower the road truly required, and how meager its benefits ultimately would be, their enthusiasm waned—much as Chiang Kai-shek's enthusiasm had waned once Major General Claire Lee Chennault, commander of the Fourteenth Air Force based in China, had started whispering in his ear about the miracle of air power.*

To Lieutenant General Stilwell's dismay, Chennault kept using

---

*Chennault was promoted to major general in March 1943.

his trademark charm to undermine the Ledo Road. In April 1943, Chennault and Stilwell flew to Washington to meet with Roosevelt and the War Department brass, at an Allied conference codenamed TRIDENT. Madame Chiang came as her husband's emissary, installing herself (against the president's wishes) in a White House bedroom. She passed along the Generalissimo's request—obviously penned by his pal Chennault—that all American resources in the CBI be used to increase the number of cargo flights between Assam and southern China. If enough supplies could be airlifted over the Himalayan Hump, the Ledo Road would be redundant.

Having committed himself to the road just five months earlier, Roosevelt did an about-face upon meeting Chennault, whose persuasive powers were aided by his folksy drawl and impeccable manners. The Cajun general promised to do more than just save Chiang's regime: he also vowed to gain supremacy in China's eastern skies and start bombing Japan's home islands. Chennault stated that if his Fourteenth Air Force was allocated ten thousand tons of supplies per month, it would eventually sink a million tons' worth of Japanese naval vessels.

Roosevelt was bowled over by Chennault's grandiose vision. "If you can sink a million tons, we'll break their backs!" the president declared, excitedly pounding his fists on his desk.

Stilwell sneered at Roosevelt's newfound zeal for air power, though he wasn't too surprised by the president's fickleness. Vinegar Joe had always had a low opinion of Roosevelt's intellect, dating back to their first meeting in February 1942. He found the president to be self-important and overly loquacious, not to mention a Democrat—anathema to a lifelong Republican like Stilwell. "Cordial and pleasant—and frothy. Unimpressive," Stilwell jotted about Roosevelt after their initial tête-à-tête. "Acted as if I were a voter calling on a Congressman. Rambled on about his idea of the war—'a 29,000 mile front is *my* conception,' etc. etc. Just a lot of wind."

Stilwell pushed for the Ledo Road's preservation in his typically abrasive style, making no effort to conceal his disdain for both Roosevelt and the lower-ranking Chennault. He argued that Chennault's planes should be used to support the budding ground campaign in northern Burma—the offensive led by Chinese troops from Ramgarh, aimed at clearing the road's intended path. Stilwell also warned against catering to Chiang's latest whim, emphasizing that the Generalissimo surely had ulterior motives: he forthrightly described the Chinese leader as "a vacillating, tricky, undependable old scoundrel who never keeps his word."

Correct though he may have been about Peanut, Vinegar Joe's gruffness did him no favors at the TRIDENT conference. Unlike *Life* or *The New York Times*, Roosevelt wasn't impressed by Stilwell's aversion to diplomacy. The president was tempted to kill the Ledo Road altogether, in favor of granting Chiang's request in full. All that saved Stilwell from total humiliation was the last-second intervention of some War Department friends, who lobbied for the ground campaign's continuation. Roosevelt relented, but made sure that Chennault would get his desired supplies—at Stilwell's expense.

In the months following TRIDENT, as American destroyers slugged across the Pacific and GIs stormed up the Italian peninsula, the CBI faded into the war's forgotten theater. The Ledo Road fell out of vogue in Washington, as did Stilwell's plans to retake Burma, a mission that even his admirers increasingly viewed as inconsequential. This happened in part because more crucial matters—such as preparations for D Day—took precedence, but also because Chiang overplayed his hand. After his minor victory at TRIDENT, Peanut had the gall to ask for a billion dollars in gold, threatening once again that China's economy would collapse without the lucre. Yet Chiang still resisted Allied calls for him to commit more and better troops to Burma. The United States finally began to see Chiang for what he was: not an Asian version of George Washington, but an extortionist whose regime was basically useless to the Allies.

As the military historian Maurice Matloff would later write, the War Department realized that the CBI had become a classic military quagmire: a pullout was untenable, as it would be interpreted as a sign of weakness, yet there was no discernible upside to staying the course:

> By the beginning of 1944 the War Department General Staff had few illusions about the value of China in the war against Japan. Washington intelligence estimates recognized frankly that China had little desire to do any actual fighting, although it might engage in limited offensives to secure a voice at the peace table. . . .
>
> The land route to China would not be ready in time to assist U.S. Pacific operations nor would the Chinese Army be able to take a port on the China coast. . . . It was becoming evident that the U.S. investment in the CBI had reached a point where, although it had to be sustained for political and psychological reasons, it had become militarily and economically a losing proposition.

Lord Louis Mountbatten, Stilwell's British counterpart in Asia, tried adapting to the post-TRIDENT reality by suggesting a scaled-down version of the Ledo Road. He proposed a highway that would only extend as far as Myitkyina, the site of Japan's key air base in northern Burma. Liberating that town, Mountbatten believed, would make transporting cargo to China much safer; pilots would no longer have to fly over the Himalayas from Assam, but instead could steer an easy course from Myitkyina to the Chinese city of Kunming, the Burma Road's terminus.

Yet Stilwell wouldn't consider shortening the road by 40 percent, and not just because he ridiculed the dashing Mountbatten as a "glamour boy" with "nice eyelashes." Stilwell still dreamed not just of reconquering Burma, but of driving his divisions across China and putting the squeeze on Japan itself. Anything less would be insufficient revenge for the drubbing he'd received in 1942. And abbreviating the road would give air power a bigger role in the theater, a de facto win for Chennault—another outcome that Stilwell couldn't countenance.

The White House and the War Department's growing indifference seeped down to the press, which took to branding the Ledo Road a massive folly. Stilwell brusquely defended the project, telling a prying *Time* reporter in Delhi that the jungle highway had "stood up very well to monsoons," and that, at the very least, its construction provided an excellent excuse to kill Japanese soldiers in Burma.

Yet even the bullheaded Stilwell was privately wavering. He would never admit as much to the media, lest he disappoint his adoring public. But in his private notes, Stilwell acknowledged the obvious: "[Chiang Kai-shek] is blind. . . . Solution—Open the Road? For What? If CKS handles supply, this means only hoarding for maintenance of [Chinese Nationalists]." Rather than serve as a path for Stilwell's divisions to march toward the East China Sea, the Ledo Road would serve only to enrich the detestable Peanut.

Still, the Army barreled forward. There was simply too much ego staked on the road's completion, no matter how many lives were lost to malaria, tigers, or Japanese snipers, or how little the highway meant to the Allied cause. Saving face was more important than acknowledging—and then fixing—a grave mistake.

FOR THE OFFICERS supervising the Ledo Road's construction, losing men was a minor inconvenience compared to losing equipment. Washington's lack of interest in the project meant that fresh Cats and 6x6s were rarely shipped to India. So whenever the clutch on one of the 849th's trucks gave out, or a bulldozer's tread wore completely through, Herman Perry and the other engineers were forced to scavenge for replacement parts. They reworked cogs from scrapped machines, welded together junked radiators, and learned how to jerry-rig radios out of used apple boxes. The GIs' technical improvisation saved the Ledo Road from ruin.

With heavy machinery constantly on the fritz, much of the construction had to be done by hand. The most grueling manual tasks were assigned to coolies, who had previously worked in Assam's tea gardens and coal mines. The coolies, like the African American engineers, languished at the bottom of a rigid pecking order. The gin-sipping British plantation owners topped Assam's racial hierarchy, followed by the Marwaris, an Indo-Aryan people trusted by the raj; they ran the tea plantations' day-to-day operations. Beneath the Marwaris were the middle-caste Bengalis, who worked as accountants or shopkeepers. And then there were the dark-skinned, illiterate coolies, whom their countrymen dismissed as less than fully human. Born into lives of indentured servitude, they could hope for nothing better than reincarnation (if Hindu) or paradise (if Muslim).

While awaiting their divine reward, male coolies obeyed the Americans' orders to clear the jungle, using shovels, pickaxes, and bare hands. Female coolies, who had worked as tea pickers prior to the war, carried off rocks in saucer-shaped baskets atop their heads; they poured these stones into conical grinding machines, which spit out chunky gravel used to coat the road's surface. African American

Coolies clearing the jungle with hoes and pickaxes.

GIs, meanwhile, worked side by side with the native laborers, hacking away at the jungle rot with pocket knives—machetes were in short supply.

Bulldozers and trucks were prone to getting stuck in the mud, so the Ledo Road's commanders resorted to low-tech alternatives, starting with the horse-drawn *tonga* carriages used in Bengali cities. But the diminutive horses proved ill suited to rough terrain and heavy loads; their skinny legs frequently snapped in two. The Army had more success with Indian elephants: the craggy pachyderms moved gracefully through the postmonsoon sludge, bundles of timber cradled in their trunks. Yet at $3,000 to $8,000 per elephant, the cash-strapped Army could afford relatively few of these ivory-tusked assistants. Given how much each elephant cost, it was especially tragic when passing Chinese soldiers, en route from the Ramgarh Training Center to the Burmese front lines, entertained themselves by shooting the gentle animals.

The CBI's supply crunch trickled down to the Army shops, or PXs,* which charged exorbitant sums for everyday goods. A tin of chicken soup went for $1—about $12 in today's dollars—while a pack of razor blades cost $1.20. These prices were beyond the means of Perry and his fellow privates, who scraped by on $2 a day. They had to envy the 849th's lieutenants, whose compensation, including a housing allowance and meal money, amounted to nearly $300 per month—enough to purchase the stores' $20 bottles of whiskey.

Forsaken by Washington and stiffed by their Army paymasters, the GIs felt perversely entitled to swipe cargo bound either for Chongqing or the pricey shops. "The most lucrative black market in the world was operating right under our noses," said Private Clyde

---

*An abbreviation for "post exchange."

Blue, an African American 6x6 driver from Chicago. "Everybody was involved. . . . Everybody had an angle."

The 849th, for example, specialized in stealing beer. Each enlisted man was supposed to receive a case of beer per month, usually a thin lager such as Hyde Park or Stegmeier, but the Army too seldom made good on this promise. Thirsty for suds, Perry's comrades targeted moving trucks headed to restock PXs. As a 6x6 lumbered up the Patkais, moving at just a mile or two per hour, a gang of engineers would run up from behind and unload cases of brew; they'd skedaddle once the truck reached the summit and started picking up speed on the downslope. "It should be noted that this petty pilfering of PX convoys along the Ledo Road has now shown signs of reaching an accute [sic] stage," read one military police report concerning the 849th's racket.

Similarly audacious scams were everywhere. At the Hellgate checkpoint in Assam, members of the 699th Military Police Company confiscated bottles of whiskey from officers, then resold them at outrageous markups; warehouse guards in Burma shooed away Chinese burglars, then swiped cartons of cigarettes by the armful; and 6x6 drivers sold pilfered goods in Namti, a Burmese village infamous for its black-market bazaar. By the end of 1944, the MPs estimated that $4 million worth of cigarettes, dollars, jewels, and fountain pens had either been stolen or smuggled in the CBI; the true amount was certainly far higher.

There was a brisk trade in humans, too, a situation exposed in the so-called Bordello Affair. Indian women were secreted on cargo flights from Assam to southern China, with the expectation that, should they survive the perilous journey, they would work as prostitutes in Kunming's brothels. When Stilwell was alerted to this sex trafficking, he was enraged to discover that his flyboy rival, the Cajun who'd charmed both Roosevelt and Chiang, had signed off on the scheme. "Officers pimping!" Stilwell raged in his diary. "Hauling whores in our planes. Sent for Chennault. He *knew*. . . . More dope on gas-stealing ring."

African American engineers like Perry, who spent their days slogging through the jungle rather than airborne over the Hump, had no stake in the Bordello Affair. They were instead active in the illicit arms trade, though as buyers, not sellers. Chinese soldiers did a brisk business in pistols, which they'd been issued at the Ramgarh Training Center for the purpose of fighting the Japanese. The black GIs, whose commanders often forbade them to carry weapons when off duty, were avid consumers of these bootleg guns. If a racial incident were to spark a violent clash, turning the jungle into Camp Van Dorn, the black engineers wanted to be able to respond with something deadlier than sharpened broomsticks.

While the Chinese trafficked in guns, the native laborers earned extra cash by peddling intoxicants. When the men of the 849th couldn't steal sufficient beer from moving trucks, they settled for Indian or Burmese moonshine. Variously known as jungle juice, bamboo juice, or local joy juice, these beverages ranged from *zu*, a cloudy rice beer beloved by the Nagas, to distilled spirits that smelled and tasted like sweetened kerosene. Quaffed mainly by the brave or foolish, the drinks caused epic hangovers, a rough malady to endure while clearing trees in 110-degree heat.

The second-most popular native intoxicant was marijuana. The various Indo-Burmese hill tribes had long cultivated the drug on their terraced farms, selling it to tea workers at the lowland bazaars. The British outlawed the trade in 1878, partly on the grounds that Naga dealers weren't paying taxes on their scraggly "hill ganja." But with the prescribed punishment amounting to nothing more than a small fine ranging between ten and fifteen rupees, the marijuana business never stopped bustling.

A twist of *Cannabis sativa*, called "gunga" by the GIs, could be purchased for a song and smoked on the sly, often while crouched in the bushes during a midday break. And so a number of engineers passed their days with cobwebbed minds, a trick the coolies had long used to paper over their misery. The Army was appalled to discover that its soldiers were indulging in this native habit; the marijuana addict was a feared archetype in American culture, reputed to be sexually insatiable and on the fast track to insanity. Proving oneself to be a gunga user was one of the two most reliable ways to obtain a psychological discharge and escape the Ledo Road; the other was claiming to be homosexual, then considered a form of psychopathy.

The black GIs found buying ganja and moonshine much easier once they picked up Urdu and Hindi, two languages that officers rarely mastered. The 90 Day Wonders preferred to keep their distance from the coolies, the low men on the Ledo Road's racial totem pole. They instead relayed their instructions through black sergeants, who ran the day-to-day show in the jungle. These soldiers in turn dealt directly with the Indian "contractors" (as the coolies were often called in Army documents), using hand signals at first, then native words as the months wore on. The GIs' linguistic talents surprised their higher-ups, who'd been raised on pseudoscientific drivel about Negroid cranial deficiencies.

Establishing a rapport with the Nagas was trickier than with the coolies, and not just because the tribesmen spoke a tricky Tibeto-Burman language. Unlike the coolies, the Nagas refused to work construction. They preferred to take advantage of the Americans' relative wealth by swapping scrawny chickens for bags of flour, or by selling polished agates at town bazaars. Many Nagas also worked as porters, carrying air-dropped supplies to units deployed beyond the reach of trucks. Since paper money was seldom used in Naga society, the tattooed tribesmen demanded alternative compensation. The keys from sardine tins were a coveted form of payment, as they could be fashioned into stylish earrings; swatches of parachute cloth were prized as well. But what the Nagas most desired from the Americans was opium, and plenty of it. The MPs maintained footlockers of the tarry narcotic, purchased from the British; hardworking Nagas were rewarded with pebble-size chunks. In a typical month, the Army doled out fifty-five pounds of opium to porters—enough for thousands of Nagas to get high daily.

Described by an Army handbook as "thick-legged, muscular aborigines," the Nagas were the phantoms of the Ledo Road. They'd emerge from the tree line like tattooed wraiths, then vanish back into the tribal realms where the GIs dared not follow. "They never let us see the points at which they entered or left the trails leading to their small villages," said Evelio Grillo, a sergeant with the African American 823rd Engineer Aviation Battalion. "They lived deeper in the jungle and much higher than the camps we had established."

Sometimes Naga men thumbed rides aboard American 6x6s, despite the Army's ban on picking up hitchhikers. Mystified by these loinclothed passengers who always carried their square-bladed *daos*, the GIs regarded the Nagas as primitive, even childlike; it was said that if a Naga could be taught to count to a hundred, then an ape could learn to count to fifty. There were also several apocryphal tales of Nagas marveling at the physiques of shirtless blacks, or learning to urinate while standing after observing the Americans.

Yet the GIs rightfully feared the tough, suspicious tribesmen who lurked in the woods. They heard disturbing gossip from the coolies, who spoke of Naga villages decorated with racks upon racks of human skulls. The brass heads that adorned Naga necklaces, the fearful coolies added, were not mere ornaments, but rather symbols of how many foes the wearer had decapitated.

Only the most senior American officers, however, realized the full extent of the Nagas' yen for heads. In November 1943, a memo from a British political officer was circulated among Army higher-ups, describing an alarming flare-up in an ancient Naga feud: "It is reported that a combination of Chingmei, Nokluk, Pangsha, Ponyu, Tsaplaw, and Tsawlaw and possibly some other small villages attacked and destroyed Law Nawkum, taking between 250 and 300 heads." The official concluded that "no action be taken," since the head-hunting didn't directly threaten the Ledo Road.

An OSS Detachment 101 agent named Jerry Pettigrew makes friends with a Naga chieftain. Note the two brass heads on the chief's necklace.

Despite such barbarism, the Office of Strategic Services, an American intelligence agency, tried wooing the Nagas to the Allied cause. The OSS realized that Naga aid could prove critical in rescuing downed pilots, who might otherwise perish before trekking out of the jungle. An OSS unit codenamed Detachment 101 sent agents to several Naga villages, to inform the tribesmen that any and all help would be handsomely rewarded with trinkets, coins, and opium.

Among those who owed their lives to Detachment 101's outreach program was CBS Radio's Eric Sevareid. In August 1943, Sevareid's plane to Chongqing went down in the jungle, a victim of engine failure: Sevareid parachuted out of the doomed C-46 just before its final nosedive. While searching for a radio air-dropped by a rescue party, he heard humans yelling in a strange, singsong tongue. Sevareid hid in the bush and watched the Nagas approach:

> They were fifteen or twenty in number: short men with deep chests and muscular legs, coffee-brown in color and quite naked save for narrow black breechcloths pulled up tightly under the crotch. They had straight black hair, cut short around the head so that the effect was that of a tuft of trimmed thatch. Some had faded blue tattoo markings on their chests and arms. All carried long spears with splayed metal points, and some also held wide-bladed knives, a couple of feet long, heavy and slightly curved, almost like a butcher's cleaver.

Unsure of whether these well-armed men were friends or foes, Sevareid gambled on the former: "Some instinct, born no doubt of the Wild West novels of childhood, prompted me to step a pace forward, raise my palm, and say: 'How!'" The gambit worked: these Nagas were among those who'd heard that downed Americans could be exchanged for drugs. And despite the protestations of some "younger hotheads" among the tribe, who demanded that the foreigners' skulls be taken, the Nagas took care of Sevareid and his comrades until help arrived. The tribesmen even went so far as to drink goat's blood with their unexpected guests, as part of a sacred bonding ritual.

Yet the Nagas weren't always so agreeable, especially when it came to protecting their women. The American GIs, deprived as they were of female companionship, were sorely tempted to proposition Naga girls, whose Mongolian features and bare breasts were a sight to behold. Yet Naga beauties were off-limits to outsiders—a rule that Naga elders elucidated by making the slit-throat motion toward GIs caught leering.

This wasn't an empty gesture. "Naga tribesmen were normally smiling and shy, but they were ferocious when provoked," said Lloyd Kessler, a member of the 209th Engineer Combat Battalion. "Two men from Company C found a lone Naga girl on the outskirts of their village and took turns raping her. Naga justice was swift. Responding to the girl's screams, men of the village caught the second soldier in the act and promptly cut off his head."

Herman Perry's sunny disposition quickly evaporated in the jungle, destroyed by the sweltering heat and ceaseless routine of corned willy, leeches, and toil. By the start of October, Perry had developed the surly attitude of a veteran, always griping about the workload, the weather, and the perks enjoyed by the 90 Day Wonders.

On October 4, a lieutenant from South Carolina named Emanuel Sterghos gave Perry an order—to work an extra hour, perhaps, or to spit-shine some moldy boots. Perry either refused outright or responded with a crude remark. He likely expected that his minor insubordination would earn him nothing more than a barked reprimand or a night's duty scrubbing pots. But Sterghos, like so many of the 849th's junior officers, was fond of court-martialing GIs who challenged his authority. Perry was arrested for his insolence and subjected to a special court-martial.

Within twenty-four hours of his arrest, Perry was convicted of behaving with disrespect toward a superior and refusing to obey a direct order. His sentence: to be confined at hard labor for a maximum of three months, and to forfeit $32 of his $60 monthly pay through the following March. Perry was then trucked back to Ledo, where he'd convalesced at the Twentieth General Hospital just weeks earlier. This time, however, he was headed for the notorious Ledo Stockade.

A section of the stockade was reserved for a smattering of malnourished Japanese scouts, whom Chinese soldiers taunted with insults and stones. Later on, the prison would also house captured "comfort girls," Korean women brought to Burma to service sex-starved Japanese troops. Yet most of the stockade's residents were men like Perry, African American GIs who'd wisecracked or slacked off. Clyde Blue, who was incarcerated around the same time as Perry, and for exactly the same offense, described the prison with bitter clarity:

> The stockade was a barbed wire enclosure with watchtowers at each corner. The men lived in tents which appeared to be a block long. They slept on cots practically touching each other and were allowed one blanket though it got quite cold there at night. The captain in charge had been a big cheese in the Georgia chain-gang penal system. He had a ball practicing his trade, sadistic brutality.
>
> The day I entered the gates of the Ledo Stockade I was greeted by a white guard who started a tirade of obscenities each of which was modified by the adjective "black." I watched his performance

and said nothing. Angered by my silence he said, "Oh one of those smart niggers!"

The labor component of Perry's sentence was every bit as grueling as his routine with the 849th. From dawn until nightfall, he joined the other convicts in digging sump pits, chopping wood, stripping busted vehicles for parts, and burying dead animals. If caught loafing for even a second, a prisoner was assigned several hours of extra work. Other infractions worthy of mention in the stockade's punishment book were smoking while working, using profanity, wearing one's hat while eating, sitting down without asking, and reading magazines.

Habitual offenders of the stockade rules were progressively subjected to punishments viler than additional chores. Some incorrigible GIs were forced to walk in tight circles for hours, until they'd burrowed ankle-high trenches into the ground; they were then ordered to start a new circle. By far the worst punishment, though, was confinement in an isolation cell, which prisoners called "the Box." The windowless, concrete Box was just four feet long and two feet across, and the corrugated metal roof was so low that a man couldn't stand up all the way. "Few men were able to walk out of this contraption," said Blue. "The guards dragged them out." So cruel were the Box's effects that the Army eventually forced the stockade's commanders to increase the cell's size, in order to bring it in line with regulations regarding the humane treatment of prisoners.

The change in the Box's dimensions came too late for Perry, who rebelled at every turn while locked up. No matter how many times he was punished, he kept on complaining about the disproportionate severity of his sentence. Perry knew the guards were trying to break him, to make him see the wisdom in keeping his trap shut. But staying mum wasn't in the garrulous Perry's nature.

About two weeks before Christmas, Perry received a letter from Edna. She inquired as to whether her older brother had written to a girl in Monroe who'd expressed a romantic interest. Perry wrote back as cheerfully as he could, never once revealing that he was languishing in the stockade—or that he'd recently spent time in the prison's infirmary, due to a painful case of anal fissures. Yet halfway through his letter, he let slip his increasingly desperate state of mind:

Hi Edna

Hows the young lady and the family fine I hope. so far I am making out o.k. I received your letter a few days ago but this is my first chance to answer.

young lady I wrote the girl you asked me to but she has not answered. young lady you had better make her answer my letter or I will write and tell her what I think of her freezing up on me.

Hows xmas treating you Lewis and the family. to be truthful its not so good with me. this will really be a dead xmas for us. no where to go and nothing to do. and no body to help you do that its a rather raw life but we are doing o.k.

I wont even be able to buy a xmas card there arent any here. so heres a letter to wish you a merry xmas and Happy new year. any present you can send will be welcomed "indeed so" guess Ill have to close here write soon.

Yours
Herman

Originally scheduled to rejoin his unit before New Year's Day, Perry was kept in the stockade for several days (perhaps as many as eighteen) beyond his promised release date—a final, morale-crushing punishment cooked up by the guards.

Devoid of legal recourse, Perry could only fume and fantasize about revenge. His laid-back optimism gave way to ranting victimhood, an attitude tinged by visceral hatred of the "peckawood" guards who reveled in his agony and humiliation.

At some point during his extended incarceration, Perry contracted a nasty ulcer on his penis—not a venereal disease, but rather an icky skin condition typical of unhygienic, overcrowded conditions. So when he finally emerged from the stockade in early January, Perry went directly to the hospital to undergo a round of dermatological treatments.

The mounting misery was more than Perry could bear. As he traveled past the Hellgate sign once more, en route to rejoining his unit on January 13, his thoughts were darker than the Box at night. If Perry was to survive the Ledo Road, he would need some way to cope, some way to salve the pain of jungle life. The balm he chose is one that flourished in the hills, growing in the bulbs of bright red poppies.

SEVEN

The monsoons had tapered off while Herman Perry was imprisoned, and the milder weather allowed the engineers to finally make some headway. Mudpits congealed in the dry autumn air and landslides no longer erased the Army's gains on a daily basis. Bulldozers resumed smashing through the Indo-Burmese jungle, clanging down the Patkais' eastern slopes past the icy Lake of No Return. The neck-high elephant grass of Burma's Hukaung Valley—termed "the ancestral home of the leech" by the British—lay ahead.

Overseeing this progress was the Ledo Road's new chief engineer, Colonel Lewis Andrew Pick. His ousted predecessor, Brigadier General John C. Arrowsmith, had become Lieutenant General Stilwell's scapegoat for the project's monsoon-induced woes. Vinegar Joe had personally sacked the hapless Arrowsmith in August, blasting him as a layabout in a telegram to Delhi headquarters: "Engineer in charge regards [the road] as just a job and not the contest of his life. He accepts setbacks complacently instead of tearing into them, is content to stick around office, and generally lacks drive and pep."

Pick, by contrast, was a cranky World War I veteran who reminded Stilwell of his pugnacious self. On the night of October 17, 1943, his first as the project's commander, the ruddy-faced, pear-shaped Pick delivered a Stilwellesque ultimatum to his new subordinates: "The Ledo Road is going to be built—mud, rain, and malaria be damned."

The fifty-three-year-old Pick took pains to cultivate a charismatic image, one not too dissimilar to the tell-it-like-it-is character favored by his acerbic patron. One of Pick's first orders of business was to fashion himself an ornate bamboo walking stick; he used it for dramatic emphasis when issuing orders, waving the gnarled staff in the direction he wanted the road to go. He also replaced several middling officers with more cantankerous men. "I went through all the files of the engineer board," he told an aide, "and I asked for the toughest, most pigheaded men—men that didn't have enough brains to quit."

Pick's crotchety theatrics earned him two nicknames among the rank and file: the Old Man with the Stick and, more poetically, Old Mud and Ruts. The colonel was certainly an old-timer, having graduated from Virginia Tech in 1914, before virtually every soldier under his command had been born. Yet he also brought an undeniable competence to the Ledo Road, due to his familiarity with the ravages of excess water. He had helped New Orleans recover from the Great Mississippi Flood of 1927, and he'd managed flood-control operations in the Missouri River Basin. Pick's mundane specialty was building drainage systems, a skill that came in handy along the frequently waterlogged road.

A taskmaster as well as an engineering wonk, Pick ordered the men to work around-the-clock shifts; the nighttime path was lit with flares bobbing in buckets of oil. He bullied battalion commanders who didn't perform to his liking, once awakening the 849th's Lieutenant Colonel Wright Hiatt at 3:00 A.M., demanding to know why one of the unit's rock crushers wasn't running. Other officers received spiteful, handwritten notes branding them "wash-outs" (or worse) if Pick questioned their devotion. Everyone in a position of authority was made to feel as if he were one mistake away from sharing Brigadier General Arrowsmith's shameful fate.

A crew of engineers and coolies gathering rocks along the Ledo Road.

Whether due to Pick's mind games or simply the drier weather, the engineers increased their pace severalfold, completing a mile's worth of road per day in November and December 1943. Two days after Christmas, as a forlorn Perry seethed in the Ledo Stockade, the builders reached Shingbwiyang, the village that Major John Ausland had visited during his dispiriting 1942 reconnaissance mission. In a strategic show of magnanimity, Pick rewarded the troops with candy, doughnuts, and 9,600 cans of warm beer.

With the road now jutting nearly seventy miles into Burma—22 percent of the way to the planned endpoint at Mongyu, on the Chinese border—the ground campaign ramped up. Stilwell's Chinese divisions, trained at Ramgarh, had been engaging the Japanese in northern Burma for several months. Joining them were the Chindits, a British commando unit led by the larger-than-life Major General Orde Charles Wingate, whose prewar missions had included training Jewish security forces in Palestine and battling slave traders in Sudan. He was rarely seen without his trademark pith helmet.

Named after a winged lion from Burmese lore, the Chindits specialized in traversing fearsome terrain, a talent that served them well during their long-range forays. In early 1943, Wingate's commandos had marched five days west of Burma's Irrawaddy River—well beyond the road's reach—losing nearly nine hundred men to disease and firefights. Now, powered by a diet of hard cheese, dates, and biscuits—high-calorie foods that resisted jungle rot—the Chindits aimed to establish Allied airfields deep within Burma. Their assault plan, to be launched on March 5, 1944, was codenamed Operation Thursday.

Not to be outdone by the British, whom Stilwell considered pansies, the Americans were readying their own group of commandos: the 5307th Composite Unit (Provisional). Comprised of 2,900 seasoned jungle fighters, veterans of a bloody campaign in the Solomon Islands, the 5307th would soon be better known as Merrill's Marauders, after its commander, Brigadier General Frank D. Merrill. The Marauders were tasked with capturing the Burmese town of Myitkyina, through which the Ledo Road was eventually supposed to run. To reach their isolated target, the commandos would have to travel over 250 miles on foot, accompanied only by pack mules.

The 5307th came marching down the road that February, to the envy of many black engineers who pined for the supposed glory of combat, as opposed to their workaday roles as laborers. As the commandos passed by on their way to Shingbwiyang and points beyond, the 858th Engineer Aviation Battalion's band strutted right behind, feting the Marauders with rousing renditions of "Dixie" and "God Bless America." The band's trumpets still pealing across the hills, Merrill's troops then disappeared into the Hukaung Valley, bound for one of the war's ghastliest ordeals. By year's end, 80 percent of the 5307th's men would be either dead or wounded, all in the name of advancing the Ledo Road.

Perry glumly watched the Marauders from his new camp near Tagap Ga, a Burmese village twenty-four miles north of Shingbwiyang. The 849th had moved along with the road, widening the nascent highway to accommodate two-way 6x6 traffic. Tagap Ga was marginally more pleasant than the 849th's digs at the Pangsau Pass, though buzzing flies frequently turned the sky a mottled black. Everyone knew that it was only a matter of weeks before the monsoons returned, at which point the region would again devolve into a malarial everglade.

The Herman Perry who arrived at Tagap Ga wasn't the same man who'd boarded the *West Point* six months earlier. The jungle and the stockade had conspired to erode his boyish good looks, leaving his cheeks sallow and his brow creased. Even more noticeable was the road's effect on Perry's personality: the formerly upbeat playboy from D.C. was now dour and combative, seemingly bent on inviting another court-martial. To anyone who'd listen, he'd rail against his treatment by the stockade's guards, harping on the days he'd been held beyond his promised release date. The failure of even the black sergeants to acknowledge this perceived injustice ate away at whatever remained of Perry's morale. He requested a transfer out of the 849th, but headquarters turned him down.

By late February, Perry's intransigence had become such a problem that word reached Lieutenant Colonel Hiatt. Preoccupied with Colonel Pick's incessant needling, the young and heartsick Hiatt had little time to coddle willful GIs. But nevertheless, he called Perry to his office for a chat. Perry used the opportunity to gripe about the rough treatment meted out by the 849th's officers; most likely, he also reiterated his grievance regarding his extended stay behind bars. Hiatt agreed that Perry was getting the short end of the stick, but declined to help smooth things over. He instead offered a sympathetic ear:

> All I said was that [he] should try to get along with his company commander, and the [sergeants] for his own good, and I didn't like to come into a company and take any action when that was actually a function for the company commander. However, I said I was interested in each individual soldier in the battalion and I had always maintained a policy of taking an interest in their problems. In other words, if they were in trouble they had a right and privilege to talk to me about it.

With that reassurance, Perry was dismissed and returned to work, and to the risky form of recreation he'd discovered in the jungle.

THE MONOTONY AND loneliness of life on the Ledo Road vexed many GIs to the edge of madness. Bone-tired after finishing yet another interminable work shift, and often feverish from malaria, an engineer could do little but choke down yet another slab of Spam, stare at the jungle's wall of trees, and fantasize about "Uncle Sugar," as they called the United States. After a few hours of fitful sleep, repeatedly interrupted by howling gibbons and blood-slurping mosquitoes, it was back to the Cats and the rock crushers for another steamy day of toil. The routine never varied.

Men with fragile psyches had a hard time with the tedium, especially when disease or injury added to their woe. Freak-outs, as Sergeant Evelio Grillo of the 823rd later wrote, were alarmingly common:

> The three horsemen of our own particular apocalypse were malaria, amoebic dysentery, and emotional breakdown. . . . Emotional disorders did not have the recognition they enjoy now. The result devastated the afflicted, since they were judged to be either malingering or simply "crazy." Some men would have extended bouts of depression, go on crying jags, or become belligerent and assault other soldiers.

There were, indeed, many nasty episodes of soldier-on-soldier violence on the Ledo Road, often centered around card games or petty jealousies, or involving the abuse of moonshine. In one such incident, Private John Gladney of the 823rd plunged a hunting knife through the neck of a staff sergeant, as the victim watched movies at a makeshift cinema near Hellgate. Gladney committed the assault after not so cryptically telling a friend, "I killed one man, I'm going to kill some more," implying that he'd gotten away with murder once before. In another case of irrational carnage, Private Willie Delaney of the 1883rd Engineer Aviation Battalion "killed by .30 calibre rifle a soldier of his company whose first name is Thomas but whose last name is unknown"; this mysterious and unfortunate Thomas, Delaney claimed, had been cheating at craps.

The men loved gossiping about the freak-outs, but Army censors kept the incidents under wraps: the Ledo Road's few reporters were compelled to convey only wholesome news. In lieu of dwelling on craps games and stabbings, the *Chicago Defender*'s Denton J. Brooks portrayed the jungle's leisure opportunities as similar to those at summer camp:

> "Why haven't these men cracked up," I wondered when I saw under what conditions they had lived for so long a period of time, without any normal modes of recreation, seeing only themselves. There was only one answer—they have made their own recreation.
>
> They had cleared a space behind camp and there with jungle background I saw one of the sweetest softball games I have ever witnessed. Each company has a team fully equipped with gloves, balls and bats, part of the equipment they brought from home, and they play every night the weather permits.
>
> Volley-ball was in progress in another clearing and coming down the road was a detachment, spic and span in freshly laundered suntans with shining shoes sparkling against a tropical sun marching in close order drill formation.

The Army-run *CBI Roundup*, meanwhile, focused on the solace that black GIs found in music. Articles hailed the ingenuity of soldiers who built guitars out of cargo crates and aluminum scrap, or described the sweet rhythms of an a cappella group, named Four Notes in Harmony, that once serenaded Stilwell with Hawaiian folk tunes. Excluded from the Bamboo Bar, a whites-only officers' club near Ledo, the African American enlisted men founded the Bamboo

Inn, a combination church and juke joint, complete with an in-house band that specialized in an allegro version of "Praise the Lord and Pass the Ammunition." "I sat through a jive session with about 100 colored troops," reported an eager *Roundup* writer in early 1943. The band's leader, he continued, "acted as a master of ceremonies, calling on the men to 'jump right in the mood with us and get in the jive. Let me see your foots move.' "

If only music and softball had been enough to distract every engineer from the day-to-day grind. But many of the road's GIs, brimming with the vim and foolishness of youth, yearned for baser pleasures.

Sex, of course, topped their list of cravings. Men who desired other men were the lucky ones, since eligible women were a rarity in the jungle. Homosexual liaisons were common enough, though clandestine—such behavior was punishable by imprisonment. Sergeant Earle Ennis of the 4048th Quartermaster Truck Company, who claimed to have bedded between twenty-five and twenty-eight men over a six-month period, was among those nabbed for homosexuality. According to one witness against Ennis, the sergeant specialized in forced seductions:

> "I had been drinking heavily and Sergeant Ennis had played with my penis. . . . [He] approached me several times later and questioned me about getting a 'blow job'. . . . Sergeant Ennis got me intoxicated and I 'passed out,' when I 'came to' Corporal William H. Duhart [of the] 4048th QM Truck Company informed me that Sergeant Ennis had been 'sucking' my penis. . . . I am normal and I got no pleasure from action of this type."

Straight men, on the other hand, usually had to content themselves with furtive peeks at bare-breasted Naga women. A small number of industrious soldiers arranged to rent coolies' wives for *jig jig* (sex), at about ten rupees a throw. Others patronized the road's few prostitutes, though there was always a danger of a paid sexual encounter spiraling into a rape allegation. In one such instance, a Burmese woman named Ma Thein Khin claimed that several black GIs had forced themselves on her, and she demanded compensation. Army investigators soon uncovered that Ma Thein Khin was in fact a hooker who'd accepted the soldiers' money, and they recommended that the accused be punished only for using American vehicles to journey to and from their tryst.*

With sex a chancy rarity, soldiers with sordid appetites were forced to choose among gambling, drink, and "native intoxicants." Herman Perry, already teetering on the brink of mental collapse in the early months of 1944, chose the last of these three as his primary solace.

VIETNAM IS SUPPOSED to have been the first druggie war, the first conflict in which American troops chose grass and heroin over liquor as their preferred chemical comforts. Yet American soldiers were getting stoned—albeit involuntarily—at least a century before the nation's anti-Communist adventure in Southeast Asia. The advent of the hypodermic needle in 1853 made morphine a handy battlefield painkiller, and the drug was used extensively throughout the Civil War. Once hostilities ceased between North and South, a number of veterans realized that their healed bodies still longed for morphine: if they tried quitting the opiate cold turkey, awful sickness ensued. Veterans hampered by addiction were said to be suffering from "the

---

*At least two GIs were alleged to have satisfied their sexual desires in a most uncouth manner. On September 30, 1944, two privates from the 4276th Quartermaster Service Company were arrested for sodomizing a goat in Ledo. The men were allegedly caught red-handed, still holding the poor goat.

soldier's disease." One ex-Confederate saddled with the ailment, John Stith Pemberton, tried squelching his morphine jones by ingesting a cocaine-laced tonic of his own invention: Coca-Cola.

The active ingredient in Pemberton's beverage was much in vogue by the start of World War I, and many Doughboys coped with Europe's trenches by downing slugs of coca-infused wine, or by inhaling lumps of white powder. Moralists, however, fretted over the drug's deleterious effect on a soldier's willingness to fight. "It will, for the hour, charm away his trouble, his fatigue and his anxiety," opined the London *Times* at the height of the war. "But it will also, in the end, render him worthless as a soldier and a man." The British government, fearing that the widespread availability of cocaine in London's West End was part of an ingenious German plot, forbade sales of the Andean stimulant to soldiers.

The medics of the American Expeditionary Force, meanwhile, were lugging a form of marijuana to Europe: the War Department recommended that for every thousand men in the field, Army medics keep a bottle of "*Cannabis indicæ* tinctura" tablets on hand, for the treatment of headaches, insomnia, and cramps. It was not until the early 1920s that the War Department expressed concern over the recreational use of marijuana. Members of a Puerto Rican regiment stationed in the Panama Canal Zone were first noted as smoking the drug in 1916; the military's report on their habit referred to cannabis only as "a weed which caused unusual symptoms." The next official reference came six years later, in a memo stating that marijuana smoking had become widespread in the Canal Zone, and that "there were cases of delinquincy [sic] attributed to its use." The Zone's military authorities promptly outlawed the drug.

Exhibiting an unusual degree of open-mindedness for a quasi-colonial official, the Zone's American governor, Meriwether L. Walker, appointed a blue-ribbon panel to investigate whether marijuana deserved the blanket ban. The committee came back with a report that ran contrary to everything the yellow press was printing about the "demon weed" and its potential for turning average men into sex-crazed loons: "There is no evidence that marihuana as grown here is a habit-forming drug in the sense in which the term is applied to alcohol, opium, cocaine, etc. or that it has any appreciably delete-rious influence on the individuals using it. . . . [We recommend] that no steps be taken by the Canal Zone authorities to prevent the sale and use of marihuana."

The marijuana prohibition in the Canal Zone was lifted in ac-cordance with the committee's recommendation, and bored soldiers happily resumed puffing away. Yet their commanders remained con-vinced that the drug was incompatible with the martial spirit, and they pressed for a fresh study. They finally got their wish in 1931, and this time the results were more to the Army's liking. The new study found that 20 percent of the soldiers at Panama's Fort Clayton were marijuana smokers; of these men, "62 percent were constitutional psychopaths and 23 percent were morons." The study's conclusion was clear: marijuana melted the mind.

This viewpoint became the conventional wisdom at the War De-partment throughout the 1930s, and suspected addicts were barred from service; during World War II, those who lied about their mari-juana use on draft-board questionnaires were subject to five-year prison terms. In 1944, a pair of Army doctors released a study, *The Marihuana Addict in the Army*, based on their observations of thirty-five marijuana users (all African Americans) who'd been hospitalized for self-mutilation, "chronic somatic complaints," and other curious ailments. The doctors recommended "that government institutions be created to which such confirmed marihuana users may be com-mitted for long-term treatment and rehabilitation, or for indefinite custody."

While excoriating marijuana users as fit only for asylums, the Army was simultaneously encouraging the use of a more potent drug. Benzedrine tablets, first marketed in the 1930s as a treatment for narcolepsy, were freely distributed to soldiers during World War II in order to enhance alertness. The Army Air Forces, for example, recommended that all flight-crew members carry two five-milligram "bennies," and pop both in case of physical exhaustion. Doctors observed that troops on Benzedrine jags tended not to eat; after the war, they'd prescribe millions of pills to aspiring dieters who couldn't control their hankerings for bacon and Bundt cake. The medical establishment would eventually realize that the risks of steady amphetamine consumption outweighed the benefits, though this revelation would come too late for thousands of addicts.

Despite the perils of getting caught smoking a muggle in lieu of popping a bennie, marijuana use was surprisingly common among GIs, who discovered that American jazzmen were hardly the drug's only aficionados. Private Clyde Blue, the truck driver who spent time in the Ledo Stockade with Herman Perry, bought strong hashish in Egypt while on shore leave from his transport ship: "The poor natives can't afford liquid intoxicants so they get high on their native grass, which grows wild. They use it and sell it. I should say it's not the cut junk you buy in the states; it is pure. When we left the ship no problems, no hangovers, no addicts."

Marijuana was similarly available and pure in the Patkais, peddled by Nagas who cultivated patches of cannabis on hillside farms. But the Nagas themselves preferred a stronger means of pharmaceutical escape: opium. Used for centuries as a cure-all, opium had become even cheaper and more widespread under the raj. To satisfy Chinese demand, colonial plantations produced a glut of the drug—at one point in the nineteenth century, opium accounted for one-sixth of India's gross domestic product. Licensed opium shops flourished in North-East India and the number of addicts soared. Coolies were particularly avid consumers of the narcotic; in addition to making them temporarily forget their cares, opium suppressed both sex drive and appetite, two desirable side effects when deprived of female affection and subsisting on rationed rice.

Opium addiction also escalated among the Nagas, amid accusations that the British covertly nurtured the drug's spread as a way to lull the famed headhunters into passivity. If this allegation is true, then perhaps the British underestimated opium's allure; by the early twentieth century, colonial administrators were forced to start rationing schemes, lest entire Naga villages vanish into narcotic oblivion.* In the areas of the Indo-Burmese jungle where they held sway, British officials insisted that inveterate opium eaters be confined to houses reserved for addicts. This regulatory experiment, launched in the early 1920s, didn't go quite as planned; it was undercut by the widespread availability of bootleg opium from eastern Burma and the Himalayan foothills. Indian coolies also sold small quantities of the drug, in order to support their own habits.

Though opium was actually part of the Army's medicine chest, prescribed in tincture form to treat dogs suffering from diarrhea, the drug was far more frightening to GIs than the familiar marijuana. They were scared in part by warnings that Japan was manufacturing opium for the sole purpose of turning the Allies into zombies. *Time* reported that resistance was nonexistent in occupied Nanjing, Chiang Kai-shek's erstwhile capital, because the Japanese had flooded the city with five-cent packets of opium. And a Japanese factory in Seoul churned out upward of three thousand pounds of

---

*Early in his career as an advocate for Indian independence, Mahatma Gandhi expressed grave concerns over North-East India's high levels of opium addiction. He organized an antiopium campaign in Assam in 1921, collecting over a quarter of a million signatures on a petition demanding that the sale of the drug be banned. Yet Gandhi's main objection wasn't to the drug's soul- and body-killing effects, but rather to the fact that the British were profiting from the venture: "The vice has existed in India from time immemorial. No one organised the vice, as the present government has, for the purposes of revenue."

heroin per month; the shipments went overland to Manchuria, and were used to pacify locals who might otherwise have chafed under the brutal Japanese yoke.

The Ledo Road's soldiers also saw firsthand the ugly pitfalls of opium addiction among the coolies and tribals, the way in which hunger for the drug blotted out all earthly concerns. A military policeman stationed in Burma recalls entering a village's opium den in 1945, while searching for black-market goods. The druggie squalor disgusted him: "There's this old woman, just an old crone, lying there on the floor. She gives me this big toothless smile and opens up her legs, and she points at her, y'know. She's inviting me to have sex with her! All I wanted to do was get out of there."

So though opium was perhaps the Ledo Road's most readily available drug, few American soldiers dared try it. The bedraggled Herman Perry, desperate to lose himself in fantasy, was one of the exceptions.

The fortunes of the Perry brothers could scarcely have been more divergent as March 1944 began: while Herman careened toward darkness, Aaron was on the cusp of boxing stardom. The Anvil had reeled off thirteen straight victories over the likes of Kid Lewis, Tuffy Cummings, and, most impressively of all, a brick-fisted thug named Vic Creelman. There was a hiccup in Aaron's path toward a title shot when it was revealed that he'd been lying about his age; when he'd turned pro he was only seventeen, a year shy of the legal threshold for fighters. But his manager, Harry Garsh, had worked things out with the District Boxing Commission, and a major bout with Billie Banks was on tap for March 10.

So bright were the Anvil's prospects that a wealthy Washington restaurateur, Tom O'Donnell, offered to buy a 50 percent stake in

Aaron for the princely sum of $5,000. Garsh declined; he was already lining up a match with former world champion Henry Armstrong, which would yield a payday deep into five figures. Aaron and Roscoe, the eldest brother, had big plans for the money that was soon to be pouring in. They dreamed of opening a dry cleaners together, and of chasing every skirt from Fairfax to Baltimore.

Letters from family members kept Herman apprised of Aaron's exploits, but they weren't enough to prevent his unraveling. Sick, exhausted, and still fuming over what had happened in the stockade, Herman was losing touch with reality—a condition exacerbated by his growing drug use. He spent hours daydreaming about an alter ego named Johnny, whom he imagined as married to Alma Talbot back in Washington. Perry carefully collected his young girlfriend's letters, using them as talismans to make his fantasy seem more real. He would later summarize his mindset in March 1944 with six choice words: "I was pretty well messed up."

When the 6:00 A.M. bugle sounded on March 3, every able-bodied member of the 849th's Company A reported for duty, save for Perry. The company's commander, Lieutenant Gene Carapico, saw Perry lolling about camp later that morning, seemingly unconcerned with his pick-and-shovel duties. Carapico instructed one of his trusted black sergeants, Booker Stitt, to order Perry to work the second shift. Perry grunted an assent to Stitt's command, but still showed up for duty four hours late that afternoon.

Perry missed reveille again the following morning, and this time he was nowhere to be found. The other soldiers in Company A shrugged their shoulders when asked about their comrade's whereabouts; they had bigger things to worry about, particularly the booby-trapped Japanese artillery shells that had just been discovered alongside the road.

When informed of Perry's absence, Carapico asked Stitt to find the wayward private and bring him in for a serious talking-to. The commander planned not only to deliver a lecture about responsibility, but also to arrest Perry and send him to the company's guardhouse, a prelude to another stint in the Ledo Stockade. Enough, Carapico had decided, was enough.

Stitt looked all over for the AWOL private, to no avail. That's because Perry was holed up in the woods, getting high on opium and ganja. Even with his pay docked, he could still afford the narcotic release peddled by the Nagas; given the tribesmen's proclivity for American rations and trinkets, and their aversion to paper money, the drugs could even be obtained in exchange for canned food or safety pins.

Perry smoked until late, floating through a fuzzy reverie while gibbons gracefully swung by. As if solely to enhance his buzz, the jungle to the north lit up with a false dawn: a powerful gasoline fire was burning near the village of Loglai, consuming twenty-five thousand gallons of fuel and providing the Ledo Road's night crew with a crude pyrotechnic show.

Stoned to the gills, Perry snuck back to camp just a few hours ahead of his shift. When reveille was called at 6:00 A.M. sharp that morning, Perry slept right through the din of his comrades slipping into their moldy boots and overalls. He was dead to the world atop his cot, enjoying a rare moment of peace.

Stitt shook Perry out of his slumber, demanding to know where he'd been for the last twenty-four hours. The groggy Perry shrugged off the query, then stumbled out of bed in search of breakfast.

Familiar as he was with Perry's erratic behavior, Stitt had prepared for whatever ugliness might accompany the arrest. He'd told a fellow soldier, Staff Sergeant Jeff Gobold, that he'd probably need help taking Perry into custody. The plan now was to wait until Perry was in the mess hall, where he'd presumably be hesitant to make a scene in front of the entire company.

Stitt and Gobold approached Perry right as he was joining the chow line. Stitt broached the topic of the three of them heading over to Carapico's office, carefully avoiding any hint that a trip to the guardhouse was sure to follow. Still, Perry seemed in no hurry to comply. "Wait 'til I eat breakfast," he told the pair.

"Wait until he eats breakfast, and then carry him down," Stitt whispered to Gobold, as Perry attempted to cure his hangover with forkfuls of Spam and rice. Gobold went back to his tent and strapped on Stitt's .45 pistol. He wasn't personally authorized to carry such a weapon, but something about this Perry situation seemed dicey. Gobold thought it best to arm himself, just in case.

After Perry had finished eating, Stitt escorted him to the company's unadorned office tent. Carapico entered a few minutes later, along with his morning's breakfast companion, Lieutenant Harold Cady. The two had just been discussing Perry's recalcitrance, as well as the fact that Carapico was going to place the private under arrest. This doubtless pleased Cady, who was known around the 849th as a stern disciplinarian. A few months earlier, in an incident much discussed in the battalion, Cady had smacked around a GI who'd been slow to respond to an order. He claimed the soldier had been drinking, and though Lieutenant Colonel Hiatt said he disapproved of such methods, Cady wasn't punished.

Carapico asked Perry why he'd missed reveille that morning. "Reveille?" Perry answered, sounding as if he'd never heard the word before.

Carapico was expecting either an excuse or an apology, and didn't quite know how to handle Perry's tactic of playing dumb. The commander next asked why Perry had missed work the previous day.

"Work?" Perry answered, again pretending that he barely grasped the English language.

Carapico had no patience for games, nor for being made to look a fool in front of Cady, his subordinate. "All right, Perry, you turn in your rifle and your cartridge belt, you are under arrest," he said. "You are going to the guardhouse. Sergeant Stitt, see to it that he does it."

Perry froze and stared at Carapico. He knew what a trip to the guardhouse meant: a special court-martial would follow, and then another spell in the Ledo Stockade. And though he'd seemingly been bucking for exactly that fate since January, Perry now realized what lay ahead: sadistic guards, hard labor, and sweltering punishments in the Box.

"What's it all about?" asked Perry. "Do you plan to send me back to the guardhouse?"

"That's right."

As Perry left the office, headed to retrieve his rifle and cartridge belt, Stitt heard him mumble an ominous rejoinder: "That's what you think, Lieutenant."

FIFTEEN MINUTES LATER, Stitt and Gobold entered Perry's tent. They found the private there alone, sitting on his cot looking dazed. As soon as he saw the sergeants coming, Perry reached over to the foot of the bed and picked up his .30-caliber M1 Garand rifle, the one he'd been issued to fend off Japanese snipers. Gun in hand, he began frantically looking around the tent. Stitt and Gobold figured he was scanning for ammunition, and worried that their straightforward arrest of an AWOL soldier was about to get seriously out of hand.

"Perry, what are you going to do with that rifle?" asked Stitt.

"I'm going to carry it down to the supply room and turn it in."

"No, Perry, leave it here. We'll carry it down."

"No, I'm going to carry it myself."

There was silence for a moment as Stitt pondered Perry's request. Something seemed unwise about letting an arrested man carry a firearm, even for a few hundred feet. Then again, Perry sounded lucid enough; perhaps he just wanted to go down with a little dignity.

"All right," Stitt said, turning to Gobold. "Carry him down to the supply room and let him turn it in."

The supply tent was manned by two clerks, Staff Sergeant Earl Rawlins and T/5 Fred Underwood,* who were in charge of disbursing tools and guns to the 849th. Gobold called out for Rawlins, who was relaxing in his quarters behind a canvas partition.

"Sergeant Rawlins, Perry wants to turn in his rifle," Gobold informed the supply sergeant. Rawlins was perplexed—men were always trying to wheedle weapons from him, but they rarely, if ever, gave up their guns voluntarily. But then he saw the .45 on Gobold's waist, and it all made sense: Gobold wouldn't bend the rules and pack a pistol unless he was escorting a potentially violent prisoner.

Contrary to the submissive attitude he'd struck just a few minutes earlier, Perry now chafed at Gobold's order. "Me?" Perry asked, in mock confusion. "I ain't going to turn my rifle in."

"If I was you, I wouldn't get into no more trouble," warned Gobold. He assured Perry that the rifle would be returned in due time, and that he might even be able to talk his way out of the arrest by appealing directly to Hiatt: "Go down and talk to the colonel. You know he is a mighty good man and maybe he won't send you to the guardhouse."

The word *guardhouse* echoed in Perry's fearful mind. Calmly, as if merely discussing the weather, he made clear that he was

---

*T/5 is short for Technician Fifth Grade, a discontinued rank that was one notch above Private First Class.

through with Army justice: "I'll die and go to hell before I go to the guardhouse."

Underwood, who'd come out from behind the tent's partition midway through the argument, now tried to play the peacemaker. "What's the matter, Perry?" he asked.

"They want to take my rifle. Nobody is going to get my rifle. Even my mother wouldn't get this rifle."

Underwood stammered something about how turning in the M1 was the smart move, but Perry brushed off the advice. "I'm not going to the guardhouse anymore. If I do, I'm going dead."

Perry now turned to face the startled Gobold. "Go on and leave me alone," he said. "I don't want to make trouble for you. Let me go and see the colonel alone. I don't need anybody to take me."

With that, Perry took the M1 off his shoulder and pulled back the bolt. A fresh cartridge glistened inside the chamber. The three men surrounding Perry interpreted this act of "showing brass" as a tacit threat: *Get in my way, get this bullet.*

Perry shut the bolt closed, then stomped out of the tent with his rifle slung across his chest. As he departed, he locked eyes with Rawlins and offered one last indication that he wasn't to be messed with.

"Don't try to stop me. I mean business this morning."

Gobold, wisely, didn't give chase. He instead ran to Carapico's office to report an escaped prisoner.

PRIVATE JAMES WALTON, a dump-truck driver with the 849th's Company C, had been working since six that morning, hauling gravel to Shingbwiyang. He was on his way back to camp when he noticed something odd: a fellow African American soldier hastily trotting northbound up the Ledo Road, a rifle in his right hand. What was this lone GI doing out here, especially armed like that? Rifles were only supposed to be used on construction jobs, not brandished when walking about.

The armed pedestrian craned his neck to see the approaching truck, then held out his left hand—the universal symbol for "stop." Walton was happy to oblige; hitchhiking was the norm for Americans, coolies, and Nagas alike. Herman Perry, whom Walton recognized as a member of the 849th, circled around the front of the truck and hopped in the passenger's seat. Perry didn't say a word, just laid the rifle on his lap.

Unnerved by the silence, as well as by Perry's frantic gaze, Walton shifted back into gear and resumed driving at twenty-five miles per hour. He noticed that Perry was fidgety, nervously shifting the M1 splayed across his legs.

At one point, when Walton hit a sharp curve, the rifle slid over and hit him in the thigh. Perry snatched it back and secured it between his knees.

CARAPICO AND CADY were chatting about one of the company's malfunctioning bulldozers when Gobold came rushing into the Company A office tent. Upon learning that an armed Perry had broken arrest, Carapico called the military police and instructed them to keep an eye peeled for the runaway soldier at the road's checkpoints. Satisfied that Perry would shortly be captured without incident, he told Cady to forget about the matter and go check on the Cat they'd been discussing.

Cady took one of the 849th's jeeps and offered a lift to three engineers he met in the motor pool: Sergeant Harry Bethel, T/5 Robert Griffis, and T/4 George Waites.

Coming around a hairpin turn, Cady saw a dump truck lumbering ahead of him. He veered his jeep into the left-hand lane, in an attempt to pass. When he pulled even with the truck, Cady glanced over to make sure the driver was aware of his presence. In that split second, Cady saw Perry in the passenger's seat, the muzzle of an M1 peeking out from between his knees.

Cady frantically honked his horn and waved for the truck's driver to pull over. The puzzled Walton brought his vehicle to rest on the road's left shoulder; Cady, meanwhile, abruptly halted his jeep in the middle of the road.

"Soldier, get out of that truck and get in this jeep," an irate Cady yelled up to Perry.

Perry stepped out, holding the rifle diagonally across his torso, the muzzle pointing at the sky. He circled around to the right side of the jeep, placing one hand on the door. But he said nothing.

Cady, still sitting in the driver's seat, ordered his passengers to exit the jeep and get in Walton's truck. Once the three engineers were clear, Cady focused on Perry. "Soldier, get in this jeep," he commanded.

Perry took a step backward, still clutching the rifle to his body. "No, I'm not going to get in the jeep," he said. "I'm going to report to Colonel Hiatt." The reason Perry had gone trotting up the road in the first place was finally clear: he was hoping to take Hiatt up on his offer of a sympathetic ear, and perhaps talk his way out of a court-martial.

But Cady wasn't having it. He pulled the emergency brake, stepped out of the jeep, and circled around the hood toward Perry. Tears now welling in his eyes, Perry started walking away toward the opposite side of the road, nervously peering over his shoulder at the approaching Cady.

"Get back!" Perry yelled at his pursuer. "Get back!"

The lieutenant rephrased his command as a threat: "You will either get in this goddamn jeep or I'll throw you in!"

Perry spun around and pointed the M1 at Cady's chest. His hands were shaking, his sobbing now uncontrollable. From the driver's seat of the truck, Walton heard the M1's safety click off. Perry sputtered out a warning: "Lieutenant, don't come up on me."

But Cady had a tough-guy rep to uphold. Crouched low like a wrestler, he moved in closer. Perry raised his voice to a scream and repeated: "Lieutenant, don't come up on me!"

Right hand in front of left, just a few paces from the sobbing, trembling Perry, Cady reached for the rifle. Or perhaps he was reaching for the neck of the disobedient black man holding it.

Gunfire. Twice in quick succession, followed by a plume of smoke wafting from the M1's muzzle. The men in the dump truck saw Cady fall forward, his head lolling to the side like a rag doll's. For the longest time, no one moved. Perry sniffed at the air, now acrid with the smell of spent gunpowder.

Then Perry started running sideways down the road, his smoldering M1 trained on the truck and its frightened occupants. When he reached the road's edge, a little cliff that dropped off into virgin jungle, he stopped and placed his rifle against a mound of dirt.

Perry stared at the four men in the truck, and they stared back with mouths agape; not a single word was spoken. Perhaps in his fellow engineers, who'd stoically accepted their Army lot, Perry glimpsed the other path he could've chosen. The jungle was a bitch, for sure, and so was all the Jim Crow bunk. But the Perrys were supposed to be survivors; after all, they'd made it out of Monroe's fields to thrive in cutthroat Washington. Maybe Herman, like his comrades, should have swallowed his pride and toughed out the road—for Alma's sake, and for his daughter, Portia.

But having just shot a white man through the heart, Perry knew he'd never get that chance. He picked up his M1 and jumped over the embankment, disappearing into the dense green thicket below.

Safe from further gunfire, the four witnesses raced to Cady's side. The blood spurting from his perforated heart had created a muddy, scarlet pool where he'd fallen. Yet Cady had somehow managed to raise himself up on his hands and crawl to the road's left edge. He picked up his dust-covered head and begged the soldiers standing over him: "Don't leave me, boys! Don't leave me, boys!"

EIGHT

The scent of gunpowder lingered in Perry's nostrils as he fled into the hills. Rifle still in hand, he replayed the shooting in his mind a hundred times, fixating always on Cady's expression. That first brass round had been the killshot, tearing through the apex of Cady's heart and piercing his spinal column. As the bullet minced vital organs, Perry had seen the anger flush from Cady's face, replaced by a mixture of bafflement and dread. Perry didn't remember pulling the trigger a second time, and thus didn't know that he'd pumped an additional round into Cady's stomach.

As he stumbled through the jungle's miasma of trees and rotting ferns, the enormity of his deed began to dawn on Perry. All he'd wanted was an audience with Lieutenant Colonel Hiatt, a chance to argue that "you don't put a man in the guardhouse for missing reveille." His pursuit of that modest goal had somehow ended with his shooting an unarmed officer to death.

So now what? Keep running or surrender? Run where? Without the road to orient himself, Perry was essentially lost; in every direction, there was nothing to see except thick walls of vegetation. There was no food in his pockets, nor anywhere to rest except the sludgy earth. And tigers were known to lurk in these parts.

Perry tried clearing his panicked mind, the better to ponder his next move. But that same odor kept on ricocheting about his skull—the burnt, chemical smell curling from the M1's muzzle. A debilitating wave of nausea washed over Perry; he thought he'd vomit if he ever caught another whiff of M1 powder.

It was not yet eight o'clock in the morning. Perry had been a fugitive for less than forty-five minutes.

THE THREE GIs who'd been riding with Cady now scrambled to save the twenty-eight-year-old lieutenant's life. They carried his limp body back to the jeep, propping him up in the passenger's seat; blood oozed from the two exit wounds in Cady's back. T/5 Robert Griffis took the wheel while Sergeant Harry Bethel and T/4 George Waites hopped in back. Griffis made a U-turn and jammed on the accelerator. There was a field hospital back near the 849th's camp, where the 151st Medical Battalion worked wonders on the gravely injured.

The jeep had gone just fifty feet when Cady let out a loud gasp. He was silent the rest of the way.

A mile later, the three soldiers saw Lieutenant Gene Carapico driving toward them from the opposite direction. Confident that the MPs would handle the Perry matter without incident, Carapico was heading out to check on a maintenance crew. Bethel and Waites waved furiously at their commander, begging him to stop. As Carapico braked, he saw Cady slumped over with his eyes shut. A bloody puncture mark was clearly visible beneath his breast. He looked dead.

Carapico jumped in next to Bethel and Waites as Griffis floored it for the hospital. The medics there laid Cady on a stretcher and cut away his overalls. The shredded flesh around the wounds had already turned a sickly, oxygen-starved blue. Everyone could see there was no point in attempting resuscitation.

The medics went through Cady's pockets that afternoon, cataloging the lieutenant's possessions: a lighter, a pack of cigarettes, a handkerchief, a wallet containing 530 rupees. They dabbed his wounds with soapy water, dressed him in fresh clothes, and placed him in a casket for burial near Ledo.

It would take five days for word of Cady's death to reach his widow, Myrtle, back in Woodhull, New York. The War Department told her only that Harold had been killed in action. The Cadys' daughter, Paula Jean, was still too young to comprehend her father's death.

CADY WASN'T THE first member of the 849th to die at a comrade's hands. In December 1943, for no discernible reason, T/5 Ben Smith had shot and killed a private named Willie Johnson. But Perry's crime was far more taboo: he'd killed a white officer, not a fellow black GI. And he was a deserter, too, having disobeyed Carapico's orders and broken arrest. In the Army's eyes, Perry was a villain of the highest order.

The MPs launched their investigation within hours of Cady's death. They sifted through Perry's belongings, finding his trove of letters from Alma Talbot but not much else. Roadblocks were erected between Tagap Ga and the Indian border, and the trunks of northbound vehicles were carefully inspected; the police assumed that Perry would try and get to Ledo's train station. The MPs also grilled members of the 849th for leads, but the GIs stayed mum, loath to betray one of their brothers in misery. "They were quite close-knit, [so] they zipped up," said Orville Strassburg, a lieutenant with the

502nd Military Police Battalion. "We got nowhere with that unit." The only exceptions were the four soldiers who'd witnessed the shooting, though they could add little beyond the fact that Perry had last been seen leaping into the jungle.

Rumors swirled regarding the circumstances of the crime, with the details differing according to the color of the gossipmonger's skin. Cady was a notorious hard-ass, so the black engineers readily believed that he'd provoked the killing. The word around the enlisted men's tents was that Cady had literally kicked Perry's butt as a reprimand for laziness. Perry obviously went too far by responding with bullets, but the GIs in the 849th could understand where he was coming from. Who among them hadn't fantasized, if only for a microsecond, about plugging a couple of M1 rounds into the chest of an obnoxious 90 Day Wonder?

The 849th's officers, on the other hand, blamed the shooting on Perry's ganja addiction. Early police reports noted that Perry was a heavy user of the demon weed, though they made no mention of his opium habit. As later recounted by Colonel William Boyd Sinclair, a CBI veteran who became the theater of operations' unofficial historian, the scuttlebutt was that Perry had first turned to marijuana as a way to enhance trysts with tribal prostitutes. The drug, Sinclair wrote, slowly corroded Perry's ability to differentiate right from wrong, fantasy from reality:

> One of the effects of the various extracts of the scraggly, yellowish-green hemp herb—*ganjha,* hashish, marijuana, bhang, *kif, charas*— is the uncoiling of time, in which an instant becomes an hour, a second a season, and an interval an eon. To the addict who smokes the leaves, flowers, and resins of this ragweed-looking *cannabis sativa,* the vast, wheeling clock of the universe tells time rather than the passages of this planet and its guiding star. Everything takes

longer, including lust and libido. *Ganjha* could, to Perry, have made sexual contact seem longer.

All the dubious rumors tended to gloss over the simplest explanation: unable to cope with the prospect of another prison term, the mentally precarious Perry had finally snapped. He was just another jungle freak-out, but one who'd killed an officer while breaking down. And the Army couldn't forgive the subversion of its hierarchy during wartime, regardless of whether or not Perry had been compos mentis when he killed.

Cady was by no means blameless in the tragedy. Eager to burnish his macho reputation, he'd tried using force against an obviously unstable individual. Cady should have backed off and waited for the MPs, or coaxed the gun out of Perry's hands with soothing words. But such levelheaded tactics were reserved for white psychiatric casualties, who were treated as lost souls rather than troublemakers. A lieutenant with the 1007th Engineer Special Service Battalion in Burma, for example, recalled how he dealt with a white soldier caught in a situation similar to Perry's:

> I had one soldier who was drunk with a drawn pistol. I could see that he was beyond reasoning about the pistol. I talked to him. Talked to him about his wife and daughters. He handed me the pistol. He continued to cry and talk. He was lonesome and blue. Christmas Eve was a time when he wanted to be home. We talked until he became sleepy. I led him into his tent and saw him in bed.

Yet the Ledo Road brass spent little time, if any, pondering how Cady might have better handled the confrontation. They were too busy worrying that Perry's crime might embolden the enlisted men and beget more violence. The road's success depended, after all, on the black engineers' accepting their roles without complaint. What if the men instead followed Perry's mutinous lead?

The official alarm only increased the day after Cady's death, when two privates from the 849th, both zooted on jungle juice, opened fire on their own camp. They wounded no one, but the attack from within convinced the battalion's officers that the rank and file were once again veering toward insurrection—much as they had back at Camp Kilmer, New Jersey.

Perry needed to be found and punished before the situation spiraled out of control. The longer he avoided justice, the more his reputation would grow among his comrades. Hoping to hasten the manhunt, Cady's fellow officers pitched in to offer a one-thousand-rupee reward for information leading to Perry's capture, dead or alive.

TRAUMA CAN WARP the mind in many ways. In Perry's case, it blanked his memory; upon first grasping how truly screwed he was, he drifted into a dissociative state. His first seventy-two hours on the lam were a blur, though there probably isn't much to tell—he was alone in the jungle, sleeping amid leeches and fumbling in the dark. Only the occasional echoes of dynamite blasts or downshifting 6x6s made Perry realize that the road wasn't far.

After three days of muddling through an amnesiac haze, the famished and haggard Perry decided he'd had enough of the jungle. By that point, he couldn't quite remember why he was wandering in the first place. He had a powerful sense that he'd done something terrible, something that made returning to camp a risky proposition. But he couldn't for the life of him recall what that something was. So he might as well go back and grab some rations, then deal with the consequences once his belly was full. Anything was better than another night in the jungle sludge.

Perry followed the din of human commotion back to the road, then back to camp in the predawn hours of March 8. It had rained the day before, and the morning air was thick with steam—monsoon season was just around the corner. Soaked to the bone after three nights in the jungle, Perry built himself a bonfire at the edge of camp. While getting himself toasty and dry, Perry heard the horn of reveille. Still dazed, he started walking down the camp's main path, between the rows of log-and-canvas huts where the GIs bunked.

Groggy men emerged from those huts to the most baffling sight: their wanted comrade Perry, a man with a one-thousand-rupee price on his head, casually strolling along with the very M1 he'd used to kill Cady. Jaws dropped: every MP within a hundred-mile radius was out for Perry's scalp, and he'd actually returned to camp as if everything was copacetic? Surely he was mad, or just ballsy beyond belief. Or maybe a little bit of both.

While dozens of weathered faces gawked, one GI strode right up to Perry and grabbed him by the arm. He asked what in the hell Perry was doing back at camp, given the circumstances. When Perry mumbled a low, nonsensical response, the soldier shook him hard, trying to restart his brain. The frustrated Good Samaritan eventually had to resort to throwing cold water in Perry's face, a tried-and-true method for reviving the semiconscious.

"From the time I shot the officer until the time that the soldier threw water in my face, I knew I did something wrong," Perry later said. "But [I] couldn't remember what it was." Soaked anew after drying out by his bonfire, Perry finally snapped back to reality—and to the dismal realization that, whatever the jungle's hardships, he'd made a huge mistake by returning to the 849th's digs near Tagap Ga.

Perry's anonymous savior dragged him to a tent, one in which the lanterns were turned off, the better to conceal the fugitive from the prying eyes of passersby. Another GI who'd witnessed the clamor at reveille soon showed up, holding a clump of letters addressed to Perry. The letters had been written over the previous three days by several members of the 849th, who figured they might spot Perry while out working. If such an unplanned rendezvous were to occur, the engineers knew it would be safer to quickly palm off a note than attempt a conversation.

Each letter said the same thing: that the MPs were looking for Perry because he'd killed an officer, and that he would be shot on sight. The way Perry understood it, "as soon as I [threw] my gun down and say 'I am Perry,' I would be shot." And the triggerman would receive a nice bundle of cash for his troubles, courtesy of the 849th's officers.

Perry had every reason to believe his comrades; if the Army could stuff a man in the Box for backtalk, why not lynch a murder suspect? Perry and his allies thought it best that he split at once. Someone handed him extra ammunition for the M1, and perhaps a pack or two of C rations. Perry then crammed the warning notes into the pockets of his olive drab fatigues and scampered back into the wilderness, before any 90 Day Wonders got wise to his presence.

Though Perry now had his bearings, he quickly grew despondent. Hours after fleeing the 849th's camp, he built a fire in a jungle clearing and sat down to reread his friends' letters. He couldn't believe the bind he was in: giving himself up would be tantamount to suicide, but so, too, would roughing it in the hills. Things had been bad enough in the Army; now he was without ample food, shelter, or medicine. How long until the water of some Burmese stream saddled his gut with parasites, or mosquitoes injected malaria into his veins? And then there were the tigers to consider.

As he burned each letter into ash, Perry made a decision: he would take his chances with the MPs. True, they might gun him down on sight, but maybe their trigger fingers weren't as itchy as the letter writers warned. If Perry survived the initial encounter, at least he'd be given Spam and shelter—after three nights in the jungle, even a jail cell sounded dreamy. And when the court-martial took place, Perry would get to tell his side of the story. Maybe there were other men like Lieutenant Colonel Hiatt in the Army's upper echelons, good-hearted men who'd understand that he wasn't cold-blooded, just shattered and aggrieved.

On the night of March 9, Perry made his way back to the road, intending to find a passing MP jeep to which he could surrender. As he neared the road's shoulder, he saw a bridge up ahead, spanning the burbling Namyung River. Perry figured that was as good a place as any to wait; a patrol was bound to come by sooner or later.

To minimize his odds of being shot, Perry chose to proceed unarmed. He laid his M1 against a log and placed his ammunition belt beside it. Then he walked to the swaying pontoon bridge on the Namyung and waited for the cops.

The crack of gunfire ended Perry's surrender attempt just minutes later. The noise had nothing to do with him: it could have been snipers, hunters, or (most plausibly) moonshine-addled drunks taking potshots at birds. But Perry's first thought was that his pals in the 849th were right, and the MPs were out to kill him then and there. Surrendering, he instantly surmised, would be the same thing as placing an M1 against the roof of his mouth and blowing out his brains.

Perry's survival instinct kicked in: jungle life, however daunting, was preferable to death above the Namyung. He bolted for the tree line, so panicked that he forgot about his rifle lying against the log.

He ran deep into the pitch-black woods before remembering, by which time it was too late. Aside from lacking food and potable water, Perry was now without a weapon, too.

THERE WAS BIG news from the front that March, as the Chindits and Merrill's Marauders took the fight to the Imperial Japanese Army. The Chindits' Operation Thursday, launched on the same day as the Cady shooting, had met with good initial results. Major General Orde Charles Wingate's troops had used gliders to infiltrate northern Burma, and were now engaging Japanese forces near the town of Indaw. The fighting continued despite Wingate's death in an airplane accident on March 24, while flying back from a command powwow in Imphal, India.

The American Marauders, meanwhile, took the village of Shaduzup after surviving some of the war's grisliest combat. Merrill's heroically scruffy troops, their ranks drastically thinned by typhus, ambushed the Japanese camp at 3:00 A.M. on March 28, using bayonets to dice their sleeping foes. Once the battered Japanese had fled, the Marauders were elated to discover a supply truck filled with that most precious of battlefield commodities: fresh underwear. The Americans triumphantly donned their vanquished enemies' clean undies, then dined on the fish and rice that had been left simmering on the camp's fires.

The joy was short-lived. Japanese remnants rained shells upon the Americans' foxholes that night, and the shrieks of dying, mutilated soldiers rang out for hours. But Shaduzup still belonged to the Marauders; their campaign's main objective, the town of Myitkyina and its crucial air base, was within reach.

Still, the main topic of conversation along the Ledo Road wasn't the Chindits or the Marauders, but the elusive Herman Perry. The grapevine buzzed with a million rumors about the killer's location; with each passing day, the list of alleged hideouts grew longer. And with each passing day, the splotch of egg on the Army's face grew larger: a supposedly ganja-addled private from D.C. was making a fool of the military police.

The man in charge of the manhunt was Captain Eugene Kirk, the provost marshal* of Ledo. His job was complicated not only by the relative inexperience of his force, full of 90 Day Wonders who mainly handled traffic and drunks, but by the Army's shoddy record keeping. When Kirk tried to obtain a photograph of Perry, he discovered that the Army had none; a mug shot had to be sent from Washington.

Other blunders were more directly attributable to Kirk's shortcomings as a detective. In the all-points bulletin he sent to MPs in the field, Kirk misstated Perry's Army serial number, as well as basic facts about the suspect's appearance. He was slow to spread the word to forward-deployed battalions, and he wasted considerable effort convincing the Washington police to monitor Perry's mother's mail—as if Perry was not only dumb enough to betray his location in writing, but would also stick around the same place for the weeks it took nonmilitary mail to cross the oceans.

Kirk nonetheless seemed confident that he was hot on Perry's trail. Exhibiting the sort of fallacious logic that has ended many a military career, Kirk reasoned that, given the inborn African American penchant for sexual voraciousness, Perry would try and whore it up as much as possible while on the lam. Since paid sex was hard to come by in the jungle, Perry would likely head for the nearest center of sin: Calcutta.

---

*An officer who supervises the military police.

Yes, he had to be in Calcutta. So in mid-March, that was where Kirk dispatched one of his most trusted lieutenants, David Smith, to lay a trap throughout the city's infamous brothels.

THE FALL OF Burma in 1942 had been catastrophic for Calcutta, a city already accustomed to its share of sorrow. After capturing Rangoon in March of that year, the Japanese had halted the export of Burmese rice, a staple of the Bengali diet. Then in October, a cyclone devastated Bengal's fishing grounds and livestock. Famine inevitably followed, and malnourished Bengalis either wasted away or fell victim to cholera and smallpox. The London-based *New Statesman* estimated that three million Indians perished. "Whole areas are almost depopulated," *The New Republic* reported in May 1944. "Sometimes the survivors are too weak to bury the dead, and leave them to the competition of dogs and vultures." The few relief workers who made it to the Bengali countryside were shocked at the profusion of skeletal beggars, "some longing for food with a piteous look, some lying by the wayside approaching death hardly with any more energy to breathe."

Tens of thousands of survivors squeezed onto trains bound for Calcutta, Bengal's capital, in hopes of finding sustenance. They rarely did; the famine had boosted rice prices by 500 percent, and the government was stingy with handouts. Refugees were reduced to foraging in the city's railyards, looking for errant grains of rice buried in the trackside muck.

Calcutta's colonial elite didn't share in the suffering. Their oak-lined clubs still served scotch and steaks, and they amused themselves with cricket as the masses starved. CBS Radio's Eric Sevareid was struck by the disparity between the city's haves and have-nots:

In the Calcutta stock exchange, enormously fat brokers dozed in their deep leather chairs, surfeited with their heavy lunches; they sprawled out with their feet apart, their snoring mouths wide open. You went down the stairs and sidestepped to avoid a totally naked Hindu who was foraging with his head in the garbage pail. You stepped over the frail, white-swathed bodies of women who lay on the sidewalk in front of your hotel, dying quietly with their babies clutched to their breasts.

American GIs on furlough in the Bengali capital were similarly appalled by the famine's toll. "The great obscenity of Calcutta was the dead bodies," wrote Sergeant Evelio Grillo of the 823rd. "They would lie on the sidewalks waiting for the trucks that circled the city constantly, picking up the bodies unceremoniously and pitching them atop the bodies already loaded. Walking down the sidewalk, we had to cross from one side of the street to the other and back to avoid dead bodies. The experience of Calcutta made the return to the jungle welcome."

As ghastly as it was, famine-wracked Calcutta was the only R & R option available to the Ledo Road's black GIs. There were eleven American rest camps scattered throughout India, and white soldiers could opt for such exotic destinations as Kashmir (with its excellent skiing) or Darjeeling. But of these eleven camps, blacks could only stay at one. It was located in Howrah, a five-minute ferry ride across the Hooghly River from Calcutta, and its conditions were deplorable. The *Chicago Defender*'s Denton J. Brooks described the segregated riverside digs as "little better than those [the black GIs] had left in the wilds of Burma," with the supposedly vacationing soldiers housed in field tents and served the same Spam-and-rice dinners they ate in the jungle. The corpses of beggars, unable to afford even the thirty rupees it cost to be cremated atop a pile of bullock dung, floated by the tents, dousing the entire camp in the stench of death. The Army would eventually make small improvements by adding mattress-covered beds and hiring three black Red Cross girls to distribute doughnuts, but not until the war's final days.

Rather than endure the broiling tedium of the Howrah camp, which also meant making another excruciating trip along the Bengal-Assam Railway, many black GIs turned down the chance to go on leave; engineers often spent two and a half years straight in the jungle, the monotony broken only by sporadic trips to Ledo. Those who made the trek spent as little time as possible in Howrah, preferring to ferry across the Hooghly and drink in Calcutta's strange mélange of redbrick Victorian architecture and Hindu pageantry. The culturally curious checked out the Hooghly ghats, where thousands of Calcuttans bathed in the grimy river. Or they'd weave through streets that reeked of fried sardines and sandalwood, the path blocked every few steps by fly-plagued cows or sinewy rickshaw pullers naked from the waist up. GIs with genteeler tastes—whether black or white—could enjoy a proper British tea service at the Kyd Street mansion of Sir David Ezra, a Jewish real-estate magnate. And at night, soldiers filtered over to the Winter Garden, a swank, integrated nightclub where the house band was led by Teddy Weatherford, an expatriate African American jazzman.

But after months without female companionship, many of the vacationing GIs had only one form of recreation in mind upon arriving in Calcutta; an army travels not only on its stomach, as Napoléon Bonaparte once observed, but also on its loins. Fearful of its already tenuous forces being further decimated by the clap and syphilis, the Army forbade its men to visit neighborhoods known for open prostitution. GIs caught traversing brothel-lined Karaya or Acre roads were arrested on the spot.

British administrators had long tolerated a cluster of brothels staffed by registered prostitutes, who submitted to regular medical checkups in exchange for legal protection. But the Americans, abetted by a puritanical Indo-British club called the Association for Moral and Social Hygiene, forced the Calcutta government to shutter many of these whorehouses during the war. The city's licensed sex workers protested the closures in a petition submitted to the American military police, arguing that soldiers would merely satiate their sexual desires in less savory places:

> It must be borne in mind that we are the only registered prostitutes in the city who are continually under the supervision of the Calcutta Police, but there are some 30,000 to 50,000 unregistered prostitutes who are housed in Rembagen, Senagachi, Dhakaria Bagan and hundreds of other places throughout the city, over which the police have practically no control, as they are repeatedly moving from one area to another. Your lads will be taken by broker to these Indian brothels, where they will in the majority of cases contract venereal disease.

The protesting prostitutes were correct. The MPs might have been able to keep Calcutta's out-of-bounds districts free of horny soldiers, but the famine had forced countless families to pimp their women, and flush foreign soldiers were the obvious johns of choice. "In many famine-devastated areas of Bengal, womanhood has been dishonoured," lamented the Bengali novelist Bhowani Sen. "A section of the contractors has made a profession of selling girls to the military. There are places . . . where women sell themselves literally in hordes, and young boys act as pimps for the military."

In Calcutta, these baby-faced pimps were often shoe-shine boys. They'd swarm around men in uniform, waving their gunk-encrusted

rags and pleading, "Shine, sahib?" When a soldier declined, the boy
would instead offer a liaison with his sister, cousin, or mother. Official estimates placed the number of Calcutta sex workers at around
forty thousand, but the specter of starvation had turned almost any
woman into a potential whore. As a result, large numbers of GIs
contracted venereal diseases during their Calcutta leaves.

The GIs had to follow the shoe-shine pimps back to the city's
ghettos, where assignations were conducted in shacks and lean-tos.
The Army brass, however, didn't have to hazard Calcutta's squalor in
order to procure willing girls. Along with a daily two-egg breakfast—
equivalent to half a month's egg ration in England—the palatial
Grand Hotel on Chowringhee Street offered a laissez-faire attitude
toward sexual shenanigans. When the MPs raided the hotel in
March 1944, they were scandalized to discover American colonels
partying with "a goodly number of Eurasian and coloured girls aged
between fourteen and sixteen." The girls were expelled from the
premises, but the officers apparently avoided punishment.

Had he been even vaguely familiar with Calcutta's sex scene,
Captain Kirk would have realized the futility of his plan to ensnare
Perry in flagrante delicto. A horny GI intent on dodging the MPs
would obviously tap the services of a shoe-shine pimp, rather than
risk the well-patrolled brothel districts. And given that Calcutta's
houses of ill repute numbered in the thousands, many of them un-
registered and cloistered in dicey outlying neighborhoods, Lieutenant Smith and his four assistants couldn't cover them all in a decade,
let alone a few days.

Yet Smith readily bought into Kirk's proposition that not only was
Perry definitely headed for Calcutta, but that hookers-*cum*-informants
would be key to a successful manhunt. Within days of arriving in
Calcutta, Smith sent a triumphant telegram back to Ledo, bragging to
Kirk that he and his men had "laid out a dragnet" among the city's

brothels. Smith ended the communiqué with a sentence fragment that oozed confidence: "Impossible for him to remain free."

HAVING LEFT HIS rifle near the Namyung bridge and burned his comrades' disturbing letters, Perry was now traveling with nothing except the olive drab fatigues on his back. All that saved him from starvation that first week in the jungle was his knack for rapping with tribesmen—the same knack he'd already used to score ganja and opium. As he scaled the wispy, brush-strewn trails that coiled up the Patkais, Perry would sometimes come upon a Naga field *basha*, a bamboo hut where farmers stayed while tending to their hillside plots. Using the snippets of tribal lingo that he'd picked up on the road, Perry begged these farmers for rice. They were glad to oblige: the black Americans were usually kind to the Nagas, offering them truck rides, tins of Spam, or well-thumbed copies of *CBI Roundup* as souvenirs. A bowl of rice was the least they could provide in return.

But the Naga hospitality stopped at food. Perry didn't rest in the field bashas, but instead kept clawing through the jungle, following the setting sun westward toward the Indian border. The pleasure dens of Calcutta were probably nowhere in Perry's thoughts as he tore away branches with his bare hands and shooed off giant insects. His only objective was to survive another day, a task that would become even tougher once the monsoons hit.

On or about March 18, an exhausted and reeking Perry heard human voices chattering through the trees. Creeping closer, he realized they were speaking English, though tinged with a lilting accent he recognized from his time in India—limeys, for sure. Desperate for provisions, Perry decided to gamble that the British would be unfamiliar with the Cady shooting. He called out to them.

The British troops were likely part of a civil-affairs patrol, checking in with villages loyal to the Crown—usually smaller settlements that needed protection against head-hunting raids. The Brits were surprised to find an American so casually wandering about the tribal hinterlands, and a black American at that. They knew their allies used blacks as manual laborers, but had never heard of an African American jungle scout. And even if such a thing existed, why would he be in the British-controlled Patkais, rather than out on the front lines far to the southeast?

Perry coolly allayed any suspicions the Brits might have, explaining that he was "attached to a liaison officer"—in other words, he was a man Friday for one of the OSS Detachment 101 agents who plied Naga chieftains with gifts of tin and opium. He'd simply become lost during a mission, and was trying to make his way back to camp. Could they perhaps help with a little food for a hungry ally?

Hoodwinked by Perry's trademark charm, the British pitched in with whatever rations they could spare. It would be enough to get Perry through a few more days of running, but the food obviously wouldn't last forever. He needed to figure out a long-term alternative to depending on the kindness of strangers, or else he'd surely die.

In need of better shelter than the jungle's arboreal canopy, Perry searched for a native village where he could hole up for a while, at least until he figured out a plan. He now had cans of Western food, which the Naga prized for their rarity as well as for their heavy caloric content. Perry might be able to exchange them for a few nights' worth of room and board—enough time, perhaps, for him to gather his thoughts and plot a course to safety.

A day or two after bidding farewell to the British, while hiking along a narrow mountain stream, something on an uphill ridge caught Perry's eye: a sharply peaked roof covered with dried palm leaves. The house was positioned to give its inhabitants an eagle's-eye view of the forested country below. Beneath a bamboo porch, fat pigs rutted around in piles of trash and human waste.

Crossing the stream to get a closer look, Perry noticed something else about the house. Just outside its walls were cords of vine, hung from poles like washing lines. And dangling off these vines were several scrubbed and polished human skulls, with the horns of water buffalos affixed to their sides.

Herman Perry had discovered his new home.

NINE

In January 1880, a correspondent for *The Englishman*, a Calcutta newspaper, filed a gruesome dispatch from eastern Assam. A few days earlier, a band of Naga tribesmen had raided one of the province's foremost tea gardens, decapitating several coolies and leaving the headless corpses to fester in the sun. Genuine shock tinged the reporter's description of the massacre's aftermath: "The whole was a horribly sickening scene, and a complete wreck; and such surely as none but the veriest of devils in human form could have perpetrated."

The correspondent's revulsion suggests that he was a newcomer to raucous North-East India, where such violence was numbingly routine. Naga headhunters, always keen to acquire skulls and slaves, had been raiding the Assamese lowlands for centuries, sowing terror with their square-bladed daos. Their fortunate victims were granted quick, if painful, deaths; the unlucky were spirited off to the jungle, held captive for months, then speared or ritually beheaded as offerings to the gods.

Head-hunting was the linchpin of Naga society, the means by

which men established their bona fides and villages asserted their supremacy over rivals. Keith Cantlie, a British colonial official, described the Nagas' raiding style in his diary: "Heads were taken by ambushing usually. A woman's head was an object prized as greatly as that of a man. To get the head one had to go near the enemy's village. The horrible act of killing children did not seem repulsive or shameful to a Naga." The heads of infants, in fact, were especially prized—the logic being that babies are exceptionally tough to kill, since they're so diligently guarded by their parents.

There was no glory to be had while dying on a raid; if detected while crouching in the bush, a Naga head-hunting party would flee instead of fight. Some men, desirous of a headtaker's prestige yet too cowardly or feeble to risk their lives, bought slaves to behead. Such a slave would be taken to the edge of his captor's village and told he was finally free, after weeks or months in bondage. But it was all a cruel trick: the Naga who'd purchased the slave would be lying in wait along the path, ready to score an easy kill. Heads obtained through this shortcut were considered no less magical than those culled from more challenging prey.

Naga headhunters returning from a successful raid were greeted with boisterous adoration, as log drums were beaten and women danced manic jigs. Christoph von Fürer-Haimendorf, an Austrian anthropologist, described how Naga villages in northeastern Assam typically celebrated the arrival of a freshly taken head:

> The captured head was put down and the senior men of all the clans involved in the capture smashed raw eggs on the head, intending by magical means to blind the kinsmen of the dead foe. Then, a clan elder poured rice beer into the mouth and said, "May your mother, may your father, may your elder and younger brothers all come, may they drink our beer and eat our rice and meat. May they all come!"

These ritual words were intended to compel the deceased to call his relatives so that they too might fall victims to the spears of the victors. . . .

The next day all the men of the village dressed in ceremonial clothes and ornaments and painted their bodies with lime. In solemn procession the head was carried either to two stones standing in front of the chief's house or to the upright stone newly set up in a ritual place. There, the senior descendant of the village founder, acting as priest (*niengba*), cut off small pieces of the ears and tongue and called again on the kinsmen of the dead man. He took a small chicken and, sprinkling its blood on the stones, repeated the same incantation. Next, he examined the intestines to see whether the omens were propitious for the slaying of more enemies. The carcass of the chicken was left lying on the stone, but the captured head was taken to a tree close to the [house] of the captor and hung up there to dry. Throughout the day there was dancing and feasting, and the whole village observed a day of abstention from work in the fields.

Once the festivities were over, the mutilated heads were turned into trophies. A warrior's wife might boil off the flesh in a pot of chilies, then adorn the denuded skull with buffalo horns and grass tassels. Another popular approach was to pierce the mouth and eye sockets with sharpened sticks, "to give the spirit pain in the next world." Once dried and stripped of skin, skulls were displayed in a variety of ways: corded on vines, impaled on posts, lined up on bamboo shelves, hung from "head trees" like ghoulish Christmas ornaments. The man responsible for the decapitation was thereafter entitled to wear a symbol of his achievement: a skull-shaped pendant made of brass, a figure-eight tattoo across the face, or an orchid-stalk headdress garnished with tufts of human hair.

There are numerous theories as to why certain cultures devel-

A Konyak Naga named Wong holding a skull trophy, early 1920s.

oped a zest for head-hunting—not just in Southeast Asia, where one-third of the population engaged in the sadistic pastime before the 1700s, but in Oceania, the Amazon, and the Balkans. Anthropologists have speculated that head-hunting may be a primitive anger-management technique; a ritual meant to boost a population's fertility; a crucial rite of passage for teenage boys; a way for young men to convince young women of their marriageability; or perhaps a crude strategy for limiting casualties from warfare, as a single captured skull was usually enough to satiate a village's collective bloodlust, at least for a while.

The Nagas themselves explained simply "that heads were taken as they were the only fit morsel (sacrifice) for the spirits." Their animist religion taught that the soul resided in the neck, and that decapitation was the surest means of acquiring this vital force. This belief raises a chicken-and-egg question: did the Nagas start hunting heads because their priests told them to, or did the priests contort Naga dogma in order to justify head-hunting as a religious obligation?

Whatever the Nagas' deep-seated psychological reasons for head-hunting, their appetite for skulls had a very pragmatic effect: it convinced outsiders that the Nagas, however destitute and lacking in the accoutrements of civilization, were a people to be feared—and, if at all possible, avoided. As if their menacing reputation required further burnishing, the Nagas were also said to be avid lycanthropists, capable of possessing the bodies of leopards and tigers during the moon's waning phases. "Possession is not confined to men," the British anthropologist J. H. Hutton observed. "Women also become were-leopards and are far more destructive as such than men are. Of men, those who have taken heads are the most dangerous, and are believed to kill as many men as leopards or tigers as they have done as warriors."

For the six centuries prior to the Brits' arrival, Assam had been ruled by the Ahoms, a Hindu dynasty of Burmese origin. Their kingdom's official records, the *Buranjis*, boast of several military campaigns against the Nagas, though these accounts are likely exaggerated; the Ahoms knew better than to overly antagonize a group of head-hunting lycanthropists. The Ahoms interacted only with the Nagas who abutted the plains, leaving alone the isolated mountain villages that were largely impervious to attack. A deal was cut with the more accessible Nagas, offering them land and fishing rights in exchange for minor tribute—elephant tusks, spears, and cloth. Forging economic ties with the Nagas, the Ahoms surmised, would reduce the frequency of head-taking raids.

Soldiers of the British East India Company first encountered the Nagas in 1832, while searching for a navigable passage between Burma and Assam. Accustomed to relative independence under the Ahoms, the Nagas did not take kindly to these Westerners who fancied themselves South Asia's masters. The Nagas made clear their displeasure by taking several fair-complexioned heads, a rude welcome that immediately soured the British on their new subjects. "They are the wildest and most barbarous of hill tribes, and looked upon with dread and horrour by the neighbors of the plains who consider them as ruthless robbers and murderers," observed John McCosh, a Scottish surgeon, in 1837.

The British had no designs on the Nagas' mountainous territory, covered as it was with toxic jungles. The Naga realms were not only short on arable land, they were also malarial, waterlogged, and plagued by hungry tigers; one colonial official described trekking "through a country devastated by tigers which had literally eaten up the population; each day we passed deserted village sites." But the British also realized that head-hunting posed a serious threat to the nascent Assamese tea industry; murdered coolies, after all, cost money to replace. So the British launched a series of punitive expeditions, torching Naga villages accused of raiding the plains and bayoneting any tribals who resisted.

But the military solution failed to scotch the raids, in large part because the British did not yet comprehend a key fact about the Nagas: they were not members of a single, unified tribe, but an ethnic group divided into dozens of tribes and subtribes, each with its own distinct customs, religious tenets, and even language.

These tribes were linked by common ancestors, most likely inhabitants of eastern Tibet or western China who had migrated to the Indo-Burmese hills in ancient times.* This shared heritage accounts for the Nagas' distinctive physical appearance, often described as quasi Mongolian and similar to that of the head-hunting Dayaks of Borneo. There were also cultural threads that connected the disparate tribes, such as the affinity for trophy skulls and the use of slash-and-burn agriculture (a practice called *jhuming*).

But the tribes felt scant kinship toward one another, an estrangement reinforced by the Nagas' broad geographic distribution. Tribes resided throughout the vast Indo-Burmese border region, from the Manipur Hills in the south to the northern tip of the Patkais, with the majority inhabiting a forested range known as the Naga Hills. A member of the Tangkhul Naga tribe living near Imphal had little or nothing to do with an Ao Naga from outside Mokokchung, 110 miles to the north. And that Ao, in turn, was a virtual foreigner to a Tangsa Naga living by the Pangsau Pass, another 120 miles northeast.

Even more confusingly, a Naga's first loyalty was to his village, not his tribe. Neighboring villages often raided each other for heads, regardless of whether their populations shared a tribal affiliation.

---

*In the seventh volume of his colossal *Geographia*, written during the Roman Empire's heyday, Ptolemy briefly mentions a barbarous, flat-nosed people who inhabited a land east of the defunct Indo-Greek Kingdom. He refers to this land as *Nagalog*, or "realm of the naked"—proof, Naga historians claim, that their people have lived in the Indo-Burmese wilderness for at least two millennia.

Vendettas between Naga settlements could last for years, to the point that everyone forgot why they'd started seizing tit-for-tat skulls in the first place; for a young man to emigrate from a village embroiled in such a blood feud was considered the equivalent of military desertion. When the British burned a village, then, the surrounding Nagas weren't cowed, but rather delighted—that meant one fewer competitor for local resources and, as a special bonus, a lot of charred corpses from which heads and their attendant souls could be harvested.

By 1851, the British had concluded that their military campaigns were only exacerbating the Naga problem. So the colonial government switched to a noninterference policy, whereby the Nagas were largely left to their own devices. Instead of devoting their resources to burning villages, British troops created a line of defense just below the hills. Punitive expeditions were undertaken only in the event of particularly egregious head-taking raids; as long as the Nagas didn't decapitate too many coolies, the British let them be. Furthermore, the British invited an ethnic group from southern Assam, the Kukis, to resettle in the foothills of the Indo-Burmese frontier. Colonial administrators hoped that Kuki villages would create a buffer zone between the Nagas and the tea gardens.

The British erred, however, by covertly encouraging the Kukis to snatch away Naga farmland. Kuki pioneers clashed with the incumbent Nagas, who in turn felt betrayed by the British; if the noninterference policy was a sham, then there was no reason for the Nagas to keep their head-hunting in check. The ensuing upsurge in raids aggravated British military officers, since the noninterference policy precluded them from avenging each and every Naga incursion.

The British were soon compelled to change strategies once again. This time, they would gradually pacify the Nagas by extending the raj's political influence. As part of this so-called Forward Policy, the

British built schools, roads, and hospitals in the hills, hoping to convince the Nagas of modernity's benefits. More cleverly, they realized that feuds between Naga villages were a societal weakness that could be exploited. The British identified vulnerable villages and made them tempting offers: protection from the predations of more formidable Nagas in exchange for fealty to the colonial government.

The mightier Naga enclaves resisted the Forward Policy, attacking British political agents sent to cement the raj's grip on the hills. In 1875, a 197-person party headed by a Lieutenant Holcombe was ambushed while surveying an uncharted jungle zone. Within minutes, eighty members of the group, Holcombe included, had been hacked or speared to death, and another fifty-one gravely wounded. Several Naga villages were burned in retaliation, but the British were unable to recover Holcombe's head.* From that point on, interlopers steered clear of the hills' remotest corners.

The peak of Naga resistance to the Forward Policy came in 1878, when several thousand Angami Nagas laid siege to the city of Kohima, a British administrative capital about 150 miles southwest of Ledo. After initially massacring more than 50 soldiers, the Naga army surrounded Kohima's central garrison and tried to starve out its 545 men, women, and children; the Nagas' tactics included poisoning the fort's water supply with a severed head. "It is certainly a very awful thing, after a great disaster and massacre, to be shut up in a weak stockade built of highly inflammable material, and surrounded by 6,000 howling savages who spare no one," wrote Sir James Johnstone, a British political officer sent to quell the disturbance. The besieged Brits nearly made the tremendous blunder of surrendering

---

*In the 1920s, a British political officer named Charles R. Pawsey renewed the hunt for Holcombe's head, finally locating it in 1925. "Holcombe's head is still in the La-wong's morung in a position of honour above the rest," he wrote in his diary. "Those of the sepoys are with common herd." It is not clear whether Pawsey reclaimed the trophy skull, though he seemed incensed at the failure of previous British expeditions to punish its owners. According to colonial scuttlebutt, Pawsey was obsessed with the head because he was actually Holcombe's illegitimate son.

the garrison, a move that, in Johnstone's opinion, would have led to "545 headless and naked bodies . . . lying outside the blockade." But reinforcements arrived in the nick of time, and British artillery decimated the rebels.

Resistance diminished thereafter, at least in the southern and central regions of the Nagas' mountainous homeland. The glut of cheap opium eroded the tribes' martial spirit, as did the introduction of Christianity. American missionaries had first arrived in the Naga Hills in the 1830s, and found the Nagas disinclined to abandon their cherished beliefs in sky gods, demons, and entrails-reading oracles: instead of welcoming the Lord's salvation, the Nagas raided the missions for heads. But in 1872, the Reverend E. W. Clark finally succeeded in establishing a viable mission, one that converted many members of the Ao Naga tribe to an abstentious strain of Baptism. The converts, no longer interested in typical Naga pursuits like getting wasted on rice beer and taking heads, were often ostracized from their villages and forced to settle elsewhere. Such schisms delighted the British, who viewed Christianity as an effective tool for weakening the Nagas. "It cannot be doubted," noted Johnstone, "that a large population of Christian hill-men between Assam and Burmah [sic] would be a valuable prop to the State."

By the early twentieth century, the British had brought sizeable swaths of the Naga Hills' western slopes under their political control. They governed with a light touch, burning villages suspected of excessive head-hunting and registering opium addicts, but otherwise staying out of day-to-day Naga affairs. The British political officer E. T. D. Lambert explained the tacit arrangement to the Royal Geographical Society in 1937:

> Administration in these backwards tracts does not amount to as much as it does in the ordinary districts of India. The Indian Penal

Code and other similar Indian laws are not in force, and the people are ruled as far as possible under their own laws and customs. They pay a small poll or house tax varying from Rs.2 to Rs.5, and in return for this Government provides an administrative officer, schools, and dispensaries. Head-hunting and human sacrifice are banned, and the people are given protection from raids across the frontier. An attempt is made to improve the economic lot of the inhabitants.

Yet the British, like the Ahoms before them, stopped short of extending their influence to the more isolated Naga tribes, especially those inhabiting the Patkais. This seldom-traversed "Tribal Territory" was simply too forbidding for the British to control, and the natives too belligerent. As a result, the tribes living in the Patkais' northern jungles, such as the Wancho and the Heimi, continued to live as they had for centuries. Many villages on the Patkais' Burmese slopes, in particular, were only vaguely aware of their supposed British overlords.

The difference between these two Naga domains—one nominally under the British thumb, the other virtually untouched by modernity—was starkly apparent to Americans who roamed the jungles during World War II. Among them was William R. Peers, commander of OSS Detachment 101, the secret unit whose mission included currying favor with Naga chieftains:

> Two lines divide the Naga Hills; crossing over the "outer line" one found pleasant, relatively safe villages, and might cross paths with an occasional British or Indian Civil Affairs Officer. Should one trek on twenty miles into the hills, he crossed the so-called "inner line." Here a party depended on weapons for safety and was on the watch for Nagas; alert, hardy warriors, these Nagas were at times friendly, but could for one cause or another turn into enemies.

The Naga village that Herman Perry stumbled upon in March
1944 was well beyond that inner line.

THE PEAKED, palm-covered roof that first caught Perry's eye belonged to a *morung*, or bachelors' dormitory, the focal point of every
Naga village. Decorated with carvings of elephants, leopards, or
human couples in coitus, morungs were positioned to give their inhabitants the clearest possible view of the countryside below; the
dorm's residents were charged with keeping watch for head-seeking
raiders. In the Patkai foothills where Perry found himself, about
eight to ten miles west of Tagap Ga, morungs were traditionally built
atop bamboo poles, creating porches where bachelors gathered to
socialize and, more odiferously, shit; pigs were kept below, where
they fattened up on human excrement.

The more pungent smell that wafted down to Perry as he approached the morung, however, was that of rotting bodies—not
headless victims of the dao, but deceased Nagas laid out on raised
funeral platforms, bundled in cloth or straw and surrounded by animal skulls. Once a dead Naga's body had reached the advanced
stages of decomposition, the head was removed and buried in an
earthenware pot, or secreted inside a stone phallus. The tattoos that
an important man had carried during his lifetime were often carved
into his skull, so that the spirits might recognize his soul's grandeur
as it journeyed into the gated Land of the Dead.

As Perry hiked the last few yards to the village's center, his arrival
caused a stir; solo travelers rarely chanced these parts, to say nothing
of black Americans. But the villagers, likely members of a Heimi
Naga subtribe, were at least familiar with the presence of African
American soldiers in Burma: at its nearest point, the Ledo Road was

just over six miles away. The village's inhabitants were among the Nagas who sold chickens, knives, and ganja to GIs, then melted back into the jungle like leathery, tattooed ghosts.

But the Nagas' past dealings with Americans by no means guaranteed Perry's safety. As Peers had learned in his jungle travels, the Nagas who had remained beyond the raj's grasp were an ornery and suspicious lot, still in love with ritual violence and its attendant magic. Perry certainly couldn't help but notice the plethora of festooned human skulls that hung outside the morung, nor the fact that every male villager had a dao slung across his chest or back.

Head-hunting was officially a relic of the past, as the British had outlawed the practice in the low-lying Naga areas it administered. In villages that had complied with this directive, either willingly or under threat of the torch, a soul-crushing torpor had ensued. All the affected Nagas could do was dream of bygone days, when men were men and fresh heads regularly graced the village trees or trophy shelves. "If you talk to a Phom or Konyak on such tedious topics as theology, economics or social organization he quickly slips away to have a refreshing drink of rice-beer," the British anthropologist Verrier Elwin would write about two major Naga tribes a decade later. "Open the question of head-hunting and his eyes light up, his whole body comes to life and a torrent of exciting and highly improper information pours from his lips."

Yet in the forests of the eastern Patkais, where Perry was on the lam, head-hunting had never vanished. On the rare occasions that a British administrator showed up, the Nagas simply hid their trophy skulls until the foreigner departed. "Even if we want to stop head hunting, I don't see how we can do so at present," a colonial official admitted in 1943, when asked to report on a wave of intertribal violence in the Patkais.

The head-hunting indeed continued throughout World War II, as an American lieutenant discovered on a survey mission through the Patkais:

> I was investigating trails with an interpreter a while back, when a Naga chief invited me into his hut to show me his 70 skulls. Listening to his palaver I thought he was bragging until the interpreter informed me that the chief was apologizing for the shortage of his stock, explaining that he had 200 skulls in his *basha* hut which burned. He begged me to return soon and promised to have his collection back to 100.

Nagas from rival villages were the headhunters' preferred prey, since killing fellow tribals was unlikely to invite British reprisals. But some opportunistic warriors, of the same craven ilk who had no qualms about killing slaves, weren't picky about their victims. Stories circulated of downed Allied pilots falling victim to the dao, the head-takers having decided they'd rather have a soul-filled skull than the opium that the Americans promised in exchange for rescued fliers.

So as Perry made his way toward the Nagas that March day, whether he'd survive the encounter was anyone's guess. He was now surrounded by armed, seminaked men with wavy blue tattoos running down their cheeks and necks. At any moment, the village *ang*, or hereditary chief, could order his warriors to take the stranger's skull.

But Perry had two things working in his favor: the effortless charm that had served him so well in courting girls in Washington, and the tins of chow he'd copped from the British. There was actually no better way to impress the Nagas than with gifts composed of lightweight metals, which Naga craftsmen had yet to master. When visiting a Naga village for the first time, for example, members of OSS Detachment 101 would elicit a royal welcome by distributing coins and trinkets. Once the ang felt properly honored, and his warriors had shown off the chunky brass pendants that symbolized the heads they'd taken, the Americans would plead through an interpreter for help with saving pilots, or for land on which to build lookout posts. An Army captain who went on one such mission recalled "purchasing" an entire mountain from an ang named Tong, for the princely sum of nine dollars' worth of silver and a jackknife. The sale included Tong's solemn oath that his warriors would decapitate any Japanese soldiers they encountered, and add the skulls to his personal trophy shelf.

Perry didn't want anything as grandiose as a mountain, just a place to rest and hide. He smiled and passed out British rations, then signaled that he needed shelter. Disarmed by Perry's kindness, the Nagas invited the tallest, darkest man for miles around to stay awhile. The ang told Perry that the Burmese called their village Tgum Ga. Perry couldn't quite pronounce those alien syllables, so he mangled the village's name into something that more easily slid off his tongue: Glau.

PERRY HAD ARRIVED in Glau just as the farming season was getting under way. The Nagas had recently planted rice on their meager hillside plots, using sticks and daos to till the feeble soil. Weeding was done by hand, a backbreaking chore made bearable by the regular ingestion of rice beer. Drinking, as Perry discovered to his delight, was integral to village life; the Nagas enjoyed few things more than a heavy buzz. Imbibing was particularly popular among young, unmarried men and women, as recounted by Fürer-Haimendorf:

Toward the end of the weeding the boys of the gang would entertain their girlfriends in one of the field huts, and on that occasion they took pride in providing sufficient rice beer to make their guests drunk. If the girls could not walk unaided the boys would carry them home on their backs and deposit them proudly at the houses of their parents.

A few days later the girls would return the hospitality, and then it was their ambition to make the boys drunk. Two girls might then drag or carry one of their intoxicated friends up the hill to the village.

The drudgery of subsistence agriculture was further broken by song and dance, two art forms for which the Nagas were justly renowned. Drums and horn flutes sounded nearly every night, as boys and girls joined hands in single-sex circles and swayed in time. On more festive occasions, warriors donned trapezoidal helmets outfitted with boar's tusks and mimicked the frenzy of battle, waving their daos

Young Konyak Naga men in their finest garb, early 1920s.

skyward while cursing their enemies. Boys of marrying age, meanwhile, wooed girls with tender love songs, accompanied by the twangs
of bamboo mouth harps.

As an erstwhile gentleman of leisure who'd been deprived too long
of female company, Perry vibed to the sexual energy that crackled
between Naga bachelors and bachelorettes. Fourteen or fifteen was
considered the right age for a girl to become sexually active, and pre-
marital liaisons were permitted, even encouraged—should a girl become pregnant from such a tryst, it was taken as an admirable
testament to her fertility. The girls paraded around with pert, bare
breasts, framed by piles of beaded necklaces. Perry was hardly the first
Westerner to be enchanted by their beauty, as well as by the permis-
siveness of Naga culture.

The Nagas' easy sexuality had shocked many a prudish Brit over
the years. Touring through the hills in 1923, J. H. Hutton had been
scandalized by the willingness of Naga women to gratify the visitors:
"When we got to the village, we found a bevy of the village beauties
sitting outside the gate in wait for us. One or two had washed their
faces, and showed very fair skins with a touch of pink underneath. . . .
They put up one of their own menfolk to tell us how much they
would like to have children by us—and they [were] married women
and their husbands [were] listening!"

No such offer was immediately forthcoming for Perry, although
he took an instant liking to one of the ang's daughters, a comely
fourteen-year-old. As village royalty, she was entitled to wear the
finest skirts, skillfully embroidered and decorated with glass beads
and locks of goat hair. Girls of such elevated lineage also sported
long, flowing tresses, in contrast to the cropped hairdos of commoners. Perry thought he caught her giving him the Naga equivalent of
a come-hither look—"the glad eye," as he'd later call it. But he was
scared to work his game; there was the language barrier, for starters,

but also the fact that she was the ang's daughter. Still bewildered by Naga culture, Perry feared that one faux pas could lead to his expulsion from Glau—or, far worse, his murder.

Perry realized that the surest way to win the Nagas' trust, and thus permission to court the headman's daughter, was to provide them with more of the Western goods they craved. And so he gathered his courage and hiked the six miles down to the Ledo Road, emerging wraithlike from the murky jungle as he'd seen so many Nagas do before. As suicidal as it sounded, Perry was going to round up some American rations.

The details of how Perry managed to flag down a 6x6 and secure such loot is an aspect of his story that remains unknown, and unknowable. After a month on the lam, Perry was fast becoming a folk hero among the black engineers, a righteous outlaw whose freedom was an embarrassment to the Army. No question there were American soldiers eager to assist the Butch Cassidy of Burma, even if it meant risking an accessory-to-murder charge.

But which truck driver slowed down for the disheveled hitchhiker on the road's shoulder, only to discover that the CBI's most wanted man wasn't whoring it up in Calcutta, but rather living in the jungle less than a dozen miles from the crime scene? Who figured out how to make several boxes of Spam and fruit cocktail disappear from their battalion's larder, and snuck them out to Perry without being detected? The name or names of those who risked their necks for a killer, rather than betray him for the one-thousand-rupee reward, will forever be a mystery. All that's known is that Perry's gambit worked: he showered the Nagas with gifts, filling one of Glau's bashas with cases of tinned food. Since there were only steep footpaths leading from the Ledo Road to the village, Perry would have needed several Nagas to help carry back the haul.

Perry's Army buddies also stole him an item far more precious than ninety pounds worth of syrupy fruit cocktail: an M1 Garand rifle to replace the one that Perry had abandoned near the Namyung bridge. The Nagas were still using swords, clubs, and crossbows, along with the occasional muzzle-loading flintlock rifle. In addition to being the gracious provider of strange and wondrous foods, Perry was now the village's best-armed man. And he was generous with the weapon, letting the Nagas borrow it for their jungle hunts. These hunts were often for monkeys, which the Nagas then skinned and roasted to create a delicacy that bore a queasy visual resemblance to a human baby.*

Tigers, however, were the feral prey most prized by Naga hunters. The area around Tgum Ga was so infested with these predatory cats, it was a wonder that Perry hadn't been mauled during his jungle wanderings. Men who killed tigers were entitled to wear the animal's jaw around their necks, a treasured symbol of masculinity passed down from generation to generation. Naga mythology taught that man and tiger were spiritual brothers, created simultaneously at the dawn of time by "the first spirit"; this connection explained why so many Nagas possessed lycanthropic powers. Respect thus had to be accorded a tiger's corpse, or it would attack its slayer in the afterlife. Some hunters wedged the animal's mouth open with sticks before disposing of the carcass, in the belief that doing so would prevent the tiger's ghost from chomping them in the Great Beyond.

By providing the Nagas with the means to kill more monkeys and tigers than they'd ever dreamed possible, Perry's stature within the village soared. The ang took notice of the newcomer's largesse; he

---

*Though their dietary staples were quite plain, the Nagas enjoyed several culinary treats that struck Westerners as unpalatable. According to Sir James Johnstone, the Angami Nagas loved a dish whose preparation began by pouring many pounds of rice down a dog's gullet. Once suitably bloated with grain, the dog was bludgeoned to death and roasted. The flesh was greedily consumed, but the most prized part of the meal was the undigested rice scooped out of the dog's stomach.

urged his daughter to make nice with the tall, dark stranger in the olive drab fatigues.

It was not unheard of for an ang to offer girls to an American. One lucky recipient of such a proposition was Dr. Harold Scheie, an ophthalmologist stationed at the Twentieth General Hospital in Ledo. At the request of British political agents trying to win the Nagas' friendship, an ang named Rang Lang was brought to Scheie. The elderly chief's vision had been completely ruined by cataracts. "He had two relatives with him, one on each end of a bamboo pole possibly twelve feet long, and he holding onto the middle for guidance," Scheie recalled. "He was wearing little but a loincloth, his legs bare. . . . He had bamboo spikes through his hair to hold it up and also through his perforated ear lobes. His teeth were stained a brownish-red color from eating betelnuts."

Two operations were required to restore the ang's sight, a result that must have seemed miraculous to Rang Lang, whose previous idea of sophisticated medicine was a plug of opium. Upon regaining his vision, Rang Lang was further pleased to discover that his bamboo earrings had been replaced with metal safety pins, prized doodads among the Nagas. "He showed his appreciation by offering me a hundred chickens and two wives from his village," said Scheie. The doctor politely declined.

Perry was more receptive to the notion of settling down with a Naga lass. Compared to life with the 849th, Glau was a paradise, especially now that he'd earned his way into the ang's good graces. No one bossed him around in the jungle, or treated him as less than fully human because of his race. If anything, Perry was now atop the pecking order, by virtue of his .30-caliber rifle and his strategic generosity. Plus there was drinking, and dancing, and pretty teenage girls who leisurely milled about topless—a twenty-one-year-old man's dream.

In late April or early May, just before Perry turned twenty-two, his American comrades had a change of heart. "They helped me for the first month or so, but then they got yellow," Perry would later complain, though his accomplices really can't be faulted for getting spooked; they had everything to lose should they be caught abetting a murderer. The GIs stopped stealing rations for Perry, and stopped meeting him surreptitiously at the jungle's edge.

So Perry could no longer depend on cartons of Army grub with which to supplement his diet and, more important, gratify his Naga hosts. He was still an honored guest because of the M1, but Perry needed a deeper connection to Glau, one that wouldn't evaporate should his rifle break or his ammunition run out.

Marrying the ang's daughter would do the trick.

It was not a decision to be made lightly: once wed, Perry would be sealed forever to the village, obliged to battle raiders and forbidden to emigrate. Unbeknownst to Perry, he'd also be the first Westerner ever to cast aside the modern world in favor of joining a Naga clan. Missionaries and anthropologists might have spent appreciable time in the hills, but none went so far as to marry a Naga—and certainly not a Naga from the wild Tribal Territory of the eastern Patkais, where head-hunting and human sacrifice persisted.

Yet what choice did Perry have? As hostile as the jungle had been in March, when he first went on the lam, conditions were bound to get worse once the monsoons hit in May. Perry's options boiled down to two: go native with the Nagas, or take his chances in the wilderness.

Perry knew his future was in Tgum Ga, and that whatever hopes he'd had of seeing Washington and Alma Talbot again were pipe dreams, nothing more. He cast his lot with the headhunters.

"I intended," he would later state, "to pass the remaining years of natural life in the jungles . . . and live with the Naga girl who I claim as my wife."

———————

THOUGH THEIR UNION was arranged by the ang, Perry and his prospective bride were still required to observe the rituals of courtship. That suited Perry fine—romance had been his forte back home in Uncle Sugar. But Naga dating wasn't quite like picnicking in Meridian Hill Park with Alma. The process began with the boy giving gifts of betel nuts, to which the girl was expected to respond coyly. Christoph Fürer-Haimendorf described what happened next:

> Ultimately the suitor would persuade the girl to retire with him into the dark porch of [her] house. If the girl, as one of my informants put it, "refused with her mouth, though she consented in her heart," the young man might be bold enough to drag her into the porch and it was there, on a small bamboo bench, that the first intercourse would take place. The lovers were not afraid of being detected by the girl's parents, but to be seen by the girl's brother was considered embarrassing.
>
> Once the lovers knew each other better, the girl would agree to spend the whole night with her boyfriend. The ideal places for such prolonged meetings were the sheltered verandas of the granaries on the outskirts of the village. There, couples of lovers could remain undisturbed until morning. . . .
>
> At cock's crow the couples parted. The girls crept back to their parents' houses, where they were soon busy husking rice and carrying water. The boys were less energetic. They returned to the morung to sleep.

The Nagas who lived in the hills west of Namyung were known for quick weddings, sometimes just a matter of hours after a couple's betrothal. Grooms were supposed to obtain permission from the bride's parents by offering several balls of opium, but this is a custom from which Perry would have been exempt. The ang was more than happy for his daughter to wed the dark-complexioned American, the esteemed giver of gun and rations.

Her arms weighed down with biceps-hugging brass rings, Perry's young bride would have been fortified with rice beer on the day of their wedding; drinking zu prior to the ceremony was customary for guests and participants alike. Perry, though by no means a devout Christian, surely would have found the Nagas' spiritual customs a tad bizarre—the chicken rubbed on his bride's hair, then strangled as an offering to the gods; the indecipherable chants directed at the spirit who'd created the sky.

The ang had a basha built for the newlyweds. Perry used some of his remaining rations to purchase seeds for planting—rice, of course, but also opium poppies and ganja. He had enough wealth left over to hire several Nagas to till his fields; Perry himself preferred to spend his days hunting monkeys with the M1. At night he'd return to the basha, where his wife and copious piles of fragrant ganja awaited. As the sounds of log drums, flutes, and stomping feet poured out of the nearby morung, Perry would smoke and watch the nocturnal jungle come alive with fireflies, bats, and those cacopho-nous gibbons.

Stoned, enveloped by music, and apparently safe from harm, Perry couldn't believe his good fortune. A month before, he'd seemed headed for the stockade, or even the gallows. Now, just miles from the scene of his violent nadir, he'd found a curious peace among the Nagas and their trophy skulls. A second-class citizen no more, he got to toke, screw, dance, and otherwise revel in life's simpler pleasures.

Herman Perry had arguably become the world's first hippie.

TEN

As Perry happily adjusted to tribal life, the Army's manhunt was hitting a brick wall. Lieutenant David Smith's brothel dragnet in Calcutta had yielded only a smattering of dead-end leads; the tips elicited by the one-thousand-rupee reward were all worthless. Perry's trail would have gone entirely cold if not for a coolie who answered nature's call on the morning of April 16, 1944.

The coolie in question was working on a rock-crushing crew near the Namyung River bridge, under the supervision of Private Arquillus Q. Pearson of the 849th's Company C. Shortly after eleven o'clock, the man asked for and received Pearson's permission to take a leak in the bushes. While going about his business, the coolie spotted something out of place: a mud-caked rifle lying beneath a log. He brought the gun back to the road and gave it to Abdul Tiban, an Indian *babu* (clerk) helping Pearson run the crew. Tiban, in turn, showed the rifle to his American boss, who asked where it had been found. The coolie guided Tiban and Pearson to the spot where he'd been peeing, about fifty feet from the drainage ditch that marked the road's edge.

Pearson inspected the rifle, a .30-caliber M1 Garand. The initials *HP* had been carved into the gun in five places: twice on the muzzle, three times on the stock, with the P reversed in spots. The weapon was in dismal shape, flecked with rust and dirt. Pearson tried opening the bolt, and in doing so accidentally fired a round; it hadn't occurred to him that someone might leave a loaded rifle in the jungle. Pearson finally managed to remove the M1's clip, which contained seven cartridges of ammunition bearing the imprint SL 43, indicating that they'd been manufactured at the St. Louis Army Ammunition Plant.

Pearson cleaned and oiled the rifle, hoping to get it back in working order, but to no avail: the muzzle was bloated beyond repair, and the front sight cracked when he nudged it. Resigned to the uselessness of his seemingly lucky find, Pearson turned over the M1 (though not the seven bullets) to Company C's supply sergeant. It took another two days for word of the damaged, monogrammed rifle to filter up to Lieutenant Warren Oley, Pearson's commanding officer. Oley had the rifle brought to his office, where he checked its serial number (479312) against the battalion's records. The wrecked M1 had been issued to Private Herman Perry in 1943.

The military police were baffled. They'd always assumed that Perry had tried to make his way to Ledo, the closest transport hub. But the abandoned rifle near the Namyung bridge indicated that Perry had instead fled into the central Patkais, an unruly region from which there was no obvious means of escape. The only logical conclusion was that Perry, whom the MPs had yet to catch sight of, had been dead for weeks—stricken with dysentery, mauled by a tiger, or beheaded by a Naga. There seemed no way an unarmed punk from Washington could make it in the jungle alone.

————

FERTILITY WAS A cherished virtue among the Nagas, and Perry and his young bride were expected to get right down to reproducing. It didn't take long for the newlyweds to comply; the fourteen-year-old girl was soon with child. As the father of a potential future ang, Perry was treated with the utmost respect and deference by his new relations. When he contracted malaria that May, for example, a villager was dispatched all the way to Ledo, some eighty miles up the road, to procure medicine. And laborers tilled Perry's rice, opium, and ganja plots on his behalf, leaving him free to hunt, smoke, and learn the tribal language.

Down on the road, meanwhile, Perry's comrades in the 849th were slogging through another vicious monsoon season. Flash floods crashed down the streams of Burma's Hukaung Valley, washing out bridges that had taken weeks or months to build. Colonel Richard Selee of the Forty-fifth Engineer General Service Regiment chronicled each day's rainfall in his diary, assessing its impact on the road's progress (or lack thereof). "Very dismal," Selee wrote the day after a pair of crucial bridges were pulverized by torrential downpours. "Prospects about as poor as they have ever been." A short time later, upon enduring a sixth straight day of heavy rains, he whittled his commentary down to a single word: "Hell."

The 849th's primary mission that spring was to build a timber trestle across the swollen Namyung. No sooner had they finished the chore, however, than a deluge whisked it all away; the pristine bridge, recalled Colonel William Boyd Sinclair, "flushed down the Namyung like toilet paper in a sewer line." In one forty-eight-hour span, seventeen inches of rain drenched the Hukaung Valley, destroying around three hundred bridges and culverts.

The monsoons may have frustrated the Ledo Road's builders, but there was good news from the Burmese front. On May 17, a battalion of Merrill's Marauders, in conjunction with one of Lieutenant General Stilwell's Chinese regiments, finally captured the Japanese airstrip outside Myitkyina. After months of barely surviving on air-dropped rations, the Marauders were finally able to resupply in full, as well as fly in much-needed reinforcements. Most important, Japanese fighter planes could no longer harass Hump flights, making the Assam–Kunming cargo route far less perilous to navigate.

Tens of thousands of Japanese troops, meanwhile, were embroiled in a last-ditch counterattack to the west of Myitkyina: the long-anticipated invasion of India. The offensive's mastermind was Lieutenant General Renya Mutaguchi, an egoist notorious for committing his troops to meat-grinding battles of dubious value. He'd been a regimental commander during the Marco Polo Bridge Incident, a 1937 clash that Japan had used as a pretext to overrun Beijing. Now Mutaguchi was certain that by invading North-East India, he would forever be known as the general who'd both started and ended the war: "If I push into India now, by my own efforts and can exercise a decisive influence on the Great East Asian War, I, who was a remote cause of the outbreak of this great war, will have justified myself in the eyes of our nation."

Mutaguchi's plan called for his army to march across the southern Naga Hills toward the cities of Imphal and Kohima, taking them both in a mere three weeks. Having been neglected by the Tokyo generals, who were preoccupied with affairs in the Pacific, the invaders lacked the resources to establish supply lines over the hills; they planned to survive on confiscated tribal livestock and captured enemy rations. Mutaguchi's forces were also short of aircraft, trucks, and tanks, so they were forced to use animals to bear their ordnance through the jungle: 12,000 horses and mules, 30,000 oxen, and over

1,000 elephants were pressed into service. By the invasion's end, only a handful of elephants would remain.

Joining the Japanese in this campaign was the Indian National Army (INA), led by the Bengali radical Subhas Chandra Bose. An anticolonial zealot who rejected Gandhi's doctrine of nonviolence, Bose had fled to Berlin in 1941, dodging several British assassination attempts along the way. From there he'd made his way to Japanese-occupied Singapore, where he raised an army committed to liberating India from the raj.

Like the leaders of the Burma Independence Army who'd helped take Rangoon, Bose was deceived by Japan's "Asia for the Asiatics" canard. He promised the Japanese that once the INA was well established inside India, the native population would revolt against British rule. Mutaguchi thought such a rebellion would destroy the Allies' ability to fight in northern Burma, since American and British combat troops depended on Indian bases for support.

Among the INA's members were a small number of Nagas, most notably a young intellectual named A. Z. Phizo. An Angami Naga who'd received a Western education from Baptist missionaries, Phizo was one of the earliest proponents of a sovereign Naga homeland, which he hoped to carve out of eastern Assam. Like Bose, Phizo had been duped into believing that abetting the Greater East Asian Co-Prosperity Sphere was a first step toward that romantic goal.

A few other southern Nagas joined the Japanese cause, guiding the invaders to British ammunition stashes. But the majority sided with the Allies—some because they were Christians, others because they felt indebted to the British for establishing schools and hospitals, and for keeping head-hunting in check. Then there were the Nagas who'd witnessed the suffering of refugees two years earlier, when the triumphant Japanese had forced a mass exodus from

Burma to India. Many Nagas admired the fortitude of the retreating British soldiers, who cheerfully trooped across the hills despite hunger pangs and gangrenous wounds.

The Nagas were poorly outfitted for modern warfare, rarely possessing more than a few antiquated muskets in addition to their daos and spears. But their military contributions nonetheless proved invaluable. Adept at creeping through the jungles undetected, Naga scouts provided prime intelligence on Japanese troop movements and defensive positions. "The quantity and quality of operational information received from the local inhabitants has been a major factor in our success to date," a British intelligence officer reported back to Delhi in the summer of 1944. "A high percentage of our successful air strikes have been the direct result of local information."

Some Nagas, masquerading as compliant porters, conned their way into Japanese camps and swiped classified battle plans. In one celebrated instance, a Naga spy delivered an operational map to a British general, who figured the document was pretty much useless; surely the Japanese would alter their tactics upon discovering the theft. But when the battle commenced, the Japanese followed their original plan to the letter. The startled British later learned that the Japanese knew a Naga had taken the map; they had just assumed that the thief, as a member of a supposedly inferior race, wouldn't have the brainpower to realize what it was.

Violence was more of a Naga specialty than spycraft, and the tribesmen were ecstatic when Charles R. Pawsey, the British administrator in the Naga Hills, ordered them to kill as many Japanese stragglers as possible. He asked only that the Nagas refrain from taking their victims' heads, out of fear that such atrocities would lead to reprisals against British POWs. "Instead of this he authorised them to remove a finger and an ear," one of Pawsey's assistants recorded in his diary. But the Nagas didn't always heed Pawsey's wishes: the jungle was soon littered with headless corpses whose uniforms bore the insignia of the Rising Sun. There would have been even more beheadings had the invasion gone through the rougher Naga realms to the north, where Pawsey and the British had far less influence.

The most organized Naga fighting unit was led not by a respected ang, but rather by Ursula Graham Bower, a twenty-nine-year-old British anthropologist who lived off and on among the Zemi Naga tribe. Bower had rebelled against her privileged, boarding-school up-bringing by traveling repeatedly to North-East India, where she pho-tographed scenes of splendidly attired Nagas dancing, drumming, and cutting one another's hair. Bower was able to gain such extraor-dinary access to the normally reclusive Nagas in part because of her natural charm, but also thanks to an unbelievable stroke of luck: some Nagas regarded her as the reincarnation of a cult leader named Gaidiliu.

A teenage priestess of a messianic sect that blended Hinduism, Christianity, and animism, Gaidiliu had been an accomplished char-latan. She and her mentor, whom the British eventually hanged for conducting human sacrifices, had grown rich off donations from fellow Nagas, who were promised divine favor in return. She later turned to faith healing and, more absurdly, to touting her ability to turn British bullets into water. Prior to being arrested and impris-oned for murder in 1929, Gaidiliu told her followers that she'd some-day return in an unrecognizable form. To Nagas who still kept the faith, Bower was Gaidiliu in a white woman's cloak. The British press would soon dub her "Queen of the Nagas."

Like Perry, Bower had found bliss among a people whom West-erners widely dismissed as rank savages. Bower exulted in the Nagas' fondness for beer, music, and fellowship, and grew to regard British society as dreary in comparison:

I think the Zemi [Nagas] were a great deal happier than we. There one derived pleasure from small and transient things, from kindnesses, friendships, loyalties and the like, which because of their simpler, barer state were more deeply felt and of greater meaning. Then, too, there was always the sense of mortality and impermanence to quicken appreciation. Death was never very far from anyone in that malarial, doctorless country, and thinking back, I believe it was chiefly that which held one so firmly in the present and prevented too great building of hopes for the future. Certainly, to enjoy every simple pleasure as though it were for the last time sharpened the sense and gave life extraordinarily rich texture.

At the behest of British agents, Bower organized a Naga battalion to patrol the hills; the unit's 150 volunteers were paid ten to fifteen rupees per month, a small fortune in an impoverished Zemi village. Armed with nothing more than a few nineteenth-century rifles, the Nagas were no match for the advancing Japanese; the British eventually sent a detachment of Gurkhas* to save Bower's battalion from annihilation. But the unit, as Bower herself readily admitted, was an excellent propaganda tool. The British spread exaggerated news of its accomplishments in order to win Naga sympathies and boost morale.

By the time the Japanese invaders reached the Indian plains, they were in no shape for victory. Starting on April 6, they laid siege to Kohima, where Sir James Johnstone had crushed the Angami Naga rebellion more than six decades earlier. The Japanese managed to shell the city for weeks, but ultimately ran out of supplies. The British rations they had captured proved insufficient, and they lacked planes capable of air-dropping much-needed food and ammo. Kohi-

---

*Members of a Nepalese ethnic group renowned for their martial prowess, and employed by the British as soldiers beginning in the early nineteenth century.

ma's British and Indian defenders, on the other hand, enjoyed thousands of tons of airlifted goods, plus a steady stream of fresh soldiers.

Even more damaging to Lieutenant General Mutaguchi's plans, however, was the failure of Bose's promised uprising to materialize. As much as they detested the oppressive raj, the Indian masses saw no reason to pin their hopes for independence on Japan's starving, battered army.* Rather than face total destruction, the Japanese were eventually forced into a humiliating retreat. Eighty thousand Japanese troops perished during Mutaguchi's foolhardy attempt to conquer India—many from disease, and many from using grenades to commit *seppuku* (ritual suicide).

ON MAY 22, as Merrill's Marauders celebrated the liberation of Myitkyina's airstrip and Japanese troops outside Kohima anguished over their empty stomachs, 15,421 spectators poured into Griffith Stadium in Washington, D.C., for a blockbuster ten-round fight: thirty-two-year-old former world champion Henry "Homicide Hank" Armstrong versus eighteen-year-old wunderkind Aaron "the Anvil" Perry. Less than a year since going pro, Perry was up against one of the greatest pound-for-pound boxers of all time.[†]

Aaron came out like a bull in the first round, tagging the ex-champ with his big right hand. But it was all downhill from there for the teenage underdog. Taking advantage of Perry's tendency to teeter

---

*Officially, Bose was killed in a plane crash on August 18, 1945, while fleeing to Tokyo. There is widespread speculation, however, that he was actually imprisoned by the Soviets after the Japanese surrender, and died in a Siberian gulag some years later.

[†]At one point in his storied career, Armstrong simultaneously held world titles in three different weight classes: featherweight, lightweight, and welterweight. At his zenith in 1938, Armstrong recorded twenty-seven knockout victories in a row. His lifetime record is officially 151 wins (101 by knockout), 21 losses, and 9 draws. But this tally is probably short several fights that Armstrong fought under a pseudonym, Melody Jackson (his given middle and last names).

off balance after jabbing with his left, Armstrong pounded the Anvil's midsection and temples. By the time the fight was stopped in the sixth round, Perry had hit the canvas seven times. "The kid's got guts and he's plenty game," the victorious Armstrong said afterward, "but he doesn't know enough for the big time." Fans grumbled that Perry's manager, Harry Garsh, had rushed the kid for the sake of earning a quick payday.

Eating a postbout bowl of ice cream, Perry shrugged off the loss and challenged Homicide Hank to a rematch. "I coulda fought him all night if they'd let me," he told a reporter from *The Washington Evening Star*. "He never hurt me when he knocked me down."

As the Anvil oozed confidence in Griffith Stadium's locker room, he hadn't the slightest clue about his brother's escapades some eight thousand miles away. Although the Army was secretly monitoring the family matriarch's mail, it hadn't informed the Perrys that Herman was a wanted man. As far as they knew, Herman was dealing with the Ledo Road's "raw life" with his characteristically cheerful aplomb.

Herman, meanwhile, would have given anything for news of Aaron's boxing exploits, or a letter from Alma Talbot cooing about their dates in Meridian Hill Park. As much as he enjoyed Naga life, especially its abundance of psychoactive drugs, Perry was still far from forgetting where he'd come from. His most tangible reminder of the past was the stockpile of Army rations he'd secured that first month on the run. But those tins of fruit cocktail were gradually disappearing from the basha larder, consumed by the ang and his warriors. Soon enough, Perry's only mementos of his former life would be his M1 and his tattered olive drab fatigues, which he still insisted on wearing each day.

Not yet fully accustomed to the jungle's isolation, Perry suffered through sporadic pangs of homesickness. Even though his Naga wife was plenty affectionate, Perry retreated at times into the fantasy world he'd created while working the road, the one in which he imagined himself safely back in Washington, married to his darling Alma. In the course of one such daydream, Perry carved the initials *JT* on his rifle: Johnny Talbot, his alter ego.

Still recuperating from malaria, Perry started asking around Glau about how to get American goods on the black market, especially those packs of cigarettes that 6x6 drivers were always skimming off their shipments. A Naga eventually volunteered to trek down to Namyung, where bootleggers traded in the shadows of the town's bazaar.

On one of these trips, Perry's runner blabbed to someone—a black-market merchant, perhaps, or a fellow Naga who appeared trustworthy—about the dark-skinned foreigner who'd married the ang of Tgum Ga's daughter. No matter how many oaths of secrecy might have been sworn, news that strange was bound to spread. There was a British-run rice station in Namyung, where Nagas from miles around gathered for handouts. As they waited for their gratis sacks of grain, the Nagas would gossip about events in the hills. It didn't take long for every man with a dao to hear about the black American in their midst.

Once all the Nagas in Namyung had heard about Perry, it was only a matter of time before the rumor reached Captain Southerland, the British liaison officer who ran the rice station. Overseeing the delivery of freebies had helped Southerland cultivate deep contacts among the grateful hill tribes, which was partly why the British had started the program in the first place. In the second week of July, one of Southerland's Naga informers passed on the startling news: a black American soldier had become a village bigwig in Tgum Ga.

Southerland was floored. On July 18, during a visit to Shingbwiyang some thirty miles south, he shared the sensational rumor with Captain Walter McMinn, the town's American provost marshal. There had been plenty of false reports regarding Perry's whereabouts, placing him everywhere from Assam to southern China. Yet McMinn thought something about the British officer's tip rang true. At the very least, it was worth checking out.

But how? Tgum Ga didn't appear on any maps, and there certainly weren't any drivable roads leading to the Naga backcountry. McMinn could dispatch some MPs to hike up the Patkais, but odds were they'd get lost in the shadowy jungle and never be heard from again. The safe move, McMinn decided, was to enlist the aid of Sun Baw, a Naga ang who ruled a village near Namyung, and whose loyalty the Allies had earned with gifts.

Sun Baw dispatched a Naga scout to Tgum Ga on the nineteenth, to see whether the American was really there. At noon the following day, the scout returned to Namyung, where McMinn anxiously awaited. The Naga confirmed the whispers: there was, indeed, a black American living in the village, which was located approximately eight miles southwest of Namyung. And the man was armed with a rifle.

McMinn showed the Naga a picture of Perry. Yes, the Naga nodded. That's him.

ON JULY 19, as Sun Baw's scout was ascending the Patkais, Perry had sent a young Naga down to Namyung for rice. The boy returned that evening with a warning for his American taskmaster: get out of Tgum Ga, pronto. Perry's linguistic skills weren't sharp enough to grasp the exact nature of the threat, but he trusted the Nagas' instincts on matters of security. The next day, he bid his pregnant wife farewell and headed for a nearby *noksa*, or satellite village, about a mile and a half away.

A family in the tiny noksa, which Perry called "Doo City," agreed to take in the ang's son-in-law. Perry leaned his rifle against one of their basha's bamboo walls, crouched by the cooking fire, and began to ponder: after five months on the lam, was the Army finally closing in? If so, he had no one to blame but himself. It had been reckless of him to risk detection for the sake of American cigarettes, a selfish craving that now threatened to obliterate everything he'd built: a marriage, a family, a life of relative privilege and bliss.

As the flames licked at his careworn face, Perry surely realized he had much to lose—more than he'd ever had back in Uncle Sugar.

BY 2:30 P.M. on July 20, McMinn had formed his posse in Nam-yung. Four of the group's members were from McMinn's outfit, Company C of the 502nd Military Police Battalion: Lieutenant Or-ville Strassburg, Sergeant Charles Kulp, Corporal Earl Wilson, and Private First Class Willis Whiteman. Sergeant Robert Davis of the Criminal Investigation Division was the sixth soldier to volunteer for the mission. Suitably bribed with opium, Sun Baw arranged for the posse to take three Naga guides, who'd walk them along the obscure footpaths that led to Tgum Ga. None of the Nagas spoke a word of English, and none of the soldiers knew the Nagas' tongue. Hand signals would have to suffice.

The trek was harrowing, up narrow, root-strewn trails concealed by trees dripping with Burma's Technicolor array of leeches. It took three and a half hours to reach the mountain stream that ran beneath Tgum Ga's morung. The cautious McMinn sent a guide up the hill to the village, to find out which basha belonged to Perry and his wife. The Naga returned minutes later, shaking his head and pointing to the distance. The MPs got the message: Perry was gone.

One of the posse's Naga guides signed that he was familiar with the satellite village where the fugitive was reportedly holed up. McMinn sent the Naga onward to the noksa, with orders to "establish if Perry was at this other village, and also if Perry had a rifle with him." Approximately ninety minutes later, the guide returned with news: the posse's target was definitely there.

The Naga guide also had a surprise in his hands: Perry's M1.

Citing his distant familial ties to the noksa, the guide had talked his way into the basha where Perry was staying. Once inside, he'd taken advantage of the American's celebrated generosity by asking to borrow the rifle for a nocturnal monkey hunt. Accustomed to assisting his Naga protectors whenever possible, Perry had naively agreed. After months of nothing but friendship from his tribal hosts, it had never occurred to Perry that a Naga might betray him.

Kulp and Whiteman were left outside Tgum Ga while the rest of the posse followed the cunning guide along another series of twisting, shrouded paths. They reached the smaller village after 8:00 P.M., by which time the jungle was enveloped in a moonless night. The four Americans scanned the noksa's perimeter with flashlights, trying to locate Perry's hideout. The beams glinted off clumps of thick-leaved trees before alighting on a grassy clearing. In the clearing's center lay a thirty-foot-long basha, its broad porch propped on bamboo stilts. The frond-covered roof of the hut's closest neighbor was barely visible in the background, a good fifty yards away.

The Naga guide pointed at the basha and nodded. That's where he'd tricked Perry out of the M1.

The MPs switched off their flashlights and crept from the tree line to the grass, hoping for a better look. A fire glowed through the hut's windows, and voices could be heard chattering away in a melodic language. Davis thought he recognized one of the speakers' accents as belonging to a black American, though he couldn't be sure.

McMinn and Davis got down on their bellies and wriggled toward the front of the hut, drawing themselves to within ten feet of the porch. Strassburg and Wilson, meanwhile, snuck around the back. With their flashlights off and the moon absent, they couldn't see more than a few inches ahead. Strassburg, for one, was scared to death. Here he was, a kid from outside Buffalo slithering blindly through the Burmese muck, home to venomous snakes and blood-slurping leeches and Lord knows what else. But McMinn had drilled the importance of this mission into his men: they might never get another shot at Lieutenant Cady's killer. Strassburg swallowed hard and inched his way into position. He and Wilson stealthily flanked the back porch, a man on either side.

McMinn could have ordered his men to storm the basha. But if Perry had obtained one rifle while on the lam, perhaps he had other weapons: a bootleg .45 pistol or a box of black-market grenades. And what if the MPs ran in there with guns blazing, only to discover they'd killed some innocent Nagas? American heads might be taken in retaliation.

McMinn preferred to wait for exactly the right moment—when they knew Perry was in there, for starters, but also when they had a clean shot. So the posse's four members kept still. Fifteen minutes passed. Then another fifteen, and another fifteen. Facedown in the pitch-black jungle, the surrounding woods vibrating with the hum of insects and the croak of frogs, it seemed more like forever.

As he'd been eating dinner and socializing with his Naga hosts, Perry had noticed something odd through the windows: beams of light flickering outside the front of the basha. It looked like people waving flashlights around, and Perry was pretty sure the Nagas didn't own any flashlights. The thought of making a dash for the jungle crossed his mind, but he remembered that the country behind the noksa was crawling with tigers; even the bravest Nagas didn't venture there at night.

The lights disappeared within a few seconds, and Perry decided against stepping outside to investigate. Strange things happened in the jungle at night; there was probably a perfectly reasonable explanation for those flickers. He remained around the basha's cooking fire, communicating as best he could in the tribal tongue.

Separated from his wife and preoccupied with the warning he'd received the previous evening, Perry tried comforting himself by whistling an American tune. The sweet trill of his whistle wafted out to the MPs; Davis tried his best to summon the song's title, but kept drawing a blank. But one thing he knew for certain now: an American was inside that hut.

Davis was getting antsy—he wanted to move on the basha. But McMinn whispered, "Lay still." It took a moment or two, but Davis finally figured out the reason for McMinn's caution: a Naga woman was approaching from a few dozen yards away. McMinn didn't want her getting wise to the posse's presence in the grass; she might call out for Perry to start running.

As the woman drew closer, McMinn and Davis realized they were directly in her path: if she kept walking straight, she'd literally trip over their prone bodies. The pair inched forward on their elbows, even closer to the basha, hoping to avoid detection.

A dog inside the hut started barking. Perry's wariness instantly morphed into grave concern; the village dogs never barked at the Nagas. He peered out the front window and saw three silhouettes within ten yards—one walking upright, the other two pressed flat against the ground. Perry looked for his M1, but then remembered that he'd just lent it out. He grabbed a dao instead, as well as a bamboo staff that he stuck in the fire until its top was ablaze. Lightly armed and bearing a crude torch, Perry ventured out to see what might have caused his hosts' dog to yap like that. The basha's married owners crept behind.

When he saw Perry walk onto the front porch, McMinn leaned over to Davis and told him to turn on his flashlight. Davis trained the yellow beam right on Perry's eyes. McMinn popped up from the ground, his carbine* fixed on the startled fugitive's head.

"Don't move, Perry!" he yelled.

Nearly blinded by the flashlight, all Perry could see was a gun's muzzle peeking out of the darkness. Hadn't his comrades in the 849th warned him that it might end like this—mowed down by officers bent on revenge? Perry chucked his torch and dao and turned to run back inside the basha.

McMinn fired. Perry heard the crack of the carbine, felt the bullet whiz between his head and the head of the Naga man. He bolted through the long hut, praying that no one was covering the back.

Strassburg and Wilson heard the gunshot, followed by McMinn loudly cursing his misfiring gun. Then there was the frenetic *whump-whump* of boots sprinting across bamboo boards. A figure came flying off the elevated back porch, landing in a crouch. Behind him, a flashlight's beam bobbed up and down inside the basha, growing in intensity. Davis was giving chase.

"Halt!" yelled Strassburg, as he and Wilson stood up and raised their rifles. The frazzled Perry looked right at Strassburg, just fifteen feet away. Surely he'd be killed if he tried to run. But he might be killed if he surrendered, too.

Tigers be damned, Perry made a break for the jungle that lay several dozen yards behind the two MPs. He took three steps forward. Strassburg fired. Then Wilson. But Perry zipped past them in

*A short-barreled rifle.

a blur. The MPs spun and unloaded their clips into the darkness, firing as many as thirty shots between them. When their ammo was spent, they listened for the sounds of an injured man's gurgle or a corpse crumpling to the ground.

Nothing. Strassburg could have sworn he plugged a round right in Perry's chest. Lieutenant Cady's killer should've been lying at their feet, either dead or dying. But he was nowhere to be seen.

HAVING JUMPED OVER the ravine that marked the jungle's edge, Perry crashed through the darkened woods as fast as his legs would carry him. He was running downhill, knocking away branches with his flailing arms. Nearly a quarter of a mile later, he came to a small stream. He stopped to listen for pursuers, but the night yielded nothing except the jungle's normal chirps and wails.

Perry now realized that he was thirsty, thirstier than he'd ever been in his entire life. He tried kneeling down at the stream's edge for a drink of water. As he lowered himself to the ground, he felt dizzy and lost his balance. Tipping over, he felt a burning sensation in his chest. He pawed around his olive drab shirt. It was damp, soaked through with something warm and viscous. Blood.

Perry writhed slowly in the dirt, unable to right himself for a sip of water. He rolled onto his back and looked up at the moonless sky. He listened to the peaceful babble of the stream, now fat with monsoon rain. Bright, pretty lights washed over him as the world receded.

GATHERED AROUND THE basha's back porch, the four MPs bemoaned their rotten luck. After months of futility, they'd finally located the CBI's most wanted man. They'd hiked nearly ten miles through the jungle, waited until Perry was in their sights, and then squeezed off thirty shots at close range. Yet what did they have to show for all their fine police work? Perry had eluded their well-laid trap, apparently without so much as a scratch. And now he had what seemed to be an insurmountable head start through the jungle, where Naga friends and relatives could aid his flight. For all the MPs knew, Perry would be halfway across the Patkais by dawn.

Once his frustration ebbed, however, McMinn turned incredulous. Strassburg and Wilson were decent shots; could they really have missed thirty times between them, from just fifteen feet away? The MPs couldn't tell if there was any blood spattered in the grass, but maybe Perry had been wounded after all. There were plenty of tales of soldiers carrying on with major gunshot wounds, adrenaline inuring them to the excruciating pain—at least for the first few minutes.

McMinn ordered Strassburg and Wilson to flick on their flashlights and search the woods behind the basha. The two MPs soon spotted a trail of snapped branches. They followed the wrecked foliage down a hillside, praying all the while that a Bengal tiger wasn't lurking nearby.

As they neared the hill's bottom, Strassburg and Wilson heard a faint human groan. They waved their flashlights toward the sound's source, alongside a wispy stream.

The two MPs yelled up to their commander. They'd found Perry, and he appeared near death.

McMinn and Davis scrambled down the hillside. They removed their raincoats and lashed them to a pair of bamboo poles, creating a makeshift stretcher that the four Americans used to carry Perry back to the basha. The frightened Nagas could do little but allow the Americans to set Perry on their porch and bandage his wound.

Given the severity of his injury, it was a wonder that Perry was still alive. He'd been shot above one of his nipples; the bullet had perforated his lungs before ricocheting off a rib and exiting the chest. Every time he breathed, the MPs could hear air hissing out of the two puncture marks—the classic sign of pneumothorax, a condition colloquially known as a sucking chest wound.

It would have been easy enough for McMinn to dispense with Perry right then and there by denying him medical attention. But contrary to the rumors going around the 849th, the MPs weren't out for vigilante justice. At about 10:00 P.M., with Perry obviously in no shape to walk, McMinn volunteered to hike back to Namyung and find not only a doctor, but also extra soldiers to help bear Perry's stretcher down to the road.

As Perry clawed his way back to consciousness, the first thing he heard were voices speaking in English. Too groggy to understand what they were saying, he opened his eyes and recognized the stars above, a light distinct from the more ethereal glow that he'd glimpsed while teetering between life and death. But he wasn't lying by the stream anymore; he was back on the same porch where he'd felt that carbine round zing by his ear. And it felt like there was a scalding iron sitting on his chest.

Hearing Perry's moans for the first time in a while, Davis leaned over the supine fugitive and asked, "Are you Herman Perry?"

Perry slowly shook his head. Davis unfolded a WANTED poster from his pocket and scrutinized the photograph. The man lying before him looked older and more weathered than the boy on the poster, but there were some obvious similarities: a fleshy, flattened nose, a slightly cauliflowered ear. No question, this was Perry.

Davis asked again, this time eliciting a verbal response. "My name," insisted Perry, "is Johnny Talbot." The Naga guide who'd led the posse to the basha brought forth the M1 he'd borrowed under false pretenses. Davis could see the initials *JT* etched into the stock and muzzle.

The game went on and on as everyone awaited McMinn's return: Davis kept asking Perry to admit his identity, and Perry kept replying, "No, no, you've got it all wrong, my name is Johnny Talbot." Davis mentioned all the details he knew about Perry's life back in Washington, hoping to prod him into a confession. He told Perry he knew about his career as a butcher, and about the jail time he'd served for missing his draft-board physical back in 1941. He held the WANTED poster right in front of Perry's nose and begged him to admit the obvious. But Perry stuck with the Johnny Talbot line.

As more and more of Perry's thoracic blood dribbled down his rib cage, however, his will to lie faded. He began to realize that he'd probably die out there in the jungle, and so perhaps it was best he got right with . . . well, not God exactly, since he was never much one for religion. But a man is supposed to spill secrets on his deathbed, isn't he? Even if that deathbed's nothing more than a pair of canvas raincoats tied together.

An hour into the interrogation, then, Perry broke down. Yes, he was who Davis thought he was, and, yes, he'd killed that lieutenant back near Tagap Ga. But he also wanted Davis to understand something very important about what had gone down. "Perry readily admitted to the shooting of Lt. Cady," Davis recorded. "But [he] kept insisting that this said officer would have struck him, had he not shot him."

Now Perry turned loquacious. He told Davis how he'd tried surrendering at the Namyung bridge; about his marriage to the daughter of the ang of Tgum Ga; and how he'd started growing rice, opium, and ganja in the hills. Davis asked Perry how much assistance he'd gotten from members of the 849th, fishing for the names of coconspirators. But Perry refused to squeal. When pressed on how he'd acquired the new M1, he changed the subject to the hunting he'd done near Glau.

Dawn was fast approaching and Perry's strength was almost gone; he was on the verge of bleeding out. Around five thirty in the morning, McMinn finally returned with a medic, some more MPs, and, surprisingly, Lieutenant Colonel Wright Hiatt of the 849th. Hiatt confirmed what everyone already knew: the shirtless soldier who lay dying on the basha porch was Private Herman Perry of Washington, D.C.

The medic rebandaged Perry's wound and dosed him with a shot of morphine. Then the whole crew began the slow trudge down the Patkais. The footing on the jungle paths was bad enough under normal circumstances, and now the MPs had to deal with carrying a stretcher and its 170-pound payload. It took more than nine hours for the party to reach the Ledo Road, where an ambulance was waiting to take Perry to Shingbwiyang, site of the Seventy-third Evacuation Hospital.

Torn from his blissful jungle life, the wounded Perry enjoyed one small blessing on the journey: he was passed out.

ELEVEN

Dripping water and the briny stench of iodine finally ushered Perry back to consciousness. He groggily surveyed
the scene: a clammy hospital ward crammed with thirty
cots. Warm rain seeped through the poorly thatched roof. Men
moaned weakly as nurses in knee-length skirts made the rounds,
dressing wounds that teemed with maggots. Feverish patients swad-
dled themselves in scratchy wool blankets, oblivious to the monsoon broil.

Perry mined his memory for clues on how he'd gotten here. He
dimly recalled collapsing next to a mountain stream, then being
hoisted off a basha porch and borne into the jungle. Everything beyond that was a blur; unbeknownst to Perry, his thoughts were being
dulled by painkillers. The drugs were all that made his sucking chest
wound bearable.

As the world slowly sharpened into focus, Perry realized that a
day had passed. A few hours after he awoke, around eight o'clock in
the evening, a doctor came by with three loaded hypodermics. In
addition to the antibiotic sulfadiazine, Perry received eight milli-

grams of morphine sulfate and one hundred milligrams of the barbi-
turate Phenobarbital. The injections knocked him for a loop:
morphine tends to exacerbate Phenobarbital's soporific effects, especially in trauma patients who have lost large amounts of blood.*
Perry spent the night of July 22 in the figurative clouds, a place far
preferable to Ward B-3 of Shingbwiyang's Seventy-third Evacuation
Hospital.

Perry's first visitor the next morning was Sergeant Robert Davis,
the Criminal Investigation Division agent to whom he'd babbled in
the jungle while awaiting medical attention. Davis sidled up to Perry's cot and renewed the interrogation he'd started on July 20. He
was joined by another CID agent, Corporal Frank Nurthen Jr., as
well as Corporal Earl Wilson, one of the two MPs who'd covered the
basha's rear three days earlier. Nurthen duly informed the weakened
Perry of his right against self-incrimination. From that point on, everything Perry said could be used against him in court.

Having already heard the bulk of Perry's story, Davis just wanted
to glean a few last details. The investigators huddled around their
bleary suspect, out of earshot of the hospital's staff. Davis asked the
questions, jotting down Perry's often disjointed answers. At one
point, Nurthen handed Perry an unloaded carbine. "Show me about
what position that you held the gun when Lieutenant Cady come up
on you," Davis demanded. Propped up in his cot, Perry wrapped his
right hand around the trigger assembly and gingerly pressed the
stock against his hip.

After a few last questions about Perry's opium and ganja use, the
investigators departed. Davis headed for the hospital's spartan office

---

*Perry received transfusions of blood from African American donors only. During World War II, the Army
ordered the Red Cross to segregate its blood supply, so that wounded soldiers would be given blood from
donors of the same race. The American Medical Association objected, stating that there was "no factual
basis for the discrimination against the use of Negro blood or plasma for injection in white people." But the
Army wouldn't relent, on the grounds that GIs might refuse surgery should they fear being pumped full of
the opposing race's blood.

to turn his notes into a typewritten narrative of Perry's crime, flight, and capture.

At one o' clock that afternoon, Davis, Nurthen, and Wilson approached Major Carl Goetz, the hospital's head administrator. Davis had a three-page statement in hand—a summary, he said, of what Perry had told the CID agents that morning. He asked Goetz to accompany the three investigators into Ward B-3 in order to administer a legal oath to Perry. Once sworn in, Perry would be asked to review and sign the statement.

Perry was still supine with a gaping hole in his chest and a bevy of sedatives coursing through his veins. But Goetz thought the alleged killer looked "cheerful and respectable," and he administered the oath with no qualms. In accordance with Davis's instructions, Perry read through the brief statement he was supposed to sign. Despite his wooziness, Perry expressed concerns: key details were either absent or distorted, and there were a few sentences he couldn't remember saying. Davis offered assurances that signing was no big deal: "That's all right, soldier. We just want the general idea of how it was."

Perry made one inconsequential correction, crossing out an assertion that Lieutenant Cady had told the passengers in his jeep to get in Private James Walton's dump truck. He initialed each page and signed his name at the bottom in shaky script. Goetz notarized the document.

Perry was then left alone to resume convalescing, seemingly unaware of the terrible mistake he'd just made.

A FOLLOW-UP STATEMENT was taken by Davis five days later, and again notarized by Goetz. This second statement focused mainly on the events immediately leading up to Cady's death, with a couple of key addenda. In one, Davis asked Perry whether he knew Cady prior to the shooting. "I didn't know him personally," responded Perry, "and I didn't know him by sight, but I knew his name and have heard the boys talk about him." Perhaps sensing that Perry was about to mention Cady's belligerent reputation, Davis backed off this line of inquiry.

In another passage, Davis asked Perry how he'd obtained an M1 while on the lam. The original text of their exchange reads:

Q: Will you tell me how you got rifle 420033?

A: No.

Q: Did you steal this rifle?

A: Yes, I stole it.

Q: When did you steal this rifle?

A: I don't know when I got the rifle, I would rather not talk about it.

Before signing the statement, Perry crossed out "Yes, I stole it" and replaced it with "No answer."

Given that Perry had been sobbing during his confrontation with Cady, it was obvious to Davis and his CID bosses that the defendant's mental state could be an issue at trial. A psychiatric evaluation was in order, but no one at the Seventy-third Evacuation Hospital was qualified to conduct such an exam. It would have to wait until Perry was well enough to be transferred to the larger Twentieth General Hospital, where he'd already been treated twice before.

That transfer occurred in early August. Perry was ambulanced 103 miles up the boggy road to Ledo, past all the sights he thought he'd left behind: malnourished coolies hacking away at boulders, 6x6s marooned in rust-hued mud, malarial engineers who resembled the living dead. As he traveled west past Hellgate and descended into the Brahmaputra Plains, the forest-shrouded Patkais faded behind Perry. So, too, did his hopes of ever reuniting with his wife and unborn child.

On August 8, Perry was judged well enough to be released from the Twentieth General Hospital. His next stop was the Ledo Stockade, the very place he'd tried so hard to avoid some five months earlier. But a day later, the doctors called him back for a psychiatric exam. The Twentieth General Hospital had received an order from the office of Brigadier General Lewis Andrew Pick,* the Ledo Road's chief engineer, requesting that Perry be "mentally observed" in order to determine whether a "disease of the mind" had factored into his crime.

On the tenth, the chief of the hospital's Neuro-Psychiatric Section filed a one-paragraph report in response to Pick's request:

> The results of the examination are as follows: The soldier knew right from wrong at the time of the offense. He did not act under an irresistible impulse from a disease of the mind. He is of sound mind and capable of standing trial.

This conclusion, delivered without further explanation, would make the already tricky task of defending Perry that much tougher. And that task fell to an officer whose criminal-law experience consisted largely of defending drunk drivers.

DURING WORLD WAR II, the Army's general courts-martial, which handle the most serious criminal offenses, were convened according

---

*Pick had been promoted from colonel to brigadier general in February 1944.

to the Articles of War—a set of rules originally adopted by the Continental Congress in 1775. The articles' sketchy guidelines regarding courts-martial had been roundly criticized following World War I, due to numerous complaints about overly harsh sentences, an opaque appeals process, and a lack of rights for the accused. Important revisions were made to the articles in 1920, prescribing uniform procedures and punishments. But by the standards of civilian justice, the document remained a dinosaur. The defendant was granted a right to counsel, for example, but the articles said nothing about that counsel's minimum qualifications. Nor did accused GIs have the right to request that at least some of the court's members—who serve as both judges and jurors—also be enlisted men, rather than officers. This meant that black defendants such as Perry were virtually guaranteed to face all-white tribunals.

The commanders of the CBI's Services of Supply, the Army branch in charge of the Ledo Road, were entrusted with organizing Perry's court-martial. On August 7, the SOS appointed eight officers, ranging in rank from captain to colonel, to serve as the court's members. The Eighth Article of War mandated that when possible, the tribunal's head, known as the law member, be an officer of the Judge Advocate General's Department. But JAGD officers were apparently hard to come by in Assam; the job was instead given to a major from the Quartermaster Corps, Bruce Waitz.

The task of prosecuting Perry was assigned to Lieutenant Bernard Frank, a former standout tennis player at the University of Miami. Prior to joining the 502nd Military Police Battalion in 1942, Frank had spent several years as a criminal defense attorney in his native Miami, primarily working robbery and assault cases. In 1943, shortly after arriving in India, he'd been asked to defend a black engineer accused of killing a coolie—the victim had allegedly refused to make his wife available for jig jig. Frank won a rare acquittal, a victory that brought his legal talents to the attention of the CBI brass. He was thereafter made the Army's top prosecutor in Assam, responsible for trying hundreds of cases ranging from insubordination to murder.

As for the position of defense counsel, the SOS's brain trust appointed an officer much greener than Frank: Captain Clayton Oberholtzer, who oversaw a battalion of African American truck drivers. The SOS tapped Oberholtzer because he'd been an attorney back in civilian life, albeit a novice one. After graduating from Cleveland's Western Reserve University School of Law in 1939, Oberholtzer had opened a solo practice in Medina, Ohio. Like any good small-town lawyer, he handled whatever cases came his way—civil disputes, probates, bankruptcies, criminal misdemeanors. Violent felonies were a rarity in Medina, and thus not part of his repertoire.

Oberholtzer enlisted in the Army in February 1941 and was initially assigned to train for medical duties. He disliked the gory work, however, and requested a transfer. He was then kicked over to the Quartermaster Corps and sent to Officer Candidate School, where he earned his commission. All was going swimmingly until Oberholtzer committed a major gaffe during a training exercise in California: he misread a map and inadvertently led a truck convoy into the desert. As punishment, Oberholtzer was shipped off to Ledo and put in charge of an African American unit.

Now, after months of managing shipments and other humdrum duties, the thirty-one-year-old Oberholtzer was being asked to defend a man who, if convicted, faced the death penalty. At least he would have help: the Army appointed Lieutenant Louis Ritz, an Indiana lawyer in the Quartermaster Corps, and Lieutenant George Bodamer, a Tennessee clerk in the Chemical Warfare Service, to assist with Perry's defense.

The trio had less than a month to prepare for trial, and limited access to their client as he languished in the Ledo Stockade. Yet these were the least of their worries. Far more troubling was the apparent strength of the prosecution's case, which included numerous eyewitnesses and Perry's sworn confession.

Oberholtzer realized that, given the indisputable fact that Perry had pulled the trigger, a full acquittal was improbable. His best bet was to argue that the shooting amounted to manslaughter, rather than capital murder, and thus spare his client's life. This meant Oberholtzer would have to counter the prosecution's claim that Perry had acted with "malice aforethought," or some degree of premeditation. Establishing Perry's mental frailty would be the most obvious way of accomplishing this, but the prosecution could easily neutralize that strategy by citing the psychiatric report. Oberholtzer therefore opted for a blame-the-victim defense: he would portray Cady as partly responsible for his own demise.

This was precisely the defense strategy that Frank hoped he wouldn't have to contend with. Though he could never admit as much in court, the veteran prosecutor agreed that Cady had acted foolishly. "Here's a man [Perry] who hadn't done anything really that bad, and the colonel of his battalion had told him, 'Come see me if you ever get in trouble,'" said Frank. "[Cady] would have still been alive if he had let [Perry] go see the colonel." Though he couldn't foresee the defendant getting off scot-free, Frank worried that the court might view Cady's aggression as a mitigating circumstance, and refuse to convict on the murder count.

Murder, however, wasn't the only charge that Perry was facing. He was also accused of desertion and multiple counts of willful disobedience, stemming from his refusal to turn in his rifle and submit to arrest on March 5. The desertion charge alone carried a possible death sentence, though the Army had yet to execute a soldier for this offense during the war.* Nor had the Army executed any of the CBI's quarter-million American troops.

Yet the theater's commanders had the knives out for Perry, who had embarrassed their MPs and, more important, had stoked racial tensions along the Ledo Road: it was one thing for an African American soldier to slay a coolie over jig jig, quite another for him to kill a white officer. "There are no features about this case that would indicate any real difficulty in proving all charges and specifications," wrote Lieutenant Colonel Jay Scovel, a JAGD official based in Delhi, in an August memo that stated the Army's formal stance. "The offense committed and the circumstances surrounding the offense are such as would justify an extreme penalty of death."

Though Perry was potentially the first soldier in the CBI to be sentenced to death, such punishments were not uncommon in other World War II locales. The Army would eventually execute seventy of its own soldiers in Europe, primarily for murder, rape, or a combination of the two. Of those seventy, fifty-five were black, despite the fact that African American troops made up less than 9 percent of the Army. And of the twenty-one executions ordered by General Douglas MacArthur in the Pacific, eighteen involved black soldiers.

THE COURT-MARTIAL OF Private Herman Perry came to order at 9:00 A.M. on September 4, 1944, in a tea planter's house near Ledo. Only seven of the court's eight members showed; one of the officers had begged off, claiming "special duty" elsewhere. The remaining seven members sat behind a long wooden table that was likely bor-

---

*During World War II, 21,049 soldiers were convicted of desertion. Of these, forty-nine were sentenced to death on that charge alone. But only one of these soldiers, Private Eddie Slovik, was actually executed, on January 31, 1945. Slovik's tale is well known thanks to a 1954 biography, *The Execution of Private Slovik*, that was later made into a TV movie; Martin Sheen played Slovik.

rowed from the plantation's formal dining room. Spectators crammed in despite the stifling heat, packing the makeshift courtroom so tightly that the lawyers had scant room to move.

Wearing a fresh set of olive drab fatigues, Perry was escorted in from the stockade. Frank commenced the proceedings by asking the defendant to name his counsel, a legal custom. Oddly, Perry requested that he be represented by Oberholtzer, and Oberholtzer alone; Ritz and Bodamer, the two cocounsels appointed by the court, were excused. The mission to save Perry's life was now entirely up to the untested lawyer from Medina.

Oberholtzer's first move on Perry's behalf was to challenge the participation of one court member, Major Paul Grove of the Medical Corps. The challenge was peremptory, so no cause was given; it's possible Oberholtzer feared that Grove, having heard the hospital chatter about Perry's gunshot wounds, would lack impartiality. Whatever the reason for the challenge, Grove immediately withdrew from the court-martial. That left just six members to decide Perry's fate, an abnormally low number for a death-penalty case.*

The numerous charges were read aloud, and Perry pled "not guilty" to each. Then Lieutenant Colonel Wright Hiatt took the stand for the prosecution.

Frank confined his questions to the rote: how Hiatt knew Perry, and whether Perry was on active duty when the Cady shooting occurred. Once he'd wrapped up, Oberholtzer declined to cross-examine. But he requested that Hiatt remain on the stand, this time as a defense witness. The court's members seemed puzzled by this unorthodox maneuver, yet Frank declined their offer to object. Oberholtzer went to work.

---

*During the Korean War, the laws governing courts-martial were overhauled in order to make procedures consistent throughout all branches of the military. This Uniform Code of Military Justice (UCMJ) now requires that, barring extraordinary circumstances, "in a case in which the penalty of death is sought, the number of members shall be not less than twelve."

He first asked Hiatt to recount his February meeting with Perry, the one in which he'd told the troubled young private that the 849th's enlisted men "had a right and privilege to talk to [Hiatt]" about their woes. This was a clever ploy: Oberholtzer was establishing that, on the morning of March 5, Perry didn't set out to harm anyone; he just wanted to air his grievances to Hiatt, per the lieutenant colonel's invitation.

Next came the linchpin of Oberholtzer's strategy: painting Cady as the heavy.

Q: Was Lieutenant Cady a member of your command at that time?

A: Yes.

Q: Had you ever had any trouble relative—or had Lieutenant Cady ever had any disciplinary trouble that you know of?

Prosecution: Objection to as immaterial and irrelevant.

Law Member: What does your question relate to, Counsel? Does it relate to disciplinary action taken against Lieutenant Cady, or to Lieutenant Cady in enforcing disciplinary action in his command?

Defense: To Lieutenant Cady in enforcing disciplinary action in Lieutenant Cady's command.

Q: Objection overruled. Defense will reframe your question.

Q: Do you know whether or not Lieutenant Cady has ever had any trouble in enforcing disciplinary action in his command?

Reluctantly, Hiatt acknowledged an ugly incident in the fall of 1943, in which Cady had slapped a soldier to "bring him to consciousness to get him to execute [an] order." On cross-examination, Hiatt claimed that, although the assaulted soldier wasn't drunk, "there was evidence to the effect that he had been drinking." Frank, who'd heard about Cady's rough handling of black GIs, was satisfied that he'd minimized the damage to his case. But he resolved to head off any further swipes at Cady's character.

Oberholtzer needed to elicit more evidence of Cady's alleged brutality. But the next witness from the 849th's officer corps was more tight-lipped about his fallen comrade's behavior. Lieutenant Gene Carapico, Perry's company commander, successfully parried Oberholtzer's inquiry:

> Q: Do you know about Lieutenant Cady getting into some disciplinary trouble, or having trouble in disciplining men in the Headquarters & Service Company?
>
> A: No, sir, I don't know about it. I heard about it.

After Carapico came the 849th's African American noncommissioned officers, starting with Sergeant Booker Stitt, the man whom Carapico had sent to arrest Perry. Stitt was followed by Staff Sergeant Jeff Gobold, who'd accompanied Perry to the supply tent to turn in his rifle. Oberholtzer, seeking to buttress his contention that Perry only wanted to meet with Hiatt before giving up his rifle, queried Gobold on something he'd said to the defendant:

> Q: Did you not say, "If I was you," that's referring to Perry, "I'd turn that rifle in and go down to [Headquarters & Service] and talk to the colonel, because you know the colonel is a mighty good man and you can't tell what he may do, he may not send you to the guardhouse?"
>
> A: Yes, sir.
>
> Q: "He may not send you to the guardhouse?"
>
> A: Yes, sir. Those are my statements.
>
> Q: In other words, you left the impression that if he would go down

and see Colonel Hiatt that the trouble may have been patched
up and it may have not been necessary to turn the rifle in?

A: No, sir.

Q: That was all right with you if he went to see Colonel Hiatt.

A: Yes, sir, but I didn't want him to go alone.

Frank realized that Oberholtzer was scoring points. The prosecution's case depended on the court seeing Perry as a hardened felon
bent on murder. But Oberholtzer was starting to make his client
sound fairly rational, interested in talking out his problems rather
than resorting to violence.

Frank jumped in for a redirect on Gobold, bringing the court's
focus back to Perry's menacing actions on March 5:

Q: When Private Perry left did you follow him?

A: No, sir, I did not.

Q: Why, as a guard, didn't you follow him?

A: Because he pumped his rifle and told me not to fool with him
any more, and I was afraid to follow him.

Prosecution: That is all.

It was now time for Sergeant Earl Rawlins, chief of the 849th's
supply tent, to testify for the prosecution. Unlike his two predeces-
sors in the witness chair, Rawlins was clearly reluctant to help the
Army convict his comrade. He confirmed that Gobold had encouraged Perry to go see Hiatt, but was otherwise a difficult witness,
offering Frank vague or evasive answers. When asked whether
Perry had said, as Gobold claimed, "Don't stop me this morning, I
mean business," Rawlins would state only that he'd heard "words
to that effect." He emphasized that Perry had acted respectfully

throughout the supply tent encounter, never pointing his gun at anyone.

After a short recess, the court reconvened at 10:25 A.M. for the testimony of Private James Walton, the dump truck driver who'd picked up the hitchhiking Perry. Oberholtzer probed Walton's recollection of the verbal spat between Perry and Cady, trying to get the court to understand what had provoked his client:

Q: You say that Lieutenant Cady drove up in his jeep and stopped your truck and told Perry to get out?

A: Yes, sir.

Q: What tone of voice did Lieutenant Cady use?

A: It was a harsh tone, he meant business, he swore, he said, "Get out of that God damn truck."

Frank couldn't believe his ears. Walton hadn't mentioned any swearing in the statement he'd made to the CID in early June. Nor was Frank prepared for Walton's next revelation: that Cady had told Perry to "get in the jeep or I'll throw you in."

Oberholtzer followed this minor triumph by pressing Walton to describe Perry's mental state on the morning of the shooting:

Q: Was Perry mad?

A: No, sir, he wasn't mad.

Q: Did he seem upset?

A: Yes, sir, he seemed to be afraid.

Q: How do you know that?

A: He was crying.

Q: Any other physical manifestations?

A: He seemed to be trembling.

Q: He told Lieutenant Cady to stay away from him, or not to come
up on him?

A: Yes, sir.

Q: And Lieutenant Cady kept coming up on him?

A: Yes, sir.

Q: Didn't that seem rather a foolhardy thing for Lieutenant
Cady to do?

Frank speedily objected to this last question, and his challenge
was sustained. Still, Oberholtzer's game plan was working as well as
could be expected: Cady was coming off as a bully. Frank knew he
had to go on the offensive.

He redirected on Walton, highlighting the discrepancies between
the driver's testimony and the statement he'd given investigators three
months earlier. Somewhat incoherently, Walton blamed the interrogation tactics of Staff Sergeant Otto Bowman, a CID agent who'd grilled
the witnesses in June: "When [Bowman] questioned me I only answered
what he asked me. . . . I was asleep when the Staff Sergeant woke me
up, he turned the questions in every way and I had to answer."

Walton's testimony had done Frank's case no favors, but the prosecutor didn't panic. He had supreme confidence in his next witness:
Private Harry Bethel, one of the soldiers who'd been riding in Cady's
jeep. A trucker from Logan County, Ohio, with just a grade school
education, Bethel proved unflappable on the stand. Oberholtzer did
his best to get Bethel to crack, to admit that Cady had at least uttered a lone "God damn." But he got nowhere:

Q: What did Lieutenant Cady say?

A: Nothing—Lieutenant Cady said, "I have got to put you into
the jeep."

Q: Just like that?

A: Yes, sir.

Q: Did Lieutenant Cady use any profanity?

A: No, sir.

Q: Did Lieutenant Cady say, "Get in that God damn jeep or I'll put you in with my fist?"

A: No, sir.

Q: You realize that you are testifying under oath?

A: Yes, sir.

Q: You realize the accused is charged with a serious crime?

A: Yes, sir.

Q: And you still say that Lieutenant Cady didn't use profanity?

A: Not that I heard.

Oberholtzer would try the same approach with the two other eyewitnesses from Cady's jeep, T/5 Robert Griffis and T/4 George Waites. He got Griffis to testify that he'd heard some profanity, but Waites mimicked Bethel's denial. So avidly did Oberholtzer pursue the cursing issue that he neglected to ask the two men more salient questions—he never got Waites to describe Perry's sobbing and trembling, for example, and neither witness was queried about Cady's reported penchant for using his fists. Oberholtzer did ask Griffis the same question he'd posed to Walton, about whether Cady's advance toward the armed, crying Perry seemed "foolhardy." But Frank's sustained objection meant the court would never hear the answer. After a morning's worth of conflicting testimony, the court's six members had learned nothing conclusive about the shooting—except that Perry had, indeed, pulled the trigger.

Just before the court broke for lunch, Sergeant Robert Davis of the CID took the stand. He told the court how he'd questioned Perry on the basha porch, and how Perry had "readily admitted to me, in

the presence of Lieutenant Strassburg and Corporal Wilson and
Captain McMinn, all of the 502nd Military Police Battalion, that he
did shoot Lieutenant Cady."

This was an equivocation: McMinn had left to get medical help
while Perry was claiming to be Johnny Talbot, so he couldn't have
heard the alleged confession that came an hour later. But the unas-
sailable fact remained that Perry, thinking himself a goner, had come
clean about his involvement in Cady's death. Davis's testimony, despite its holes, was damaging.

Oberholtzer objected on the grounds that Davis had no evidence
that Perry's jungle confession—made while Perry was both dying and
unadvised of his legal rights—had been voluntary. The court was
inclined to agree until Frank pointed out that he also had a written
confession from the accused: the statement that a wounded, sedated
Perry had carelessly signed on July 23 while convalescing in Shingbwiyang. The defense objection was overruled.

Though he'd certainly been aware of the written statement, Oberholtzer was unsure how to counter it. He asked Davis to describe
Perry's physical condition during the interrogation at the hospital,
then abruptly switched gears and inquired about the shooting in the
jungle. He asked how far McMinn had been from the basha when
he yelled "Don't move, Perry," and—bizarrely—what Perry had been
wearing that night. A few questions into the cross-examination,
Oberholtzer announced that he was done with Davis. The court
recessed for lunch.

The flustered Oberholtzer needed the break. After a promising
start to the trial, his defense was faltering; his efforts to characterize
Cady as the aggressor had ultimately been a wash, and he'd botched
the cross-examination of Davis. All would be lost unless he could
swing the court's attention back to the issue of whether Perry had
been provoked.

Oberholtzer began the court-martial's afternoon session by recalling Davis. He asked the CID agent to again recount the details of
Perry's capture, and got him to admit that, before firing, McMinn
hadn't identified himself as a military policeman—a minor point that
did little to bolster the defense. Oberholtzer asked nothing more
about the signing of the statement, saving those questions instead
for the prosecution's next witness, Major Carl Goetz of the Seventy-
third Evacuation Hospital.

Goetz authenticated Perry's statement, which Frank then read
aloud for the court. Much of it was boilerplate, a rehash of what had
been said in court earlier—there were parts about going to see Hiatt,
and about hopping a ride in Walton's dump truck. Perry's description
of the shooting itself was consistent with his claim that he feared a
beating:

> This officer then told me that if I didn't get into the jeep, he [the
> officer] would put me in it with his fist. I was surprised at this officer
> for ordering me around as he never stated why he wanted me to get
> in the jeep. This officer then drew his fist back. I remember my gun
> exploding, the smell of the M-1 powder and the expression on the
> officer's face. If I ever smell the powder again, I would get sick at
> my stomach. After I shot this officer I ran away.

Yet there were other parts of the statement that didn't sound like
they'd come from Perry's mouth, as well as several glaring omissions.
There was no mention of Perry's tenuous mental state, for example,
only a quick reference to his consumption of opium and ganja on the
night of March 4. And then there was a damning line: "I never intended to return to the Army, nor did I intend to return to the United
States of America." This sentence's stilted phrasing was out of sync
with the rest of the statement's more natural tone; it appeared tacked

on by Davis. Yet its inclusion was sufficient proof that Perry was a deserter. And if Perry had really just acted in the heat of the moment, the prosecution's logic went, why would he then compound his crime by deserting? Desertion, Frank believed, was irrefutable evidence of malice aforethought.

Now Oberholtzer really had his work cut out for him. He needed to get the statement thrown out, or his chances of saving Perry's life were slim. He started in on Goetz:

> Q: I now show you the body of this statement, as you see, most of it is in narrative form. It leaves the impression that when it was taken, Private Perry related it in narrative form. Is that a fact, or were questions asked of Perry and then put in narrative form by a reporter?
>
> A: I was not there when the original questions were asked him, but when I first saw the deposition it was typed out and I was told that it was taken from Perry in that ward. I don't know whether the questions were asked, it was my impression that it was his own words.
>
> Q: In other words, when this statement was actually taken from Perry you were not present?
>
> A: No.
>
> Q: In other words, it was given to you later and they told you that it was Perry's statement?
>
> A: Yes, that's correct.

Oberholtzer had uncovered a flaw in the prosecution's case, one that called into question the veracity of Perry's alleged confession. He promptly objected to the statement's admission into evidence. But when a member of the court demanded clarification on the reasons for the objection, Oberholtzer inexplicably withdrew his protest and went on questioning Goetz. He asked about how much medication Perry had been administered prior to the interrogation—Goetz didn't know—then ended his cross-examination.

The prosecution rested. Oberholtzer had missed a golden opportunity—his only opportunity—to have Perry's statement tossed.

THE DEFENSE'S CASE was wafer thin. Oberholtzer opened by motioning for several of the charges against his client to be dropped, citing "an unlawful multiplication of charges." The court refused, leaving Oberholtzer to call his first witness: Walton, the truck driver.

Having veered away from his initial strategy in response to the introduction of Perry's written statement, Oberholtzer now returned to trying to tar Cady. Frank was ready for this gambit:

Q: Do you know Lieutenant Cady's reputation relative to handling men in his organization?

Prosecution: We'll object, immaterial and irrelevant.

Law Member: What do you hope to prove by this?

Defense: I wish to prove that Lieutenant Cady's reputation in handling men was open to question. In other words, it is a character trait that has a direct bearing on this altercation between Lieutenant Cady and Private Perry. In other words, what is his character relative to disciplining men in his organization.

The court sustained Frank's objection, and sternly warned Oberholtzer that "the officer is not on trial." Exasperated, Oberholtzer asked virtually the identical question twice more. Twice more Frank objected, and twice more the objection was angrily sustained. "What I am trying to show is that Lieutenant Cady had trouble in handling men in his command," Oberholtzer pleaded. But the court's members had made up their minds—after earlier granting the defense some latitude to impeach Cady's character, they would no longer permit Oberholtzer to speak ill of the dead.

The stymied defense counsel had just one more witness to call: Perry.

As Perry approached the witness chair, one of the court's members cautioned him about the risks of testifying. "You further understand that you do not have to make a statement which may be used against you, do you understand that?" he asked, before adding several more legal caveats. The member seemed to be warning Perry, *This is a very, very bad idea.*

But Perry took the oath, stated his full name, rank, and serial number, and started talking.

Perry spoke uninterrupted for the next several minutes—about the events of March 5, his life among the Nagas, and the "bright, pretty lights" he'd glimpsed while drifting toward death. His testimony was long-winded and jumbled, betraying how little time Perry had spent with Oberholtzer in preparation for the court-martial. Sometimes the details were microscopic, as when Perry described the few seconds leading up to the shooting: "He kept walking, I saw that he was going to catch me, I stopped, I asked him not to come up on me, and he slowed down and looked me right in the eye, he kept on coming, he dropped his hands down and kept on coming and I kept walking back, I was glancing back at him, and I asked him a couple more times not to come up on me." Other times, Perry skipped over weeks in a heartbeat, or confused the order of events.

Oberholtzer followed up with a couple of superficial questions: one about whether Perry ever intended to desert ("No, sir"), another about his state of mind on the morning of March 5 ("I was pretty well angry, I was crying").

Now it was Frank's turn. Realizing that Oberholtzer had failed in his efforts to discredit Perry's signed statements—the primary one made on July 23, as well as the supplemental statement taken five days later—the prosecutor gleefully used the confessions as cudgels:

Q: Perry, these two statements that you signed, did you read them before you signed them?

A: I can't remember what I read, at that time I was kind of sleeping.

Q: But you signed them?

A: I did.

Q: Did anybody force you to sign them?

A: No, sir.

Q: You want this court to believe you would sign something that you really didn't think was the truth?

A: That's the way it is, he didn't take the whole statement as it is there, he didn't take it that way, he asked me the questions and brought it back that way.

Q: Isn't it a fact, that the real reason why you signed these two statements is that you wanted to come clean about everything?

A: Will you repeat the question?

Q: Isn't it a fact that because you wanted to come clean about the entire altercation that you signed these statements?

A: I signed them because he asked me to sign them.

Q: Are you in the habit of signing something that is wrong?

A: That's the first time I signed anything.

Frank then shifted his cross-examination to the topic of desertion, asking Perry why he didn't stick around the Namyung bridge and wait for the MPs on March 9. "If you were in a nervous condition as I was at that time," Perry snapped back, "when you walked out to the road and you heard the shooting and saw the MPs, I think you would have run too unless you wanted to be shot."

Frank wasn't cowed by Perry's increasingly surly attitude on the stand. He moved in for the legal kill:

Q: Isn't it a fact that you shot Lieutenant Cady because you didn't want to go to the guardhouse?

A: I didn't want him to whale me, I was under the impression that he was going to whale me.

Q: He was going to do what?

A: Whale me.

Q: So you thought you would take your rifle and shoot him?

A: I tried to get away from him but I couldn't.

It was a masterful bit of lawyering. Oberholtzer had tried to paint Perry as an ordinary man with a rightful fear of being beaten. Frank was now effectively portraying Perry as a trigger-happy liar, with a temper to boot.

As Frank wrapped up his cross-examination, Perry seemed alternately frazzled and defiant:

Q: Isn't it a fact that you knew that Lieutenant Cady would send you to the guardhouse, and that the only reason he reached out towards you was to get that weapon out of your hands?

A: I don't know Lieutenant Cady.

Q: Did you ever hear of the man?

A: He didn't tell me anything at all.

Q: He didn't tell you anything?

A: He told me to get in the jeep.

Q: You didn't know why he wanted you to get in the jeep?

A: He didn't give me any explanation.

Q: Are you in the habit of waiting for an explanation?

A: When a man speaks to you in that tone of voice, I think he has
   an explanation due a man.

And with that, the prosecution rested. The court recessed until
2:55 P.M.

AFTER A STRONG performance in the early going, the frustrated
Oberholtzer had succumbed to hopelessness as the trial wore on.
Frank's constant objections, the court's obstinacy, and Perry's insolence had combined to make mincemeat of his case. As he rose to
begin his closing statement, Oberholtzer was at a complete loss
about what to say.

Oberholtzer started his speech clumsily, by simply reading the
entire statute defining manslaughter, a dense chunk of legalese that
included irrelevant sections pertaining to adultery and unlawful imprisonment. It took several minutes for Oberholtzer to shift into his
blame-the-victim riff, by far his strongest material:

> Evidence shows that Perry had been crying, that he was trembling,
> his passion had been aroused to a point where it was uncontrollable.
> In spite of this, Lieutenant Cady kept on coming. Lieutenant Cady
> was unarmed, I'll grant that. Lieutenant Cady, with a gun pointed
> directly at him, seeing that Perry was trembling, was lacking control,
> kept walking up on the accused, a very foolhardy thing to do. If
> Lieutenant Cady hadn't persisted in advancing on Perry, he would
> be alive today, and the accused would not be in this court room.

This was exactly the argument that Frank had identified as the
only one capable of saving the defendant's life. But it was too late

for Oberholtzer's most valid point to do much good, especially sand-wiched between rambling passages on adultery, Captain McMinn's failure to identify himself as an MP, and the technical definition of military desertion. The argument that should have been the crux of Oberholtzer's case, that murder was too severe a charge because Cady was partly culpable for the shooting, instead came off as a mere aside.

Oberholtzer ended his muddled oration by addressing the issue of the written confession: "I maintain that it should be closely scru-tinized, and that Perry did not have a clear mind, and that other evidence also shows that he intended to remain in the service, and it should be given its relative weight." And with that underwhelming conclusion, the defense counsel returned to his seat.

Frank couldn't have asked for a better setup for his rebuttal. He knew that Oberholtzer's attempts to vilify Cady had gone over poorly, and that Perry's lack of contrition on the witness stand had incensed the court. All Frank had to do was depict the slain officer as a hero, and mock the opposing counsel while he was at it:

[Oberholtzer] tells you that Lieutenant Cady approached Perry and he didn't act polite, he didn't tell a man who is under arrest, "Please, Private Perry, you are under arrest, please, get in the jeep, I want to talk to you; I am Lieutenant Cady. . . . "

I say here sits a man who killed another man in cold blooded murder, he tells you that the only reason why he shot Lieutenant Cady, and I believe that was brought out in the summation by the defense, is because Lieutenant Cady was coming up on him. Gen-tlemen, what Lieutenant Cady did is just what every man would do under the same or similar circumstances. It is just like a man who was pushed off into the river and was drowning, he would grab any-thing in order to save his life. That's why I tell you that Lieutenant

Cady was going down there performing his duty and was attempting to take a rifle out of the accused's hands and put him in the stockade where he rightfully belonged, and I ask that you gentlemen first find this man guilty of all specifications and charges, and bring in a sentence commensurate with the crime.

The six court-martial members retired to scribble their verdicts on secret ballots. Upon returning, they announced that the vote had been unanimous: Perry was guilty of murder, desertion, and disobeying a commissioned officer. He was acquitted of the most minor charges, involving disobedience and disrespect toward a noncommissioned officer. But those hardly mattered.

The court briefly reconvened and Perry's previous conviction, for disobeying Lieutenant Emanuel Sterghos in October 1943, was read into the record. The prior conviction would be weighed by the court's members during their sentencing deliberations.

Those deliberations took only a few minutes. At 3:30 P.M., the court handed down its sentence: Perry was to be dishonorably discharged, to forfeit all pay and allowances due or to become due, and to be hanged by the neck until dead.

The court-martial of Private Herman Perry, including two breaks and lunch, took just six and a half hours.

TWELVE

Midway through September 1944, a one-page letter arrived at 3217 Warder Street NW, a redbrick row house in Washington, D.C.'s quaint Park View neighborhood. A month earlier, with the financial assistance of her son, prizefighter Aaron Perry, Flonnie B. Johnson had purchased the two-story residence for $2,410. Home ownership was a milestone for Johnson, cementing her family's status as a Great Migration success. The budding boxing career that had made the acquisition possible, however, was temporarily on hold: shortly after his mother closed on the house, Aaron had started Army basic training at Fort Meade, Maryland.

Flonnie hadn't heard from Herman since winter, so the War Department letterhead surely made her fear the worst. But this wasn't the standard "We regret to inform you" notice. The text instead stated that Private Herman Perry had been found guilty of murdering Lieutenant Harold Cady, and that a general court-martial had decided the appropriate punishment was death by hanging. In accordance with the Articles of War, the letter continued, the case would be reviewed by three members of the Judge Advocate General's Department. These Delhi-based Army lawyers would have to confirm the trial's fairness, and the verdict's correctness, before the sentence could be carried out.

Flonnie was stunned. Herman was the gentlest of her sons, the one who'd avoided boxing for fear of spoiling his pretty face, and who fancied himself a sharp-dressed Romeo rather than a thug. He'd played truant and dabbled in other delinquent vices, to be sure, but he'd also worked a nine-to-five job. Yet there it was in stark black type: Flonnie's second-born child was a condemned killer.

The letter failed to mention the specifics of Herman's crime. Nor did it describe how, or even if, Flonnie might help her son. But her maternal instincts kicked in: she gathered what cash she could and headed downtown to Fifth Street NW between D and E streets, the block that was home to D.C.'s criminal defense bar. There she hired one of the most colorful attorneys ever to haunt Judiciary Square: Robert Ingersoll Miller, popularly known as Judge Not Guilty or, more insidiously, Bankroll Bob.

The sixty-eight-year-old Miller had been a successful horse trainer before opting for law school. He cut his legal teeth in the 1910s, defending pimps, tavern owners, and cocaine peddlers. He later earned a reputation for taking on seemingly unwinnable murder cases, especially those involving bootleggers and other underworld figures. *The Washington Post* estimated that Miller averaged a trial per day, every day, for thirty years straight.

Miller also had close ties to Washington's African American community, stemming from his friendship with prominent black attorney Armond W. Scott, a fellow Republican activist. Unlike some of his white peers on Fifth Street, Miller had no qualms about taking on black clients accused of heinous crimes, as long as the defendant was willing to pay a nonrefundable cash fee up front.

As a result of this slightly fishy payment policy, Miller's pockets always bulged with wads of bills—hence the nickname Bankroll Bob. He needed hard currency in part because he was an infamous greaser of palms; he once handed a judge a casebook with a $100 bill marking the relevant citation. The government prosecuted Miller for an array of ethics violations in 1938, but political connections got him off the hook; Miller counted former vice president Charles Curtis among his confidants, by virtue of their mutual passion for playing the ponies.

But when Herman Perry's mother walked through Miller's door in September 1944, Bankroll Bob was at the peak of his notoriety for reasons that had nothing to do with bribery: eight months earlier, he'd shot and killed his wife's lover in broad daylight.

The salacious crime had scandalized Washington society. Miller's wife, Marguerite, had long been carrying on with her shrink, the esteemed Dr. John E. Lind, an expert in criminal insanity who was related to Abraham Lincoln. On February 21, 1944, Miller approached the adulterous couple as they sat in a black sedan outside the Woodward & Lothrop department store, by the corner of Eleventh and G streets NW. Miller then shot Lind in the head and chest with a .38-caliber revolver. He claimed self-defense, saying he'd only fired after seeing his romantic rival pull a .32-caliber pistol from the car's glove compartment.

A Woodward & Lothrop porter disputed this version of events, contending that he'd witnessed Miller toss the second gun onto the passenger's seat. At the trial, however, two psychiatrists took the stand in Miller's defense, asserting that the cuckolded attorney was suffering from "severe compulsive psychosis" at the time of the shooting. "An accumulation of severe mental strain caused mental aberrations that resulted in his killing an individual without consequences of right or wrong," testified Dr. Antoine Schneider. The defense also called Marguerite, twenty-five years Miller's junior, who declared her boundless love for the dean of the Fifth Street bar.

The jury took just eighty minutes to acquit Miller of first-degree murder, a verdict that burnished his credentials as master of the seemingly impossible. If anyone could save Herman's life, Flonnie hoped, it was the slippery, well-connected Bankroll Bob.

But military justice wasn't Miller's strong suit. In fact, he had no real inkling of how to help Herman, as evidenced by the letter he sent the Army on September 28: "Please advise me regarding the procedure of an appeal in a case such as this where the reviewing authority is in the field."

As MILLER PUZZLED over the esoterica of military law, the post-trial process mandated by the Articles of War progressed at a sluggish pace. In addition to the three-lawyer review panel in Delhi, two generals had to sign off on Perry's sentence: Major General William E. R. Covell, commander of the CBI's Services of Supply, and General Joseph Warren Stilwell.*

On September 21, Major Charles Richardson Jr., acting staff judge advocate at CBI headquarters in Delhi, forwarded a report on Perry's court-martial to Covell. Unversed as he was in military law, Covell would decide whether or not to endorse the hanging based solely on Richardson's counsel.

The report was riddled with unintentional errors, most of them minor. For example, Richardson misidentified the month in which Perry had been previously convicted of insubordination, and he misstated the distance between Cady and Perry when the shooting took

---

*Stilwell had been promoted to full general in August 1944.

place. But one of the brief's most critical statements was egregiously wide of the mark:

> This being a case in which a death penalty has been imposed, this reviewing authority has only the power to approve or disapprove the sentence in its entirety and has no power to order execution of the sentence, or to grant commutation thereof.

This directly contradicted the Forty-seventh Article of War, which held that a court-martial's convening authority (in this case, the SOS) had "the power to approve or disapprove the whole or any part of the sentence." In other words, Covell could commute Perry's sentence to imprisonment—a common practice during World War II. But Richardson's report gave Covell the false impression that his only options were to okay the death sentence or let Perry go free.

The major general unsurprisingly chose the former. Now it was Stilwell's turn.

Militarily, at least, things were going splendidly for Vinegar Joe as the summer of 1944 segued into autumn. Myitkyina had finally fallen to the Americans and their Chinese allies on August 3, two and a half months after Merrill's Marauders had seized the vital airstrip on the city's outskirts. The British-led Chindits, meanwhile, had shelled the Japanese out of Mogaung, another key town along the Ledo Road's intended route. Reeling from these losses as well as their catastrophic invasion of India, the Japanese were rapidly losing their grip on Burma.

Before Stilwell's monsoon season victories in the plains of northern Burma, the War Department had seriously considered canceling the Ledo Road altogether. Swayed by the antiroad arguments of Major General Claire Lee Chennault, Stilwell's flyboy rival, as well as by the Brits' continued pessimism, the department had briefly recommended that all Army engineering resources be redirected to boosting the number of Hump flights. But after the mid-May capture of the Myitkyina airstrip, the road had come back into favor: the Washington bureaucrats feared that, should they quash the project, they'd be accused of having let the Marauders die in vain.

When the annual rains started tapering off in September, the engineers zoomed forward with their coolies and Cats. By month's end, "Pick's Pike" had reached Warazup, a village approximately halfway between Shingbwiyang and the Irrawaddy, Burma's longest river. The relatively flat and well-trodden territory ahead was far less problematic than what the engineers had overcome in the Patkais and the Hukaung Valley. With the Japanese in retreat and fresh equipment arriving from Calcutta, the SOS commanders hoped the Ledo Road might join up with the Burma Road, which lay 276 miles from Warazup, before the 1945 monsoons.

There was, however, a bitter irony to the success of Stilwell's forces in northern Burma: by clearing the way for the Ledo Road, they'd made the road more irrelevant than ever. Capturing the Myitkyina airstrip had essentially ended the Japanese aerial harassment of Hump flights. Since they no longer had to fear the predations of Japanese fighter planes, Assam-based pilots bound for Kunming could now take more southerly routes, thereby avoiding the deadliest sections of the Himalayas.

As a result, it was now feasible to supply China solely by air. Though obviously biased, Brigadier General Stuart Godfrey of the Army Air Forces made a convincing pro-airlifts case in an October briefing. Godfrey calculated that in August 1944, seventy-five C-47 cargo planes had delivered twelve thousand tons of goods from North-East India to Myitkyina, with each plane making two to three trips per day. Had the Ledo Road been open that far, he estimated that it would have taken twelve hundred trucks and four thousand men operating around the clock in order to deliver the same amount of cargo—an impossible assignment. Furthermore, Godfrey argued, building additional airfields would require 80 percent less manpower than completing the Ledo Road.

One person who could vouch for the growing efficiency of the airlifts was none other than Chiang Kai-shek. In April 1944 his government had received thirteen thousand tons of Allied goods over the Hump; in August that figure had soared to twenty-nine thousand tons, due largely to the removal of Japanese planes from the northern Burma skies. Despite his continued avowals of support for the Allied cause, Chiang kept stacking these supplies in his Chongqing warehouses, for use against the Communists once the meddlesome foreigners had departed, or for resale on the black market. Chiang's cronies even went so far as to trade American goods with the Japanese, their supposed sworn enemies.

Though aware of these underhanded dealings, Stilwell was more galled by the Generalissimo's failure to provide the Allies with fresh, halfway competent troops. Chiang now insisted that most of his conscripts train in China rather than at the American-run facility in Ramgarh, India. The Chinese camps were dreadful at turning peasants into warriors; thousands died of malnutrition while training, and those who survived the ordeal were mostly useless in combat. "The [Chinese soldiers] were generally so diseased, so spiritless, so badly led, so utterly devoid of any technical training, that it was a criminal waste to give weapons to any but those we had taken in hand and trained from the basic rudiments on up," concluded CBS Radio's Eric Sevareid after a visit to Chongqing.

At his wit's end, Stilwell tried brokering a deal with Mao Zedong's disciplined Red Army, hoping the Communists would agree to unite with Chiang's forces against the Japanese. But Chiang said he'd accept such a deal only if he were personally put in charge of distributing weapons to the Communists—yet another scam to fatten his own arms cache.*

A crisis came in mid-September when Chiang threatened to pull his divisions from Lungling, a besieged Chinese city along the Burma Road, just north of the planned junction with the Ledo Road. A defenseless Lungling would be easy pickings for the Japanese, who'd doubtless slaughter the city's inhabitants and build a fortified base. The occupiers would then be able to halt any future ground shipments between Assam and southern China, rendering the Ledo Road worthless. And as Washington had decided that it couldn't spare any more combat units for the CBI, Stilwell would be hard-pressed to break a Japanese blockade.

Vinegar Joe was apoplectic over Chiang's threat, raging in his diary:

> The crazy little bastard. The little matter of the Ledo Road is forgotten. The only point on the whole trace we do not control is Lungling, and he wants to give that up and sabotage the whole God-damn project—men, money, material, time and sweat that we have put on it for two and a half years just to help China. Unthinkable. It does not even enter that hickory nut he uses for a head. . . . Usual cock-eyed reasons and idiotic tactical and strategic conceptions. He is impossible.

Having had enough of Peanut's machinations, Stilwell decided it was time for an ultimatum. He demanded that Chiang give him complete, unfettered control of the entire Chinese military, or else

---

*Many American officials didn't view Mao Zedong and his followers as "real" Communists, but rather as admirable revolutionaries bent on solving China's chronic woes. Stilwell referred to the Communists as "agricultural liberals," while others in Washington preferred the phrase "agrarian reformers." Few in American government anticipated Mao's zeal for taking Marxist dogma to dark extremes.

he would see to it that the United States "would withdraw entirely from China and India and set up base elsewhere." President Roosevelt backed Stilwell's gambit, sending Chiang a stern telegram ordering that Vinegar Joe be granted "unrestricted command of all your forces. . . . It appears plainly evident to all of us here that all your and our efforts to save China are to be lost by further delays."

After personally witnessing Chiang's dismay at reading the president's note, Stilwell thought he'd finally gained the upper hand. In a letter to his wife, he jotted a gleeful poem oozing with contempt for the Generalissimo:

I've waited long for vengeance—
At last I've had my chance,
I've looked the Peanut in the eye
And kicked him in the pants.

The old harpoon was ready
With aim and timing true,
I sank it to the handle
And stung him through and through.

The little bastard shivered,
And lost the power of speech.
His face turned green and quivered
As he struggled not to screech.

For all my weary battles,
For all my hours of woe,
At last I've had my innings
And laid the Peanut low.

But Stilwell had gloated too soon; his adversary hadn't become China's despot by lacking in tenacity. Chiang sent a sharp riposte to Roosevelt, implying not so subtly that unless Stilwell was fired forthwith, the alliance between the United States and China would forever be ruined: "The appointment of General Stilwell as field commander would immediately cause grave dissensions in the new command and do irreparable injury to the vital Chinese-American military cooperation."

Chiang knew that Roosevelt, a lifelong Sinophile, was desperate for China to become a postwar Great Power, a bulwark against any potential revival of Japanese militarism. Forced to choose between that vision and Vinegar Joe, the president caved to Peanut. In mid-October, he ordered Stilwell back to Washington and split the CBI theater in two: the India-Burma theater, commanded by Lieutenant General Daniel I. Sultan, and the China theater, led by Lieutenant General Albert C. Wedemeyer. The wily Generalissimo had once and for all defeated his American nemesis.

Preoccupied with his struggle against Chiang, Stilwell couldn't be bothered with trifling legal duties. It wasn't until October 25, the day after he officially stepped down as commander of the CBI, that Stilwell finally reviewed Herman Perry's case. He didn't read the court-martial transcript, but rather relied on an advisory memo written by Colonel C. C. Fenn, a JAGD member in Delhi. Fenn urged the general to approve the death sentence, calling the trial "fair and impartial" and noting that "the evidence fully supports all findings of the court."

The memo also included a backhanded compliment to Perry meant to dispel any patronizing sympathies Stilwell might have for his black GIs: "The accused does not appear as a simple minded, ignorant negro [sic] soldier. His use of words and handwriting indicate an agile, trained mind."

Vinegar Joe predictably signed off on Perry's hanging. But the fact that Stilwell was no longer the theater's commanding general technically voided his approval. The case file was thus forwarded to Lieutenant General Sultan, the new boss, who was busy acclimating to the post: dealing with enlisted men's courts-martial was not high on his list of priorities. Furthermore, Sultan still needed an official letter from Secretary of War Henry L. Stimson in order to validate his powers, which included the endorsement of executions.

While this hierarchical chaos ensued in Delhi and beyond, Perry sat in the Ledo Stockade, waiting for his date with the noose to be set. And as the weeks rolled by with no word on his fate, Perry began to scheme.

PERRY'S DEATH ROW was a cramped tent reserved for the Ledo Road's worst offenders. The canvas dwelling was surrounded by its own barbed-wire enclosure, with a lockable gate opposite the front of the tent. Two of Perry's cellmates were rapists serving life terms; the other two were deserters doing twenty-five years each. All four of these fellow inmates were white—the stockade's ramshackle high-security wing was one of the CBI's few bastions of integration. Perry, however, was the only man in the tent, as well as in the entire CBI, who'd been sentenced to death.

Because he'd humiliated the Army by eluding justice for so long, Perry was singled out for uniquely callous treatment. In the weeks following his September 4 conviction, Perry was kept perpetually handcuffed and shackled at the ankles. The shackles were in turn chained to a log buried beneath the tent's dirt floor, so that Perry couldn't wander more than a few feet in any direction. The guards meant for Perry to spend his last days living like a chastised dog.

But the handcuffs had rusted in the monsoon rains, and Perry kept jiggling them until they cracked off his wrists. The stockade didn't have a replacement set, and requisitioning a new pair was apparently too much of an administrative hassle. Soon after the handcuffs broke, Perry's leg shackles were commandeered by a military police battalion for use in the field. During daylight hours, Perry was now free to roam the stockade and commune with other prisoners. He was even put to work on the stockade grounds, chopping wood and digging garbage pits.

Perry developed a fast friendship with Private Lucius Weaver, a fellow African American member of the 849th who'd been sentenced to ten years at hard labor for attempted murder. As part of his punishment, Weaver was daily sent outside the stockade on work details, which included stripping vehicles and cleaning mortar off used bricks. The work crews operated like chain gangs, with shotgun-wielding officers, called "chasers," watching the prisoners toil beneath the blazing sun. Several months of good behavior was enough to earn a prisoner trustee status, meaning he could work without an armed guard present. But Weaver was too much of a troublemaker for that: he was repeatedly reprimanded for sitting down without permission.

The guards may have been good at spotting layabouts, but they were lousy at preventing smuggling. They neglected to pat down inmates returning from outside work details, and they never bothered to search the tents for contraband. None of this was lost on Perry and Weaver.

A COPY OF the court-martial transcript didn't arrive at Robert I. Miller's Fifth Street office until October 18, giving him little time to prepare a brief on Perry's behalf. The letter that accompanied the transcript noted that "there is no procedure by which an 'appeal' can be made in any court-martial case in the sense used in the civil law." But Miller's brief, the letter added, would be given "careful consideration" by the three-person panel reviewing the case in Delhi.

Miller was given two weeks to write his brief, but he wound up taking nearly a month. Like Captain Clayton Oberholtzer, Perry's defense counsel, Miller argued that the shooting of Lieutenant Cady amounted to manslaughter rather than murder. He cited a 1941 precedent, *Bullock v. United States*, in which a federal appeals court had ruled that "appreciable time" must elapse between the decision to kill and the act itself in order for the crime to be judged deliberate, as opposed to merely impulsive. "In the case of Private Perry," wrote Miller, "no premeditation or deliberation was shown the Court and nothing in the record shows that such evidence was offered."

Since Perry had also been convicted of desertion, and this crime alone was punishable by death, Miller ended the brief by arguing that his client was guilty only of being absent without leave, a much less serious infraction. "The record shows that defendant never was more than eight miles from camp and that he always wore his uniform," Miller wrote. "Common sense tells us that a man wanting to desert would discard the uniform as soon as possible and would also travel as far from his base camp as possible." This laughable excuse was offered instead of the most honest one: that Perry had feared being lynched should he surrender.

Miller made no mention of Perry's mental frailty—a curious omission, given that Miller himself had recently beaten a murder rap by claiming to have suffered from "severe compulsive psychosis." True, there was the cursory Army psychiatric report to contend with, the one that asserted Perry wasn't suffering from any disease of the mind. But if anyone could find a reputable shrink to offer a convincing alternative opinion, it was Bankroll Bob. Reading Miller's brief, one gets the feeling he devoted a minimum of effort to Perry's case—a level of effort perhaps commensurate with the nonrefundable cash fee paid by Flonnie.

The citation of *Bullock v. United States*, however, was spot-on. There was certainly nothing in the trial record to indicate that Perry had planned to kill anyone on March 5. In fact, Perry had made a point of walking away from Cady when first confronted, and had repeatedly warned the lieutenant, "Don't come up on me." He fired only after Cady reached forward, an act the traumatized Perry had interpreted as a provocation.

On November 15, Miller submitted his three-and-a-half-page brief to Colonel R. E. Kunkel, chief of the Military Justice Division at the Washington-based Office of the Judge Advocate General. Five days later, Kunkel mailed a copy to Delhi, for the benefit of the two entities that still needed to sign off on Perry's execution: Lieutenant General Sultan, commander of the newly created India-Burma theater, and the review panel. But the brief didn't arrive in time to affect Sultan's decision; he reconfirmed the death sentence on November 24.

That left Perry's life in the hands of the three reviewers, all of them experienced judge advocates: Lieutenant Colonel John O'Brien, Lieutenant Colonel Itimous Valentine, and Lieutenant Colonel Robert Van Ness. They'd begun working on the case without Miller's brief in hand, believing that it might never be forthcoming. But upon learning that Kunkel had mailed the document on November 20, they decided to wait for its arrival before completing their report.

So the lawyers in Delhi bided their time. And weeks flew by.

THE LEDO STOCKADE was a far cry from Alcatraz. There were only two guard towers, positioned diagonally opposite each other;

Perry's tent was located near one of the prison's two towerless corners. Between midnight and dawn, the perimeter barbed-wire fence was patrolled by a lone watchman, who took fifteen minutes to circumnavigate the grounds. Another guard was stationed in front of Perry's tent at night, but men assigned to this duty were often seen sitting against the gate, daydreaming or catching some shut-eye. None of the stockade's guards carried flashlights; the only artificial illumination was provided by the towers' searchlights, which lacked the wattage necessary to penetrate the thick Assamese fog.

Then there were the drainage ditches that ran beneath the perimeter fence. Designed to prevent monsoon flooding, these troughs brimmed with water between April and September. But once the rains of 1944 had ended, the stockade's warden, Lieutenant Sidney Dennis, had neglected to fill them in. It didn't take long for the inmates to discover this oversight, and exploit it.

The first inmate caught making use of the ditches was Private Nathaniel Jackson. Jackson's aim was more modest than outright escape: he only wanted to return to his unit's camp at night, enjoy some liquor or dice, then slip back into the stockade in time for breakfast. Jackson treated himself to several of these unauthorized furloughs, until the morning a tower guard spotted him preparing for reentry. The guard shot and wounded Jackson, thereby ending the private's run of eight-hour vacations.

But nothing was done about the ditches once Jackson's forays came to light. It wasn't until early December, after two more prisoners escaped briefly through the channels, that Dennis ordered them blocked. But instead of using pipes or boulders, the apathetic guards deployed coils of barbed wire. Sporadically strewn throughout the ditches, these prickly barriers were hardly impassable.

Captain Eugene Kirk, the Ledo provost marshal who'd sent MPs to case Calcutta's brothels in March, rightly feared that Perry might be the next inmate to attempt a jailbreak. In November, Kirk had requested that Dennis, one of his subordinates, move Perry somewhere less flimsy than a tent. There was a two-hundred-square-foot brick building on the stockade grounds, which housed an officer serving a five-year sentence. Kirk suggested that this privileged inmate be relocated so that Perry could be placed in the cell. But Dennis refused; the brick structure had been built specifically to house the incarcerated officer, and he saw no reason to deviate from that plan.

In early December, the nervous Kirk went up the chain of command, asking Brigadier General Pick's office to approve Perry's transfer to a more secure stockade: there was one at the nearby Chabua Air Base, from which no one had ever escaped. Pick's people forwarded a summary of Kirk's wishes to Services of Supply headquarters in Delhi. On December 11, the office of Major General Covell, the SOS commander, rejected the transfer request without comment.

ON DECEMBER 15, Lieutenant General Sultan transmitted a classified message to the Office of the Judge Advocate General back in Washington. "File in case of Private Herman Perry has not been received," he wrote. "Did you send same by courier mail? Suggest you send a copy of brief by courier mail if this means of transmission was not used in original transmission."

Had Miller's brief arrived in Delhi as planned, the review panel might have wrapped up its work by late November, and Perry either would have been hanged or been granted a reprieve shortly thereafter. But the document had somehow vanished in transit, and now the panel was weeks behind schedule. Perry's postconviction limbo was dragging on for an unseemly long time.

That evening in Ledo, Kirk met with Dennis to reiterate his

fears about Perry busting out of the stockade. Dennis was miffed at his boss's lack of faith. "Perry isn't going anywhere," he bluntly proclaimed.

JUST LIKE THE July night when Perry had been captured near Tgum Ga, the moon was entirely absent from the sky on December 15, 1944. The stockade's two low-powered searchlights could barely pierce the darkness, let alone the pea-soup haze that enveloped the inmates' tents.

Sometime after midnight, Perry tiptoed to the front of his tent and peeked outside. A soldier stood watch a few yards from the entrance flap, his back to the prisoners' canvas hovel. Like most other stockade guards assigned to late-night duty, he appeared bored and indifferent. His mental energies were likely devoted to dreaming of the hearty Spam breakfast that awaited him at shift's end.

Perry crept to the tent's rear, lifted up the loose edge, and gently rolled onto the dusty earth outside. Then he crawled to the barbed-wire fence that encircled the tent—the only barrier between him and the drainage ditches along the stockade's perimeter.

Perry had spent weeks preparing for this moment. He dug into his pocket and pulled out strips of coarse wool that he'd cut from his prison-issue blanket. He draped them over the wire, then unsheathed the centerpiece of his plan: a pair of wire cutters, probably smuggled into the stockade by his pal Weaver. The guards' failure to search inmates returning from work details, or to conduct snap inspections of the stockades' tents, was about to bite them in the ass.

Cutting a suitably sized hole into the fence was an arduous task. The wire was arranged in a checkerboard pattern, so numerous squares of metal had to be snipped apart. But Perry did so fearlessly; he knew the searchlights' beams couldn't reach the spot where he was working, especially on such an exceptionally dark and foggy night. And after months of observation, he also knew the lazy guards never circled back to the rear of the tent. As long as the wool strips muffled the sound of his cutting, Perry could take his sweet time.

Once he'd created a fissure big enough to wriggle his 170-pound body through, Perry crouched low and made a beeline for the drainage ditches. Since these ditches were now being watched somewhat carefully due to previous escapes, Perry probably hid nearby until he heard the perimeter guard walk by. Having timed this ritual, Perry knew that once the guard passed, he'd have fifteen minutes to clamber through a trench, then dash for the copse of betel-nut and banana trees that lay just beyond the stockade's edge.

Perry heard the scrunch of the watchman's boots grow louder, then peak in volume and begin to fade. Once the footsteps were no longer audible, Perry dove headfirst into a drainage ditch and began to crawl.

As he writhed along on his belly, Perry surely did so with a hand thrust forward in order to push aside the barbed wire that blocked his path. Perhaps, to prevent the spiked obstructions from dicing his palm and fingers, he wrapped the last few wool strips around his fleshy probe.

Whatever his means of dealing with the ditch's feeble barriers, Perry soon emerged on the other side of the stockade's fence. Filthy and exhausted from the night's exertions, he didn't yet have time to rest. He sprinted for the trees, praying that the patter of his scampering feet would fail to grab anyone's ear, and that a tower searchlight wouldn't suddenly flare to life and swivel toward his backside.

Nothing of the sort occurred. Perry entered the woods and heard only the natural sounds of Assam—the ululating insects, the thrush of nocturnal critters scurrying about. No sirens, no growling dogs, no shotgun pumps, no southern accents yelling about a man escaped.

Perry was free. But he was also a good eighty miles from his Naga kin on the Patkais' eastern slopes. To get back to Glau, he'd have to walk across mountains that would soon be teeming with MPs, along with the usual assortment of tigers, leeches, and potentially hostile tribesmen. And he'd have to start his journey carrying neither food nor weapons.

It was an almost identical situation to the one he'd faced in early March, after abandoning his rifle near the Namyung bridge. Except this time, self-preservation wasn't his only goal: Perry now had a wife and unborn child to find.

THIRTEEN

Livid over Herman Perry's death-row escape, the Army brass demanded that heads roll in Ledo. Investigators were dispatched from Delhi to determine who was responsible for the stockade's porous security. They quickly placed the lion's share of blame on Captain Eugene Kirk, Ledo's provost marshal and the man who'd once thought Perry was holed up in the brothels of Calcutta.

Mediocre as he might have been, Kirk was nothing more than a convenient scapegoat; he had, after all, begged his superiors to move Perry to a more secure facility. It was the office of Major General William E. R. Covell, head of the theater's Services of Supply, that had refused to take action. But Kirk was precisely the sort of mid-level officer who usually takes the fall for the blunders of higher-ups. He was stripped of his command and replaced by Lieutenant Colonel Elliott Stoutenburgh, who was instructed to make Perry's recapture his top priority. Meanwhile, the Ledo Stockade's warden, Lieutenant Sidney Dennis, was formally reprimanded for negligence, as were eight of his guards.

Considering their rank ineptitude, Dennis and the guards got off lightly. And their bungling continued right through the postescape investigation. When the stockade guards searched Perry's tent the morning after the jailbreak, for example, they turned up nothing of value. But when Stoutenburgh's men combed the tent a week later, they discovered a stack of Perry's handwritten notes stashed behind a canvas flap. The MPs were dismayed that Dennis's guards could have missed such an obvious clue.

Disjointed and partly illegible, the notes didn't reveal where Perry might be heading. But they made clear the depth of his rage toward the Army. Perry seethed over his first court-martial conviction for insubordination, which had netted him a three-month sentence in October 1943. It wasn't the trial that bugged Perry so much as the inequities of the Ledo Stockade, particularly the guards' decision to extend his confinement by several days. He also complained about late pay, excessive punishments, and his denied request for transfer out of the 849th Engineer Aviation Battalion.

As for the time he'd spent among the Nagas, smoking ganja, hunting monkeys, and romancing a fourteen-year-old, Perry summed up his feelings with a sentence fragment: "Not a bad life."

CBI ROUNDUP, the official Army newspaper read from Bombay to Chongqing, advised soldiers to keep their eyes peeled for Perry. "WANTED FOR MURDER," a December headline blared in all-capitalized boldface, accompanied by the mug shot taken during Perry's 1941 arrest for draft evasion:

> Sentenced to death by court-martial for the murder of an Ameri-
> can Officer and awaiting final action on his record of trial, Private
> Herman Perry, 13074419, colored, escaped from the stockade at

Ledo at 0200 Saturday, 16 December 1944. This general prisoner is 5'8½" in height, weighs approximately 170 pounds, has a husky build with broad shoulders, has black bushy hair, complexion of chocolate brown, and wears a size 10½D shoe. He is a nervous type of individual, smokes cigarettes in chain fashion, and is addicted to marijuana.

His escape may have been abetted by outside help, and it is very likely that he is now equipped with arms. Knowing that his life is forfeit, he will actively resist any effort toward recapture. Perry is a fast and smooth talker with no southern or Negro accent, well educated and exceedingly dangerous. All military personnel are urged to be on the look-out for this man. Any information pertaining to this case should be reported to the nearest military authorities, the Provost Marshal, Military Police or the Criminal Investigation Division without delay.

Other media outlets picked up the Perry story, too. Radio stations, both Army and civilian, broadcast the fugitive's description in a multitude of languages. A thousand new WANTED posters were printed up, with Perry's vital statistics translated into Burmese and Kachin on the flip sides. KUMHPA GUMHPRAW 1000, the poster's Kachin section promised—a new one-thousand-rupee reward for information leading to Perry's capture. The photograph used on these posters was not the 1941 mug shot, but a picture taken in the Ledo Stockade. Perry's hair is bushy to the point of wildness, his once-bright face contorted into a dead-eyed snarl. Dog tags dangle crookedly from his sinewy neck, framed by the open collar of his olive drab fatigues.

Unsure of how to reach the most remote Naga villages, the MPs enlisted the aid of John Walker, a British political agent trusted by the tribals. Walker counseled his Naga contacts to betray Perry should they have the chance, rather than harbor the fugitive and risk

Bilingual WANTED *poster offering one thousand rupees for information leading to the capture of Private Herman Perry, early 1945.*

American reprisals. British plantation owners were also informed of Perry's flight, and asked to have their coolies watch for a black man hiding amid the tea plants.

The MPs were split on Perry's intentions: would he try to vanish into the jungles, or was he planning to avenge himself on the officers who'd sentenced him to swing? The court-martial members, as well as witnesses who'd testified for the prosecution, were told to watch their backs, lest they wind up with a dao or bullet in their spines. Lieutenant Bernard Frank, the prosecutor who'd battered Perry on the witness stand, took to sleeping with an M1 by his bedside. Hearing footsteps approach his cot late one night, the jumpy lawyer grabbed the rifle and nearly blasted his unwitting roommate.

In hopes of discerning Perry's plans, the MPs bugged the stockade tent where he'd been living; perhaps he'd blabbed to one of his fellow convicts about a jungle hideout. But the microphone revealed nothing except inane chatter.

The MPs also struck out with their policy of stopping and searching black soldiers at random, on the off chance one might be smuggling supplies to Perry. If anything, these humiliating gunpoint friskings only hardened the resolve of many African American troops—even if they feared or hated Perry, no way in hell were they going to help the heavy-handed MPs.

While teams of heat-addled German shepherds unsuccessfully sniffed around Ledo in search of Perry's scent, small aircraft dropped WANTED posters on the Patkais. Among the villages hit by the leafleting was Tgum Ga, Perry's adopted home. The illiterate Nagas, lacking a written language of their own, were unable to read the posters. But they were nonetheless pleased, even awestruck, to see photographs of the ang's son-in-law raining from the skies. The Nagas gathered all the posters they could and plastered them on the walls of his family's basha—a shrine to a brother thought lost forever, but who was now perhaps preparing for a triumphant return.

Sometimes black engineers came across the air-dropped posters, too. More often than not, they'd tear them to shreds.

THOUGH PERRY WAS no longer in Army custody, the three judge advocates in Delhi proceeded with their review of his case. Robert I. Miller's brief was dispatched from Washington via courier mail on December 18, reaching the panel right before Christmas. Just a few days later, on December 27, the panel issued a twelve-page report in the matter of *United States v. Pvt. Herman (NMI) Perry, 13074419, Company A, 849th Engineer Aviation Battalion, Advance Section #3.*

Most of the report was a straightforward rehashing of the evidence presented at trial. On page ten, however, the judge advocates raised a red flag: "It is believed that a serious irregularity appears with respect to the admission in evidence of the accused's written confessions." They expressed skepticism over whether the wounded Perry's utterances on the basha porch, which were incorporated into his written statement three days later, could be considered voluntary—there was nothing in the trial record, for example, to indicate that Perry had been informed of his rights while awaiting medical attention. And the panel worried that Perry's self-incriminating remarks had been elicited through "improper inducements"—say, a promise of speedier first aid, or an assurance that coming clean would lessen the eventual punishment.

The report criticized Captain Clayton Oberholtzer, Perry's attorney, for not pressing these issues at trial. And the court-martial members were skewered for admitting Perry's comments from the basha porch, as well as the statements he'd signed while doped-up at the Seventy-third Evacuation Hospital. Since the jungle interrogation had been improper, all of Perry's subsequent statements were tainted—"fruit of the poisonous tree," as the legal adage goes.

The Board of Review had no choice but to toss out all of Perry's pretrial confessions, both written and oral, as "illegal evidence."

Had Perry's case been handled by a civilian court, such a finding would almost certainly have been enough to warrant a new trial. But military law was less forgiving to defendants, especially those accused of the most heinous crimes. With the statements excluded, the panel now pondered whether the evidence that remained (essentially just the testimony offered at trial) was sufficient to warrant a murder conviction—and, more important, a death sentence.

The judge advocates focused on a claim that Perry had made on the stand: that Lieutenant Cady was preparing to "whale" on him in the moments before the shooting. "Mere fear of being struck by an unarmed man is not in itself sufficient to reduce the killing, with a firearm, from murder to manslaughter," they wrote.

The Board of Review never directly addressed Miller's central argument: that Perry had acted with an impulsiveness that made him guilty of manslaughter, not murder. But the judge advocates noted that Perry's repeated acts of disobedience on the morning of the shooting—his refusal to turn in his rifle, his flouting of Cady's orders to get in the jeep—indicated to them that he was "heedless of social duty" and "fatally bent on mischief." "Such a condition of the mind evidences malice," the panel concluded, "the characteristic which distinguishes murder from voluntary manslaughter."

The report ended with the Board of Review's affirmation that Miller's brief had been given "careful consideration," and that they had "subjected the record to intense scrutiny." And despite the illegal inclusion of Perry's statements at trial, the judge advocates saw no reason to overturn the conviction, nor commute the death sentence.

Had Perry still been at the Ledo Stockade, he would have been hanged without further delay. He had escaped just in time.

IN ADDITION TO the coming of the new year, the engineers had much to celebrate on the last day of 1944. They'd recently completed a 1,150-foot pontoon bridge across the Irrawaddy, and the road now extended fifteen miles beyond that mighty Burmese river's eastern bank. Chinese infantrymen were busy clearing Japanese remnants out of Wanting, a town thirteen miles north of where the Ledo and Burma roads were supposed to meet. Brigadier General Lewis Andrew Pick, the road's commander, was optimistic that the entire route from Ledo to Kunming would be navigable by early

February. He was already making plans to lead the road's first ceremonial convoy, an event designed to showcase Pick's leadership for the American press.

As the troops prepared for a beer-soaked New Year's Eve, a tip reached the ears of Major John Murray, a Criminal Investigation Division agent stationed in Ledo. A black American had been spotted at a deserted timber camp about five miles to the southwest. The camp, located in a clearing near the Burhi Dihing River, was one of countless clusters of abandoned huts that speckled the Assamese countryside.

While the engineers drank themselves into joyous oblivion that night, Murray and a posse of MPs marched toward the timber camp. Reaching their destination at sunrise, the first dawn of 1945, Murray signaled for his men to surround the derelict huts. Once the MPs were in position, their rifles trained on the bashas' doorways, Murray would call out for Perry either to surrender or face a hail of bullets. With an armed MP stationed at every turn, the fugitive would have nowhere to run.

The lightness of Perry's slumber ruined Murray's plan. The whoosh of boots brushing against grass snapped Perry into the waking world. He scanned the tree line, now backlit by the rising sun, for signs of movement, either human or tiger. He spotted several men in olive drabs darting behind the betel-nut trees, M1s slung across their backs.

Perry's mind rewound to the first time he'd been caught, when he'd foolishly dismissed the glint of Army flashlights as fireflies or some other harmless jungle phenomenon. He wasn't going to make the same mistake twice. Without so much as a second's pause, he bolted from his basha.

Still fanning out around the camp, the MPs were caught off guard by Perry's sudden flight. They unslung their rifles and fired round after round in the fugitive's direction. Yet when their ammunition ran out, there was no bullet-riddled corpse to be found—just trampled grass leading off into the woods.

Murray and his disappointed men searched the empty basha where Perry had been hiding. They found just one item of note: a loaded .45 pistol, of the sort that black GIs often bought from Chinese soldiers. Perhaps Perry had snuck into a battalion's camp and swiped the gun from a carelessly stored holster. But given how he'd obtained an M1 during his first time on the lam, the more plausible explanation was that Perry was once again receiving help from sympathizers. And if that was indeed the case, then he'd have another .45 soon enough.

WINDED FROM HIS sunrise sprint, Perry finally stopped for a breather deep within the forest. His chest was moist with sweat, not blood, and his limbs appeared free of holes. The only thing amiss was a tingling sensation in his left foot. He checked the appendage and discovered a streak of singed, torn flesh—a classic grazing wound. Had the bullet's trajectory varied by just a fraction of an inch, it would have smashed Perry's bones and left him hobbled. Fortune was smiling on him.

But his .45 was gone and the MPs were closing in. He needed to come up with a way out of Assam, and fast.

PERRY RETURNED TO being a virtual ghost after the timber-camp incident. On January 11, an Indian reported seeing a lone black American near Jaipur, about twenty miles west of Ledo. But by the time the MPs got there, Perry was nowhere to be found, and neither was the native tipster.

After that, the trail went cold. The reward money prompted plenty of leads, but most were absurd. A Kunming merchant would report having just sold Perry a scoopful of rice; a few hours later, a Calcutta madam would swear that Perry was giving the business to one of her girls. The MPs feared that, in reality, Perry had realized the Patkais were too hot to cross, too crawling with cops and natives who craved the one-thousand-rupee reward. The conventional wisdom now was that Perry had followed the Burhi Dihing to the southern bank of the Brahmaputra River, then paid a ferryman for passage to the other side. Above there lay the Miri Hills, a wild range where the Americans held no sway. If Perry had indeed traveled north of the Brahmaputra, he was doubtless gone for good.

Perry's legend grew each day, burnished by dubious scuttlebutt. GIs gossiped that Perry had only been caught the previous summer because his Naga wife had tipped off the Army; she was said to have been furious over his affair with another tribal beauty. Others whispered that Perry had been tacking taunting notes to Army bulletin boards after sneaking into camps and making off with food and guns.

Regardless of rank, the consensus was that Perry was too crafty to be taken alive. "We were all saying, They're not going to catch him," said Lieutenant Bernard Frank. "Never, ever." Newspaper reporters in India and Burma, apprised of Perry's royal status among the Nagas of Tgum Ga, gave the fugitive an adulatory nickname: the Jungle King.

As the MPs' hopes of finding Perry diminished, Brigadier General Pick was getting ready for his triumphant first drive to Kunming. The Japanese still controlled slivers of territory near Wanting, as well as the Burmese village of Namkham, twenty-six miles west of the Ledo Road's junction with the Burma Road. But Pick had been assured that the route into China would be clear by the end of January, if not sooner. The road itself wasn't really complete: several stretches were short of gravel, and many streams lacked permanent bridges capable of handling heavy traffic, to say nothing of the coming monsoons. But in the mild January climate, the road was robust enough to handle Pick's convoy.

On January 12, 113 arms-laden vehicles lined up on Ledo's outskirts; the lead truck was draped with a banner reading PICK'S PIKE—LIFE LINE FROM INDIA TO CHINA. Lieutenant General Daniel I. Sultan, commander of the recently created India-Burma theater of operations, had flown in from Delhi for the occasion. At the convoy's front, he greeted Pick with a salute and a congratulatory handshake. "You have done a splendid job," he told the Old Man with the Stick. "I am confident this is the first of many convoys to go along this road to our Chinese allies." With that, the trucks pulled out toward Hellgate, led by two white-gloved MPs on motorcycles.

The *Chicago Defender*'s Denton J. Brooks was the only reporter to accompany the convoy across the Patkais and the Hukaung Valley; the rest of the media was waiting in Myitkyina, where there'd be plenty of photo-ops as the trucks refueled and the drivers rested. Brooks observed that, although the road was in far better shape than when he'd first arrived, it was still a work in progress: "As we rolled through the late afternoon sun and into the night, there were still thousands of colored boys mounted atop bulldozers and tractors and gravel crushers widening and improving—for weather being what it is in this section of the world, this is a job which will never be completed."

Brooks also noticed the roadside engineers scanning the convoy's trucks, searching for black faces among the drivers. They were inevitably disappointed: although the majority of the road's 6x6 drivers were African American—95 percent, according to Brooks—only whites had been selected for this mission.

The convoy reached Myitkyina on the fifteenth. Here, to Pick's frustration, the journey was forced to halt for longer than planned: heavy fighting had flared up near Bhamo, less than one hundred miles from the roads' junction at Mongyu, Burma. On the plus side, the break allowed Pick to mug for the cameras; his favorite pose was to stand in the road's center and point his bamboo cane in the direction of China.

Of the forty journalists in Myitkyina, just two were black: Brooks and the *Pittsburgh Courier*'s Frank E. Bolden.* They were the only ones to ask Pick about the convoy's utter lack of African American drivers. Pick wisely realized that no good could come of this obvious racial slight, especially if it became a cause célèbre in the black press. So orders were sent back to Ledo for nine black drivers to double-time it to Myitkyina. It was a token number, representing fewer than 3 percent of the convoy's total manpower; the Ledo Road's day-to-day American workforce, by contrast, was at least two-thirds black. But nine drivers was better than nothing, and Pick's gesture was enough to coax Brooks and Bolden into keeping their journalistic fangs at bay.

The convoy finally departed Myitkyina on the twenty-third, moving jerkily up the road. The motorcade would stop upon receiving reports of artillery fire, then start again once the Imperial Japanese Army's scrappy remnants had been shelled into submission. The trucks passed countless signs erected by horny engineers, featuring pneumatic pinup girls with safety messages scrawled beneath their breasts: LISTEN, CATS / I AIN'T JIVIN' / TAKE IT EASY / WHILE YOU'RE DRIVIN'. On breaks, the drivers would explore the ruins of temples

---

*A legend of the black press, Bolden had turned to journalism when discrimination kept him out of the University of Pittsburgh's medical school. After covering the Ledo Road, which he termed a "green hell," Bolden spent fifteen days interviewing Mahatma Gandhi. Nearly two decades later, while covering the 1964 Republican National Convention, he bribed a hotel bellboy to let him into Barry Goldwater's room, where the Arizona senator was taking a bath. "I didn't know [newspapers] hired you people," a startled Goldwater told Bolden, before agreeing to an impromptu interview.

wrecked by bombs; golden Buddhas sat atop mounds of rubble, having somehow survived the onslaughts. Scattered all around were the corpses of soldiers, sun-bleached ribs protruding through their tattered, bloodstained uniforms.

The trucks reached Mongyu and the Burma Road on January 28, sixteen days after leaving Ledo. From there they proceeded the few miles north to Wanting, described by *Time*'s Theodore White as "a ruined little border town of gray, drab buildings roofed with corrugated iron." The convoy stopped for the night to rest up for the remainder of the journey; it was still another 566 miles to Kunming.

*The first official convoy over the Ledo Road passes
through Wanting, January 1945.*

The Americans awoke the next morning to find Wanting transformed. A frond-covered gate draped with gold and crimson banners now straddled the town's plank bridge, and rope archways festooned with tin plates dangled over the streets. Spectators thronged the roadsides as a Chinese band played "The Star-Spangled Banner."

Another ceremony was in order. In Wanting's dusty town square, a galaxy of American and Chinese generals addressed the cheering masses. Pick and Sultan took turns at the podium, as did Major General Claire Lee Chennault, who'd long opposed the road as part of his ego clash with the departed General Stilwell. Vinegar Joe himself, now licking his wounds in Washington, was relegated to tele-gramming a brief statement that hailed "the men who fought for [the road] and built it."

The convoy next followed the Burma Road across the Salween River Gorge, then up the steep slopes leading toward the switchback highway's terminus: seven-thousand-foot-high Kunming. They stopped to grab naps, and the drivers were surprised to awaken with driblets of frost dangling from their eyebrows; after years in the Indo-Burmese broil, they'd forgotten that cold weather existed.

Having logged nearly eleven hundred miles, the convoy reached Kunming on February 5. Long Yun, the one-eyed, opium-addicted warlord who ruled the city, greeted Pick at Kunming's western gate. Long had an important message to relay from Chiang Kai-shek: the Generalissimo had ordered that the combined Ledo and Burma roads be renamed the Stilwell Road, in honor of the former CBI commander's contributions to China's prosperity. The rechristening was an inspired insult: Chiang had ensured that Stilwell's name would forever be connected to a project widely dismissed as folly. With a proclamation that didn't cost him a single yuan, Peanut had forever tarnished Vinegar Joe's legacy.

The convoy was feted in Kunming's brick-lined streets, hailed by flag-waving residents and the scream of fireworks. "Painted prostitutes . . . mingled with merchants dressed in conservative American business suits," wrote Colonel William Boyd Sinclair, the

CBI's unofficial historian. "Coolies in rags crowded the curbs, and proud mothers and fathers held tiny children above the crowd to see the convoy." After the convoy's haul of weapons was unloaded, the Americans were treated to a grand banquet at Long's palace, where the operatic soprano Lily Pons performed.

The only Americans made to feel unwelcome in Kunming were the nine black truck drivers. There had long been a tacit understanding between Chiang and Stilwell that no African Americans would set foot on Chinese soil; it was rumored that Madame Chiang had personally insisted on the ban. The denizens of Kunming had never seen black men before, and so treated the drivers like freak-show curiosities, staring and tittering as the soldiers rolled through town. One African American sergeant described the experience as akin to being naked in public, surrounded by thousands of pairs of leering eyes.

The black drivers were sent back to India within forty-eight hours. And despite Pick's jubilant entry into Kunming, the Stilwell Road was still months away from completion.

LIKE MANY OF the railroad towns between the Brahmaputra and Ledo, Makum was known for its bustling black market. The town's woven-mat shacks housed all manner of illicit peddlers, who stocked bottles of Canadian whiskey and cartons of Lucky Strikes "liberated" from Allied shipments along the Bengal-Assam Railway.

Staff Sergeant Raymond Toomer and T/4 Otho Troxler were among the Americans availing themselves of Makum's black-market services on the evening of February 19, 1945. The two black engineers, both New Yorkers originally from the South, had come to buy some liquor. They were about to complete the transaction when Herman Perry stormed the bootlegger's shack, brandishing yet another .45 pistol—a replacement for the one he'd been forced to leave behind at the timber camp.

Perry stole ninety-five rupees from Toomer and Troxler, then forced the poor bootlegger to cook him dinner while the two GIs watched at gunpoint. As he tore into his obviously much-needed meal, Perry chatted up his countrymen. Assuming that their shared skin color made them natural allies, Perry asked Toomer and Troxler to do him a huge favor: he wanted them to bring him a truck stocked with food, fresh clothes, a tent, a knife, and ammunition for his .45. And he needed it all within twenty-four hours.

Scared of being shot should they refuse, Toomer and Troxler agreed to bring a loaded truck to Makum the following night, and then drive Perry past some nearby Army checkpoints. Satisfied that he was on the verge of acquiring the supplies and wheels he needed to flee Assam, Perry said his good-byes and slipped off into the darkness.

Toomer and Troxler were in a serious bind. It would have been one thing to get food and clothes for Perry, even a weapon. But an entire truck? The road might have been a messy operation, but someone was bound to notice a 6x6 missing from the motor pool. And if the theft were traced back to Toomer and Troxler, and their link to Perry revealed, the pair would spend the next few decades in prison.

They could, of course, just not show up for the rendezvous. But what if Perry came after them? There were rumors that Perry was out to assassinate the members of his court-martial; Toomer and Troxler didn't want their names added to the hit list.

Then there was a third option: Toomer and Troxler could tip off the police. Doing so might qualify them for the one-thousand-rupee reward, equivalent to about five months' pay. But they'd be risking the lethal wrath of their fellow African American engineers; if word got out that they'd helped the MPs nab Perry, they'd be branded the worst sorts of Uncle Toms. The Army's Jim Crow ways had convinced a lot of black GIs that their first allegiance was to their race, and then to their commanders. Besides, many among the rank and file considered the Jungle King a folk hero, a Robin Hood of the Indo-Burmese wilderness. Those soldiers wanted Perry's tale to have a happy ending, one commensurate with the courage and ingenuity he'd displayed while on the run. Heroes aren't supposed to hang.

Involuntarily sober thanks to Perry's holdup, Toomer and Troxler debated their options' pros and cons on the way back to camp. By midnight, they'd made their decision: they flagged down an MP patrol jeep and said they had some valuable information regarding Herman Perry. The MPs drove the pair to the headquarters of the 159th Military Police Battalion at nearby Chabua Air Base. There they were ushered into an emergency meeting with the 159th's commander: Major Earl Owen Cullum.

In LATER YEARS, when asked to cite what he loved most in life, the tall, taciturn Cullum wouldn't mention God or family. The two great passions that defined his character, he'd say without a hint of irony, were national defense and law enforcement.

Yet Cullum had a third obsession, one he shared with countless other born-and-bred Texans: storytelling. Though not particularly deft with the written word, Cullum would fanatically chronicle his life in letters, articles, and even a self-published, spiral-bound booklet. Without Cullum's compulsion to leave behind a detailed record of his achievements, without his yen to be remembered as the Perfect Texan, Perry's saga might have faded into obscurity. The embarrassed Army tried hard to destroy evidence of the Perry imbroglio; Cullum, for reasons both selfish and sincere, made sure the story stayed alive.

An avid genealogist, Cullum traced his family's roots back to William the Conqueror. He was born in Corpus Christi in 1913, and proudly claimed that his "first outing in a baby buggy was to the nearby Alamo." Cullum grew up in Dallas and attended North Dallas High, where he was a ROTC cadet and football letterman; he played in the inaugural high-school game at the Cotton Bowl, now a Texas landmark. Cullum's next stop was Texas A&M University, with its celebrated ROTC program, but the Depression forced him to drop out and work at his father's grocery store.

Cullum joined the Army's reserve corps in 1937, then the Dallas Police Department two years later. When World War II began, he

Major Earl Owen Cullum poses in his jeep, circa 1945.

had the ideal résumé to become a military policeman. He wound up a captain at Michigan's Fort Custer, teaching 90 Day Wonders how to direct traffic using hand signals. In August 1943, he was ordered to the CBI, where he was first assigned to investigate thefts from the Calcutta docks. Cullum quickly worked his way up the MP ranks, becoming the provost marshal of Chabua in less than a year; he liked to point out that he was "responsible for 1,250 men, more than a George Washington regiment, or Harrison's army at Tippecanoe, or Houston's army at San Jacinto, or Stuart's force that rode around General McClellan's army." Cullum, like Brigadier General Pick, also enjoyed posing for flattering photographs: in one of his favorites, he's casually perched in the driver's seat of his jeep, the right side of his face artfully shaded by jungle flora. He looks like a leaner version of William Holden in *Force of Arms*, with a smoldering gaze and oversize ears.

Before Toomer and Troxler showed up, Cullum's involvement in the Perry manhunt had been minimal. He'd taken a surveillance flight over the Patkais and had been a member of the posse that took a futile trip to Jaipur on January 11. Like many of his comrades, Cullum figured that Perry had long since left the Ledo area, and was likely on the northern side of the Brahmaputra by now—a theory disproved by the engineers' late-night tip.

Cullum proposed setting a trap, with Toomer and Troxler as bait. The two GIs would show up as promised in a supply-filled truck. When Perry appeared and began to approach the 6x6, MPs crouched in the roadside trees would pounce, firing if necessary—Perry was condemned anyway, so there was no good reason to bring him in alive.

For safety's sake, Cullum refused to stock the truck with .45 ammunition; in case Perry somehow made it to the vehicle, he didn't want his MPs pinned down by gunfire. And Cullum swore his men to secrecy regarding Toomer and Troxler's complicity in the trap; if word got around that the two GIs had betrayed the Jungle King, they'd face violent retribution from their peers.

About an hour past sunset on February 20, as the MPs tiptoed into position, Toomer and Troxler parked the loaded truck just south of Makum. Cullum knelt down alongside a Criminal Investigation Division agent named Edwin Wheeler, who was armed with a sub-machine gun. Wheeler had worked for the Border Patrol back in Texas; Cullum felt he could trust him.

A figure finally appeared along the foggy road, moving toward the truck. But it wasn't Perry—it was a dhoti-clad native, most likely a coolie. And he wasn't alone: Cullum could see other similarly attired men emerging from the haze, walking shoulder to shoulder with one another. Pretty soon there was a slew of Indians marching in the direction of the 6x6; it was too dark to tell if Perry was hiding in their midst.

The MPs were at a loss. Even if one of them managed to spot Perry, they couldn't just open fire on a pack of coolies. Strict orders precluded them from doing so: the Army needed to avoid antagonizing the Indian laborers, without whom road construction would stall.

Cullum reckoned that Perry might have engaged the coolies as errand boys to pick up the truck and drive it elsewhere. Perhaps Perry was even watching this curious scene from a safe distance, waiting to see if the MPs pounced.

Whatever his game, one thing was certain: Perry had anticipated a trap, and had hatched an ingenious plan to avoid it. It seemed he'd put the ninety-five rupees he'd stolen the previous night to good use, hiring the coolies to befuddle any potential ambushers.

As the bewildered MPs looked to one another for guidance, Perry suddenly rose up from the middle of the huddle and sprinted for the rear of the canvas-covered truck. The natives immediately scattered, melting back into the woods.

Cullum swallowed hard as Perry ran, praying that his men wouldn't fire. Even the most expert sniper couldn't have hit Perry, so quickly did the fugitive dash from behind his coolie shield to the 6x6. Shooting would just blow the MPs' cover, and thus play right into Perry's hands.

To Cullum's great relief, his MPs didn't panic. Having made it into the truck without being shot at, Perry presumed that his black comrades hadn't squealed—no way the trigger-happy MPs wouldn't try and cut him down if given half a chance.

So Toomer and Troxler had passed the test of racial allegiance; they were solid. Perry tapped the cab and ordered Troxler, the driver, to get a move on.

Toomer knew it was time to set Cullum's backup plan in motion: if the initial trap failed, Toomer was supposed to tell Perry that the first MP checkpoint lay just a few hundred yards ahead. He'd then suggest to Perry that they get out, walk around the checkpoint, and meet Troxler and the 6x6 on the other side. While they walked, the MPs would creep from behind and reset their trap.

Perry trusted Toomer at this point, so he agreed to hop out and hoof it around the checkpoint. Troxler promised that he'd be waiting down the road after feeding the guards a bullshit line about his destination.

As arranged that morning, Toomer guided Perry toward a grassy patch that Cullum had designated as his Plan B hideout. Toomer moved as slowly and circuitously as possible, giving the MPs ample time to take up their new positions.

Squatting silently in the grass, Cullum waited until he could see two sets of fatigue-clad legs striding along the road's edge—the informer and the target. The most wanted man in South Asia was just a few yards away.

Cullum sprang to his feet, followed by the heavily armed Wheeler. Cullum repeated the words that Captain Walter McMinn had uttered exactly six months earlier near Tgum Ga: "Don't move, Perry."

Toomer hit the ground. Perry turned and ran for the other side of the road.

Cullum expected the next sound he heard to be the splutter of Wheeler's submachine gun perforating Perry's back with bullets. But there was a long pause, followed by only a single shot: Wheeler had flicked off his gun's automatic setting. Cullum was sure it was because the border patrolman lacked the heart to kill.

Cullum whipped out his pistol and emptied his clip into the Assamese gloom; his MPs followed suit with more than two dozen shots. But as at the timber camp in December, there was no sign of Perry once the smoke had cleared, save for a smattering of trampled vegetation.

When Cullum stepped forward to check which way Perry had fled, he felt something warm and squishy in his left shoe: blood. He'd been hit in the leg by friendly fire, probably a ricochet off a boulder. He needed to sprinkle the wound with sulfa powder or else gangrene would set in. The manhunt would have to wait.

PANTING IN THE pitch-black woods, Herman Perry checked his body for bullet holes. He'd been nicked by grazing shots to his hip and left foot, but neither injury was worse than a bad scrape. The only wound that really stung was on his right foot—a bullet had passed in and out of the flesh near his Achilles tendon. No bones had been broken, but blood was pouring out at an alarming rate.

Given the unsanitary nature of the jungle, it wouldn't take long for an infection to develop.

Perry felt around the surrounding trees. When his hand alighted on a fuzzy patch of moss, he ripped off a hunk and stuffed it in the wound—a Naga trick he'd learned in Glau.

Perry checked the waistband of his olive drabs. The .45 was still there.

FOURTEEN

E ven with the bleeding stanched by tree moss, Perry's foot was throbbing. He needed to put some distance between himself and the MPs who'd just tried to kill him, but the pain was too intense. He'd have to find a place to rest, then figure it out from there.

Perry hobbled through the darkened woods until he came to a rice paddy. The monsoons were still weeks away, so the soil beneath the plants was dry. The paddy's edge struck Perry as a decent hideout; he could take cover amid the thin green stalks, nibbling on husks for sustenance. Hopefully his foot would improve in a few days' time. And while he was on the mend, he could hatch another plan to flee Assam, one that didn't rely on the kindness of fellow soldiers. Perry had learned the hard way that no one could be trusted, no matter the color of their skin.

He curled up in the dirt and dozed for hours, until his sleep was interrupted by the frenzied barks of German shepherds. Perry rose up to see members of the Army's War Dog Detachment weaving through the betel-nut trees. Trained to scout for Japanese machine-gun nests, these dogs had been deployed to great effect at the battle of Myitkyina. They'd have no trouble sussing out a warm human body between the rows of rice.

Perry had to suck up the pain and move. He broke across the dried-out paddy, his torso well above the three-foot-high plants. He was now a clear, if moving, target for T/5 Robert Fullerton, one of the German shepherds' handlers.

Fullerton lifted his carbine and waited for Perry to cross his field of vision. He aimed for the fugitive's head.

A bullet zinged past Perry's face, so close he felt the breeze. Perry just kept on running until he reached the paddy's other side, where a copse of trees provided cover.

Perry clawed at his face, startled to have survived such a close encounter with a carbine round. That's when he realized there was a nick of flesh missing from the tip of his nose; the bullet had clipped him ever so slightly. Perry rubbed another clump of moss into the wound, then sped on as best he could.

Fullerton and his dog-team cohorts couldn't believe Perry's luck. For the third time since New Year's Day, the Jungle King had evaded bullets, then disappeared. There was something almost supernatural about Perry's knack for elusion, as if he just wasn't meant to be caught.

HIS RICOCHET WOUND salved with powder, Major Earl Owen Cullum returned to his office on the morning of February 22. On his desk was a buckslip* from Brigadier General Joseph A. Cranston, Cullum's boss at Chabua Air Base. Cranston had heard about the botched trap at Makum, as well as the previous day's near miss in

---

*A package insert the size of a dollar bill, used principally to list contents.

the rice paddy. He had decided to blame Cullum, head of the 159th Military Police Battalion, for all of the manhunt's failings.

"Perry is giving you the 'runaround' literally," Cranston chided in his two-line note. "Are you going to let him get away with it?"

For an organization man like Cullum, so religiously devoted to the Army way, Cranston's rebuke was a powerful motivator—a small testament, perhaps, to the general's managerial genius. Cullum was genuinely ashamed to have disappointed a superior, and determined to work himself out of the doghouse. He felt no special enmity toward Perry; truth be told, he found himself oddly admiring of the fugitive's grit. But as long as Perry roamed free, Cullum would reside on Cranston's shit list. And that was something he couldn't abide.

Cullum folded up the general's snide note and stowed it in a drawer for safekeeping.

PERRY FINALLY LIMPED back to the Ledo (now Stilwell) Road on the twenty-second, with a new plan in mind. This time he'd take a cue from the 849th's beer-stealing scheme, in which engineers had unloaded cases of lager from slow-moving trucks. Perry would similarly creep behind a lumbering 6x6, but instead of filching beer he'd hop aboard and ride over the Patkais, concealing himself behind crates. Once he felt the road's gradient start to level out—an indication that the truck had traveled well into Burma—he'd leap off and roll into the bush.

Stowing away on a 6x6 was a major gamble: MP checkpoints were everywhere, and inspections were the norm. But Perry was skidding into despair. He'd take the risk.

Hunkered down in the roadside weeds, Perry saw an eastbound truck crawl by. He gave chase, steadily gaining ground as the 6x6 puttered along. A few feet from the rear bumper, Perry jumped for the truck's canvas-covered back. But he'd misjudged how much his gimpy foot would affect his hops: he fell short of the mark, glancing off the bumper and crashing to the gravel. His .45 pistol skittered out of its holster, ending up yards away from his body.

Splayed out on the road, skin scraped raw and bones rattled, Perry watched his ride to Burma disappear. He then realized that he wasn't the only spectator: a coolie stood gawking by a culvert, having witnessed the whole sorry affair. Before the coolie could call for his sahib, the dazed Perry picked himself up off the gravel and staggered back into the woods. He left the .45 behind.

Perry had once again failed to make it out of Assam, except this time he'd lost his pistol and suffered a crunching fall as well. His foot ached; his stomach gurgled with hunger pangs. And the unraveling situation was about to take a dire turn: the microorganisms that cause dysentery were swimming through Perry's gut, an inevitable consequence of drinking from the Burhi Dihing River and its tributaries. However awful Perry felt in the moments right after his futile leap, he was about to feel a whole lot worse.

UNAWARE OF THEIR hero's fraying health, many black engineers continued to revere Perry. The outlaw's popularity became clear when Staff Sergeant Raymond Toomer and T/4 Otho Troxler, the two GIs who'd snitched to Cullum and had helped set up the Makum trap, foolishly mentioned their duplicity to some comrades. Word quickly spread that Perry's admirers were keen to murder Toomer and Troxler in revenge; the Army had to evacuate the threatened pair from Asia.

The Jungle King's saga bore an uncanny resemblance to that of Corporal David Fagen, a veteran of the Spanish-American War. In 1899, Fagen's unit, the African American Twenty-fourth Infantry

Regiment, was transferred from Cuba to the Philippines, which a defeated Spain had recently ceded to the United States. The Filipinos, however, were not interested in swapping one colonial overlord for another: the nationalist leader Emilio Aguinaldo had declared the Philippines an independent republic. By the time Fagen arrived, an anti-American insurgency was in full swing.

Fagen, who'd fought alongside Teddy Roosevelt's Rough Riders at the battle of San Juan Hill, felt gravely wronged by his commanders in the Philippines. He complained about being assigned to menial jobs despite his extensive combat experience, and he was disturbed by the frequency of American atrocities; during one campaign, a general instructed his soldiers to "kill everyone over the age of ten." Such brutality, Fagen believed, was enabled by the racism of his white comrades, who disparaged the Filipinos as "niggers," "black devils," or "goo goos." In letters home, American soldiers often described their mission as the extermination of all so-called goo goos; one declared that shooting Filipinos "beats rabbit hunting all to pieces."

Aware of the racial friction within their enemy's ranks, the native *insurectos* did their best to encourage defections. They disseminated leaflets addressed to "The Colored American Soldier," which characterized Filipinos and African Americans as oppressed brothers and compared southern lynchings to the atrocities committed against Filipino villagers. Black soldiers who deserted to the insurectos were promised officers' commissions, an honor they could never receive in the segregated U.S. Army.

On the night of November 17, 1899, Fagen snuck out of his regiment's camp to meet an insurecto agent, who was waiting with two horses. The pair galloped off to the slopes of Mount Arayat, a dormant volcano and guerrilla stronghold near the city of Angeles. After swearing his allegiance to the Filipino cause, Fagen was promoted

to the rank of captain by his new compatriots. He would soon become one of the nationalists' most brilliant and feared commanders,
specializing in the harassment of American units on the island of
Luzon. Fagen was said to enjoy taunting his former superiors in the
heat of battle, once announcing an ambush with the pithy declaration, "Captain Fagen done got yuh white boys now!"

The Americans posted a sizeable dead-or-alive reward for Fagen's
capture, but the defector proved a slippery target: his flair for escap-
ing close calls, even when surrounded and hugely outnumbered,
defied belief. In December 1901, however, a Filipino turncoat finally
claimed the bounty by delivering a severed black head to an Army
camp. The *Indianapolis Freeman*, an African American newspaper,
lamented the apparent end of Fagen's run: "Fagen was a traitor and
died a traitor's death, but he was a man no doubt prompted by honest motives to help a weakened side, and one he felt allied [to] by
bonds that bind."

Many in the Philippines refused to believe that the brave and wily
Fagen had met such an ignominious end. They speculated that the
head belonged to one of Fagen's ambush victims, and that he'd orchestrated the ruse to throw the Army off his trail. Fagen, his admirers swore, lived out his natural life in the jungles of Luzon, along
with his gorgeous Filipina wife.

Compared to Fagen, a man driven by moral outrage, Perry was a
rather uninspiring character. Perry hadn't deserted for political reasons, nor had he taken up arms against his country; he far preferred
licentiousness to battle, and his only real cause was self-preservation.
When Fagen felt wronged by the system, he defected to a foreign
army; when Perry felt similarly aggrieved, he medicated himself with
ganja and opium, then fell apart.

The accidental nature of Perry's folk heroism, however, is precisely what endeared him to the Ledo Road's underclass. Perry was

the black enlisted Everyman, treated with contempt from the day he was drafted, judged too dim for anything more complex than crushing rocks. When this decidedly ordinary GI lashed out, many of his comrades thought they grasped the reason why. And perhaps they secretly wished they had the guts to do the same.

On top of that, Perry had embarrassed the 90 Day Wonders again and again, armed only with his wits and a couple of dinky .45s. The Army had obviously wasted Perry's talents by putting a shovel in his hand; his jungle feats disproved the Jim Crow lie.

But one man's folk hero is another man's villain. The MPs chafed at Perry's growing legend, and their grumbling soon turned ugly. In the mimeographed pages of the *Assam Police Gazette*, published by members of Cullum's battalion, Perry was nicknamed the "Chocolate Brown Kid . . . the possum of the Possum Hunting Club sponsored by the Assam Military Police." The *Gazette*'s reporters exhibited a modicum of respect for Perry's cunning, but also took disconcerting pleasure at the prospect of seeing him hang:

> A colored Houdini from the USA aided by a few Naga tricks is sure playing "hob" with the traps that have been set for him. He has turned cart-wheels and tap danced over and through rice paddies and tea patches with the grace and abandon of a Gypsy Rose Lee in her best strip tease. Firstly, he slides by his enemy taking off a cap then as the chase warms he discards a jacket following with true professional "art," a shoe and lastly, in utter disregard for feelings in this "mad stripper" gaily tosses away his shoulder holster and his "heater" (pistol to you). Woe be unto that colored boy when he takes off his rabbit's foot cause then he is through and I mean all finished. . . .
>
> Do not be dismayed men, one day the "Stripper" will lose his luck and then it will be our turn to make him "dance."

———

CULLUM KNEW THE manhunt would fail if he just waited around Chabua for a lucky break. In order to reach the air base's offices, tips on Perry's whereabouts had to wend their way from natives to local officials to Army underlings, a process that could take hours, even days. If Cullum wished to follow up on one of these belated leads, he'd have to drive out to the fugitive's reported location, perhaps thirty miles away or more; by the time he got there, Perry would almost certainly be long gone. Returning to Chabua empty-handed, Cullum would then be subject to more of Cranston's scolding, or to the not-so-gentle ribbing of his peers.

Cullum decided it was better to go mobile with the manhunt. Along with a handpicked crew of MPs, he packed up some rations and struck out for Perry's last-known coordinates near Ledo. Cullum and his men started to live like fugitives themselves, overnighting in backcountry huts instead of returning to base. They supplemented their diets with parched grub worms and scoops of monkey stew purchased from Assamese villagers. And they slept fitfully on five-foot-long bamboo racks, which couldn't quite accommodate the six-foot-two Cullum.

Rather than radio back to Chabua for third-hand leads, Cullum relied on intelligence gathered by the Assam Police, a British-led civilian force that patrolled the Brahmaputra Plains. Cops fanned out to the villages and tea gardens that abutted the Bengal-Assam Railway, gleaning tales of a black man seen begging for food, or of barking dogs that heralded the presence of a stranger. Villagers told of finding piles of human excrement in odd places, a surefire sign of a trespasser. These reports of suspicious activity were collected and shared with Cullum, who called on local police stations daily.

Analyzing these scattershot clues revealed a discernible pattern: Perry was moving south, away from the well-trafficked Stilwell Road. He appeared to be heading in the direction of Namrup, a railroad town where the Disang River bends into a gentle U. If Perry followed the river's southeastern branch, it would lead him straight up the Patkais. It was hardly the most direct route back to Tgum Ga; if he crossed the Indo-Burmese border at Pongchau, a village near the Disang's source, Perry would have to hike another fifty to sixty miles over rough terrain. But he would also be among friends: ten miles south of Namrup was an unofficial gateway to the Naga heartland. On both sides of the Patkais' jungled slopes, Perry might encounter some tribals with whom he shared a language, or even family ties.

Cullum knew he'd be the scapegoat should Perry vanish into Burma, much as Captain Eugene Kirk, the Ledo provost marshal, had taken the rap for Perry's jailbreak. Given the fugitive's apparent pace, Cullum had a few days left before the trail dead-ended at the Patkais. After that, there would be an eternal blemish on his law-and-order record; Perry would be Cullum's white whale.

Fortified by hunks of roasted dog, Cullum marched through the desolate villages that stretched along the train tracks: Bardubi, Duliajan, Naharkatiya. The police there told stories of a black man seen gnawing on stolen stalks of sugarcane, grubby olive drabs hanging off his increasingly sickly frame.

Cullum reached Namrup on March 9, taking a much-needed breather at an office run by the 748th Railway Operating Battalion, an Army maintenance unit. Inspector K. Dutta, one of Cullum's valued Assam Police sources, stopped by for a chat.

As the two compared notes on alleged Perry sightings, an Indian named Arun Handrique came calling. Handrique, the assistant police chief in nearby Jaipur, spoke rapidly to Dutta in Assamese. Cullum didn't have a clue what was being said, but Dutta was obviously rapt. When the conversation ended, Dutta told Cullum in his stiff English, "I think we get the man now."

Perry, Dutta explained, had been spotted sleeping in a basha just south of the Disang. Handrique, who'd been tipped off by some farmers, warned that Perry might have a pistol tied to his wrist.

Cullum quickly assembled a posse, starting with Dutta, Handrique, and their English boss, Superintendent Baker Routledge. Rounding out the group were three of Cullum's most trusted MPs, who'd been accompanying him through the boonies of Assam: Sergeant Earl Gainor, Corporal Bernard Black, and Private George Crosby. The seven men piled into jeeps, bound for Perry's rumored hideout.

The basha was truly remote. Cullum and his posse drove three miles down a country lane, then parked and hiked another two miles along a railroad spur.* The spur eventually halted at the shallow Disang. Beyond that lay a jumble of trees, crowned by the haze-shrouded Patkais.

Cullum thought back to his botched trap near Makum. He'd identified two major flaws with that plan: too many MPs to manage, and a wingman who'd lacked the guts to kill. Cullum decided that only he, Handrique, and one other soldier would cross the Disang. He selected Crosby, who'd been an infantryman before transferring to the 159th. Looking into Crosby's eyes, Cullum could tell the young man had the balls to shoot a fellow American, at point-blank range if necessary.

Night had now fallen. The trio removed their boots, rolled up their pants, and waded across the cold Disang. Handrique guided Cullum and Crosby through the woods to a small clearing. An open-

*A railway line that branches off the main tracks. This particular spur was used to haul tea to the Bengal-Assam Railway.

fronted, one-room basha lay ahead. To its side, three dhoti-clad natives were warming their hands around a fire.

From a distance, Crosby silently trained his submachine gun on the natives as Cullum tiptoed toward the hut. He peered inside—empty.

Cullum now looked over at the men around the fire. Something about the group struck him as not quite right.

HIS INTESTINES SHREDDED by dysentery and his vigor sapped by malnutrition, Perry was rapidly losing hope. He'd stayed alive these past few weeks by begging Assamese farmers for handfuls of rice, taking advantage of the Hindu creed that householders "should not turn away any who comes at eating time and asks for food." But aware of the one-thousand-rupee price on his head, Perry never lingered too long in anyone's company. Even the most generous friend could have ulterior motives.

When he'd lived in Tgum Ga, Perry had refused to swap his Army fatigues for Naga dress. But he'd come to realize that his insistence on American clothing was foolish: olive drabs made him conspicuous in the fields of northern Assam. So he had coaxed a farmer into lending him a dhoti, then pared back his increasingly wild Afro into something less outrageous. Perry hoped to pass for a coolie, at least from a distance or at night.

Having spent the day convalescing in a farmer's field basha, Perry now huddled around his host's fire—Assamese hospitality at its finest. He was feverish from the dysentery, so the warmth of the flames surely felt good against his clammy flesh. The radiant moon, just six nights shy of full, revealed the outline of the nearby Patkais; the range's foothills lay less than ten miles to the south.

The Naga heartland was just two days' walk, maybe three. With a bit more of his trademark luck, Perry might even be able to resume his "not bad," proto-hippie life in Tgum Ga before the first monsoon hit. And if he managed to do so, he'd likely have a newborn to welcome him—nearly eight months had passed since he'd last seen his pregnant wife.

But Perry was also tired, very tired, having endured a lifetime's worth of hardships in a single year. He now bore little resemblance to his prewar self, the upbeat lover from Florida Avenue. Not yet twenty-three years old, he could easily have passed for a decrepit thirty-five. Sunburnt skin hung off his emaciated frame, giving him the weathered appearance of a desert-island castaway. His face was wrinkled with paranoia, his once-luminous eyes now scrunched and heavy with suspicion.

As close as the Patkai foothills were, the way up the mountains was daunting; there'd be plenty of tigers en route to Tgum Ga, and plenty of rocky, vine-choked trails to torment his injured foot. Even if Perry survived the trek, how long until the MPs tracked him down again—they'd found Tgum Ga once before, why not again? Or what if a Naga betrayed him for the thousand rupees? Constant fear was the only certainty in Perry's future.

How far he was from the days of promenading through Meridian Hill Park, a dapper playboy walking arm in arm with Alma Talbot, the scent of perfume wafting off her neck.

While taking comfort in the fire's heat, Perry noticed something out of the corner of his eye: a lanky white man approaching from the basha, a carbine in his hand. Perry was unarmed—despite reports to the contrary, he hadn't managed to score another .45 after his failed leap two weeks earlier.

As he ran up on the trio of dhoti-clad men, Cullum noticed one of them trying to hide behind the other two. Cullum lunged and grabbed the shrinking violet by the wrist.

Sick, injured, and exhausted, the Jungle King could muster only three meek words: "You got me."

Cullum dropped his carbine to the ground, stomping his foot on the gun so no one could make a dive for it. Not that Perry's two friends had any interest in doing so: they'd already split for the woods. Crosby, Cullum's gun-toting wingman, wisely held his fire.

Cullum tossed the weakened Perry to the ground, pinning him down with a knee to the sternum; he instantly sensed how dysentery and malnutrition had eroded Perry's strength. He pulled out a flashlight and fixed the beam on Perry's naked chest: two bullet-size scars, clear as day.

There hadn't been any handcuffs in Namrup, so Cullum bound the Jungle King's wrists with strips torn from the prisoner's dhoti. He remembered that Handrique's informants had spoken of a pistol tied to one of Perry's wrists, and Cullum wondered if it was hidden in the bush. But there was no time to look now—all that mattered was getting the theater's most wanted criminal back to Chabua.

Cullum led Perry through the woods, back to the southern bank of the Disang. Cullum told Crosby and the other MPs to open fire if Perry made a false move. But escape was no longer on Perry's mind. Instead he pulled Cullum's hand close as the two traversed the river, squeezing tightly to steady himself atop the pebbly streambed.

Cullum was taken aback by the resignation evident in his captive's manner. He'd always respected Perry as a worthy adversary. But now that they'd come face-to-face, had clasped hands while wading across the Disang, Cullum realized that it wasn't just respect he felt—it was something closer to empathy. Looking at the withered young man he'd soon help hang, a curious thought occurred to Cullum: how easily their roles could have been reversed, by nothing more than accident of birth.

That riddle of existence, unsolvable and also sad, would come to haunt the Perfect Texan.

THE POSSE DROVE through the night, first stopping at Namrup so Cullum could wire the Delhi bigwigs:

CONDEMNED ESCAPEE MURDERER HERMAN PERRY CAPTURED 2000 HOURS NINE MARCH NEAR NAMRUP BY CULLUM AND 159 MP BATTALION SEARCH TEAM. NO GUNFIRE AND NO INJURIES. KILLER APPEARS IN GOOD CONDITION. BEING TAKEN TO 234 GENERAL HOSPITAL FOR EXAM AND TREATMENT OF EXISTING WOUNDS. THEN TO CHABUA STOCKADE FOR SAFEKEEPING.

From Namrup they proceeded north to the Burhi Dihing, loading their jeeps one by one onto a flimsy bamboo raft. Before daybreak they reached Chabua, where Perry was admitted to the hospital. All things considered, the doctors were astounded by his fitness. The moss had kept his wounded nose and foot free of infections, and Perry had somehow avoided diseases far grislier than dysentery.

Cullum went to his office and pulled out Cranston's note. He'd waited eighteen days to answer the general's cutting question: "Are you going to let him get away with it?"

On the same buckslip, Cullum scribbled out a face-saving rejoinder sure to earn him a promotion:

No sir! Please excuse the delay. Perry was captured at 2010 on 9 March by M.P. Pvt. Crosby and myself. He is in our stockade now.

All credit is due to Mr. Routledge and his Assam Police. They got the info and led us to him.

A full report will be submitted following a little sleep.

And now—will you erase that "Black Mark" from our score sheet?

When he arrived for work that morning, Cranston found the buckslip on his desk. The general immediately wrote a letter to the Delhi brass, informing them of Cullum's fine work: "I am happy to report to you that Perry is in custody again and hope that he will remain there 'till the noose takes over."

Less thrilled to hear about the imminent execution was Arun Handrique, the Assamese policeman who had crossed the Disang with Cullum. It was not until Handrique reached Chabua that he

Perry, Cullum (center), and an Army medic at the Chabua Stockade.

learned of Perry's death sentence; as a devout Hindu, he was morti-
fied to have played a role, however small, in the killing of a fellow
human being. "If I had known that he was going to be hanged,"
Handrique confided to an American acquaintance, "I wouldn't have
reported him."

Bandaged and dosed with sulfa drugs, Perry was released from the
hospital after only a few hours. He was taken to the Chabua Stockade
and locked in an isolation cell surrounded by its own barbed-wire
fence. Sergeant Gainor, one of the MPs who'd accompanied Cullum
on the arrest mission, was put in charge of the guard detail. Security
could scarcely have been tighter if Hitler himself were the prisoner:
whenever Perry went to answer nature's call, for instance, MPs armed
with Tommy guns trailed him to the john and watched.

Gainor tried coaxing Perry into revealing how he'd obtained his
pistols, and to name the engineers who'd abetted his flight. But Perry
wouldn't snitch. According to Gainor, Perry just claimed to be halfway relieved he'd been caught, since "it's no fun to be hunted like a
wild beast, knowing that any minute it may end with a slug in the
right place." He expressed regret over Cady's death, but hastened to
add that he'd have killed his pursuers if given the chance. As for his
impending punishment, Perry seemed nonchalant: "If I hang for it,"
he told Gainor, "I'll hang like a man."

The instructions for the hanging came straight from Delhi: the
execution was scheduled for the morning of March 15, on a gallows
to be built outside Ledo Stockade. The date was to be kept secret,
even from Perry, for security's sake: there were reports that black GIs
were stocking up on munitions in order to rescue their hero, or at
least start a massive, bloody riot in his honor. These rumors reached
Brigadier General Lewis Andrew Pick, the road's chief engineer. He
wired an urgent message to Delhi, pleading that Perry be held at
Chabua until the hanging: "IT IS IMPERATIVE THAT PERRY NOT REPEAT

NOT BE RETURNED TO LEDO FOR CONFINEMENT." Pick worried that the stockade's notoriously inept guards couldn't withstand an organized assault by black engineers.

So Perry was to be imprisoned at Chabua until the appointed hour, never given the slightest hint as to when he'd be carted off to the gallows. This was in violation of official Army policy, which mandated that condemned prisoners be notified twenty-four hours in advance of their executions. But Cullum, normally a stickler for the rules, saw fit to break this one: the threat of a racially charged uprising was simply too great.

PERRY WAS SHAKEN awake well before dawn on March 15. The guards led him to a line of five jeeps, placing him in the third. They tied his shackled hands to an eyebolt on the jeep's floor. A wool blanket was tossed over his body to shield him from the early morning chill.

There were seventeen MPs in the escort convoy, including Cullum. They were under strict orders: should gunfire erupt from the roadside, Perry was to be summarily shot.

The ambush didn't happen. The convoy made it to Ledo at 6:15 A.M., just as the sun came peeking over the Patkais to the east. Perry could see the gallows' crossbeam jutting over a canvas-draped fence. Dozens of guards ringed the site, their backs to the scaffold and guns at the ready—the attack might still be coming. The Army, cognizant of avoiding the appearance of a lynching, had made sure that several of the guards were black. All of the stockade's inmates, meanwhile, had been moved to a distant exercise yard—ostensibly for calisthenics, but really to minimize the odds of a riot.

Upon seeing precisely where his neck was to be snapped, Perry turned to Cullum: "Now," he said, "the Hell will start."

Just inside the stockade's gates, the death warrant was read aloud. Perry was asked if he had any last requests. Yes, he answered—a pencil and paper, so he could write a farewell letter to his brother Aaron. Last Herman had heard, Aaron was undergoing basic training at Maryland's Fort Meade. He needed his younger sibling to be the family's rock:

Dear Brother,

Heres a letter that may knock your hat to one side this a.m. I walk the last mile with the same smile I had when I saw you fight I don't want you to take it so hard Mother told me you were quite worried about me Well don't be I am safe from all harm or at least I will be in a few minutes.

I don't know what to say to cheer you up your being in the Army won't help, stick it out kid, make the best of it the army will give you a break if you do right so there.

I did wrong myself please dont make the same mistake its very easy to get in trouble but hell to get out of take it from me I know Almost three years in the army and I wind up like this. You will take my advice wont you. You must spare mother any more pain while I die once she will die a thousand times see if you can get a pass go to her spend every second with her you can she needs it

There must be someone with her at all times for a while if you can make it to her please go right away guess Ill have to close here.

Dont answer.

It was now 7:00 A.M. Escorted from the stockade to the adjacent gallows, Perry was handed a final cigarette. Cullum was among the sixty or so people in the audience; witnessing the execution was part of his job. But as Perry ascended the scaffold, Cullum walked away,

The last-known photograph of Herman Perry, March 1945.

unable to bear the sight. Pleased as he was with the manhunt's success, Cullum couldn't help but feel that he'd taken part in something slightly monstrous.

Cullum was gone, but the *Chicago Defender*'s Denton J. Brooks remained. He was scribbling notes for an account of Perry's last moments. In Brooks's nimble prose, Perry would become the epitome of the stoic black GI, nobly enduring the unendurable: "Mannerly and well-bred when not cornered, Perry won the admiration of officers forced to witness the execution for his cool courage in the face of certain death. Never once did he break, even as he walked upstairs to the gallows platform."

In the Army's segregationist spirit, a black chaplain had been assigned to offer Perry solace, and a black medic recruited to deal with Perry's corpse. The chaplain lacked the nerves for the job: standing next to the noose, he burst into tears. Perry was the one who had to do the consoling. "Don't cry, Chaplain," he said. "I'm the one who's going." Perry then asked the minister to write his mother back in Washington, and to pray for her continued health.

A guard came forward with a hood, which Perry declined. But the guard insisted: it was an Army regulation that condemned men wear hoods or blindfolds. "Oh, well, I don't want to break any rules," Perry deadpanned. The hood went on.

The CBI lacked an experienced executioner, and so the noose was crudely tied—just a slipknot, with a leather strap spliced on and angled to catch the jawbone's corner. The trapdoor was propped up with a ladder; when the moment came, an MP would pull it away and let gravity take over.

Perry, hooded and bound, slipped his head inside the rope circle. The hangman, an Army colonel, adjusted the leather strap to just beneath Perry's cauliflowered ear.

The signal was given. The ladder was pulled.

THE JUNGLE KING thrashed around for a few minutes—the crude noose hadn't worked as intended. But the struggling eventually stopped, and Perry's legs went slack.

The MPs let him swing for a quarter of an hour, just to make sure. Finally, the black medic was allowed to check the flaccid body. No pulse, no breath.

Perry was placed in a coffin and driven to the Army cemetery in Margherita, where Lieutenant Harold Cady had also been buried. They dug Perry a grave about one hundred yards from everyone else's, beneath a droopy tree and behind a foot-high hedge—forever separated from his comrades, as the Army's final show of disrespect.

The grave site soon became a macabre tourist attraction. Soldiers stopped by with their Kodaks to photograph the crooked white cross that marked the infamous Perry's resting place.

ON ST. PATRICK'S DAY, a letter arrived at the redbrick row house at 3217 Warder Street NW, in Washington, D.C.'s Park View neighborhood. Flonnie, Herman's mother, hadn't been informed of her son's escape from death row; the last she'd heard from her attorney, Bankroll Bob, the conviction and sentence were still under review.

Now this: a notice that Herman had died of "judicial asphyxiation . . . due to his own misconduct."

Flonnie's grief was matched only by her bewilderment. She still didn't know all the specifics of the case, nor anything about Herman's past three months on the run. Flonnie and her family wanted answers from the Army. None would be forthcoming.

FIVE MONTHS LATER, about a week before Japan's unconditional surrender, Captain Richard "Les" Johnston of the 382nd Engineer Construction Battalion was asked to ascend the Patkais in search of a downed cargo plane. Johnston, a Pennsylvania steelworker now stationed in Ledo, wasn't entirely up to the task: a few months earlier, he'd tripped a Japanese booby trap, and his left knee had been struck with grenade shrapnel. But he set out anyway, along with one of his black GIs and a dozen Naga porters.

They reached the plane after an arduous three-day trek over the Patkais, only to find that it had been marked with a black X—a symbol indicating that another Army unit had been there already to check for survivors. Johnston had hiked all those miles for nothing. Now his knee was killing him; the shrapnel wound had reopened and become infected.

One of the Naga porters, a young man named Nampoo, spoke rudimentary English. He told Johnston that he had relatives in a nearby village, where they could obtain medicine for the infected knee. He led the two Americans down to a cluster of bashas gathered around a peak-roofed longhouse. Johnston couldn't help but notice all the polished human skulls hanging from vines, stout buffalo horns bolted to their sides.

Nampoo brought Johnston to the hut of a woman he said was an expert healer. She treated the knee with a poultice of heated tree sap. Johnston immediately felt better, but Nampoo recommended that they spend a night in the village; dusk was fast approaching, and tigers would soon be on the prowl.

The ang invited the visitors to dine at his basha. Johnston and his GI eased down onto the bamboo floor of the chief's house and tucked into simple Naga fare—"rice and barley, very coarse." Once the guests were thoroughly sated on starch, a boy came around with a special dessert: bowls filled with artificially syrupy cubes of apple and citrus.

"I thought, Where in the hell did they get this fruit cocktail?" remembers Johnston. "This was miles off the road, we were *way* back in the jungle. They said there was this girl there who had married a black soldier, and he gave them the fruit cocktail."

Johnston knew exactly whom the Nagas meant. He'd been present at Perry's hanging, overseeing a contingent of black GIs recruited to guard the gallows; he'd witnessed Perry arrive in Ledo that morning, hands shackled to the eyebolt on Cullum's jeep. And like every other American who worked the road, Johnston knew all about the

Jungle King's exploits. As a lifelong boxing aficionado, he'd taken a particular interest in the case: he was familiar with Aaron the Anvil's work in the ring.

The Nagas could tell that Johnston was impressed by their trove of rations. The following morning, as the Americans prepared to leave, a Naga man motioned for them to come over to a basha—the only one in the village painted a bright yellow-orange. Johnston cautiously peered in: the hut was filled with crates of Army goods. And the walls were covered floor-to-ceiling with WANTED posters featuring Perry's photograph, his vital statistics listed in Burmese and Kachin.

As Johnston marveled at the scene, a young girl was brought to the basha. She was cradling a six-month-old baby, whom she held out for Johnston to see: a boy with whorls of brown hair, his skin a few shades darker than his mother's, his eyes less almond-shaped.

Perry's infant son.

"I said, 'Well I'll be damned,'" says Johnston. "It really floored me."

The boy would never be seen again.

FIFTEEN

Work continued on the rechristened Stilwell Road through the spring of 1945. It took the engineers four months to widen the stretch between Myitkyina and Wanting to two lanes, and to cover those lanes with enough gravel to withstand the coming monsoons. A heavy-duty bridge over the Irrawaddy River was completed on April 1, though it wasn't yet sturdy enough to handle more than "limited traffic." Lewis Andrew Pick, recently promoted to major general, presided over the bridge's opening ceremony, to the snickers of his underlings. "The cameras were rolling and flashing," a lieutenant wrote in his diary. "Pick is a publicity hound and a politician. That's all I can say for him. He wasted the whole day to 'set' the last bolt for the news-reel cameras. He can get his name in the news again."

The road between the Salween River and the Kunming terminus in China required constant upkeep, a chore the Army assigned to the African American 858th Engineer Aviation Battalion. Chiang Kaishek was miffed to learn of the 858th's deployment; his wife was still said to be repulsed at the thought of blacks treading, let alone living, on Chinese soil. But qualified white battalions were scarce, so the Generalissimo yielded. The 440 enlisted men of the 858th thus became the only black soldiers to be stationed in China during World War II. They accounted for 0.7 percent of America's military presence in the Middle Kingdom.

Pick finally declared the road finished on May 20, twelve days after Germany's surrender. Major General William E. R. Covell, head of the theater's Services of Supply, gushed over the achievement. The Stilwell Road, Covell promised, would "stand forever as a monument to the unstinting labor, courage, determination, and ingenuity of both the living and those who gave their lives in this remarkable accomplishment."

The monsoons did their best to prove Covell a liar. For the third summer in a row, drenching rains obliterated bridges and triggered mudslides. A reporter for *CBI Roundup* watched floodwaters engulf and smash a four-hundred-foot bridge near Warazup, Burma; the aftermath, he wrote, looked "as if a giant had come along and stamped on the span and then kicked the debris out of the way."

In August 1943, the War Department had projected that the Ledo Road would provide China with thirty thousand tons of supplies per month. But the monthly average for 1945 barely cracked twelve thousand tons: bridges were often washed out, aging 6x6s broke down almost daily, and drivers were slowed by dust pneumonia. Getting from Ledo to Kunming was supposed to take ten days, but it usually took closer to fifteen.

Army convoys shared the road with gangs of industrious smugglers. "Read a terrible report today written by a C.I.D. agent about the almost unrestricted smuggling going on here," a colonel lamented in his diary. "Caravans going and coming daily to China to the Tengchun [*sic*] cut-off* and opium coming out and all American supplies (all stolen) going in—most of the depredations by the Chinese."

The Hump air route, meanwhile, was running smoothly. By mid-summer, the Air Transport Command was flying more than seventy thousand tons of supplies per month to southern China. "It was the Hump and the Hump alone that kept Free China on her feet during the darkest years of the war," acknowledged Leslie Anders, a historian and staunch defender of the Ledo Road. Back on Capitol Hill, congressmen apprised of these tonnage figures asked whether the road should be abandoned. The moral case for keeping the road open was still compelling—namely that closing it would mean admitting that lives had been wasted. But even that argument was losing its clout.

Under pressure to justify the road's existence, the theater brass in Delhi decided to replace Pick with someone adept at supply management rather than construction. They chose Brigadier General Paul F. Yount, the officer in charge of the Bengal-Assam Railway. Having successfully overseen an epic feat of engineering, Pick didn't take kindly to his unceremonious ouster. At a dinner on June 30, he got rip-roaring drunk and berated Yount, promising to "crucify" his anointed successor when the road inevitably failed. ("About as uncalled for and unfair as anything I've ever witnessed," another dinner guest observed.)

Pick left Ledo for good less than two weeks later, and headed back to the anonymity of controlling floods along the Missouri River. The road's officers had mixed emotions about Old Mud and Ruts's departure. "Much as I have winced at things he has done, ruthless

---

*The Tengchung Cutoff, also known as the PTM Road or the Marco Polo Trail, was an offshoot of Ledo Road that ran eastward across the Kaolikung Mountains. It was built in the dry season between the 1944 and 1945 monsoons. Once the rains returned, it became useless to heavy vehicles; only three Army convoys ever passed over the Cutoff before it essentially washed away.

as he has been, there's something very fine and disarming about him," wrote Colonel Richard Selee of the Forty-fifth Engineers. "And tho I've damned his hide a thousand times, I love him."

Three months after his return to the United States, Pick was named to the Gillem Board, a panel charged with shaping "a policy for the use of the authorized Negro manpower potential during the postwar period." The board concluded that African Americans had been underutilized in World War II, and that more emphasis should be placed on training black soldiers during peacetime. But Pick and his cohorts stopped short of recommending an end to segregation; they didn't think the Army, or the country as a whole, was ready for such radical change.

Rain forced the Stilwell Road's closure for most of August, but by then the issue was moot: reeling from the atomic bombings of Hiroshima and Nagasaki, Japan surrendered on August 15. That same day, as they celebrated V-J Day with slugs of scotch, the road's commanders received new orders: all construction was to cease immediately, and they were to prepare their units for "prompt evacuation" from India and Burma.

To save on homebound shipping costs, virtually everything was left behind. Bulldozers and trucks were either turned over to the British, sold for scrap, or dumped into ravines, where jungle critters burrowed into the rusting hulks.* Surplus goods, including stockpiles of TNT, were brought to warehouses in Myitkyina in preparation for a pennies-on-the-dollar clearance sale. Chinese deserters in northern Burma, who'd coalesced into gangs of *dacoits* (bandits), kept robbing the Myitkyina depots until Gurkha mercenaries were

---

*The C-46 and C-47 cargo planes that had flown the Hump were taken to the Bengali city of Panagarh, where they were either scrapped or put on sale. In the late 1940s, the newly created Indian Air Force bought five hundred of these aircraft for $1 each.

hired as guards. The Gurkhas summarily slit the throats of anyone caught stealing, then tossed the thieves' bodies into the Irrawaddy. The dacoits learned to look elsewhere for their spoils.

The engineers turned in their rifles and packed their things for Ledo, the first stop on the long trek back to Uncle Sugar. As for the black-market pistols they'd purchased from Chinese troops, many ended up giving them to the coolies, Nagas, and Kachins they'd befriended while building the road. The GIs couldn't foresee how their gifts would help beget a generation's worth of violence.

With dwindling manpower available to fend off Mother Nature, the jungle quickly spread its fingers: "The Road hasn't folded yet," noted a *CBI Roundup* reporter, "but the jungle crouches by it like a cat waiting to take possession of its own. Vines and creepers have inched across bare places and crept up and down banks, waiting [for] a chance to cross this alien thoroughfare."

The last three American soldiers to drive the entire road, on a mission to resupply checkpoint guards with rations, arrived in Kunming on Christmas Eve 1945. The United States abandoned the road for good less than three months later, recalling its last twelve thousand troops from India and Burma. A 125-word United Press story announced the road's fate to an indifferent American public, quoting a government report's stark conclusion: "There can be no better example of the terrific waste of war and the fact that much war surplus cannot be used in the civilian economy."

In the fall of 1946, David Richardson, who'd traveled with Merrill's Marauders as a correspondent for *Yank: The Army Weekly*, returned to Burma to check on the road's condition. Upon landing in Myitkyina, he asked a British official to drive him along what remained of Pick's Pike. "You can't see much of it, old chap," the official replied. "The last monsoons did it in. Almost all the big bridges are out and the landslides have finished it in the mountains. We don't have any engineers to speak of in this part of Burma, you know, so I guess your road is through forever."

But Richardson insisted, so the Brit took him out in a jeep. Their journey was over almost as soon as it began:

> Just 18 miles south of Myitkyina, the engineers had spent nine months alone building the longest pontoon bridge in the world. Each of its pontoons was bigger than the LCTs [amphibious landing craft] that used to carry tanks in Pacific invasions. The monsoon torrents had ripped it apart and what was left of it was clinging to both shores of the river—as much of it as hadn't floated on down the churning Irrawaddy.

The road's final cost was officially placed in the neighborhood of $164 million—about $1.87 billion in today's dollars. This figure does not include the millions spent on combat in order to clear the road's path, nor such related expenses as the cost of shipping thousands of multiton trucks and Cats to the flip side of the globe. Pick himself admitted that an accurate accounting of the road's cost was impossible. In 1947, *The New Republic* quoted a true price closer to $1 billion (over $11.4 billion today). The road might have cost billions more had the bulk of its workforce not been composed of indentured servants.

The human toll is even harder to measure. The Man-a-Mile Road certainly deserved its ghoulish nickname, though it claimed few lives in the grand scheme of World War II: the Ledo Area Command reported 1,133 fatalities, just one-fifth of those killed in action at the battle of Iwo Jima. Not included in this official tally, of course, are the unknown number of Indian, Chinese, and Burmese laborers who succumbed to disease, malnutrition, mud slides, and tiger attacks.

Many of these workers were dumped in anonymous roadside graves, their impoverished families never notified. There is no way to estimate how many coolies were disposed of in such an expeditious manner.

But the road's lethality cannot obscure the wonder of its magnitude. The earth moved to build the first 270 miles totaled 13.5 million cubic yards, enough to construct a ten-foot-high, three-foot-thick wall from New York to San Francisco. Another 1.38 million cubic yards of gravel was culled from Indian and Burmese streambeds; those pebbles could fill a freight train measuring 470 miles from engine to caboose. The Army correctly referred to the road as "one of the engineering marvels of the world"; that it had been built at all, let alone during wartime, was a triumph worthy of the highest praise. Anyone requiring confirmation of man's limitless ingenuity and ardor need look no further than the muddy track that slashes through the Pangsau Pass.

Yet the road was also a testament to mammoth folly. The project's stated purpose—to stave off China's downfall—was noble at face value. But as evidence mounted that the road was, as Winston Churchill had predicted, "an immense, laborious task, unlikely to be finished until the need for it has passed," the American leadership stayed the course. And so a textbook boondoggle was born—the White Elephant Road, as the Brits cheekily called it.

Organizational disasters (or "clusterfucks," in military parlance) seldom can be ascribed to a single man, and the Ledo Road is no exception. The road's postmortems typically have ascribed the majority of blame to General Stilwell. Though advisers warned him of the jungle's cruelty and the monsoons' wrath, Vinegar Joe stubbornly insisted on the road's completion, using it as an excuse to retake Burma and avenge his humiliating defeat at the hands of the Japanese. He never relinquished his far-fetched dream of marching down the road toward the East China Sea, nor of winning his crass political struggle against Major General Claire Lee Chennault, the CBI's air-power prophet. Beloved as he was for his blunt charisma, Stilwell let egoism cloud his judgment of the Ledo Road's true worth.

But the civilians in Washington blundered, too, starting at the very top of the political ladder. Preoccupied with shaping the postwar world, President Roosevelt mistook Chiang Kai-shek for a faithful ally rather than a rank opportunist. The road was a sop to a dictator whose interests were battling Mao Zedong and enriching his cronies, not aiding the Westerners he considered uncivilized and unclean. There was perhaps no easy response to Chiang's extortionate tactics, since China's surrender would have been disastrous for the Allies. But caving to Peanut's demands for the road, then sticking with the project even as his enthusiasm waned and the Hump flourished, was an uninspired plan.

More egregious was the War Department's indecision, resulting in a worst-of-both-worlds strategy. The department's bureaucrats approved the road in December 1942; Stilwell was assured that it would be a top priority, second only to the invasion of North Africa, as Roosevelt himself promised. But the road's builders were never given the tools and resources necessary for success: CBIers didn't call their theater "Confusion Beyond Imagination" for nothing. South Asia was treated like a sideshow where stalemate was tolerable as long as casualties were kept within reason. No matter how obvious the road's impracticality became, the War Department failed either to halt or to bolster the project. It just let construction putter along, electing to squander blood and treasure rather than concede a mistake.

The neglect was obvious to the road's GIs. In a June 1945 survey, they were asked, "How important do you consider your own Army job in the total effort?" Considerably fewer than half responded "very important," an abysmal result at a time of sky-high patriotism. Some men joked about their feelings of insignificance. "Uninformed historians may attribute the sudden collapse of Japan to the U.S. Navy, the Russian Army or even to the Air Force and their pesky little atomic bombs," wrote a major with the 1880th Engineer Aviation Battalion. "But the plain, unvarnished truth is that the Japs threw in the sponge because they were utterly unable to understand whatinell the 1880th was up to. Can you blame them?"

When the road builders finally made it home, many suffering from the chronic effects of jungle ailments, they discovered that the American public, like the War Department, didn't much appreciate their sacrifice. Fixated on Tokyo and Berlin, the wartime media had paid scant attention to highway construction in northwestern Burma. The entire CBI was nicknamed the Forgotten Theater by its veterans; the Ledo Road, built largely by a feared and reviled American underclass, was that obscure theater's footnote.

Seeking camaraderie among those who'd shared their hardships, former CBIers banded together into a close-knit society, the China-Burma-India Veterans Association. The group, whose membership peaked at over eighty thousand, was organized into bashas, or local chapters. At least once a year, until attrition forced the association's closure in 2005, a basha's members would gather to reminisce and laugh about the atrocious taste of Spam and rice, the best method for burning away leeches, or the times they'd nearly flattened tigers with their jeeps.

Membership was open to anyone who'd served at least three weeks in the CBI. Yet despite this liberal policy, the association confabs were invariably lily-white affairs. "Not once have I seen a black face at *any* CBI meeting," said one officer's wife, who attended basha events for decades. The African American veterans of the Ledo Road apparently didn't feel nostalgic about their years in the jungle.

ONCE IN A great while, after an unusually bloody shoot-out in North-East India or Burma's Sagaing Division, the Nagas make a fleeting appearance in the Western press. A one-paragraph story, relegated to a boxed "World Briefing" roundup, always explains that the violence stems from an ongoing conflict between Naga separatists and Indian or Burmese security forces. The strife dates back to 1947, the year the British quit India; the Naga insurgency, as the article may mention in passing, is arguably the longest-running in modern history.

The father of Naga nationalism is A. Z. Phizo, the Baptist intellectual who fought for the pro-Japanese Indian National Army during World War II. As the end of the British raj drew near, the Phizo-led National Naga Council (NNC) called for independence from soon-to-be-sovereign India. In keeping with their warrior heritage, Phizo and his colleagues loathed the idea of being ruled by anyone who hadn't conquered them by force of arms. And they feared that racial enmity would prevent their integration into caste-conscious Indian society. As Phizo declared in a landmark speech:

> Socially, the Indians abhor the Nagas and the Nagas despise the Indians. It is better to face facts now . . . there is nothing in common between the Nagas and the Indians. The difference is too varied, the feeling is too deep, and the attitude is too wide and too malignant for the two nations ever to think to live together in peace, much less to become Indian citizens. The only way to live in peace is to live apart.

In July 1947, an NNC delegation met with Mahatma Gandhi. According to the Nagas, Gandhi was sympathetic to their cause: "If you do not wish to join the union of India," he was reported as saying, "nobody will force you to do that."

The day before India became an independent nation, the NNC transmitted a momentous telegram to Delhi, with a copy sent to the United Nations: SOUTHERN NAGAS INCLUDING MANIPUR HILLS NAGAS AND CACHAR NAGAS WITH KONYAK NAGAS DECLARE INDEPENDENCE TODAY THE FOURTEENTH OF AUGUST 1947.

This declaration of independence was ignored. But the Nagas were granted appreciable autonomy within India; the NNC was permitted to collect taxes and enforce tribal laws. A nine-point treaty between India and the NNC stipulated that this political arrangement would be reviewed after ten years. The deal could then either be extended or "a new agreement regarding the future of the Naga people arrived at."

The NNC thought this meant they could legally break from India. But Jawaharlal Nehru, India's first prime minister, had a very different interpretation. He worried that granting the Nagas independence would lead to India's dissolution; other ethnic groups would follow suit and agitate for secession. Letting the Nagas go, Nehru warned the Indian parliament, would be "completely unwise, impracticable, and unacceptable."

In 1953, Nehru paid a visit to Kohima, the city where the Japanese invasion had been repelled nine years earlier. Naga nationalists wanted to present Nehru with a proindependence petition, but they were rebuffed by his handlers. The spurned Nagas walked out on Nehru's welcome speech, a contemptuous act that enraged the prime minister. The Naga insurgency ensued.

The rebels were initially armed with guns left behind by the

Americans, but they would later receive military assistance from Pakistan, India's mortal enemy. The war quickly turned vicious: the Nagas accused the Indian Army of committing wanton atrocities:

> Mass arrests of men, women and children were done all over the country. They were mercilessly beaten, herded into concentration camps, where thousands died of starvation, torture and disease. . . . Torturing to death through ruthless beating, thrusting stick into the rectum of [sic] private parts of men and women, [and] hanging up-side down were daily phenomenon [sic]. . . . Schools and churches were razed to the ground. Scorch-earth [sic] policies were applied in every part of the land.

The NNC claimed that between 1956 and 1957, the Indians killed one hundred thousand Nagas, most of them civilians; the Indian government disputes this estimate, saying the true figure is closer to ten thousand.

The hostilities abated in 1960, when the NNC and India signed a peace accord. This led to the establishment of Nagaland, a self-governing state with its capital at Kohima. The state's northernmost tip lies less than twenty miles south of the Disang River, close to where Herman Perry enjoyed his last moments of freedom. The Nagas of the Patkais, numbering in the tens of thousands or more, were largely left out of this arrangement. Some lived east of the border in Burma, where the nationalist spirit was weak; others lived in an Indian territory known as the North-East Frontier Agency (later renamed Arunachal Pradesh).*

---

*Much of the North-East Frontier Agency was overrun by China during the Sino-Indian War of 1962. But the Chinese army mysteriously pulled back to its border after declaring victory. To this day, however, the Austria-size province remains in dispute. In November 2006, China's ambassador to India told an Indian news anchor: "The whole of what you call the state of Arunachal Pradesh is the Chinese territory. . . . We are claiming the whole of that."

Radicals within the NNC opposed the peace and kept fighting, though most of these war-weary insurgents agreed to lay down their arms in 1975. But in 1980, a new generation of guerrillas formed another separatist organization, the National Socialist Council of Nagaland (NSCN). Violence flared anew, as did allegations that the Indian Army's tactics included torture and rape.

In a confusing, semicomical turn of events, the NSCN split into two bitterly opposed factions in 1988: the NSCN-IM and the NSCN-K. The former is the larger of the two, and is the de facto power in Nagaland, funded by a tax levied on the state's citizens and businesses. (The NSCN-IM claims this tax is necessary to continue its "liberation movement"; critics, who maintain that nonpayers are beaten or killed, call it "a tax to live.") The group's shadow government has theocratic leanings: the *yaruiwo* (president) must be a Christian minister, and drug addicts and alcoholics are rounded up for compulsory treatment.

The NSCN-IM's religiosity plays well with its base: having become even more Christianized in the wake of World War II, when Baptist missionaries came in droves, devout Nagas describe themselves as having evolved "from headhunters to soulhunters." They claim that the NSCN put an end to ritual decapitations in 1980, though stories abound of more recent incidents. The last verifiable case of head-hunting occurred in the 1990s in Burma, when a party of Konyak Nagas took between twenty-five and thirty-two heads from a Chang Naga village; the Konyaks were retaliating for an earlier raid.

The NSCN-IM's objective is an independent homeland, dubbed Nagalim, which would stretch from Manipur in the south to the Patkais in the north, and span both sides of the Indo-Burmese border. This hypothetical nation would encompass a substantial portion of the tattered Ledo Road and its jungle environs, including the area in Burma where Herman Perry and his Naga family lived.

But as the British learned in the 1800s, the Nagas of the northern climes don't much care for meddlers. The NSCN-IM has virtually no influence in the Patkais; the rival NSCN-K has a little, having established training camps in Burma's Sagaing Division, but the faction is largely despised for its use of kidnapping and extortion. Most of the militants to be found in these parts are from the United Liberation Front of Asom (ULFA), a group ostensibly committed to Assamese separatism, yet more akin to a mafia. ULFA cadres hide out in the Patkais' labyrinthine forests, descending into the Brahmaputra Plains to conduct bombings and assassinations.

Subsistence, not separatism, is the foremost concern for the northern Nagas, who are much poorer than their cousins down in Nagaland. There are now some signs of modernity in the Patkai villages: high-voltage wires, an occasional television antenna. And Western attire is the rule; the Nagas chafe at the assumption that they prefer nudity to T-shirts. But life is still brutish, especially on the Burmese side of the mountains—decades of cruel dictatorship have left the economy in shambles, and Burma's military is said to force Christian Nagas to convert to Buddhism at gunpoint. Opium addiction persists to a disturbing degree; the drug is pure and cheap, with a bundle of ten strips selling for less than $3. Whole villages are slaves to the pipe.

There are few visible reminders of the billions of American dollars that once poured into this hardscrabble region: a weed-covered truck outside a Burmese police station, an out-of-order Army jeep marooned alongside rolls of chicken wire. Near the Indian town of Jairampur in Arunachal Pradesh, a dilapidated cemetery full of cracked crypts is marked by a single, rusting plaque. The message is in English:

These graves bear silent testimony to those soldiers, unlisted workers and laboures [sic] who ventured in to virgin jungle amid blistering heat; and laid down their lives in the line of duty during the Second World War; whilst part of the Allied forces against the Imperial Japanese Army. THEIR NAME LIVETH FOREVER MORE.

A few miles up the Ledo Road is Nampong, the Indian town closest to the Pangsau Pass. This is where the Hellgate once stood; the wooden gate arm is long gone, but the posts that held it remain, now painted black and white instead of army green. Hellgate is also the name of a Nampong youth soccer team that competes in tournaments in neighboring Assam. Spectators rarely grasp the name's provenance.

THE PERRYS ALL had different ways of dealing with Herman's death, some more self-destructive than others. Aaron, for one, succumbed to anger, becoming a disciplinary nightmare for his Army commanders at Fort Meade. Soon after learning of his brother's hanging, he went AWOL for fifteen days. He was eventually found in Washington, D.C.'s Rock Creek Park, lying unconscious beneath a tree. Due to Aaron's celebrity, the incident was kept under wraps; he was quietly transferred to Alabama's Camp McClellan.

Aaron made a triumphant return to Washington in June 1945, resuming his boxing career on a Griffith Stadium undercard. To the hometown crowd's delight, he scored a first-round knockout over a kid named Jimmy Taylor. His career was back on track for a while, as he racked up victories over B-listers like Vince LaSalva, Bill "Jiggs" Donohue, and Billy Furrone. But he was partying a lot, too, usually with his older brother, Roscoe, in tow. The two opened a dry cleaners with Aaron's winnings, but most of their energy was reserved for haunting D.C.'s nightspots. And as countless failed boxers will attest, hedonism can be an athlete's worst enemy.

The late nights quickly eroded Aaron's skills. He lost two big bouts in the summer of 1946; the following February he was knocked out by Earl Turner, a mediocre Californian he'd beaten just a month before. The end of Aaron's pugilistic career was in sight. Dark times lay ahead.

At first the troubles were financial. Aaron had been exceedingly generous to his family, and exceedingly profligate in Washington's taverns. He wound up $20,000 behind on his federal taxes and nearly $7,000 on his mortgage, resulting in the loss of his two-bedroom home on Gales Street NE. Trouble with the law soon followed: in July 1950, after leading cops on a high-speed chase to the Maryland border, Aaron was arrested for taking part in a home-invasion robbery. Two months later, while free on bond, he held up a dice game at Red's, a social club off U Street.

Aaron beat the robbery cases by pleading insanity. His lawyers argued that he was suffering from "undifferentiated psychosis with schizophrenic tendencies," caused by the head blows he'd sustained while boxing. Aaron was sent to St. Elizabeth's Hospital for treatment and was released eight months later.

In August 1953, Aaron got into a bar brawl over the affections of a woman named Ella Mae Pleasure. He kicked one of the combatants, a sixty-five-year-old cab driver, in the head, fracturing the man's skull. Initially charged with "assault with a dangerous weapon (shod foot)," Aaron became a murder defendant when the cabbie later died of a cerebral hemorrhage. Once again, however, Aaron essentially skated on the case; he was found guilty only of simple assault, not homicide.

It wasn't until 1957 that Aaron finally earned a lengthy prison term, when he was convicted of raping a twenty-year-old woman on the grounds of the Soldiers' Home, an estate for disabled Army vets. Though he swore that the woman, a longtime acquaintance, had consented, Aaron was given an eight- to twenty-four-year sentence. While incarcerated, he sorted out the demons that had robbed him of his promise. After serving the minimum, he took a job fixing air conditioners at the Treasury Department; at night he volunteered as an instructor for Alcoholics Anonymous.

In November 1980, Aaron was inducted into the Washington Boxing Hall of Fame. A month later, at age fifty-four, he died of cancer.

During Aaron's final years, his half brother Henry "Hank" Johnson (the product of Flonnie's rocky marriage to John Henry Johnson in the 1930s) had started digging into Herman's case. A Baptist minister and community activist in Albany, New York, Johnson was deeply suspicious of the Army's version of events. Influenced by the radicalism of the 1960s, a decade he'd spent working as a New York City schoolteacher, Johnson smelled a conspiracy. He hoped his investigation might bring Flonnie some much-needed closure; the Perry family matriarch, who would live until 1997, still ached over Herman's death.

In his spare time, Johnson pestered the Army for documents and tracked down veterans of the Ledo Road. The research was a slog: the military bureaucracy proved a maze, and the aging GIs' recollections of the Jungle King were often hazy or inconsistent. But Johnson kept at it, slowly amassing scraps of evidence in the basement of his Albany home. It wasn't until 1994, however, that he got in touch with a Dallas resident said to be an expert on Herman's case: a retired Army colonel named Earl Owen Cullum.

MOST OF THE men involved in the Perry affair rarely discussed the matter back in civilian life. They might bring it up at a basha meeting now and then, or occasionally regale their grandkids. A few of the saga's participants, saddled with heavy hearts, deleted Perry from their lives altogether: Clayton Oberholtzer, Perry's defense counsel, never once mentioned the case to his son, who succeeded him at the family law firm in Ohio.

Cullum, by contrast, obsessed over Perry. He called the manhunt "the highlight of my military service and of my entire 38-year law enforcement career." And true to the Texan storytelling tradition, he sought to share his adventure with the world.

A month after Perry's hanging, Cullum had been rewarded with a long-awaited promotion to lieutenant colonel. Upon his return to the United States, he was assigned to Fort Bliss near El Paso. It was there that Cullum realized he wasn't meant to be an Army lifer, an epiphany spurred in part by tragedy: one of his MPs accidentally killed another while playing "quick draw" with loaded pistols. "I felt I would be more comfortable being responsible for what I did or had control over," Cullum later wrote. So he switched to a more suitable career: he became an agent with the Federal Bureau of Investigation.

Cullum served thirty years in the FBI, stationed for a decade each in Oklahoma, Indianapolis, and his beloved hometown of Dallas. He specialized in bank robberies and kidnappings, and his stories of dim-witted thieves and ingenious gumshoeing could fill volumes.* He boasted of being "the #1 agent on the #1 squad" while in Indianapolis, and of receiving several personal letters of commendation from J. Edgar Hoover. Cullum also trained plenty of youngsters, including a balding misfit with a terrible temper: G. Gordon Liddy, mastermind of the Watergate burglary.

To round out his all-American résumé, Cullum attained high-ranking positions in a number of fraternal organizations: the Rotary

---

*One of the dimwits whom Cullum encountered during his Oklahoma stint was Mickey Mantle, the famed New York Yankees slugger and an Oklahoma native. One night in Miami, Oklahoma, Mantle got drunk with Yankees teammate Billy Martin, and the two proceeded to wreck a bar. Cullum hushed up the incident, arranging for Mantle to pay for the damages and avoid arrest.

Club of Dallas, the Dallas County Pioneer Association, and the China-Burma-India Veterans Association, of which he was national commander in the mid-1970s. He also became the board chairman and official historian at his prominent Methodist church. One of Cullum's proudest moments came in 1988, when he was inducted into the Military Science Hall of Honor at the University of Texas at Arlington.

But Cullum always yearned to be remembered first and foremost

Idealized illustration of Perry and his bride from the pulp magazine Real.

as the man who'd captured the Jungle King. Every so often, a journalist or amateur historian would get wind of the Perry legend and come knocking on Cullum's door. The normally aloof FBI agent was only too happy to share his thoughts and souvenirs, including pictures of himself standing next to a handcuffed Perry on the morning of March 10, 1945. Those photographs encapsulate the legacy that Cullum hoped to leave: a policeman, an Army officer, and the only man relentless enough to catch the Wraith of the Hills.

The first writer to pick Cullum's brain was Edward Hymoff, who'd worked for the Office of Strategic Services during World War II, then covered the Korean War for the International News Service. Upon returning to the United States in 1954, to work as a news manager for NBC, he latched onto the Perry story. With Cullum as his primary source, Hymoff published a sensationalized account of the manhunt in the March 1956 issue of *Real*, a pulpy men's magazine. Entitled "The Army's Most Incredible Deserter," the article was accompanied by an amusingly stylized illustration of Perry and his Naga bride: Perry with bulging, oily biceps, his half-naked wife with the alabaster skin, perky breasts, and cherry lipstick of a Hollywood starlet.

Hymoff would publish a virtually identical story eight years later in *Impact*, another pulp magazine. This time, perhaps influenced by the burgeoning civil rights movement, Hymoff tweaked the narrative to emphasize the Army's racial inequities. "Herman Perry, an American Negro, enlisted to fight—but found it was a white man's war," reads the article's swashbuckling deck. "Full of bitterness, he turned renegade killer."

After Hymoff came Henry Burns Jr., a criminologist who'd flunked out of West Point in the 1950s. A CBI aficionado who gave his son the misspelled middle name Stillwell, Burns tapped Cullum's trove of documents, photographs, and personal recollections to help compile a five-hundred-page manuscript entitled "Death on the Ledo Road." It was never published.

To keep the Perry story alive, Cullum tried his own hand at writing—at first in articles for veterans' newsletters, and later in a self-published booklet, *Manhunt in Burma and Assam*. Cullum portrayed himself as the quintessential lawman: dutiful but unafraid to speak his mind, hard-nosed but compassionate. Referring to himself in the third person, for example, Cullum characterized his refusal to witness Perry's hanging as the act of a man whose gruff exterior concealed a gentle heart: "Someone said Perry had finally found a man tougher than he was, but it turned out that his captor was just a 'softie' himself."

Cullum's official line was that, despite his squeamishness about watching the execution, he'd delivered Perry to the gallows without remorse: "I felt that Perry deserved to hang," he avowed to CBI historian William Boyd Sinclair, some fifty years after the fact. In truth, however, Cullum was more conflicted about Perry's fate. To admit as much might tarnish his law-and-order reputation, so he kept his misgivings to himself. But when the Reverend Henry Johnson phoned him in early 1994, asking for a copy of *Manhunt in Burma and Assam*, the eighty-one-year-old Cullum sensed a chance to ease his conscience. In a cover letter clipped to the booklet, he hinted at his ambivalence:

Dear Henry:

I was so glad to hear from you, and to know your family cares at least something about your brother. He will always be "Perry" to me. If I may, you will be Henry, and I will be Earl. I fully respect your title, but at my age first names are better.

Please read the booklet and send me your comments and questions.

You see that I am critical of what others did or failed to do, so you do the same to me.

I felt a personal kinship with Perry, perhaps more than anyone else involved in the manhunt. He made a mistake (a really big one) and paid for it. It could have been me, if I ever lost control like he did. And if I hadn't caught him, someone else would. After we caught him he acted like a man all the way—never any whining or self-pity.

If he had used the right attitude, and if the army had used his abilities, he could have been an excellent jungle scout. But in the 1940s he was a roadbuilder. In the 1980s Colin Powell was the highest ranking person, black or white, in all the armed forces.

In 1949 all the Americans buried in China-Burma-India were re-interred in the U.S. or in Hawaii. Perry was buried in the Schofield Barracks Post Cemetery on Oahu, in "Plot 3,* opposite Row S." The marker shows only his name and date buried there. I think that is a special location. He was buried apart from the "Honored dead" at Ledo, and probably the same in Hawaii. I hope you understand the army's thinking. Even a Methodist layman like me can, but I'm mostly army.

Please let me hear from you.

Sincerely,
Earl O. Cullum

Johnson pored over *Manhunt in Burma and Assam*, scribbling critical comments in the margins. Next to the section in which Cullum mentions the first one-thousand-rupee reward, Johnson scrawled, "Created illegal lynch mob mentality." The paragraph about Herman's

---

*This section has since been renamed Plot 9.

escape from death row is noted with a smiley face and the exclamation "I'm outta here!" And to the left of Cullum's use of the term "Jap P.O.W.'s," Johnson wrote in boldface: "Still using derogatory, ethnic descriptive terms."

Late in the booklet, Cullum excerpts a letter of commendation he received from Brigadier General Joseph A. Cranston: "Work of this character is a direct contribution to the American war effort and is gratifying to every man on duty in this theater." Johnson, who'd spoken with black veterans who were anything but gratified by Herman's death, bracketed this quote and responded, "Saying it don't make it so. . . . "

Shortly after receiving *Manhunt in Burma and Assam*, Johnson suffered a debilitating stroke. Everything he'd learned about Herman's case, including how to contact Cullum, was locked inside his stricken mind. Johnson lived out his final years in an Albany nursing home, passing away in 2003. It is unclear what happened to his basement papers, though some may have wound up scattered among his six children, who live up and down the eastern seaboard.

Cullum also endured tragedy soon after connecting with Johnson. His firstborn son, Richard, a West Point graduate and Vietnam veteran, died of bone cancer in 1994. Four years later, Cullum himself nearly perished in a serious auto accident. Newly aware of his own mortality and still grieving over Richard, Cullum found solace in his typewriter. When insomnia struck at three o' clock in the morning, he'd rehash his life in two-page tracts with titles like *Favorite Memories of a Bygone Century* or *Outstanding Arrests*. He wanted to make sure his ten great-grandchildren knew of his many deeds, especially the eighteen days he'd spent tracking the Jungle King through the backwoods of Assam.

Age and injury had dulled Cullum's memory, but some details

never varied in his accounts: wading across the Disang in darkness, the men in native dress around the campfire, Perry's meek "You got me" upon being seized by his malnourished wrist. "Five days later Perry was taken to Ledo," Cullum wrote in *Outstanding Arrests*, "and hanged as the sun rose in the Exotic East."

Cullum always wondered what had become of the Reverend Johnson, who'd seemingly disappeared after receiving *Manhunt in Burma and Assam*. He was informed of Johnson's misfortune in the autumn of 2000, when he received a phone call out of the blue from one of the minister's nieces, Celestine Perry Thompson.

A Brooklyn social worker, Thompson had been raised on tales of "Herman and the Indian Princess," envisioning her long-lost relative married to a Pochahontas-like woman in a feathered headdress. After her uncle's stroke, Thompson had taken over as the family researcher. She posted queries on Internet bulletin boards frequented by CBI buffs, asking if anyone had heard of the Jungle King. A few replies pointed her toward *Ex-CBI Roundup*, a magazine published by the China-Burma-India Veterans Association, which periodically ran articles on the Perry manhunt. *Ex-CBI Roundup*'s editors, in turn, touted Cullum as the leading authority on the case.

Thompson flew to Dallas that November. She and Cullum met at the house of Margaret Owen, a close friend of the retired colonel's and the woman he credited with saving his life after the 1998 car accident. Cullum's daughter, Kathryn, and younger son, Kenneth, also attended, curious to meet a real-life relation of this legendary Perry fellow they'd been hearing about since childhood.

Mustering all the energy he could, the eighty-seven-year-old Cullum narrated his standard yarn of Perry's flight and capture: the death-row escape, the botched trap at Makum, the predawn drive from Chabua to the Ledo Stockade. As the story neared its grisly end, Thompson thought she noticed tears rolling down Cullum's withered cheeks.

The Perfect Texan was weeping, if only softly. Thompson, who shared her uncle's belief that Herman had been railroaded, told herself that Cullum's tears were caused by pangs of guilt. Cullum's record of the meeting, *The Herman Perry Case: 55 Years Later,* certainly suggests that he found it cathartic to speak with Thompson face-to-face: "Mrs. Thompson says today's Perry family has no bitterness against the authorities. [They] just want to learn all the details of [Herman's] life and death." A photograph taken that November day in Dallas shows Cullum, his children, and Thompson sitting together on Owen's sofa. There are smiles all around.

When Cullum passed away at age eighty-nine, he did so believing that he'd made peace with the Perrys. But Thompson was upset to learn that Cullum had mistaken her interest in the case for an offer of forgiveness. Herman's death still stings the Perrys, who feel the Army has never satisfactorily explained exactly what happened in the Indo-Burmese wilderness.

Herman's last surviving sibling, Edna Wilson, views her brother as a martyr. The Army, she contends, treated the Ledo Road's black soldiers "like animals"; to her mind, Herman was singled out for punishment because he had the courage to resist. "He did what the rest of them were afraid to do," she says, with marked pride.

Wilson spent decades trying to have her brother disinterred from the Schofield Barracks Post Cemetery in Oahu, Hawaii, where his remains lay alongside those of six other executed soldiers. All were buried with their heads facing away from the cemetery's American flag, as a sign of contempt.

The soldiers clustered around Herman's grave were a thuggish lot: a GI who raped a pregnant woman at knifepoint, another who bashed in a woman's skull with a nine-pound rock. Wilson didn't want her brother to spend eternity in such company.

After years of fruitless pleas to Army bureaucrats, Wilson finally got her wish in October 2007. Using a jackhammer and a shovel, two workmen unearthed Herman's steel casket from the red Hawaiian soil. Inside was Herman's surprisingly well-preserved body, wrapped head-to-toe in a coarse beige blanket. His Army identification tag, draped atop his covered face, was still clearly legible despite flecks of corrosion.

Wilson had her brother cremated and flown back home to Washington, to rest alongside Flonnie, Roscoe, Aaron, and, eventually, herself.

NOW THAT HERMAN'S body has come home, perhaps his great-great-grandchildren will someday pay a visit to his grave. Herman has four such young descendants in the United States, thanks to the branch of the Perry family tree he created with Elizabeth Hall, his girlfriend before Alma Talbot. Their out-of-wedlock daughter, Portia, had a daughter named Cheryl, whom Flonnie and Edna helped raise in Washington's Anacostia neighborhood. Despite her family's troubled history with the military, Cheryl joined the Army upon turning eighteen; she is currently an Army reservist in Georgia, with five children and four grandchildren.

Far less is known about the other, more peculiar branch of Herman's family. No one in the Patkais seems to have any clue what happened to the Jungle King's half-Naga son. Given the immense hardships of tribal life—hunger, disease, insurgency—there is a decent chance he died quite young.

But there are also whispers that Herman Perry wasn't the only African American GI to leave a flesh-and-blood memento along the Ledo Road. "There are a lot of people around here who look black," said one Tangsa Naga resident of Nampong, punctuating his observation with a knowing laugh.

A joke, perhaps. But stranger things have happened in the jungle.

Herman Perry's Army identification tag.

ACKNOWLEDGMENTS

I can only imagine how awkward it must be to pick up the phone and hear a stranger say, "You don't know me, but I'm working on a book. . . . " Fortunately, the people most closely connected to Herman Perry's tale turned out to be an exceptionally kindhearted lot. I am humbled by their generosity, and by their willingness to share memories both joyful and sad: Edna Wilson, Kathryn Cullum Lee and Ed Lee, Muriel and Richard "Les" Johnston, Bernard Frank, Orville Strassburg, Kirk Wilson, and Celestine Perry Thompson.

Many others gave freely of their time and expertise, filling in the vital details that made this story whole: Mahon East, Todd Chisam, Jamie Saul (RIP), Milton A. Eisenberg, Chad Cullum, Eric Scheie, Janet Hoskins, Christopher Paul Moore, Charles Hack, Grace Collins, John C. Oberholtzer, Ken Johnson, Tucker Hiatt, Ben Thompson, Robert Ellis at the National Archives, the entire staff of the Military History Institute, the Pitt Rivers Museum, Alan Macfarlane (www.alanmacfarlane.com), Glenn T. Johnston, and Rafael DeSoto (www.rafaeldesoto.com).

Oken Tayeng of Abor Country Travels & Expeditions was a godsend along the Ledo Road. Without him, my journey would have ended well short of Tinsukia, instead of proceeding across the Pangsau Pass; there is no better man to have on hand when dealing with a paranoid Burmese army captain and his sketchy Nepalese translator. Thanks also to the globetrotters who offered such excellent advice on visas, transport, and fixers: Miranda Kennedy, Alyssa Banta, Angus McDonald, Amy Waldman, Nina Berman, Dan Morrison, Prateek Chawla from Outbound Travels, and Priyankoo Sarmah. Special thanks to the crooked-toothed kid at the Dibrugarh Airport who came to my aid when things looked grim, and to Mini-Me at the Jairampur Inspection Bungalow.

Several brilliant and steadfast editors have supported my writing habit through the years. Without them, I'd probably be tending bar or selling insurance rather than living the dream: James Fallows, Jim Impoco, Lincoln Caplan, Jeff O'Brien, Julia Turner, Chris Anderson, Bob Cohn, Emily Bazelon, Chris Suellentrop, Laura Conaway, Ted Halstead and the New America Foundation, Steven Clemons, Sherle Schwenninger, Alison MacKeen, Stephen G. Smith, Amy Bernstein, Damon Darlin, Bryan Curtis, Dan Engber, Nadya Labi, Mark Robinson, Nick Denton, Monika Bauerlein, Sara Sklaroff, Tim O'Brien, Jacob Weisberg, and Brian Lam.

Friends and relatives got me through the dark times, providing sympathetic ears, welcome criticism, and plentiful libations when necessary. I must have been extremely virtuous in a previous life in order to have earned such peerless fellow travelers in this one: Ryan "Ulf" Nerz, Ta-Nehisi Coates and Kenyatta Matthews, Tom Folsom, Rob Galligan, Ben Robbins, Kit Roane, Jason "Indy" Vest, John Marks, Loukas Barton, Brian Lavery, Samir Patel, Jeff Kulkarni, Jacki and David (the Angels of *vino*), Karisa King, Alysia Cotter, Ezra Edelman, Mishka Brown, Paragraph NY, Jeffrey Green, Matthew Williams, BirdByBird, WeFunk, Nick Thompson, Howe Lin, Chris and Kyla Catlett, Scott Kaylie, Tomer Seifan, Abigail Hart Gray, Brian Ashcraft, Erica Paul and Billy Lewis, Shannon and Charles Clerke, Joel Johnson, Eyal Press, Michael Kennedy, and Thomas Beug. My mother is a saint for her patience and good humor, my father a champ for (among so many other things) first reading me *Leiningen versus the Ants*.

My agent, Zoë Pagnamenta, had the utmost faith from Day One, and fought the good fight on my behalf. A better, more gifted advocate I can't imagine.

Vanessa Mobley, my editor at The Penguin Press, is a bona fide genius, without whom this book would have died on the vine. Working with her and learning from her have been among life's great pleasures. Thanks also to Vanessa's assistants, Lindsay Whalen and Nicole Hughes, for fielding all my irksome questions.

Above all, my eternal everything to Cili—half woman/half amazing, and the straw that stirs The Crew. This book is for her.

NOTES

ONE

page

1. *reputation would be ruined:* Bernard Frank interview, Mar. 2007.

1. *"Get back!":* Statement of T/5 Robert L. Griffis, June 5, 1944, Clerk of Court, U.S. Army Judiciary, Falls Church, Va.

1. *the quivering Perry:* Statement of Sgt. Otto M. Bowman, June 5, 1944, Clerk of Court, U.S. Army Judiciary, Falls Church, Va.

1. *gaunt, dark cheeks:* Statement of Pvt. James W. Walton, June 5, 1944, Clerk of Court, U.S. Army Judiciary, Falls Church, Va.

2. *Perry sputtered:* Ibid.

2. *Cady froze:* Ibid.

2. *Cady took another step:* Ibid.

2. *wrest it away:* Court-martial testimony of Pvt. James W. Walton, Sept. 4, 1944, Clerk of Court, U.S. Army Judiciary, Falls Church, Va.

3. *behind barbed wire:* Court-martial testimony of S/Sgt. Jeff C. Gobold, Sept. 4, 1944, Clerk of Court, U.S. Army Judiciary, Falls Church, Va.

3–4. *"The jungle . . . like an earthquake":* David Richardson, "The Jungle's Victory," *The New Republic,* Feb. 10, 1947.

6. *triumph for the ages:* Author's visit, Nov.–Dec. 2006.

6. *Man-a-Mile Road:* "India Prepares to Resurrect Wartime Route That Cost Allies a Man a Mile," *The Independent,* Mar. 15, 2005.

6. *Two-Man-a-Mile Road:* Leslie Anders, *The Ledo Road* (Norman: University of Oklahoma Press, 1965), 234–35.

7. *feed and care for:* Richardson, "The Jungle's Victory," 14.

7. *"I had . . . No one was fooled":* Eric Sevareid, *Not So Wild a Dream* (New York: Atheneum, 1976), 316.

7. *all of World War II:* The Army's official estimate was closer to 60 percent, but this was surely an undercount. The African American historian Nancy Brockbank quotes an estimate of 65 percent in her 1998 master's thesis, *The Context of Heroism.* Yet this revised figure also seems too low. Of the nine biggest engineer units that built and maintained the Ledo Road, seven were "colored": the 352nd Engineer General Service Regiment, the 93rd Engineer General Service Regiment, the 849th Engineer Aviation Battalion, the 45th Engineer General Service Regiment, the 823rd Engineer Aviation Battalion, the 858th Engineer Aviation Battalion, and the 1883rd Engineer Aviation Battalion. The trucking units, meanwhile, were almost exclusively black; the *Chicago Defender's* Denton J. Brooks, the dean of Ledo Road reportage, estimated that 95 percent of the project's truck drivers were black. These snippets of statistical evidence are certainly in line with what I heard from the many veterans I interviewed, who all remarked that the overwhelming majority of the road's rank-and-file was African American. For example, Bernard Frank,

the man who prosecuted Herman Perry, estimated that "about 90 percent of the troops were black."

7. *white Americans existed, too:* Author's visit.

8. *"lacking in the Negro":* Steven D. Smith and James D. Ziegler, eds., *A Historic Context for the African-American Military Experience* (Champaign, Ill.: U.S. Army Construction Engineering Research Laboratories, 1998), Chap. 8, http://www.denix.osd.mil/denix/Public/ES-Programs/Conservation/Legacy/AAME/aame4.html#8%20African%20Americans.

8. *"fuckup" by his commanders:* Bernard Frank interview.

9. *run another day:* Earl Owen Cullum, *Manhunt in Burma and Assam* (Dallas: Self-published, 1993), 20–29.

9. *rather than a man:* "Behind the Stockade Fence," *The Assam Police Gazette,* Mar. 5, 1945.

TWO

11. *the Anvil:* "Weigh In . . . With Walter Haight," *The Washington Post,* Mar. 26, 1944.

11. *Bad News: The Washington Evening Star,* Mar. 11, 1944.

11. *"District boxing history":* "3,415 Watch Negro Youth Score Here," *The Washington Post,* Jan. 22, 1944.

11. *an opponent to death:* "Boxing Champion Lew Hanbury," *The Washington Post,* Aug. 16, 2001.

11. *purses here and there:* BoxRec.com record for Roscoe Perry, http://www.boxrec.com/boxer_display.php?boxer_id=054850.

12. *jackrabbit around a ring:* According to his enlistment record, Perry measured five feet eight and weighed 154 pounds. However, the WANTED posters that were printed during the manhunts of 1944 and 1945 listed his weight as 170 pounds.

12. *disproportionately large feet:* "Wanted for Murder," *CBI Roundup,* Dec. 24, 1944. This clipping is from the private collection of Kathryn Cullum Lee.

12. *of a gentler nature:* Edna Wilson interview, Sept. 2006.

12. *sweetheart of the moment:* Photographs of Herman Perry, private collection of Edna Wilson.

12. *pose for a mug shot:* Herman Perry mug shot, private collection of Kathryn Cullum Lee.

12. *never tie the knot:* Edna Wilson interview.

12. *Perrys had once resided:* Census card for Buford Township, South Carolina (Enumeration District 82, Supervisor's District 5), Jan. 22–23, 1920, National Archives, Washington, D.C.

12. *Flossie and Vander:* Census card for Monroe, North Carolina (Enumeration District 90-11, Supervisor's District 8), Aug. 9, 1930, National Archives, Washington, D.C.

12. *the aging Edward:* Edna Wilson interview.

13. *measly nine cents:* J. Paul Lilly, "North Carolina Agricultural History," http://www.ncagr.com/stats/history/history.htm, u.d. The last year for which Professor Lilly cites farm-yield statistics is 1992, which makes it likely that this history was published in 1994 or 1995.

13. *charge of their upbringing:* Edna Wilson interview.

13. *each other's finery:* Ibid.

14. *Big Jesse yanked her along:* Robert F. Williams, *While God Lay Sleeping* (Chicago: Third World Press, 1973), 5–6.

14. *per black student than per white:* John L. Bell Jr., *Hard Times: Beginnings of the Great Depression in North Carolina* (Raleigh, N.C.: North Carolina Division of Archives and History, 1982), 75.

14. *But the illiterate Henrietta:* Census card for Monroe, North Carolina, 1930.

14. *ravaged the state's soil:* Lilly, "North Carolina Agricultural History."

14. *cotton they produced:* Bell, *Hard Times,* 5.

14. *state's starving farmers:* Ibid., 42.

14. *plate-glass windows:* Ibid., 73.

14. *keep cows or goats:* Ibid., 43.

15. *less than a decade:* David Brinkley, *Washington Goes to War* (New York: Ballantine, 1996), 23; Census data from 1930 and 1940, http://www.census.gov/prod/www/abs/decennial.

15. *spacious by comparison:* "Welcome to Washingtonians," *The New Republic,* Dec. 29, 1941, 877.

16. *cotton in the Carolinas:* Brinkley, *Washington Goes to War,* 20–23; "Washington Job Picture Proves 'Same Old Story' Despite 75-Year Battle," *The Chicago Defender,* May 29, 1943.

16. *the Great Migration:* Edna Wilson interview.

16. *along with Roscoe:* Ibid.

16. *"find a new nigger"* Brinkley, *Washington Goes to War,* 21.

17. *Gallaudet University:* Washington, D.C., City Directory (1941 edition), National Archives, Washington, D.C. According to Herman Perry's entry in this directory, his employer was Nathan B. Johnson, the owner of a grocery store at 1826 Benning Road NE.

17. *tables near Capitol Hill:* Ibid.

17. *Dunbar High School:* Edna Wilson interview.

17. *facilities for white students:* Paul Cooke, "The Cost of Segregated Public Schools in the District of Columbia," *The Journal of Negro Education,* vol. 18, no. 2 (Spring 1949): 96–98.

17. *near the Maryland border:* Edna Wilson interview.

17. *from Meridian Hill Park:* Washington, D.C., City Directory (1941 edition).

17. *permeated the urban night:* Brinkley, *Washington Goes to War,* 20–23; "Alley Dwellers Seek to Solve Own Problems," *The Washington Tribune,* 1935 (specific date unknown).

17. *busboy's monthly wage:* "Alley Dwellers Seek to Solve Own Problems."

17–18. *nowhere else to go:* "Alley Homes Fight for Respect," *The Washington Post,* May 29, 2006.

18. *on D.C.'s eastern edge:* "Alley Dwellers Seek to Solve Own Problems."

18. *"according to God's plan":* "Mrs. Roosevelt's Non-J.C. Views Blamed for Dee Cee Housing Crunch," *The Washington Tribune,* June 17, 1941.

18. *verboten list, too:* Brinkley, *Washington Goes to War,* 21.

19. *to pursue the case:* "Will Demand Action in Harvard Street Bombing," *The Washington Tribune,* Apr. 13, 1940.

19. *picked off by sniper fire:* "In the Race Riot of 1919, a Glimpse of Struggles to Come," *The Washington Post,* Mar. 1, 1999.

19. *issues of the day:* Kathryn Schneider Smith, ed., *Washington at Home: An Illustrated History of Neighborhoods in the Nation's Capital* (Washington, D.C.: Windsor Publication, 1988), 119–29; Paul T. Mills Sr., "Langston Hughes: February 1, 1902–May 22, 1967," June 20, 2003, http://dclibrary.org/blkren/bios/hughesl.html.

20. *most regal churches:* Smith, *Washington at Home,* 119–29.

20. *the Tillie Club:* "Among the Washington Clubs," *The Washington Tribune,* Apr. 20, 1935. Other prominent black clubs included the Tête-à-Tête Bridge Club, the Panther Whist Club, and the Jolly Comrades.

20. *a brown paper bag:* "For Black College Students in the 1930s, Respectability and Prestige Depended on Passing the Brown Bag Test," *The Journal of Blacks in Higher Education,* Jan. 31, 1999.

20. *that of New York:* "House Inquiry Finds D.C. Crime Rate 'Disgracefully High,'" *The Washington Post,* May 2, 1935. Unfortunately, the violence of the Depression-era capital now seems quaint. In 2004 there were 35.8 murders per 100,000 residents in Washington, D.C.—more than triple the rate in 1935.

21. *drapes and tapestries:* "Agents Raid Lavish 'Den' of Drug Ring," *The Washington Post,* Dec. 21, 1936.

21. *and classical music:* Photographs of Herman Perry, private collection of Edna Wilson; Edna Wilson interview.

21. *skinny-limbed:* Photograph of Alma Talbot, private collection of Edna Wilson.

21. *in Meridian Hill Park:* Photographs of Herman Perry, private collection of Edna Wilson.

22. *Twelfth Street Y:* National Historic Landmark Nomination, Twelfth Street Young Men's Christian Association Building, Mar. 1994, http://www.cr.nps.gov/nhl/designations/samples/dc/YMCA.pdf.

22. *Fourteenth and W streets NW:* "Nolan, Del Rio Have Eye for Style," *The Washington Times,* Nov. 26, 2006.

22. *and hockey games:* "As Decades Pass, a Coliseum's Glory Days Go to Waste," *Washington Business Journal,* Apr. 13, 2001.

22. *in the first round:* BoxRec.com record for Roscoe Perry.

22. *destructive jab:* "Age Dispute, Managerial Muss Bar Perry from Banks Fight," *The Washington Evening Star,* Feb. 18, 1944.

22. *boy from Tennessee: The Washington Evening Star,* Apr. 13, 1943. The man who defeated Aaron was a private in the Army, Art Saulsgives.

23. *Anvil's arm in triumph:* Roger Treat, "Gallows for a Jungle King," *Coronet,* Sept. 1945, 131–32.

24. *capped at nine hundred thousand:* "President Franklin D. Roosevelt Message to Congress on Extension of Selective Service Terms of Service," July 21, 1941, http://www.ibiblio.org/pha/timeline/410721awp.html.

24. *8,581 aspiring soldiers: The Washington Evening Star,* Oct. 26, 1940.

24. *on November 28, 1940:* Grand jury indictment against Herman Perry, District Court of the United States for the District of Columbia, Mar. 31, 1944, National Archives, Washington, D.C.

24. *on February 5, 1941:* Ibid.

25. *"nothing to the Negro":* "Europe's War Has Nothing to Offer Negroes," *The Washington Tribune,* Feb. 10, 1940.

25. *"Swedes, Italians, etc.":* "Conscientious Objectors," *Chicago Defender,* Jan. 9, 1941.

25. *the nation at large:* Jonathan Sutherland, *African-Americans at War* (Santa Barbara: ABC-Clio, 2003), 132.

25. *questionnaires were distributed:* "2 of 3 Brothers Plead Guilty in First District Draft Case," *The Washington Post,* Oct. 27, 1940.

26. *black men from Shaw:* "Draft Viewed as Deterrent to Crime," *The Washington Post,* Nov. 10, 1940.

26. *Commerce and Savings Building:* Complaint and affidavit in the case of *United States v. Herman Perry,* Feb. 24, 1941, National Archives, Washington, D.C.

26. *at Seventh and E streets NW:* Greeters of America, *Greeter's Guide to Washington* (Washington, D.C.: Greeters of America, 1922), 71.

26. *D.C.'s Masonic lodge:* "Masonic League Honors Turnage and Thompson," *The Washington Post,* Mar. 3, 1940.

26. *"convicted of a felony":* Grand jury indictment.

26. *"due process of law":* Complaint and affidavit in the case of *United States v. Herman Perry.*

27. *family's modest means:* Ibid.

28. *confessed to the magistrate:* Ibid. Ordinarily, the preprinted complaint form included a clause that began, "From the evidence of the said witness." However, in the Perry complaint, Turnage crossed out the word *evidence,* replaced it with *plea,* and typed *deft.* above the crossed-out word *witness.*

28. *"we decline to prosecute":* Record of proceedings in *United States v. Herman Perry* (criminal case no. 67553), National Archives, Washington, D.C.

THREE

29. *"and substance of 'Glory'":* "Fun & Blood," *Time,* Jan. 11, 1932.

29. *fled into the hinterlands:* Jonathan D. Spence, *The Search for Modern China* (New York: Norton, 1991), 443–56.

30. *burn all, loot all:* Ibid., 469.

30. *used for bayonet practice:* Sue De Pasquale, "Nightmare in Nanking," *Johns Hopkins Magazine,* Nov. 1997, http://www.jhu.edu/~jhumag/1197web/nanking.html. For further reading, please see Iris Chang's *The Rape of Nanking: The Forgotten Holocaust of World War II* (New York: Basic Books, 1997).

30. *"England and America":* Policy Adopted at Imperial Conference, July 2, 1941, http://www.ibiblio.org/hyperwar/PTO/Dip/IR-410702.html.

30. *"in Greater East Asia":* Tripartite Pact, Sept. 27, 1940, http://www.ibiblio.org/hyperwar/PTO/Dip/Tripartite.html.

31. *rivalries ran deep:* Emma Larkin, *Finding George Orwell in Burma* (New York: Penguin Books, 2006), 213.

31. *provinces went to seed:* Christopher Bayly and Tim Harper, *Forgotten Armies: The Fall of British Asia, 1941–1945* (Cambridge, Mass.: Belknap Press, 2005), 85–89.

31. *the war's European front:* Ibid., 81–83; Barbara Tuchman, *Stilwell and the American Experience in China, 1911–1945* (New York: Macmillan, 1971), 236.

31. *their fists or clubs:* Larkin, *Finding George Orwell in Burma,* 147.

31. *"Asia for the Asiatics":* Harold S. Quigley, "Asia for the Asiatics? The Techniques of Japanese Occupation," *The Journal of Modern History,* vol. 18, no. 1 (Mar. 1946): 84–85.

31. *forming in Thailand:* Bayly and Harper, *Forgotten Armies,* 13–14.

32. *to huddle in caves:* Eric Sevareid, *Not So Wild a Dream* (New York: Atheneum, 1976), 310–13.

32. *1,300-plus opium dens:* Spence, *The Search for Modern China,* 457.

32. *led by Mao Zedong:* Ibid., 451.

32. *nearest major railway:* Ibid., 444, 456.

32. *gained through bribery:* Ibid., 457.

32. *accidents, and starvation:* Ibid., 458.

32. *"mountains with fingernails":* *The Stilwell Road,* Office of War Information, 1945. This 51-minute documentary was narrated by Reagan, who was based in California throughout the war due to his nearsightedness.

33. *in China's heartland:* Policy adopted at Imperial Conference.

33. *British-controlled India:* "The CNAC Story: The China National Aviation Corporation," Mar. 29, 2004, http://www.humppilots.com/history.htm.

33. *"thousands made their living":* Sevareid, *Not So Wild a Dream,* 313.

33. *the surveyors gave up:* Leslie Anders, *The Ledo Road* (Norman: University of Oklahoma Press, 1965), 7.

34. *Indo-Burmese border:* Ibid.

34. *a sickly gray:* Author's visit, Nov.–Dec. 2006.

34. *the region's reputation:* *A Handbook for Travellers in India, Burma, and Ceylon* (London: John Murray, 1909), 320–21; "Who's Who 1891," Manipur State Archives, 1990, http://archivesmanipur.nic.in/whoswho.htm.

34. *in ninety-six hours:* William Boyd Sinclair, *Confusion Beyond Imagination: Book Three* (Coeur d'Alene, Idaho: Joe F. Whitley, 1988), 68–87.

35. *"killed by wild animals":* Henry Lionel Jenkins, "Notes on the Burmese Route from Assam to the Hookoong Valley," *Proceedings of the Royal Geographical Society of London,* vol. 13, no. 3 (1868–69): 248.

35. *"warlike people in India":* E. T. D. Lambert, "From the Brahmaputra to the Chindwin," *Geographical Journal,* vol. 89, no. 4 (Apr. 1937): 309–12, 321.

35. *Nationalist press gangs:* Anders, *The Ledo Road,* 7.

35. *from their villages:* Spence, *The Search for Modern China,* 388–89 (photographs), 478.

35. *twelve months to complete:* Ibid., 458; Anders, *The Ledo Road,* 7.

35. *more manageable 465:* Anders, *The Ledo Road,* 8.

36. *nine-figure loans:* Spence, *The Search for Modern China,* 466–68.

36. *and outright gifts:* Ibid., 469.

36. *fight in the Pacific:* Tuchman, *Stilwell,* 238.

36. *and freedom from fear:* Ibid., 239.
36. *albeit a sloppy one:* Ibid., 251.
36. *Revolutionary Alliance:* Spence, *The Search for Modern China,* 276–77.
36. *studied in Moscow:* Ibid., 338.
37. *the Communist menace:* Ibid., 353–54.
37. *gunned down in the streets:* Ibid., 361–63.
37. *advantageous positions:* Tuchman, *Stilwell,* 153.
37. *massacred by the Japanese:* Spence, *The Search for Modern China,* 448.
37. *didn't press the issue:* Tuchman, *Stilwell,* 251.
37. *"dying by the roadsides":* Sevareid, *Not So Wild a Dream,* 344.
38. *the good of the nation:* Ibid., 326.
38. *by China's air force:* Ibid., 324.
38. *than he actually possessed:* R. J. C. Butow, "A Notable Passage: Myth and Memory in FDR's Family History," *Prologue,* vol. 31, no. 3 (Fall 1999), 159–77.
38. *the Chongqing regime:* Tuchman, *Stilwell,* 322.
38. *off his boss's estimate:* William Boyd Sinclair, *Confusion Beyond Imagination: Book One* (Coeur d'Alene, Idaho: Joe F. Whitley, 1986), 209.
39. *plains to the Patkais:* Anders, *The Ledo Road,* 8–9.
39. *two and a half years to build:* Ibid., 9–10.
39. *the Burmese lowlands:* Ibid., 31.
39. *moneylending operations:* Bayly and Harper, *Forgotten Armies,* 170–71, 179.
40. *as they retreated north:* Tuchman, *Stilwell,* 276.
40. *to bury the dead:* Bayly and Harper, *Forgotten Armies,* 167–90.
40. *"crawling over corpses":* Typescript of J. P. Mills's tour diary, Mar. 4, 1927, Naga Database, http://bamdemo.lemurconsulting.com/bamdemo/db/naga. My special thanks to Alan Macfarlane of Cambridge University for responding to my inquiries regarding the database. His extraordinary body of work can be explored at his Web site, www.alanmacfarlane.com.
41. *among American officers:* Tuchman, *Stilwell,* 61–90.
41. *invasion of North Africa:* Ibid., 231.
41. *tiny brain:* Ibid., 283.
41. *term for "foreigner":* Ibid., 335.
42. *nightmare of a colleague:* Ibid., 242–43.
42. *no part of the war:* Ibid., 266–67.
42. *orders needn't be followed:* Ibid., 280.
42. *refugees headed for Assam:* Gerald Astor, *The Jungle War: Mavericks, Marauders, and Madmen in the China-Burma-India Theater of WWII* (Hoboken, N.J.: John Wiley & Sons, 2004), 88.
42. *along with his troops:* Tuchman, *Stilwell,* 288.
42. *attempt to avoid combat:* Ibid., 291.
42. *"to them does no good":* Ibid., 278.
43. *whatever Stilwell ordered:* Ibid., 278–79.
43. *Mao's Communists:* Ibid., 288.
43. *for Peanut was sealed:* Ibid., 284.
43. *missionaries in tow:* Ibid., 293.
43. *Vinegar Joe's bluntness:* Ibid., 298–300.
44. *Stilwell despaired:* Joseph W. Stilwell, *The Stilwell Papers,* ed. Theodore H. White (Cambridge, Mass.: Da Capo Press, 1991), 115.
44. *the Imperial Japanese Army:* Sinclair, *Confusion Beyond Imagination: Book One,* 216.
45. *"strike at Japan itself":* William Slim, *Defeat into Victory* (Cutchogue, N.Y.: Buccaneer Books, 1991), Chap. 12.
45. *"when I go back":* Anders, *The Ledo Road,* 86.
45. *scraggly air force:* Astor, *The Jungle War,* 13–15.
45. *Japanese plane they downed:* Ibid., 24–25.
46. *invading China proper:* "Chinese Incident," *Time,* May 25, 1942.

46. *based in China:* Astor, *The Jungle War,* 104–25.

46. *Hump flights from CNAC:* Ibid., 145–49.

46. *"flying coffins":* Sevareid, *Not So Wild a Dream,* 247.

46. *beheaded by the Japanese:* Astor, *The Jungle War,* 146.

47. *diplomatic when called for:* Spence, *The Search for Modern China,* 471.

47. *an Alabama accent:* Astor, *The Jungle War,* 15.

47. *authored by Chennault:* Williamson Murray and Allan R. Millett, *A War to Be Won: Fighting the Second World War* (Cambridge, Mass.: Belknap Press, 2000), 198.

47. *a euphemism for surrender:* Tuchman, *Stilwell,* 309–14.

47. *bombing of Tokyo:* Spence, *The Search for Modern China,* 471.

48. *War Department priority:* Anders, *The Ledo Road,* 16–26.

48. *freighters at French ports:* Ulysses Lee, *The Employment of Negro Troops* (Washington, D.C.: Center for Military History, 1966), 5; Army War College Historical Section, *The Colored Soldier in the U.S. Army,* May 1942, Center for Military History, Carlisle, Penn.

48. *Assam Tea Planters' Association:* Bayly and Harper, *Forgotten Armies,* 184, 280.

48. *sixteen cents a day:* Anders, *The Ledo Road,* 18.

48. *around two dollars:* According to the personnel files of Herman Perry and numerous other GIs, the standard wage for enlisted men along the Ledo Road was $60 per month.

48. *"need for it has passed":* "India Hopes Old Jungle Trail Can Be a New Road to Riches," *The Times* (London), May 12, 2007.

48–49. *actually kill anybody:* Harper and Bayly, *Forgotten Armies,* 270–72.

49. *a local warlord:* Tuchman, *Stilwell,* 72–83.

49. *their white counterparts:* There may be a grain of truth to the malaria theory, at least. Carriers of the sickle-cell trait, common in the descendants of sub-Saharan Africans, are believed to possess at least some degree of natural resistance to malaria. However, as will become apparent later on, black troops along Ledo Road suffered greatly from the mosquito-borne disease.

49. *pitch-black by 4:00 P.M.:* Ruth Dannenhower Wilson, *Jim Crow Joins Up* (New York: William J. Clark Press, 1944), 21; Anders, *The Ledo Road,* 9.

49. *cool to the road plan:* Sinclair, *Confusion Beyond Imagination: Book One,* 211.

49. *charge of the project:* Barry W. Fowle, ed., *Builders and Fighters: U.S. Army Engineers in World War II* (Fort Belvoir, Va.: United States Army Corps of Engineers, 1992), 330. The book's chapter on the Ledo Road was written by James W. Dunn, a former Army colonel and an expert on operations analysis.

50. *the spring monsoons hit:* Ibid., 329–33.

FOUR

51. *twice at Turner's Arena:* BoxRec.com record for Roscoe Perry. http://www.boxrec.com/boxer_display.php?boxer_id=054850.

51. *mess halls were built:* Ulysses Lee, *The Employment of Negro Troops* (Wasington, D.C.: Center for Military History, 1966), 88–91.

51. *qualified black registrants:* Phillip McGuire, ed., *Taps for a Jim Crow Army: Letters from Black Soldiers in World War II* (Lexington: The University Press of Kentucky, 1993), xxvii.

52. *they'd begin active duty:* Lee, *Employment of Negro Troops,* 91.

52. *draft official's whim:* Earl Ofari Hutchinson, "The Missing 57th Pillar in the National World War II Monument," Alternet, May 26, 2004, http://www.alternet.org/story/18801.

52. *battle on little food:* Patrick B. Miller, "The Anatomy of Scientific Racism: Racialist Responses to Black Athletic Achievement," *Journal of Sport History,* vol. 25, no. 1 (Spring 1998): 129. These anthropometrical "facts" were vigorously disputed by Dr. W. Montague Cobb, a Howard University physical anthropologist. He was famous for debunking myths regarding black athletic performance. In 1936, for example, Cobb measured the calves of

sprinter Jesse Owens, fresh off his Olympic triumph. The measurements indicated that Owens's calf muscles qualified as "Caucasoid," while those of Frank Wykoff, his white rival, were shorter and thus "Negroid."

52. *of the skull:* Ibid., 127.

53. *standards of the day:* Christopher Paul Moore, *Fighting for America: Black Soldiers—The Unsung Heroes of World War II* (New York: One World, 2005), 17.

53. *under 3 percent:* Army War College Historical Section, *The Colored Soldier in the U.S. Army,* May 1942, Center for Military History, Carlisle, Penn.

53. *"in which he is quartered":* Ibid.

53. *"drunkenness, and peculation":* Ibid.

54. *of them were chaplains:* Moore, *Fighting for America,* 17–19.

54. *cleaners, or manual laborers:* Morris J. MacGregor Jr., *Integration of the Armed Forces 1940–1965* (Washington, D.C.: Center of Military History, 1985), 3–17, http://www.army.mil/cmh-pg/books/integration/IAF-FM.htm.

54. *"generals or admirals":* McGuire, *Taps for a Jim Crow Army,* xxiv.

54. *legislation it might pass:* Redstone Arsenal Historical Information, "A Chronology of African-American Military Service, from WWI to WWII: Part One," http://www.redstone.army.mil/history/integrate/CHRON3.html.

55. *than his skin color:* McGuire, *Taps for a Jim Crow Army,* xxvi.

55. *of northern abolitionists:* Rayford W. Logan, "Make Haste Slowly," *The Journal of Negro Education,* vol. 17, no. 4 (Autumn, 1948): 508–10.

55. *"shall certainly have trouble":* Steven D. Smith and James D. Ziegler, eds., *A Historic Context for the African-American Military Experience* (Champaign, Ill.: U.S. Army Construction Engineering Research Laboratories, 1998), Chap. 8, https://www.denix.osd.mil/denix/Public/ES-Programs/Conservation/Legacy/AAME/aame4.html.

56. *"It is much more . . . of our southern people":* Memo of Rear Admiral W. R. Sexton to Secretary of the Navy, Feb. 3, 1942, Truman Presidential Museum and Library, Independence, Mo., http://www.trumanlibrary.org/whistlestop/study_collections/desegregation/large/index.php?action=docs.

57. *"O.K.":* Lee, *The Employment of Negro Troops,* 75–76. Roosevelt would employ a similar political tactic when running for a fourth term. In July 1944, the president decreed that all social facilities at Army posts, such as PXs and service clubs, should be desegregated. But he tempered this executive order with a clause giving each post's commanding officer the right to disregard the directive if he so desired. The gambit worked, as Roosevelt was endorsed by virtually every major African American leader.

57. *on July 29, 1942:* Enlistment record for Herman Perry (Army serial no. 13074419), National Archives, Washington, D.C.

57. *("very inferior"):* Rod Powers, "ABCs of the ASVAB," About.com, n.d., http://usmilitary.about.com/cs/joiningup/a/asvababcs.htm; Macgregor, *Integration of the Armed Forces,* 17–57.

57. *8.5 percent of whites:* Macgregor, *Integration of the Armed Forces,* Table 1.

58. *"techniques of modern weapons":* Smith and Ziegler, *A Historic Context for the African-American Military Experience,* Chap. 8. Fish, the scion of a prominent New York political family, was one of the NAACP's greatest allies on Capitol Hill. He had commanded the Harlem Hellfighters during World War I, and was a tireless opponent of military prejudice during the early 1940s. Fish was also an ardent isolationist and New Deal opponent, making him one of Roosevelt's least favorite congressmen. Beset by scurrilous rumors that he'd accepted money from pro-Nazi contributors, he lost the general election in 1944, to the president's tremendous glee.

58. *rather than race:* "Army Rejects More Dixie Whites Than Northern Negroes During War," *Chicago Defender,* Aug. 26, 1944. Ashley Montagu, an English anthropologist and psychologist, argued that IQ tests from World War I yielded similar results. His paper "Intelligence of Northern Negroes and Southern Whites in the First World War," published in the *American Journal of Psychology* in 1945, made him a pariah among eugenicists

and race baiters. Rather than address his argument—that socioeconomics, not race, affect group IQ scores—Montagu's enemies harped on the fact that he'd changed his name from Israel Ehrenberg, and therefore could not be trusted.

58. *"of the American people":* U.S. News & World Report, Nov. 18, 1963, 92.

58. **War Department consultant:** E. Donald Sisson, "The Personnel Research Program of the Adjutant General's Office of the United States Army," *Review of Educational Research,* vol. 18, no. 6 (Dec. 1948): 575.

58. *"person has already learned":* Francisco Gil-White, *Resurrecting Racism: The Modern Attack on Black People Using Phony Science* (Historical and Investigative Research, 2004), Chap. 9, http://www.hirhome.com/rr/rrchap9.htm.

58–59. *of his personnel file:* Perry's personnel file, like that of 85 percent of World War II veterans, was severely damaged in a 1973 fire at the National Personnel Records Center in St. Louis.

59. *efficient use of talent:* MacGregor, *Integration of the Armed Forces,* 17–57.

59. *equality in the United States:* Jonathan Sutherland, *African-Americans at War* (Santa Barbara: ABC-Clio, 2003), 130–33.

60. *at home went unpunished: Chicago Defender* microfilm, reels 48–51, July 1942–June 1944, Schomburg Center for Research in Black Culture, New York, N.Y.

61. **He cut a dashing figure:** Photograph of Herman Perry, private collection of Edna Wilson.

61. **Gunnery Range in South Carolina:** "849th Engineer Aviation Battalion," Jan. 25, 1944, Air Force Historical Research Agency, Maxwell Air Force Base, Ala.; Edna Wilson interview, Sept. 2006.

61. *whites-only showings:* "Attitudes of White Enlisted Men Toward Sharing Facilities With Negro Troops," Research Branch, Special Service Division, War Department, July 30, 1942, Military History Institute, Carlisle, Penn.

62. *were a good idea: Command of Negro Troops,* War Department Pamphlet no. 20-6, Feb. 29, 1944, 13.

62. *"dis is de Souf!":* "Stay Away from Negroes, White Soldiers Ordered," *Chicago Defender,* Jan. 29, 1944.

62. *closer to twenty:* "Obituaries," *San Antonio Express-News,* June 4, 2006; online obituary from the Porter Loring Mortuary, San Antonio, Texas, June 2, 2006, http://obit.porterloring.com.

62. *a cerebral hemorrhage:* "Mrs. Wright Hiatt Dies in New Orleans," *Union City Times-Gazette,* Nov. 3, 1942.

62. *before the new year:* "849th Engineer Aviation Battalion."

62. *for running the 849th:* Memo of Col. Ellis F. Altman, Sept. 22, 1943, records of the inspector general, Ledo Area Command, National Archives at College Park, Md.

63. *the town of Big Flats:* Census card for Big Flats, N.Y. (Enumeration District 8-4, Supervisor's District 13), Apr. 15, 1930, National Archives, Washington, D.C.

63. *before entering OCS:* Enlistment record for Harold Cady (Army serial no. 12016626), National Archives, Washington, D.C.

63. *the Pennsylvania border:* "Woodhull Officer Killed in Action," *The Canisteo Times,* Mar. 16, 1944.

63. *"darky," and "uncle": Command of Negro Troops,* 7–11.

63. *born with darker skin:* Statement of First Sgt. William R. Rawls, records of the inspector general, Ledo Area Command, National Archives at College Park, Maryland; McGuire, *Taps for a Jim Crow Army,* 59–61.

64. *drinking fountains:* "Nazi Prisoners Better Treated Than Negro Soldiers in South, Army Told," *Chicago Defender,* Jan. 29, 1944.

64. *roast pork and potato salad:* John Ray Skates, "German Prisoners of War in Mississippi, 1943–1946," *Mississippi History Now,* Sept. 2001, http://mshistory.k12.ms.us/features/feature20/germanprisonersofwar.html.

64. *"haven't got a chance":* McGuire, *Taps for a Jim Crow Army,* 63.

65. *called it "railroading":* Ibid., 143.

65. *"injustices and discrimination":* Evelio Grillo, *Black Cuban, Black American* (Houston: Arte Público Press, 2000), 113.

65. *battalion's justice "excessive"*: "Annual General Inspection, FY 1944, 849th Engineer Aviation Battalion," Feb. 1, 1944, records of the inspector general, Ledo Area Command, National Archives at College Park, Md.

65. *for days at a time:* "Report on misconduct of Enlisted Men of 849th Engineer Aviation Battalion," Sept. 10, 1943, records of the inspector general, Ledo Area Command, National Archives at College Park, Md.

66. *Camp Kilmer, New Jersey:* "849th Engineer Aviation Battalion."

66. *"sad about it or anything":* Edna Wilson interview, Sept. 2006.

67. *"three MPs killed":* Mary Penick Motley, ed., *The Invisible Soldier: The Experience of the Black Soldier, World War II* (Detroit: Wayne State University Press, 1987), 57.

67. *soldiers were arrested:* Geoffrey F. X. O'Connell, "The Mysterious 364th," *Philadelphia City Paper*, May 17–21, 2001.

67. *like common convicts:* Motley, *The Invisible Soldier*, 117.

67. *permitted to keep weapons:* Ibid., 120.

67. *three rounds into Walker:* "Sheriff Kills Chicagoan at Camp Van Dorn," *Chicago Defender*, May 29, 1943.

68. *"stark black hatred":* Motley, *The Invisible Soldier*, 127.

68. *several rocket launchers:* Ibid., 118.

68. *Alaska-Canadian Highway:* Ibid., 128. A few historians have claimed that the Army doled out a far more horrendous punishment, summarily executing more than one thousand members of the 364th. This version of events is argued for in *The Slaughter: An American Atrocity*, a 1998 book by Carroll Case. The Army followed up on Case's book with an investigation of its own, and traced the wartime whereabouts of virtually every member of the 364th. Though the Camp Van Dorn riot was no doubt bloody, the tales of mass graves and boxcars filled with executed infantrymen are highly improbable, to say the least.

68. *at least twenty casualties:* "Army Race Riots Spread; Five Outbreaks Reported," *Chicago Defender*, June 19, 1943.

68. *raping white women:* "Six Get Long Terms for Shooting at Dixie Town," *Chicago Defender*, Sept. 4, 1943.

69. *"the big Southern camps":* "The Attack on Duck Hill," *Time*, Sept. 13, 1943.

69. *twenty-five of them black:* Vivian M. Baluch and Patricia Zacharias, "The 1943 Detroit Race Riot," *The Detroit News Online*, n.d., http://info.detnews.com/history/story/index .cfm?id=185&category=events.

69. *crusade for racial equality:* "Historians and WWII: Zoot Suit Riots," National Center for the Preservation of Democracy, n.d., http://www.ncdemocracy.org/node/1146.

69. *Objectors Against Jim-Crow:* "Report on Misconduct of Enlisted Men of the 849th Engineer Aviation Battalion."

69. *Double V campaign:* Ibid. Hiatt, the report's author, specifically cited his men's "exposure to subversive elements in New York City." This appears to be a reference to a number of quasi-religious groups based in uptown Manhattan, the strangest of which was the pro-Japanese Ethiopian Pacific Movement. The movement's leader, a former Marcus Garvey disciple named Robert O. Jordan, mistakenly believed that the Japanese were committed to racial equality, and encouraged Harlem residents either to resist the draft or disobey the orders of commanding officers. He was tried and convicted of sedition, along with three of his lieutenants, in 1943. FBI operatives testified that members of the movement routinely referred to the U.S. as "the United Snakes," though the defendants argued that the agents simply misunderstood their West Indian accents.

70. *less troublesome units:* Ibid.

70. *worst sorts of Uncle Toms:* Ibid.

70. *to egg them on:* Memo of Capt. Frederick B. Zombro, Sept. 20, 1943, records of the inspector general, Ledo Area Command, National Archives at College Park, Md.

70. *his company commander:* Statement of 1st Lieut. Penneth M. Cline, Sept. 15, 1943, records of the inspector general, Ledo Area Command, National Archives at College Park, Md.

70. *witness to the fracas:* Statement of 1st Lieut. Jesse L. Coker, Sept. 15, 1943, records of the inspector general, Ledo Area Command.

71. *without further incident:* "Report on Misconduct of Enlisted Men of the 849th Engineer Aviation Battalion." Five members of the 849th were eventually court-martialed for their roles in the Camp Kilmer riot, and sentenced to terms of six months at hard labor. Private Goodwin, who claimed that he was merely trying to break up the initial fight, was among those found guilty. No white officers or MPs were punished, save for being reprimanded in Hiatt's official report.

71. *memo that September:* Confidential memo of Col. B. M. Crenshaw to Capt. D. F. Johnson, Sept. 5, 1943, records of the inspector general, Ledo Area Command, National Archives at College Park, Md.

71. *"exposure to venereal disease":* "Report on misconduct of Enlisted Men of the 849th Engineer Aviation Battalion."

71. *quarters below deck:* Interview with Milton A. Eisenberg, May 2006.

FIVE

73. *thirty thousand Virginians cheered:* Dictionary of American Naval Fighting Ships, Vol. 1-A (Washington, D.C.: Department of the Navy, 1991), 219–22; "I Christen Thee *America*," SS *America* Web site, http://www.flare.net/users/e9ee52a/America%20invite.htm. The SS *America* site is maintained by Larry Driscoll, who worked aboard the ship during its later incarnation as the passenger liner SS *United States*.

73. *Bourdelle's lacquered murals:* Photographs from the Library of Congress, American Memory Web site, http://memory.loc.gov/ammem/index.html; Photographs from the SS *America* Web site, http://www.flare.net/users/e9ee52a/S.S.%20America1.htm.

73. *"oceans of the world":* Letter from President Franklin D. Roosevelt to Rear Admiral E. S. Land, the American Presidency Project, University of California at Santa Barbara, Aug. 9, 1939, http://www.presidency.ucsb.edu/ws/print.php?pid=15789.

74. *more than eight thousand passengers:* Dictionary of American Naval Fighting Ships, 219–222; Stanley Tryzbiak, *Official Log of Cruises and Narrative History of the U.S.S. West Point AP23* (Yakima, Wash.: USS *West Point* Reunion Association, 2006), 10–12.

74. *in April 1943:* Tryzbiak, *Official Log of Cruises,* 16–30.

74. *for air and light:* Milton A. Eisenberg interview, May 2006.

75. *"Men on board . . . in the service":* Memo of Rear Admiral W. R. Sexton to Secretary of the Navy, Feb. 3, 1942, Truman Presidential Museum and Library, Independence, Mo. http://www.trumanlibrary.org/whistlestop/study_collections/desegregation/large/index.ph?action-doc.

75. *instead of manning destroyers:* Morris MacGregor Jr., *Integration of the Armed Forces 1940–1965* (Washington, D.C.: Center of Military History, 1985), 58–74, http://www.army.mil/cmh-pbooks/integration/IAF-Fi.htm. The Navy was notorious for refusing to promote black Seabees, regardless of their qualifications. Members of the 34th Construction Battalion, which served with acclaim at the battles of Guadalcanal and Tulagi, were particularly irked by this policy. In 1945, upon returning from the Pacific, one thousand of these black Seabees went on a hunger strike, demanding fair consideration for promotion. Accounts differ on how the strike ended; the NAACP claimed that it went on until the Navy caved, while the Navy claimed that the Seabees relented after "they just got hungry."

76. *"regards to inter-marriage":* Memo of Rear Adm. W. R. Sexton.

76. *"The tiers of bunks . . . in nearby bunks":* Frank H. Lowry, "USS *West Point,*" private collection of Ken Johnson, USS *West Point* Reunion Association.

76. *utter lack of ventilation:* Evelio Grillo, *Black Cuban, Black American,* (Houston: Arte Público Press, 2000), 93.

76. *fatigues and combat boots:* Ibid.

76. *well-heeled clientele:* Orville Strassburg interview, March 2006.

77. *"Considerable areas . . . is stored and prepared":* Tryzbiak, *Official Log of Cruises,* 4.

77. *black face among them:* Photographs from the Library of Virginia's online archive, http://www.ajax.lva.lib.va.us/; Rudi Williams, "Black WWII Vet Recalls Terrible Time Building 'Ledo Road,'" American Forces Press Service, July 7, 2004; Ken Ironside, "The History of the *America–West Point–Australis–American Star,*" n.d., http://www.users.zetnet.co.uk/australis/history.html.

77. *thrust their heads inside:* Lowry, "USS *West Point.*"

78. *were already roiling:* Ibid.

78. *third-class dining room:* Ibid.

78. *comrades had finished up:* Howard Zinn, *The Zinn Reader: Writings on Disobedience and Democracy* (New York: Seven Stories Press, 1997), 250.

78. *cleaned plate, took hours:* Lowry, "USS *West Point*"; Milton A. Eisenberg interview.

78. *"washing their mess gear":* Lowry, "USS *West Point.*"

78. *all 7,928 passengers:* Tryzbiak, *Official Log of Cruises,* 6.

78–79. *practiced abandoning ship:* Ibid.; Lowry, "USS *West Point.*" Enterprising black soldiers sometimes circumvented this rule by volunteering for clerical jobs. Sergeant Mose J. Davie, a senior at Tennessee State University when he was drafted, ran the mimeograph machine on the USS *Hermitage*; he was rewarded not just with fresh air, but with the right to sleep above deck (sans bedding) rather than return to his segregated quarters.

79. *Kilmer unpleasantness:* "Black WWII Vet Recalls Terrible Time Building 'Ledo Road'"; "Report on Misconduct of Enlisted Men of 849th Engineer Aviation Battalion."

79. *back to their berths:* Phillip McGuire, ed., *Taps for a Jim Crow Army: Letters from Black Soldiers in World War II* (Lexington: The University Press of Kentucky, 1993), 239.

79. *smoking below deck:* Tryzbiak, *Official Log of Cruises,* 11.

79. *first port of call:* "Davy Jones and Royal Party Welcomed Aboard," *The Pointer,* July 17, 1943; Milton A. Eisenberg interview; Ron Cooke, "Crossing the Line," SS *America* Web site, http://www.flare.net/users/e9ee52a/West%20Point%20ron_cooke.htm.

79. *speculation had to suffice:* Tryzbiak, *Official Log of Cruises,* 6.

80. *forbidden down below:* This detail, like many others associated with World War II troop crossings, is difficult to pin down due to the military's shoddy record keeping. According to the National Archives, "In 1951, the Department of the Army destroyed all manifests, logs of vessels, and troop movement files of the United States Army transports for World War II and most of the passenger lists."

80. *roses by comparison:* Grillo, *Black Cuban, Black American,* 93–94.

80. *salty water in the wound:* Lowry, "USS *West Point.*"

80. *the jitterbug contest:* "Special Services Feature," *The Pointer,* July 17, 1943.

80. *butts of unsuspecting pals:* Lowry, "USS *West Point.*"

80. *on July 31:* Tryzbiak, *Official Log of Cruises,* 6.

80. *confined to quarters:* Milton A. Eisenberg, "14th Evacuation Hospital," World War II Lecture Institute, Abington, Penn., July 15, 2003.

80. *blend into the slums:* Milton A. Eisenberg interview.

81. *from head to tail:* Ken Johnson interview, May 2006.

81. *named Tiger Nelson:* *The Washington Evening Star,* Apr. 2, 1944.

81. *a world-class fighter:* "This Morning with Shirley Povich," *The Washington Post,* Mar. 25, 1944.

81. *they'd arrived:* Tryzbiak, *Official Log of Cruises,* 6.

81. *Bombay:* The USS *West Point* went through several postwar incarnations, bearing such names as the SS *Australis,* the SS *Noga,* and the SS *American Star.* In 1994, while being towed across the Atlantic, the ship broke free of its tugboat and ran aground in the Canary Islands. As of 2007, part of the rusting, crumbling hulk could still be seen off the Spanish island of Fuerteventura.

82. *entreaties of whores:* Orville Strassburg interview.

82. *prejudice with the Indians:* McGuire, *Taps for a Jim Crow Army,* 239.

82. *'divide and conquer' propaganda"*: "Denies Bar on All Race News in U.S.," *Chicago Defender,* Jan. 2, 1943.

82. *a British rest camp:* Milton A. Eisenberg interview.

83. *slang for "crazy"*: "Wordwatch: Doolally," ABC NewsRadio (Australia), n.d., http://www.abc.net.au/newsradio/txt/s1412540.htm.

83. *saunalike conditions:* Orville Strassburg interview.

83. *the giant birds sacred:* Ibid. In the *Ramayana,* one of Hinduism's most sacred texts, a vulture is killed while trying to protect Sita, wife of the great hero Rama.

83. *"toughening up process"*: "849th Engineer Aviation Battalion."

83. *washed in fetid water:* Orville Strassburg interview.

84. *water and pray:* "Interview with John R. Leber," Jan. 15, 1999, Oral History Collection, University of North Texas, Denton, Tex.

84. *"Indians want democracy . . . idea they have of us"*: *A Pocket Guide to India* (Washington, D.C.: War and Navy Departments, 1942), http://cbi-theater-2.home.comcast.net/booklet/guide-to-india.html.

84. *might further that goal:* Ibid.

84–85. *wonder what was next:* "849th Engineer Aviation Battalion," Jan. 25, 1944, Air Force Historical Research Agency, Maxwell Air Force Base, Ala.

85. *in comfortable berths:* Orville Strassburg interview.

85. *eggs and pork chops:* Menu from Indian railway (ca. 1944), private collection of Kathryn Cullum Lee. A pork chop cost the equivalent of fifty-six cents, while scrambled eggs were thirty-four cents.

85. *slatted wooden benches:* Eisenberg, "14th Evacuation Hospital."

85. *sake of a few rupees:* William Collins King, *Building for Victory: World War II in China, Burma, and India and the 1875th Engineer Aviation Battalion* (Lanham, Md.: Taylor Trade, 2004), 31–33.

86. *intestines' painful chagrin:* "Black WWII Vet Recalls Terrible Time Building 'Ledo Road.'"

86. *of female companionship:* Orville Strassburg interview.

86. *Bengal-Assam Railway:* The Bengal-Assam Railway was created on January 1, 1942. It was an amalgamation of two existing lines, the Eastern Bengal Railway and the Assam Bengal Railway.

86. *river's shifting depths:* Orville Strassburg interview.

87. *five miles from Ledo:* "849th Engineer Aviation Battalion."

87. *were powerful talismans:* Bernard D. Wiley Collection (photographs), Military History Institute, Carlisle, Penn.

87. *in their homeland:* Richard Selee officer's papers, Military History Institute, Carlisle, Penn.

87. *a vicarious thrill:* Carl Warren Weidenburner, "Stories from India," n.d., http://warren421.home.comcast.net/stories.html. The recollections in this document come from Weidenburner's father, Warren, an Army sergeant who served on the Ledo Road.

87. *for coins or trinkets:* Interview with Eric Scheie, Feb. 2006.

88. *Camp Van Dorn fiasco:* "849th Engineer Aviation Battalion." Toward the end of the war, as it became apparent that soldiers in the CBI were generally unclear as to their role in defeating the Axis, the War Department created an introductory film strip entitled *Why We're Here.* Shown to newly arrived GIs and narrated by Lieutenant General Daniel I. Sultan, the thirty-three-minute movie characterized South Asia as a "back door to Japan" and emphasized "that there is a big job to be done and the India-Burma theater is one of the places where it will be done."

88. *Twentieth General Hospital:* 849th Engineer Aviation Battalion morning reports, Company A, Sept. 1943, National Personnel Records Center, St. Louis, Mo.

88. *chickens into their ward:* Oral History of Anna Mae McCabe Hays (Carlisle, Penn.: Senior Officers Oral History Program, Military History Institute), 21–28.

88. *on the Ledo Road:* 849th Engineer Aviation Battalion morning reports.

88. HELLGATE: Author's visit, Nov.–Dec. 2006.

88. *alive were fifty-fifty:* Ibid.

88. *a hillside clearing:* John C. Arrowsmith Collection (photographs), Military History Institute, Carlisle, Penn. This camp, at the road's Mile 37, is now an outpost of the Assam Rifles, an Indian paramilitary force.

89. *"Hello Edna . . . Love, Herman":* Letter from Herman Perry to Edna Wilson, Sept. 19, 1943, private collection of Edna Wilson.

SIX

91. *Stilwell's grand designs:* Barry W. Fowle, ed., *Builders and Fighters: U.S. Army Engineers in World War II* (Fort Belvoir, Va.: United States Army Corps of Engineers, 1992), 330–32.

92. *every few inches:* Leslie Anders, *The Ledo Road* (Norman: University of Oklahoma Press, 1969), 43–71.

92. *Indo-Burmese border:* C. M. Buchanan, *Stilwell Road: Story of the Ledo Lifeline* (Calcutta: Office of Public Relations, USF in IBT, 1945), 13.

92. *"Cooler than CBI":* Nancy E. Brockbank, *The Context of Heroism* (Ypsilanti: Eastern Michigan University, 1998), 49–54. William Boyd Sinclair's *Confusion Beyond Imagination, Book One* includes another telling quip regarding the road's brutal climate. Sinclair writes that an engineer he met along the road once told him, "The only difference between Burma and hell is hell's got a dry climate."

92. *away in the humidity:* Todd Chisam interview, May 2006.

92. *"half mile this month":* "Jungle Tale," *Time,* Oct. 11, 1943.

92. *"worth a damn":* James H. Stone, ed., *Crisis Fleeting: Original Reports on Military Medicine in India and Burma in the Second World War* (Washington, D.C.: Department of the Army, 1969), 166.

92. *on September 13:* 849th Engineer Aviation Battalion morning reports, Company A, Sept. 1943, National Personnel Records Center, St. Louis, Mo.

92. *dubbed Hell Pass:* Mahon East interview, June 2006; author's visit, Nov.–Dec. 2006.

93. *"silent as death":* Buchanan, *Stilwell Road,* 35–38.

93. *coiled in empty boots:* William Boyd Sinclair, *Confusion Beyond Imagination: Book One* (Coeur d' Alene, Idaho: Joe F. Whitley, 1986) 217, 221.

93–94. *men's flesh to pulp:* Lloyd L. Kessler, "Lloyd L. Kessler Recalls His Time in the 209th Engineer Combat Battalion in Burma," *World War II Magazine,* Mar. 2001, http://www .historynet.com/wars_conflicts/world_war_2/3038126.html.

94. *on bamboo poles:* Evelio Grillo, *Black Cuban, Black American* (Houston: Arte Público Press, 2000), 113.

94. *and shined shoes:* Orville Strassburg interview, March 2006.

94. *the exhausted GIs:* CBI Roundup, Aug. 5, 1943.

94. *brown in color:* Fowle, *Builders and Fighters,* 329.

94. *with a lit cigarette:* Todd Chisam interview.

94. *"Naga sores":* Barbara Tuchman, *Stilwell and the American Experience in China, 1911– 1945* (New York: Macmillan, 1971) 326.

94. *vulnerable orifice:* Oral History of Anna Mae McCabe Hays, Senior Officers Oral History Program, Military History Institute, Carlisle, Penn., 29.

94–95. *"One night . . . and pull it out:* William R. Peers, *Behind the Burma Road: The Story of America's Most Successful Guerrilla Force* (Boston: Little, Brown, 1963), 95.

95. *patients for surgery:* Oral History of Anna Mae McCabe Hays, 23.

95. *Oh, give me . . . dozen takes its place:* Smith Dawless, "Comment," http://cbi-theater-3 .home.comcast.net/verses/Verses_NoFrames.html. All of Dawless's poems were collected in a 1951 booklet entitled *The Ledo Road and Other Verses from the China-Burma-India Theater.* In 1949, his most famous poem, entitled "The Ledo Road" (Conversation Piece), was set to music by the composer John Klein.

95. *per every 1,000 men:* Anders, *The Ledo Road,* 80. This is not to imply that 95.5 percent of soldiers suffered from malaria; men were often admitted multiple times to the hospital for the disease, and each admission counted as one case. Nonetheless, it's fair to say that

the majority of engineers who built the Ledo Road were infected with malaria at one time or another.

95. *stay in the jungle:* Grillo, *Black Cuban, Black American,* 113; Stone, *Crisis Fleeting,* 146–48.

96. *was seldom sprayed:* Records of the inspector general, Ledo Area Command; Mahon East interview; Stone, *Crisis Fleeting,* 145–47.

96. *psychosis (true):* "The Electrical Activity of the Brain in a Case of Atabrine Psychosis," *The American Journal of Psychiatry,* vol. 110, no. 5 (Nov. 1953): 366–69.

96. *impotence (false):* James L. Howard, ed., *1007th Engineer Special Service Battalion Feb. 15, 1943–Jan. 11, 1946* (Lakewood, Colo.: Self-published, 1992), 30.

96. *throats before mealtimes:* Ibid.

96–97. *"Scrub typhus . . . a little rustic cross":* David Richardson, "The Jungle's Victory," *The New Republic,* Feb. 10, 1947, 12.

97. *bested Western medicine:* Peers, *Behind the Burma Road,* 95–96.

97. *"a/c the flood":* Richard Selee officer's papers, Military History Institute, Carlisle, Penn.

97. *for sumptuous rugs:* Howard, *1007th Engineer Special Service Battalion,* 35.

98. *never to be seen again:* Grillo, *Black Cuban, Black American,* 111.

98. *such hairpin curves:* Sinclair, *Confusion Beyond Imagination: Book One,* 222.

98. *far as two hundred feet:* Ulysses Lee, *The Employment of Negro Troops* (Washington, D.C.: Center for Military History, 1966), 611.

98. *axles were overstressed:* William Collins King, *Building for Victory: World War II in China, Burma, and India and the 1878th Engineer Aviation Battilion* (Lanham, Md.: Taylor Trade, 2004), 139.

98. *escorts riding shotgun:* Mary Penick Motley, ed., *The Invisible Soldier: The Experience of the Black Soldier, World War II* (Detroit: Wayne State University Press, 1987), 119; Mahon East interview.

98. *cobbled from scrap:* Fowle, *Builders and Fighters,* 338.

98. *in the jungle muck:* Sinclair, *Confusion Beyond Imagination: Book One,* 252.

99. *Army radio frequencies:* CBI Roundup, Apr. 22, 1943.

99. *Sergeant Two-Tone:* Mahon East interview. East added that the blast affected his ability to grow facial hair for the next two decades; he didn't start shaving again until he was in his forties.

99. *"So, we lost him":* Ibid.

99. *a top priority:* Anders, *The Ledo Road,* 22.

100. *White House bedroom:* Tuchman, *Stilwell,* 371.

100. *Japan's home islands:* Maurice Matloff, *Strategic Planning for Coalition Warfare 1943–1944* (Washington, D.C.: Center for Military History, 1990), 86–87.

100. *supplies per month:* Ibid.

100. *fists on his desk:* Gerald Astor, *The Jungle War: Mavericks, Marauders, and Madness in the China-Burma-India Theater of WWII* (Hoboken, N.J.: John Wiley & Sons, 2004), 151.

101. *"a lot of wind":* Tuchman, *Stilwell,* 249–50.

101. *road's intended path:* Astor, *The Jungle War,* 151.

101. *"never keeps his word":* Ibid.

101. *campaign's continuation:* Matloff, *Strategic Planning for Coalition Warfare, 1943–1944,* 87.

101. *at Stilwell's expense:* Astor, *The Jungle War,* 152.

102. *without the lucre:* Matloff, *Strategic Planning for Coalition Warfare, 1943–1944,* 433.

102. *"By the beginning . . . a losing proposition":* Ibid., 435–36.

103. *Burma Road's terminus:* Ibid., 435.

103. *"nice eyelashes":* Bayly and Tim Harper, *Forgotten Armies: The Fall of British Asia, 1941–1945* (Cambridge, Mass.: Belknap Press 2005), 271.

103. *squeeze on Japan itself:* Matloff, *Strategic Planning for Coalition Warfare, 1943–1944,* 434.

103. *a massive folly:* "A Difference of Opinion," *Time,* Feb. 14, 1944.

103. *soldiers in Burma:* Ibid.
103. *"[Chinese Nationalists]":* Tuchman, *Stilwell,* 365.
104. *scrapped machines:* Anders, *The Ledo Road,* 53.
104. *junked radiators:* "Uncle Sam's Negro G.I.'s in CBI-Land," *CBI Roundup,* Aug. 10, 1944.
104. *used apple boxes:* Oral History of William R. Peers (Carlisle, Penn.: Military History Institute, 1977), 10–11.
104. *paradise (if Muslim):* Author's visit.
104. *and bare hands:* Ted Price Collection, Military History Institute, Carlisle, Penn.
106. *were in short supply:* CBI Roundup, Nov. 9, 1943.
106. *snapped in two:* Bayly and Harper, *Forgotten Armies,* 280.
106. *$8,000 per elephant:* Peers, *Behind the Burma Road,* 46.
106. *the gentle animals:* Records of the adjutant general, Ledo Area Command, National Archives at College Park, Md. According to a memo dated Mar. 1, 1945, Chinese hunters shot four elephants over a three-day span that February: "One of the elephants was killed, two temporarily incapacitated. One critically wounded and not expected to survive."
106. *blades cost $1.20:* CBI Roundup, June 3, 1943.
106. *$300 per month:* Bryon Caldwell papers, Military History Institute, Carlisle, Penn.
106. *bottles of whiskey:* CBI Roundup, June 3, 1943.
106. *or the pricey shops:* "Interview with John R. Leber," Jan. 15, 1999, Oral History Collection, University of North Texas, Denton, Tex., 44.
107. *driver from Chicago:* Enlistment record for Clyde Blue (Army serial no. 36020361), National Archives, Washington, D.C.
107. *"Everybody had an angle":* Motley, *The Invisible Soldier,* 131–32.
107. *good on this promise:* Mahon East interview; interview with Richard L. Johnston, Apr. 2006. Nothing elicited gripes from a forward-deployed unit like a shipment of long-awaited beer that turned out to be awful. In 1945, Captain Harold McAtee sent a case of Stegmeier Gold Medal Beer back to headquarters in Ledo. "Purpose is to determine the condition of beer," he wrote in his communiqué. "Complaints have been received from units receiving this beer that the beer is 'flat.'"
107. *the 849th's racket:* Records of the adjutant general, Ledo Area Command.
107. *at outrageous markups:* Records of the inspector general, Ledo Area Command.
107. *cigarettes by the armful:* Todd Chisam interview. Chisam, a military policeman, noted that warehouse guards were supposed to arrest the Chinese soldiers they caught breaking into warehouses. However, the MPs realized that these failed burglars would be summarily executed for their petty crimes. The Americans thus preferred to let the Chinese off with warnings, in the interest of basic humanity.
107. *black-market bazaar:* Records of the provost marshal, Ledo Area Command, National Archives at College Park, Md.
107. *certainly far higher:* William Boyd Sinclair, *Confusion Beyond Imagination: Book Six* (Coeur d'Alene, Idaho: Joe F. Whitley, 1989), 15.
108. *"dope on gas-stealing ring":* Ibid.; Tuchman, *Stilwell,* 377–78.
108. *sharpened broomsticks:* Motley, *The Invisible Soldier,* 120–21.
108. *like sweetened kerosene:* Joseph Straub Collection, Military History Institute, Carlisle, Penn.; *CBI Roundup,* Aug. 5, 1943.
108. *epic hangovers:* Author's visit.
109. *never stopped bustling:* Extracts on Nagas from *Assam Administration Reports,* 1891–1893, Naga Database.
109. *"gunga" by the GIs:* Records of the inspector general, Ledo Area Command.
109. *form of psychopathy:* Records of the adjutant general, Ledo Area Command. Discharges due to marijuana addiction were made under the auspices of Army Regulation 615–368. Men discharged in such a manner were judged to have "undesirable habits or traits of character," and were immediately shipped home.
109. *show in the jungle:* Malcolm A. Haines, World War II questionnaire, Military History Institute, Carlisle, Penn.

109. *months wore on:* Mahon East and Richard L. Johnston interviews.

109. *bags of flour:* Kessler, "Lloyd Kessler Recalls His Time."

110. *at town bazaars:* Smith Dawless, "The Head Hunter," http://cbi_theater_3.homecom.cast .net/vertex/verses_NcFrames.html.

110. *into stylish earrings:* CBI Roundup, Nov. 12, 1942.

110. *were prized as well:* Eric Sevareid, *Not So Wild a Dream* (New York: Atheneum, 1976), 274–75.

110. *to get high daily:* Orville Strassburg interview; Stone, *Crisis Fleeting,* 166. A chronic opium addict will typically consume between four and eight grams per day, though less dependent users can get by on a smaller amount.

110. *"muscular aborigines":* Buchanan, *Stilwell Road,* 29.

110. *"camps we had established":* Grillo, *Black Cuban, Black American,* 108.

110. *count to fifty:* CBI Roundup, Nov. 12, 1942.

110. *observing the Americans:* Sinclair, *Confusion Beyond Imagination, Book One,* 213.

111. *wearer had decapitated:* C. V. Glines, "America's Headhunter Allies," *Air Force Magazine,* June 1988, 86. The British also warned the Americans to avoid antagonizing the Nagas. "Warn all forward troops under your Command to never 'beat up' Nagas for any reason whatsoever," a political officer advised the Ledo Area Command in June 1944. "Otherwise, unfortunate 'reprisals' might well be the result."

111. *threaten the Ledo Road:* Memo No. 1446G, SDO Mokokchung to the Deputy Commissioner of the Naga Hills, Nov. 26, 1943, Naga Database.

112. *coins, and opium:* Joseph Straub Collection, Military History Institute, Carlisle, Penn.

112. *"They were fifteen . . . a butcher's cleaver":* Sevareid, *Not So Wild a Dream,* 259.

112. *"'How!'":* Ibid., 260.

112. *skulls be taken:* Ibid., 284.

113. *sacred bonding ritual:* Ibid., 268.

113. *sight to behold:* CBI Roundup, Nov. 12, 1942.

113. *GIs caught leering:* Ibid.

113. *"cut off his head":* Kessler, "Lloyd Kessler Recalls His Time."

114. *special court-martial:* Evidence of previous conviction certified by 1st Lieut. Penneth M. Cline, Clerk of Court, U.S. Army Judiciary, Falls Church, Va. The specific details of Perry's run-in with Sterghos are not available because the Army did not retain permanent records related to special courts-martial.

114. *the following March:* Evidence of previous conviction. This document actually misstates the parameters of the pay reduction, quoting the duration of the decrease as one month instead of six months. But several other components of Perry's court-martial file confirm that his pay was, indeed, meant to be docked for half a year.

114. *insults and stones:* Orville Strassburg interview. Strassburg added that the MPs put a stop to the Chinese taunting by threatening to release the Japanese prisoners.

114. *sex-starved Japanese troops:* T/3 Alex Yorichi, "Japanese Prisoner of War Interrogation Report No. 49," Oct. 1944, http://www.exordio.com/1939-1945/codex/Documentos/report-49-USA-orig.html.

114–15. *"The stockade . . . smart niggers!":* Mary Penick Motley, ed., *The Invisible Soldier: The Experience of the Black Soldiers, World War II* (Detroit: Wayne State University Press, 1987), 134.

115. *and reading magazines:* Records of the Ledo Stockade, Ledo Area Command, National Archives at College Park, Md.

115. *start a new circle:* Motley, *The Invisible Soldier,* 134.

115. *"dragged them out":* Ibid., 135.

115. *treatment of prisoners:* Memo from Lieut. Col. Eliot Stoutenburgh regarding solitary confinement cells, June 9, 1945, records of the provost marshal, Ledo Area Command.

115. *severity of his sentence:* Earl Owen Cullum, *Manhunt in Burma and Assam* (Dallas: Self-published, 1993), 7.

116. *anal fissures:* Medical record for Pvt. Herman Perry (Army serial no. 13074419), Dec. 1943, private collection of Edna Wilson.

116. *"Hi Edna . . . Yours, Herman"*: Letter from Herman Perry to Edna Wilson, Dec. 14, 1943, private collection of Edna Wilson.

116. *promised release date*: Cullum, *Manhunt in Burma and Assam*, 7.

117. *agony and humiliation*: Sinclair, *Confusion Beyond Imagination: Book Six*, 38. Both Cullum and Sinclair cite the eighteen-day figure for the length of Perry's extended stay. However, I could find no primary sources to confirm this exact number.

117. *dermatological treatments*: Cullum, *Manhunt in Burma and Assam*, 7.

117. *on January 13*: 849th Engineer Aviation Battalion morning reports, Company A, Jan. 1944, National Personnel Records Center, St. Louis, Mo.

SEVEN

119. *lay ahead*: Barry W. Fowle, *Builders and Fighters: U.S. Army Engineers in World War II* (Fort Belvoir, Va.: United States Army Corps of Engineers, 1992), 329.

119. *"lacks drive and pep"*: William Boyd Sinclair, *Confusion Beyond Imagination: Book One* (Coeur d' Alene, Idaho: Joe F. Whitley, 1986), 226.

120. *"malaria be damned"*: Ibid.

120. *the road to go*: Richard L. Johnston interview, Apr. 2006.

120. *"brains to quit"*: "Interview with Richard L. Johnston," Feb. 17, 1999, University of North Texas, Oral History Collection, Denton, Tex.

120. *Old Mud and Ruts*: William Boyd Sinclair, *Confusion Beyond Imagination: Book Four*, 242.

120. *waterlogged road*: Fowle, *Builders and Fighters*, 334–35.

120. *buckets of oil*: Ibid., 335.

121. *crushers wasn't running*: Sinclair, *Confusion Beyond Imagination: Book One*, 230–31.

121. *questioned their devotion*: Richard Selee officer's papers.

122. *cans of warm beer*: Fowle, *Builders and Fighters*, 336.

122. *disease and firefights*: Gerald Astor, *The Jungle War: Mavericks, Marauders, and Madmen in the China-Burma-India Theater of WWII* (Hoboken, N.J.: John Wiley & Sons, 2004), 136–38.

122. *resisted jungle rot*: Ibid., 131.

123. *"God Bless America"*: Charles Ogburn Jr., *The Marauders* (New York: Harper, 1956), 76–82.

123. *advancing the Ledo Road*: *Merrill's Marauders: February–May 1944* (Washington, D.C.: Center of Military History, 1990), 114. The original version of this book, published in 1945, was part of the War Department Historical Division's American Forces in Action Series.

123. *north of Shingbwiyang*: Leslie Anders, *The Ledo Road* (Norman: University of Oklahoma Press, 1965), map of Patkais.

123. *a mottled black*: Author's visit, Nov.–Dec. 2006; Richard Selee officer's papers.

124. *promised release date*: Earl Owen Cullum, *Manhunt in Burma and Assam* (Dallas: Self-published, 1993), 7.

124. *turned him down*: Ibid., 22.

124. *"All I said . . . talk to me about it"*: Court-martial testimony of Lieut. Col. Wright Hiatt, Sept. 4, 1944, Clerk of Court, U.S. Army Judiciary, Falls Church, Va.

125. *"Uncle Sugar"*: Sinclair, *Confusion Beyond Imagination: Book One*, 216.

125. *"The three horsemen . . . assault other soldiers"*: Evelio Grillo, *Black Cuban, Black American* (Houston: Arte Público Press, 2000), 113.

125. *murder once before*: Report of incident, Oct. 2, 1944, records of the adjutant general, Ledo Area Command, National Archives at College Park, Md.

126. *cheating at craps*: Ibid. It was unusual, though not unheard of, for the Army to keep poor records on black soldiers, and thus be unable to identify the victim's surname in this murder case.

126. *"Why haven't . . . drill formation"*: "Negro Engineers Write History in Heroic Job on Key Ledo Road," *Chicago Defender*, 1944 (specific date unknown).

126. *aluminum scrap:* "Music 'Midst Assam Tea Patches for G.I.'s," *CBI Roundup,* 1944 (specific date unknown).

126. *Hawaiian folk tunes: CBI Roundup,* Mar. 2, 1944.

127. *"'your foots move'":* "The Joint's Jumpin' Up in Assam," *CBI Roundup,* Jan. 28, 1943.

127. *"'I had been . . . action of this type'":* Testimony of Pvt. Melvin Newby, records of the inspector general, Ledo Area Command, National Archives at College Park, Md.

127. *bare-breasted Naga women:* Grillo, *Black Cuban, Black American,* 106.

128. *ten rupees a throw:* Bernard Frank interview; Records of the adjutant general, Ledo Area Command; Eugene B. Vest, "Native Words Learned by American Soldiers in India and Burma in World War II," *American Speech,* vol. 23, no. 3/4 (Oct–Dec. 1948): 228.

128. *from their tryst:* Memo dated Mar. 4, 1945, records of the adjutant general, Ledo Area Command.

129. *Coca-Cola:* Dominic Streatfeild, *Cocaine: An Unauthorized Biography* (New York: Picador, 2003), 80–81. In fairness, it should be noted that San Francisco–based sociologist Jerry Mandel has argued that "soldier's disease" was a term invented in 1915, the same year the antidrug Harrison Act took effect. Mandel claims that prohibitionists intentionally distorted the scope of the post–Civil War addiction problem in order to justify the criminalization of opiates and other drugs.

129. *"soldier and a man":* Ibid., 154.

129. *stimulant to soldiers:* Ibid., 155.

129. *insomnia, and cramps:* Office of the Surgeon General, *Manual for the Medical Department* (Washington, D.C.: Government Printing Office, 1898), 118.

129. *outlawed the drug:* Fred T. Dick, *A Study of Opium and Other Dangerous Drugs in Relation to the Military Establishment* (Washington, D.C.: George Washington University, 1968), 28.

130. *"use of marihuana":* Ibid., 29.

130. *melted the mind:* Ibid., 31. A 1970 Army report on the drug, entitled *A Review of the Biomedical Effects of Marihuana on Man in the Military Environment,* used a more temperate tone. While acknowledging that marijuana addiction could turn soldiers unacceptably passive, the report's authors also noted some beneficial effects of the drug: "On the other hand, it may be argued with some basis in fact that the use of the drug is 'recreational' and the pleasant experience affords a temporary escape that is concluded with a restful sleep. From this euphoric experience the individual recovers with renewed vitality."

130. *five-year prison terms:* Ibid., 50.

130. *"indefinite custody":* Ibid., 37.

131. *physical exhaustion:* "Benzedrine Alerts," *Time,* Feb. 21, 1944.

131. *bacon and Bundt cake:* "A Chronology of the Far War," *The Baltimore Sun,* Oct. 18, 1998.

131. *"no addicts":* Mary Penick Motley, ed., *The Invisible Soldier: The Experience of the Black Soldier, World War II* (Detroit: Wayne State University Press, 1987), 130.

131. *gross domestic product:* Martin Booth, *Opium: A History* (New York: St. Martin's Press, 1996), 115.

132. *on rationed rice:* Ibid., 62, 177.

132. *headhunters into passivity:* Rahul Goswami, "Opium in the Naga Hills," *The Atlantic Monthly,* Sept. 1, 1999.

132. *their own habits:* J. H. Hutton, "J. H. Hutton's Tour Diary in the Naga Hills," Apr. 24, 1923, Naga Database.

132. *suffering from diarrhea:* Chief of Infantry, *Basic Field Manual, Dog Team Training* (Washington, D.C.: Government Printing Office, 1941), 63.

132. *packets of opium:* "Asparagus & Oatmeal," *Time,* Aug. 8, 1938.

133. *brutal Japanese yoke:* Dick, *A Study of Opium,* 65.

133. *"get out of there":* Todd Chisam interview, May 2006.

133. *threshold for fighters:* "Age Dispute, Managerial Muss Bar Perry from Banks Fight," *The Washington Evening Star,* Feb. 17, 1944.

134. *sum of $5,000:* "O'Donnell Bids $5,000 for Share in Aaron Perry," *The Washington Post,*

Jan. 19, 1944. According to this proposal, O'Donnell would have been entitled to half of Aaron's future earnings, minus expenses and the boxer's cut—an arrangement akin to purchasing an interest in a racehorse.

134. *deep into five figures:* "Tom O'Donnell's $5,000 Offer Declined by Perry's Manager," *The Washington Post*, Jan. 20, 1944.

134. *Fairfax to Baltimore:* Edna Wilson interview, Sept. 2006.

134. *back in Washington:* Court-martial testimony of Sgt. Robert W. Davis, Sept. 4, 1944, Clerk of Court, U.S. Army Judiciary, Falls Church, Va.

134. *girlfriend's letters:* William Boyd Sinclair, *Confusion Beyond Imagination: Book Six* (Coeur d'Alene,Idaho: Joe F. Whitley, 1989), 47.

134. *"pretty well messed up":* Statement of Pvt. Herman Perry to Sgt. Robert W. Davis, July 23, 1944, Clerk of Court, U.S. Army Judiciary, Falls Church, Va.

134. *pick-and-shovel duties:* Statement of Lieut. Gene H. Carapico, June 6, 1944, Clerk of Court, U.S. Army Judiciary, Falls Church, Va.

134. *late that afternoon:* Statement of Booker D. Stitt, June 5, 1944, Clerk of Court, U.S. Army Judiciary, Falls Church, Va.

134. *alongside the road:* Richard Selee officer's papers.

135. *the Ledo Stockade:* Carapico statement.

135. *opium and ganja:* Perry statement.

135. *pyrotechnic show:* Richard Selee officer's papers.

135. *boots and overalls:* Stitt statement.

135. *in search of breakfast:* Ibid.

136. *the entire company:* Statement of Staff Sgt. Jeff C. Gobold, June 5, 1944, Clerk of Court, U.S. Army Judiciary, Falls Church, Va.

136. *he told the pair:* Ibid.

136. *just in case:* Ibid.

136. *Cady wasn't punished:* Hiatt testimony.

137. *the English language:* Carapico statement.

137. *"that he does it":* Court-martial testimony of Lieut. Gene H. Carapico, Sept. 4, 1944, Clerk of Court, U.S. Army Judiciary, Falls Church, Va.

137. *"back to the guardhouse":* Stitt statement.

137. *"That's right":* Carapico testimony.

137. *"you think, Lieutenant":* Stitt statement.

138. *"let him turn it in":* Gobold statement.

138. *informed the supply sergeant:* Statement of Staff Sgt. Earl I. Rawlins, June 5, 1944, Clerk of Court, U.S. Army Judiciary, Falls Church, Va.

138. *potentially violent prisoner:* Court-martial testimony of Staff Sgt. Earl I. Rawlins, Sept. 4, 1944, Clerk of Court, U.S. Army Judiciary, Falls Church, Va.

138. *"turn my rifle in":* Statement of T/5 Fred L. Underwood, June 5, 1944, Clerk of Court, U.S. Army Judiciary, Falls Church, Va.

138. *"send you to the guardhouse":* Gobold testimony.

139. *"I go to the guardhouse":* Ibid.

139. *"anybody to take me":* Underwood statement.

139. get this bullet: Rawlins and Underwood statements.

139. *"business this morning":* Rawlins statement.

139. *an escaped prisoner:* Gobold statement.

140. *between his knees:* Walton statement.

140. *Cat they'd been discussing:* Carapico statement.

140. *T/4 George Waites:* Statement of Sgt. Harry Bethel, June 5, 1944, Clerk of Court, U.S. Army Judiciary, Falls Church, Va.

141. *from between his knees:* Ibid.

141. *middle of the road:* Walton statement.

141. *yelled up to Perry:* Walton testimony.

141. *out of a court-martial:* Walton statement.

142. *"Get back!":* Griffis statement.
142. *"I'll throw you in!":* Walton testimony.
142. *rep to uphold:* Bernard Frank interview, Mar. 2006.
142. *"come up on me!":* Walton statement.
142. *black man holding it:* Walton testimony.
142. *like a rag doll's:* Walton statement.
142. *spent gunpowder:* Perry statement.
142. *mound of dirt:* Walton statement.
142. *single word was spoken:* Ibid.
143. *green thicket below:* Ibid.
143. *"Don't leave me, boys!":* Bethel statement.

EIGHT

145. *Cady's expression:* Perry statement.
145. *his spinal column:* Affidavit of Capt. Richard W. Trotter, 151st Medical Battalion, Mar. 8, 1944, Clerk of Court, U.S. Army Judiciary, Falls Church, Va.
145. *a second time:* Court-martial testimony of Pvt. Herman Perry, Sept. 4, 1944, Clerk of Court, U.S. Army Judiciary, Falls Church, Va.
145. *into Cady's stomach:* Trotter affidavit.
145. *"for missing reveille":* Perry testimony.
146. *whiff of M1 powder:* Perry statement.
146. *hopped in back:* Griffis statement.
146. *the gravely injured:* Bethel statement.
146. *the rest of the way:* Ibid.
146. *a maintenance crew:* Carapico statement.
147. *oxygen-starved blue:* Bethel statement.
147. *530 rupees:* Memo to Graves Registration Officer from Capt. Wilton M. Lewis, 151st Medical Battalion, Mar. 5, 1944, Clerk of Court, U.S. Army Judiciary, Falls Church, Va.
147. *her father's death:* "Woodhull Officer Killed in Action," *The Canisteo Times,* Mar. 16, 1944.
147. *Willie Johnson:* Earl Owen Cullum, *Manhunt in Burma and Assam* (Dallas: Self-published, 1993), 8.
147. *Perry's belongings:* Orville Strassburg interview Mar. 2006.
147. *Alma Talbot:* Davis testimony.
148. *"nowhere with that unit":* Orville Strassburg interview.
148. *notorious hard-ass:* During the court-martial, Perry's defense counsel would try numerous times to introduce evidence of Cady's supposed cruelty. These attempts, most of which failed to elicit more than vague generalizations about Cady, are discussed in chapter 11.
148. *reprimand for laziness:* Mahon East interview, Jun. 2006.
148. *his opium habit:* "Wanted for Murder," *CBI Roundup,* Dec. 24, 1944. This clipping is from the private collection of Kathryn Cullum Lee.
148–49. *"One of the effects. . . contact seem longer":* William Boyd Sinclair, *Confusion Beyond Imagination: Book Six* (Coeur d'Alene, Idaho: Joe F. Whitley, 1989), 38.
149. *"I had one soldier. . . saw him in bed":* James L. Howard, ed., *1007th Engineer Special Service Battalion February 15, 1943–January 11, 1946* (Lakewood, Colo.: Self-published, 1992), 37.
150. *on their own camp:* Cullum, *Manhunt in Burma and Assam,* 8. The two shooters, privates James Edwards and Paul Wellons, were court-martialed and sentenced to five to ten years behind bars.
150. *dead or alive:* Cullum, *Manhunt in Burma and Assam,* 8.
150. *the road wasn't far:* Perry statement.
150. *what that something was:* Ibid.
151. *just around the corner:* Richard Selee officer's papers, Military History Institute, Carlisle, Penn.

151. *edge of camp:* Perry statement.
151. *the GIs bunked:* Ibid.
151. *to kill Cady:* Ibid.
151. *the semiconscious:* Ibid.
151. *"remember what it was":* Ibid.
152. *members of the 849th:* Ibid.; Perry testimony.
152. *shot on sight:* Perry testimony.
152. *"I would be shot":* Ibid.
152. *two of C rations:* Statement of Pvt. Arquillus Q. Pearson, June 2, 1944, Clerk of Court, U.S. Army Judiciary, Falls Church, Va.; Sinclair, *Confusion Beyond Imagination: Book Six,* 44. As will later be seen, though Perry fired at least two rounds while on the lam, his rifle was later discovered with a full clip—proof that he was furnished with additional ammo between March 5 and March 9.
152. *his friends' letters:* Ibid. Perry told conflicting stories of his actions on March 8 and March 9, particularly regarding the sequence of events that led up to his attempted surrender. Every effort has been made to select the most consistent and plausible elements of these accounts.
153. *chances with the MPs:* Perry statement.
153. *waited for the cops:* Perry testimony.
153. *kill him then and there:* Perry statement.
154. *town of Indaw:* Christopher Bayly and Tim Harper, *Forgotten Armies: The Fall of British Asia, 1941–1945* (Cambridge, Mass.: Belknap Press, 2005), 379–80.
154. *on the camp's fires:* *Merrill's Marauders: February–May 1944* (Washington, D.C.: Center of Military History, 1990), 54–55.
154. *rang out for hours:* Gerald Astor, *The Jungle War: Mavericks, Marauders, and Madmen in the China-Burma-India Theater of WWII* (Hoboken, N.J.: John Wiley & Sons, 2004), 241.
155. *hideouts grew longer:* Cullum, *Manhunt in Burma and Assam,* 8–9.
155. *from Washington:* Ibid., 8.
155. *to cross the oceans:* Ibid.
156. *infamous brothels:* Ibid., 9.
156. *the Bengali diet:* "The Famine in India," *The New Republic,* May 22, 1944, 697–98.
156. *grounds and livestock:* Bayly and Harper, *Forgotten Armies,* 282.
156. *"dogs and vultures":* "The Famine in India," *The New Republic.*
156. *"energy to breathe":* Bayly and Harper, *Forgotten Armies,* 282.
156. *by 500 percent:* "The Famine in India," *The New Republic.*
156. *the trackside muck:* Bayly and Harper, *Forgotten Armies,* 288.
157. *"In the Calcutta . . . clutched to their breasts":* Eric Sevareid, *Not So Wild a Dream* (New York: Atheneum, 1976), 301.
157. *"to the jungle welcome":* Evelio Grillo, *Black Cuban, Black American* (Houston: Arte Público Press, 2000), 116.
157. *bullock dung:* Richard Selee officer's papers.
158. *stench of death:* Grillo, *Black Cuban, Black American,* 116.
158. *war's final days:* Denton J. Brooks, "Open New Calcutta Rest Camp for Negro Troops," *Chicago Defender,* 1945 (specific date unknown).
158. *to go on leave:* Ibid.
158. *sporadic trips to Ledo:* Grillo, *Black Cuban, Black American,* 115; Mahon East interview; Mary Penick Motley, ed., *The Invisible Soldier: The Experience of the Black Soldier, World War II* (Detroit: Wayne State University Press, 1987), 120.
158. *real-estate magnate:* Denton J. Brooks, "Calcutta Social Whirl Happy Escape from Burma Jungle for Colored G.I.'s," *Chicago Defender,* 1945 (specific date unknown).
158. *arrested on the spot:* Sinclair, *Confusion Beyond Imagination: Book Six,* 7.
159. *"It must be . . . contract venereal disease":* Ibid., 8.
159. *"pimps for the military":* Bayly and Harper, *Forgotten Armies,* 283.

160. *cousin, or mother:* Ibid., 299.

160. *around forty thousand:* Sinclair, *Confusion Beyond Imagination: Book Six,* 6.

160. *their Calcutta leaves:* Brockbank, *The Context of Heroism* (Ypsilanti: Eastern Michigan University, 1998), 120–28. Based on an interview with a unit commander, Brockbank states that 15 percent of the 1883rd Engineer Aviation Battalion took leave in Calcutta, and that "a high percentage came back with VD." The commander was reprimanded by the CBI brass for his men's high infection rates, to which he responded with a three-page letter outlining the preventive measures he'd taken. The correspondence ended there.

160. *egg ration in England:* Bayly and Harper, *Forgotten Armies,* 298. Bayly and Harper actually overstate the English egg ration by a factor of two.

160. *avoided punishment:* Ibid., 300–301.

161. *"him to remain free":* Cullum, *Manhunt in Burma and Assam,* 8–9.

161. *farmers for rice:* Perry testimony.

161. **CBI Roundup** *as souvenirs:* "…By Planes, Jeeps, and Pack," *CBI Roundup,* Jan. 28, 1943.

161. *about March 18:* Ibid. Perry stated that he spent "about ten days" in the jungle before encountering the British unit.

162. *"to a liaison officer":* Perry statement.

162. *way back to camp:* Edward Hymoff, "The Army's Most Incredible Deserter," *Real: The Exciting Magazine for Men,* Mar. 1956, 54.

162. *they could spare:* Ibid. Hymoff also claims that the British troops gave Perry tablets of the antimalarial drug Atabrine, but this seems more far-fetched.

162. *he'd surely die:* Perry claimed several times to have joined the British troops in combat. "I spent one (1) day at the front lines with these officers and British soldiers," he swore in his statement of July 23, an assertion he repeated at his court-martial approximately six weeks later. But this claim seems fantastical: in mid-March, the British-led Chindits were preparing to attack the Burmese town of Indaw, well over a hundred miles to the south. Given that vehicular transportation was impossible through the jungle, there is no way that Perry could have made it to Indaw and back in the relatively short time period he was known to have been on the lam.

162. *mountain stream:* In *Confusion Beyond Imagination: Book Six,* William Boyd Sinclair identifies this stream as the Jum Hka. But this seems erroneous; according to the coordinates listed for the Jum Hka at TravelJournals.net and other reputable sources, the stream is too far south and east of Tagap Ga to have played a role in Perry's tale. As will be noted in the next chapter, it's possible that Sinclair confused the Jum Hka with Jum Ga, a possible present-day name for the village in which Perry settled.

163. *trash and human waste:* Perry left no records of his first impression of the village, so this description is amalgamated from four sources: Sinclair's account of the village's orientation; Captain Richard "Les" Johnston's recollections of visiting the village in 1945; numerous photographs and descriptions from the Naga Database; and the author's own visit to similar settlements in the Patkais in 2006.

163. *affixed to their sides:* As will be seen shortly, the preferred means of displaying skulls varied by village. It was Johnston who provided the detail regarding the method used in Perry's adopted home. Photographs of this method are available in the Naga Database.

NINE

165. *"could have perpetrated":* Sir James Johnstone, *Manipur and the Naga Hills* (New Delhi: Gyan Publishing House, 2002), 143.

165. *offerings to the gods:* Jamie Saul, *The Naga of Burma: Their Festivals, Customs and Way of Life* (Bangkok: Orchid Press, 2005), 181–382.

166. *"shameful to a Naga":* Keith Cantlie, "Memoir of Time in the Naga Hills as a Deputy Commissioner, 1919–1920," Naga Database.

166. *guarded by their parents:* Johnstone, *Manipur and the Naga Hills,* 47–48. "I knew a

man who had killed sixty women and children," wrote Johnstone, "when on one occasion he happened to come upon them after all the men had left the village on a hunting expedition."

166. *more challenging prey:* Christoph von Fürer–Haimendorf, *The Konyak Nagas: An Indian Frontier Tribe* (New York: Holt, Rinehart and Winston, 1969), 97–98.

167–67. *"The captured head . . . work in the fields":* Ibid.

167. *pot of chilies:* J. H. Hutton, *Naga Manners and Customs* (Gurgaon, India: Vintage Books, 1990), 30. This book was originally published in 1924 as a monograph, inelegantly titled *Diaries of Two Tours in the Unadministered Area East of the Naga Hills.*

167. *grass tassels:* Ibid., 5.

167. *"in the next world":* Ibid., 49.

167. *Christmas ornaments:* Hutton took a memorable black-and-white photograph of the last of these methods in Wanching. The photograph depicts ovoid vessels approximately two feet tall, with central cavities in which the skulls were stashed.

167. *made of brass:* Joseph Straub Collection, Military History Institute, Carlisle, Penn. This particular photo is captioned, "An old Naga chieftain wears a brass face showing that he has taken a head." In fact, the chieftain's necklace is ringed with at least two such mementos.

167. *across the face:* Saul, *The Naga of Burma,* 34.

167. *tufts of human hair:* Fürer-Haimendorf, *The Konyak Nagas,* 13.

169. *and the Balkans:* E-mail interview with Janet Hoskins, May 2006. The Montenegrin tribes were avid headhunters, with a particular yen for capturing the skulls of Muslims. Heads were also taken, and then defiled, during intertribal blood feuds. In his book *Blood Revenge* (1984), anthropologist Christopher Boehm describes one such incident: "When the agents of Prince Nicholas eventually took their revenge upon Aleksa Djilas, they cut off his head, took it home, and threw it out on a field to rot or to be gnawed on by animals." A female relative of Djilas's was sent to retrieve the head before it could be entirely destroyed, an assignment that left her "emotionally impaired for the rest of her life."

169. *at least for a while:* "Essays on Head-Hunting in the Western Solomon Islands," *The Journal of the Polynesian Society,* vol. 109, no. 1 (Mar. 2000): 6; Janet Hoskins interview.

169. *"for the spirits":* Saul, *The Naga of Burma,* 179.

169. *this vital force:* J. H. Hutton, "J. H. Hutton's Tour Diary in the Naga Hills," Apr. 10, 1923, Naga Database.

169. *"done as warriors":* J. H. Hutton, "Leopard-Men of the Naga Hills," *The Smithsonian Report for 1921,* 532–33.

170. *spears, and cloth:* Mayumi Murayama et al., *Sub-Regional Relations in Eastern South Asia: With Special Focus on India's Northeastern Region* (Tokyo: Institute of Developing Economies, 2005), 50. The report's section on Assamese history was written by Udayon Misra of Dibrugarh University.

170. *head-taking raids:* Y. L. Roland Shimmi, *Comparative History of the Nagas: From the Ancient Period Till 1826* (New Delhi: Inter-India Publications, 1988), 154–55.

170. *Burma and Assam:* Johnstone, *Manipur and the Naga Hills,* 41.

170. *in 1837:* Fürer-Haimendorf, *The Konyak Nagas,* 3.

170. *"deserted village sites":* Johnstone, *Manipur and the Naga Hills,* 67.

171. *and even language:* A. S. Shimray, *Let Freedom Ring: Story of Naga Nationalism* (New Delhi: Promilla & Co., 2005), 35.

171. *in ancient times:* Shimmi, *Comparative History of the Nagas,* 73.

171. *practice called jhuming:* E. T. D. Lambert, "From the Brahmaputra to the Chindwin," *Geographic Journal,* vol. 89, no. 4 (Apr. 1937): 312.

172. *military desertion:* Shimmi, *Comparative History of the Nagas,* 135.

172. *could be harvested:* Hutton, *Naga Manners and Customs,* 28.

172. *British let them be:* Shimray, *Let Freedom Ring,* 34.

172. *and the tea gardens:* Ibid., 36.

172. *Naga farmland:* Ibid.

172. *every Naga incursion:* Ibid., 36–37.

172. *political influence:* Ibid., 37.

173. *the colonial government:* Johnstone, *Manipur and the Naga Hills,* 57.

173. *fifty-one gravely wounded:* Col. R. G. Woodthorpe, "Notes on the Wild Tribes Inhabiting the So-Called Naga Hills, on our North-East Frontier of India," Naga Database. These notes were delivered at a meeting of the Royal Anthropological Institute in 1881.

174. *decimated the rebels:* Johnstone, *Manipur and the Naga Hills,* 141–43, 151.

174. *strain of Baptism:* Shimray, *Let Freedom Ring,* 43–44.

174. *to settle elsewhere:* Ibid.; Hutton, *Naga Manners and Customs,* 43.

174. *"prop to the State":* Johnstone, *Manipur and the Naga Hills,* 59. Johnstone was concerned, however, that unless the missionaries became more aggressive in their pursuit of converts, the Angami Naga tribe would turn to Islam—apparently a British nightmare. "Unless some powerful counter influence is brought to bear on them," Johnstone wrote of the Angami, "they will adopt the vile, bigoted type of Mahommedanism prevalent in Assam and Cachar, and instead of becoming a tower of strength to us, be a perpetual weakness and source of annoyance." Johnstone would certainly be discouraged to learn that Islam has been making great inroads in North-East India in recent years, due to an influx of Bangladeshi immigrants from the west.

174–75. *"Administration in these . . . lot of the inhabitants":* Lambert, "From the Brahmaputra to the Chindwin," 309.

175. *British overlords:* Shimmi, *Comparative History of the Nagas,* 155.

175. *"Two lines . . . turn into enemies":* William R. Peers, *Behind the Burma Road: The Story of America's Most Successful Guerrilla Force* (Boston: Little, Brown, 1963), 64.

176. *couples in coitus:* Hutton, *Naga Manners and Customs,* 39–41, 49.

176. *west of Tagap Ga:* Statement of Sgt. Robert W. Davis, July 21, 1944, Clerk of Court, U.S. Army Judiciary, Falls Church, Va. This is an estimate based on the village's reported distance from Namyung, which is a little over two miles northwest of Tagap Ga.

176. *bamboo poles:* Saul, *The Naga of Burma,* 80.

176. *human excrement:* Hutton, *Naga Manners and Customs,* 52; author's visit, Nov.–Dec. 2006.

176. *animal skulls:* Fürer-Haimendorf, *The Konyak Nagas,* 21. This passage describes how "on days following a funeral the stench of rotting flesh often caused even the Konyaks [Nagas] to hold their noses as they hurried."

176. *a stone phallus:* Saul, *The Naga of Burma,* 120; J. H. Hutton, "Tour Diary in the Naga Hills," July 10, 1926, Naga Database.

176. *carved into his skull:* Hutton, *Naga Manners and Customs,* 39.

176. *Land of the Dead:* Fürer-Haimendorf, *The Konyak Nagas,* 93–94.

176. *Heimi Naga subtribe:* Contemporary accounts from the 1940s do not mention the tribal affiliation of Perry's village. However, according to Jamie Saul's extensive research, the area due west of Namyung would most likely be home to Nagas affiliated with the Heimi tribe. However, Wanchos and Konyaks have also been known to settle in this area of the Patkais. Additionally, both Heimis and Wanchos are sometimes considered to be related to the Konyaks—their languages, for one, are closely related. The customs and traditions that I describe in this book are those of the Heimi and Konyak tribes. Great care has been taken to ensure that the traditions of more southerly tribes, such as the Angami and Ao, are not mentioned—a challenge, since the majority of British anthropological research was conducted among these more accessible tribes.

177. *six miles away:* Orville Strassburg interview, Mar. 2006.

177. *"pours from his lips":* Ramachandra Guha, *Savaging the Civilized: Verrier Elwin, His Tribals, and India* (New Delhi: Oxford University Press, 1999), 241. Guha found this quote in notes that Elwin compiled while touring the Tuensang Frontier Division in March and April of 1954.

177. *foreigner departed:* Hutton, "J. H. Hutton's Tour Diary in the Naga Hills," Apr. 10, 1923.

177. *violence in the Patkais:* Memo No. 191C from Deputy Commissioner, Naga Hills, to the Advisor to the Governor of Assam, May 12, 1943, Naga Database.

178. *"I was investigating . . . back to 100"*: "Americans Clubby with Head Hunters," *CBI Roundup*, Nov. 12, 1942.

178. *rescued fliers*: E-mail interview with Jamie Saul, Feb. 2006.

178. *anyone's guess*: Ibid.

178. *cheeks and necks*: Saul, *The Naga of Burma*, 34. Saul carefully studied the variations in Naga tattoos on the Burmese side of the border. These tattoos ranged from the solid-colored facial splotches of the Wancho to the chest triangles of the Konyak. It is impossible to pinpoint exactly which designs were favored by the residents of Tgum Ga, but Saul's research indicates that Nagas who lived between Namyung and the Indian border were marked by wavy lines that started at the cheek, and continued down the neck. These tattoos were yet another mark that the bearer had taken a head, and had thus earned the right to status within village society.

179. *personal trophy shelf*: C. V. Glines, "America's Headhunter Allies," *Air Force Magazine*, June 1988, 84–87.

179. *village Tgum Ga*: Davis statement. I have wondered whether "Tgum Ga" was a mangling of Jum Ga, a present-day village in Burma's remote Sagaing Division. Jum Ga's official latitude is 26°41'60 N, while its longitude is 96°7'0 E; these coordinates put it a bit farther south than most contemporary descriptions of Perry's location. However, there is an obvious similarity between the names. On my visit to Sagaing Division in 2006, I tried to reach Jum Ga to ascertain whether Perry had lived there some sixty-two years earlier. However, Burmese military authorities—who were displeased to find an unauthorized American trespassing in one of their nation's most off-limits areas—stopped our party well short of the village.

179. *Glau*: Perry testimony.

179. *getting under way*: Saul, *The Naga of Burma*, 114. The Naga year was divided into two seasons: one for farming (Feb. through Nov.), the other for nonagricultural chores.

179. *the feeble soil*: Fürer-Haimendorf, *The Konyak Nagas*, 32.

179. *done by hand*: Ibid., 32–33.

180. *"Toward the end . . . hill to the village"*: Ibid., 33.

181. *cursing their enemies*: Lambert, "From the Brahmaputra to the Chindwin," 312.

181. *bamboo mouth harps*: Saul, *The Naga of Burma*, 158–63.

181. *to her fertility*: Ibid., 112.

181. *"husbands [were] listening!"*: Hutton, *Naga Manners and Customs*, 9.

181. *locks of goat hair*: Fürer-Haimendorff, *The Konyak Nagas*, 10–14.

181. *hairdos of commoners*: Ibid., 58. Hutton observed that some girl slaves were compelled to keep their hair closely cropped, much like American soldiers. This is because such slave girls were responsible for cooking the ang's meals, and it was taboo for the chief to discover human hair in his food.

181. *he'd later call it*: Roger Treat, "Gallows for a Jungle King," *Coronet*, Sept. 1945, 130.

182. *worse, his murder*: Edward Hymoff, "The Army's Most Incredible Deserter," *Real: The Exciting Magazine for Men*, Mar. 1956, 54.

182. *cases of tinned food*: Richard L. Johnston interview, Apr. 2006; "Interview with Richard L. Johnston," Feb. 17, 1999, University of North Texas, Oral History Collection, Denton, Tex.

182. *to the village*: Orville Strassburg interview.

183. *Namyung bridge*: Perry statement. The M1 bore the U.S. Army serial no. 420033.

183. *flintlock rifle*: Saul, *The Naga of Burma*, 70–75.

183. *their jungle hunts*: Perry statement.

183. *to a human baby*: Cantlie, "Memoir of Time in the Naga Hills as a Deputy Commissioner, 1919–1920."

183. *generation to generation*: Saul, *The Naga of Burma*, 63, 183.

183. *lycanthropic powers*: Hutton, "Leopard-Men in the Naga Hills," 529.

183. *Great Beyond*: Ibid., 530.

184. *olive drab fatigues*: Hymoff, "The Army's Most Incredible Deserter," 54.

184. *"from eating betelnuts"*: Harold Glendon Scheie, MD, *Ophthalmic Surgery and the Scheie*

Eye Institute (University of California, Berkeley: Opthalmology Oral History Series; Regional Oral History Office, 1989), 114.

184. *politely declined:* Ibid., 115–16.
185. *would later complain:* Davis statement.
185. *joining a Naga clan:* Jamie Saul interview.
185. *"claim as my wife":* Perry statement.
186. *rituals of courtship:* Treat, "Gallows for a Jungle King," 130.
186. *"Ultimately the suitor . . . morung to sleep":* Fürer-Haimendorf, *The Konyak Nagas,* 73.
186. *balls of opium:* Saul, *The Naga of Burma,* 112–13.
187. *created the sky:* Fürer-Haimendorf, *The Konyak Nagas,* 78.
187. *for the newlyweds:* Treat, "Gallows for a Jungle King," 130.
187. *to till his fields:* Perry statement.
187. *monkeys with the Mr* Treat, "Gallows for a Jungle King," 130.
187. *ganja awaited:* Hymoff, "The Army's Most Incredible Deserter," 55.

TEN

190. *marked the road's edge:* Pearson statement.
190. *reversed in spots:* Statement of Lieut. Warren W. Oley, June 6, 1944, Clerk of Court, U.S. Army Judiciary, Falls Church, Va.
190. *Ammunition Plant:* Supplemental statement of Arquillus Q. Pearson, June 5, 1944, Clerk of Court, U.S. Army Judiciary, Falls Church, Va.
190. *Company C's supply sergeant:* Pearson statement.
190. *Herman Perry in 1943:* Oley statement; certificate of Lieut. Col. Wright Hiatt, Apr. 21, 1944, Clerk of Court, U.S. Army Judiciary, Falls Church, Va.
191. *soon with child:* This is an estimate, albeit a very educated one, based on the observations of Richard "Les" Johnston. When Johnston saw Perry's son in late July/early August 1945, he put the infant's age at six months, meaning that the child would have been conceived around May 1944.
191. *to procure medicine:* Davis statement. Davis claims that the Naga errand runner obtained quinine, but that seems unlikely given the scarcity of the medicine. Perry probably just got Atabrine.
191. *on his behalf:* Perry statement.
191. *"Hell":* Richard Selee officer's papers, Military History Institute, Carlisle, Penn.
191. *"in a sewer line":* William Boyd Sinclair, *Confusion Beyond Imagination: Book One,* (Coeur d' Alene, Idaho: Joe F. Whitley; 1986), 241–42.
191. *bridges and culverts:* Ibid., 243.
192. *much-needed reinforcements:* *Merrill's Marauders: Feb.–May 1944* (Washington, D.C.: Center of Military History, 1990), 104–7.
192. *"eyes of our nation":* Christopher Bayly and Tim Harper, *Forgotten Armies, The Fall of British Asia, 1941–1945* (Cambridge, Mass.: Belknap Press, 2005) 361.
192. *captured enemy rations:* Gerald Astor, *The Jungle War: Mavericks, Marauders, and Madmen in the China-Burma-India Theater of WWII* (Hoboken, N.J.: John Wiley & Sons, 2004), 215.
193. *elephants would remain:* Bayly and Harper, *Forgotten Armies,* 382.
193. *attempts along the way:* Sabir Bhaumik, "British 'Attempted to Kill Bose,'" *BBC News,* Aug. 15, 2005.
193. *Indian bases for support:* Wong Chee Wai, "The Effect of Material Inferiority: An Analysis of Japanese Defeat in the Battle for Imphal, 1944," *Journal of the Singapore Armed Forces,* vol. 30, no. 1 (Summer 2004): http://www.mindef.gov.sg/imindef/publications/pointer/journals/2004/v30n1/features/feature6.html.
193. *Baptist missionaries:* "Revolt in the Hills," *Time,* Aug. 16, 1956.
193. *that romantic goal:* Gavin Young, "The Nagas: An Unknown War," *The Observer,* Apr. 3, 1962.
193. *ammunition stashes:* Bayly and Harper, *Forgotten Armies,* 385.

193. *head-hunting in check:* Ibid., 203.
194. *gangrenous wounds:* Ursula Graham Bower, *Naga Path* (London: Readers Union, 1952), 157.
194. *"result of local information":* Bayly and Harper, *Forgotten Armies*, 386.
194. *realize what it was:* Ibid., 386–87.
194. *recorded in his diary:* "Tour Diary of W. G. Archer," July 1, 1947, Naga Database.
195. *far less influence:* Christoph von Fürer-Haimendorf, *Return to the Naked Nagas* (London: John Murray, 1976), 23–24.
195. *white woman's cloak:* Bower, *Naga Path*, 43–45.
195. *"Queen of the Nagas":* Bayly and Harper, *Forgotten Armies*, 204.
195. *dreary in comparison:* Ibid., 76.
196. *"I think . . . rich texture:"* Ibid., 148.
196. *Zemi village:* Ibid., 172.
196. *and boost morale:* Ibid., 204.
197. *to commit* seppuku: Ibid., 388–90.
198. *knocked me down:* "Unfeazed [sic] by Armstrong's T.K.O., Perry Wants Return Bout," *The Washington Evening Star*, May 23, 1944.
198. *cheerful aplomb:* Edna Wilson interview, Sep. 2006
198. *wearing each day:* Supplemental statement of Pvt. Herman Perry, Aug 5, 1944, Clerk of Court, U.S. Army Judiciary, Falls Church, Va.
199. *his alter ego:* Davis testimony.
199. *of the town's bazaar:* Perry statement.
199. *station in Namyung:* Earl Owen Cullum, *Manhunt in Burma and Assam* (Dallas: Self-published, 1993), 9.
200. *American provost marshal:* Davis statement.
200. *had earned with gifts:* Cullum, *Manhunt in Burma and Assam*, 9.
200. *That's him:* Davis statement. Orville Strassburg, the last surviving member of the posse that captured Perry in July 1944, tells a very different story. He credits himself with tracking down the fugitive, saying that he was tipped off by a Naga whom he'd bribed with opium. This Naga, says Strassburg, indicated Perry's whereabouts by pointing to his tooth and then pointing to the jungle; the young lieutenant took this to mean that a gold-toothed man was hiding in a village, later revealed to be Tgum Ga. But there is no other source that corroborates this account, and it should be noted that Perry did not, in fact, have a gold tooth.
200. *on matters of security:* Perry testimony.
200. *satellite village:* Jamie Saul, *The Naga of Burma: Their Festivals, Customs and Way of Life* (Bangkok: Orchid Press, 2005), 76.
200. *a mile and a half away:* Davis statement. This is an estimate based on the fact that it took approximately 30–45 minutes for the MPs to walk from Tgum Ga to the satellite village where Perry was hiding.
201. *"Doo City":* Perry testimony.
201. *led to Tgum Ga:* Davis statement. Note that Davis misspells Strassburg's name in this statement as "Strossberg." It is a sloppy oversight that calls into question the accuracy of several other questionable parts of Davis's statement, such as his assertion that Perry at one time lived in a village fifty miles south of Tgum Ga.
201. *would have to suffice:* Davis testimony.
201. *array of leeches:* Orville Strassburg interview, Mar. 2006; author's visit, Nov.–Dec. 2006.
201. *Perry was gone:* Davis statement.
202. *"a rifle with him":* Ibid.
202. *naively agreed:* Ibid.; Perry statement; Cullum, *Manhunt in Burma and Assam*, 9–10. Accounts differ as to precisely how the rifle was removed from Perry's basha. Cullum claims that the M1 was covertly swiped by one of the posse's guides, but this seems to contradict Perry's assertion that he lent the gun to a Naga for the purpose of hunting monkeys.

202. *a moonless night:* Fred Espenak, "Six Millennium Catalog of Phases of the Moon," NASA
      Goddard Space Flight Center, http://sunearth.gsfc.nasa.gov/eclipse/phase/phasecat.html.
202. *fifty yards away:* Orville Strassburg interview.
202. *he couldn't be sure:* Davis statement.
203. *snuck around the back:* Ibid.
203. *and another fifteen:* Ibid.
204. *venture there at night:* Perry testimony.
204. *the tribal tongue:* Perry statement; Perry testimony.
204. *American was inside that hut:* Davis testimony.
204. *Perry to start running:* Ibid.
204. *hoping to avoid detection:* Ibid.
204. *barked at the Nagas:* Perry statement.
204. *just lent it out:* Ibid.
205. *to yap like that:* Davis testimony.
205. *he yelled:* Ibid.; Davis statement.
205. *head of the Naga man:* Perry testimony.
206. *nowhere to be seen:* Orville Strassburg interview; Perry testimony.
206. *quarter of a mile later:* Davis statement. Strassburg remembers the distance as closer to
      150 yards.
206. *the world receded:* Perry testimony; Perry statement.
207. *bandage his wound:* Davis statement.
208. *exiting the chest:* Statement of Maj. Carl Goetz, 73rd Evacuation Hospital, July 23, 1944,
      Clerk of Court, U.S. Army Judiciary, Falls Church, Va.; Strassburg interview.
208. *sucking chest wound:* Cullum, *Manhunt in Burma and Assam*, 10.
208. *down to the road:* Davis statement.
209. *stock and muzzle:* Ibid.; Davis testimony.
209. *the Johnny Talbot line:* Davis testimony.
209. *out there in the jungle:* Orville Strassburg interview.
209. *one for religion:* Edna Wilson interview.
209. *"had he not shot him":* Davis statement.
210. *done near Glau:* Ibid.
210. *five thirty in the morning:* Davis testimony. Davis puts the time closer to 4:00 A.M. in his
      statement of July 23. But given the distance that McMinn would have traveled, the 5:30
      A.M. estimate that Davis cited in his court-martial testimony seems more plausible.
210. *of Washington, D.C.:* Ibid.
210. *Seventy-third Evacuation Hospital:* Ibid.

ELEVEN

211. *crammed with thirty cots:* "Captain Henning Tells of Army Nurse's Work," *Marshfield
      News-Herald*, 1945, reprinted by Clark County (Wisc.) Genealogy, History, Ancestry &
      Internet Library, http://wvls.lib.wi.us/ClarkCounty/clark/data/bios3/3000.htm.
211. *teemed with maggots:* David Venditta, "Rugged Passage: A Healer on the Road to Burma,"
      The Morning Call (Allentown, Penn.), Mar. 26, 2006. Nurses often left the maggots in
      place, since the larvae actually cleaned wounds before dropping away.
211. *dulled by painkillers:* Certificate of Capt. Ambrose S. Churchill, 73rd Evacuation Hos-
      pital, Clerk of Court, U.S. Army Judiciary, Falls Church, Va. The certificate is undated,
      but appears to have been written and signed in early August 1944, when the Criminal
      Investigation Division was gathering evidence for Perry's court-martial.
212. *Phenobarbital:* Ibid.
212. *against him in court:* Davis testimony; Perry statement (preamble).
212. *of the hospital's staff:* Court-martial testimony of Maj. Carl Goetz, Sept. 4, 1944, Clerk
      of Court, U.S. Army Judiciary, Falls Church, Va.
212. *disjointed answers:* Perry testimony.

212. *against his hip:* Perry statement.
213. *with no qualms:* Goetz testimony.
213. *"idea of how how it was":* Perry testimony.
213. *notarized the document:* Ibid.; Goetz testimony.
214. *"No answer":* Supplemental statement of Pvt. Herman Perry, July 28, 1944, Clerk of Court, U.S. Army Judiciary, Falls Church, Va.
214. *treated twice before:* Memo of Sgt. Robert W. Davis to C.I.D. Regional Office, July 24, 1944, Clerk of Court, U.S. Army Judiciary, Falls Church, Va.
215. *factored into his crime:* Memo of Maj. C. W. Oatley to Commanding Officer, 20th General Hospital, Aug. 8, 1944, Clerk of Court, U.S. Army Judiciary, Falls Church, Va.
215. *"The results . . . of standing trial":* Deposition of Maj. Herbert S. Gaskill, Aug. 10, 1944, Clerk of Court, U.S. Army Judiciary, Falls Church, Va.
216. *rights for the accused:* House of Representatives (66th Congress, 2nd Session), *Hearing Before a Special Subcommittee of the Committee on Military Affairs: May 4, 1920* (Washington, D.C.: Government Printing Office, 1920), 3–25.
216. *minimum qualifications: The Articles of War: Approved June 4, 1920* (Washington, D.C.: Government Printing Office, 1920), 3–31.
216. *rather than officers:* Ibid. The current Uniform Code of Military Justice, by contrast, permits enlisted men to request that one-third of the court's members be composed of other enlisted men, as long as they're from a different unit.
217. *insubordination to murder:* Proceedings of a General Court Martial, Special Orders No. 217, 7 Aug. 1944, Clerk of Court, U.S. Army Judiciary, Falls Church, Va.; Bernard Frank interview, Mar. 2007. Frank would go on to become a successful defense attorney in Miami, specializing in high-profile cases; one of his clients was the celebrated gangster Meyer Lansky.
217. *in February 1941:* Enlistment record for Clayton J. Oberholtzer (Army serial no. 35007796), National Archives, Washington, D.C.
217. *African American unit:* John C. Oberholtzer interview, May 2006.
217. *assist with Perry's defense:* Proceedings of a General Court Martial, Special Orders No. 217; enlistment records for Louis W. Ritz (Army serial no. 35151107) and George E. Bodamer (Army serial no. 34288035), National Archives, Washington, D.C.
218. *on the murder count:* Bernard Frank interview, Mar. 2007.
218. *arrest on March 5:* Arraignment of Pvt. Herman Perry, Sept. 4, 1944, Clerk of Court, U.S. Army Judiciary, Falls Church, Va.
219. *kill a white officer:* Bernard Frank interview.
219. *"penalty of death":* Memo of Lt. Col. Jay W. Scovel, Staff Judge Advocate in New Delhi, Aug. 11, 1944, Clerk of Court, U.S. Army Judiciary, Falls Church, Va.
219. *9 percent of the Army:* J. Robert Lilly , "Executing Soldiers During World War II," *Crime & Delinquency*, vol. 42, no. 4 (Oct. 1996), 491–516.
219. *involved black soldiers:* Christopher Paul Moore, *Fighting for America: Black Soldiers— The Unsung Heroes of World War II* (New York: One World, 2005), 218.
219. *house near Ledo:* Richard L. Johnston interview, Apr. 2006.
219. *"special duty" elsewhere:* Organization of the Court, Sept. 4, 1944, Clerk of Court, U.S. Army Judiciary, Falls Church, Va.
220. *formal dining room:* Richard L. Johnston interview.
220. *scant room to move:* Bernard Frank interview.
220. *olive drab fatigues:* Richard L. Johnston interview.
220. *were excused:* Organization of the Court.
221. *"he had been drinking":* Hiatt testimony.
221. *handling of black GIs:* Bernard Frank interview.
222. *"Do you know . . . I heard about it":* Carapico testimony.
223. *"When Private Perry . . . That is all":* Gobold testimony.
224. *his gun at anyone:* Court-martial testimony of Sgt. Earl I. Rawlins, Sept. 4, 1944, Clerk of Court, U.S. Army Judiciary, Falls Church, Va.

225. *"and I had to answer":* Walton testimony.

225. *Private Harry Bethel:* In his June statement to CID, Bethel is listed as a sergeant rather than a private. The latter rank seems more plausible, however, given that Bethel mentioned it himself in his court-martial testimony.

225. *grade school education:* Enlistment record for Harry Bethel (Army serial no. 35611629), National Archives, Washington, D.C.

225–26. *"What did . . . Not that I heard":* Court-martial testimony of Pvt. Harry Bethel, Sept. 4, 1944, Clerk of Court, U.S. Army Judiciary, Falls Church, Va.

226. *never hear the answer:* Court-martial testimony of T/5 Robert L. Griffis, Sept. 4, 1944, Clerk of Court, U.S. Army Judiciary, Falls Church, Va.; court-martial testimony of T/4 George Waites, Sept. 4, 1944, Clerk of Court, U.S. Army Judiciary, Falls Church, Va.

227. *objection was overruled:* Davis testimony.

228. *"The officer then . . . I ran away":* Perry statement.

228. *"United States of America":* Ibid.

230. *ended his cross-examination:* Goetz testimony.

231. *speak ill of the dead:* Walton testimony.

231. *the order of events:* Perry testimony.

234. *"explanation due a man":* Ibid.

234. *"Evidence shows . . . in this court room":* Closing argument of Capt. Clayton J. Oberholtzer, Sept. 4, 1944, Clerk of Court, U.S. Army Judiciary, Falls Church, Va.

235–36. *"[Oberholtzer] . . . commensurate with the crime":* Closing argument of Lieut. Bernard A. Frank, Sept. 4, 1944, Clerk of Court, U.S. Army Judiciary, Falls Church, Va.

236. *six and a half hours:* Record of trial by General Court-Martial of Pvt. Herman Perry, Sept. 4, 1944, Clerk of Court, U.S. Army Judiciary, Falls Church, Va.

TWELVE

237. *residence for $2,410:* Sales records for 3217 Warder Street NW, Washingtoniana Division, Martin Luther King Jr. Memorial Library, Washington, D.C.

237. *Fort Meade, Maryland:* "Boxing's Loss Is Army's Gain," *The Washington Post,* Apr. 11, 1944; enlistment record for Aaron Perry (Army serial no. 33910060), National Archives, Washington, D.C. Although Aaron Perry passed his Army physical in April 1944, he was allowed to keep boxing for several months before reporting for training. His last fight of the year was on August 18 at New York's Madison Square Garden, versus aging Angeleno Jimmy McDaniels. Disappointingly, the Anvil was knocked out in the fourth round, losing for the second time since the Henry Armstrong debacle in May.

237. *death by hanging:* Incoming classified message, CG US Army Forces China Burma and India Theater Headquarters [New Delhi] to War Department, Sept. 24, 1944, Clerk of Court, U.S. Army Judiciary, Falls Church, Va.

238. *could be carried out:* Ibid.; *The Articles of War: Approved June 4, 1920* (Washington, D.C.: Government Printing Office, 1920), 15–17. The 50½th Article of War was the one specifically dealing with the review process.

238. *rather than a thug:* Edna Wilson interview, Sept. 2006.

238. *Judge Not Guilty:* Joseph Paull, "Dr. J. E. Lind Shot in Auto At Corner of 11th and G," *The Washington Post,* Feb. 22, 1944.

238. *Bankroll Bob:* Jacob A. Stein, "Cold Cash Upfront," *Washington Lawyer,* Dec. 2002.

238. *thirty years straight:* Paull, "Dr. J. E. Lind Shot in Auto At Corner of 11th and G."

238. *Republican activist:* "G.O.P. Primary Called," *The Washington Post,* Apr. 22, 1920. Scott was a native of Wilmington, North Carolina., forced to flee to Washington by an infamous 1898 race riot. After the black-owned *Wilmington Daily Record* had published an editorial that lampooned the white hysteria over fictional black rapists, the Redshirts, a mob of Democratic thugs, burned down the newspaper's office. They then forced the city's Republican officials, including the mayor, to resign, replacing them with Democrats deemed far less sympathetic to blacks. The Redshirts celebrated this coup by murdering at least

twenty African Americans and burning dozens of black homes. Scott joined approximately 10 percent of Wilmington's residents who left town, never to return. He eventually became a judge in Washington.

239. *relevant citation:* Stein, "Cold Cash Upfront."

239. *violations in 1938:* "Officials of D.C. Go on Stand for Accused Lawyer," *The Washington Post*, Feb. 4, 1938.

239. *playing the ponies:* Paull, "Dr. J. E. Lind Shot in Auto At Corner of 11th and G."

239. *Abraham Lincoln:* Ibid. Lind was, on his mother's side, a fourth cousin of Lincoln's mother, Nancy Hanks.

239. *glove compartment:* Ibid.

239. *Dr. Antoine Schneider:* Winifred Nelson, "Miller Calm as He Tells Jury He Shot 'Other Man,'" *The Washington Post*, May 27, 1944.

240. *first-degree murder:* Winifred Nelson, "'Not Guilty,' Panel Finds, In 1 Hour, 20 Minutes," *The Washington Post*, June 1, 1944.

240. *"authority is in the field":* Letter from Robert I. Miller to Commanding General, U.S. Army Forces, Sep. 28, 1944, Clerk of Court, U.S. Army Judiciary, Falls Church, Va.

241. *"This being . . . commutation thereof":* Review by the staff judge advocate in *United States v. Private Herman Perry*, Sep. 21, 1944, Clerk of Court, U.S. Army Judiciary, Falls Church, Va.

241. *"any part of the sentence":* *The Articles of War*, 14–15. The Fourty-seventh Article of War dealt specifically with the "power to approve."

241. *during World War II:* As previously noted, forty-eight of the forty-nine death sentences for desertion were commuted to prison terms; only Private Eddie Slovik was put to death for this crime.

241. *the city's outskirts: Merrill's Marauders: February–May* 1944 (Washington, D.C.: Center of Military History, 1990), 113. The bulk of the American troops who laid siege to Myitkyina were reinforcements flown in to the captured airstrip, including two units of white engineers: the 209th and 236th Engineer Combat Battalions. (Black engineers were, of course, not welcome on the front lines.) The Marauders had simply taken too many casualties for the final assault. Of the 1,310 Marauders who reached Myitkyina, 679 were evacuated to hospitals between May 17 and June 1; however, approximately 200 remained to assist their replacements in capturing the town.

242. *die in vain:* Lesile Anders, *The Ledo Road* (Norman: University of Oklahoma Press, 1965), 146.

242. *reached Warazup:* William Boyd Sinclair, *Confusion Beyond Imagination: Book One* (Coeur d'Alene, Idaho: Joe F. Whitley, 1986), 245.

242. *of the Himalayas:* Barbara Tuchman, *Stilwell and the American Experience in China, 1911–1945* (New York: Macmillan, 1971), 484.

243. *completing the Ledo Road:* Brig. Gen. Stuart C. Godfrey, "Advantages of Air Transport," Oct. 20, 1944, Military History Institute, Carlisle, Penn.

243. *northern Burma skies:* Anders, *The Ledo Road*, 218.

243. *on the black market:* Tuchman, *Stilwell and the American Experience in China*, 489.

243. *supposed sworn enemies:* Eric Sevareid, *Not So Wild a Dream* (New York: Atheneum, 1976), 323.

243. *useless in combat:* Tuchman, *Stilwell*, 484.

243. *a visit to Chongqing:* Sevareid, *Not So Wild a Dream*, 323.

244. *his own arms cache:* Tuchman, *Stilwell*, 485.

244. *units for the CBI:* Ibid., 491.

244. *"The crazy. . . He is impossible":* Ibid., 489.

245. *"set up base elsewhere":* Ibid., 490.

245. *"lost by further delays":* Ibid., 493.

245. *"I've waited . . . And laid the Peanut low":* Ibid. 494.

246. *"military cooperation":* Gerald Astor, *The Jungle War: Mavericks, Marauders, and Madmen in the China-Burma-India Theater of WWII* (Hoboken, N.J.: John Wiley & Sons, 2004), 334.

246. *his American nemesis:* Ibid., 334–35.

246. *"agile, trained mind"* Memo of Col. C. C. Fenn to Commanding General, Oct.14, 1944, Clerk of Court, U.S. Army Judiciary, Falls Church, Va.

247. *Perry's hanging:* Memo from Commanding General India-Burma Theater to War Department, Nov. 18, 1944, Clerk of Court, U.S. Army Judiciary, Falls Church, Va.

247. *list of priorities:* Earl Owen Cullum, *Manhunt in Burma and Assam* (Dallas: Self-published, 1993), 17.

247. *endorsement of executions:* Incoming classified message, Gen. Dan I. Sultan to Maj. Gen. James A. Ulio, Nov. 18, 1944, Clerk of Court, U.S. Army Judiciary, Falls Church, Va.

247. *twenty-five years each:* Cullum, *Manhunt in Burma and Assam*, 18.

247. *inmates were white:* Enlistment records for John M. Gregal (Army serial no. 20547553), Edward A. Hahn (Army serial no. 32751209), Frank E. Hamelburg (Army serial no. 12036587), and Lawrence Schryver (Army serial no. 32748839), National Archives, Washington, D.C.

247. *feet in any direction:* Cullum, *Manhunt in Burma and Assam*, 18.

248. *digging garbage pits:* Records of the Ledo Stockade, Ledo Area Command, National Archives at College Park, Md. According to one entry in the stockade's punishment book, on December 7, 1944, Perry was given six hours extra duty as punishment for slacking off during his work detail inside the stockade.

248. *for attempted murder:* Cullum, *Manhunt in Burma and Assam*, 19.

248. *down without permission:* Records of the Ledo Stockade, Ledo Area Command. I filed a Freedom of Information Act request with the Office of the Provost Marshal General, Department of the Army, seeking additional information regarding Herman Perry's incarceration. When I didn't receive a written response within sixty days, I called the office's FOIA compliance officer for an explanation. He said that any records pertaining to Perry's stay in Ledo were destroyed long ago. Fortunately, a few key documents remained at the National Archives at College Park, Md. Those documents, along with the recollections of Earl Owen Cullum, were vital to reconstructing Perry's stockade experience.

249. *the case in Delhi:* Letter from Lieut. Col. Edwin O. Shaw to Robert I. Miller, Oct. 18, 1944, Clerk of Court, U.S. Army Judiciary, Falls Church, Va.

249. *"such evidence was offered":* Brief on behalf of Herman Perry, Robert I. Miller, Nov. 15, 1944, Clerk of Court, U.S. Army Judiciary, Falls Church, Va.

249. *"base camp as possible":* Ibid.

250. *on November 24:* General Court Martial Order No. 8, from Headquarters of United States Forces, India-Burma Theater, Mar. 10, 1945, Clerk of Court, U.S. Army Judiciary, Falls Church, Va.

250. *never be forthcoming:* Handwritten note from the Board of Review, Herman Perry case, to Theater Headquarters, Nov. 19, 1944, Clerk of Court, U.S. Army Judiciary, Falls Church, Va. The author of this note did not sign his name, but he appears to have been one of the three judge advocates assigned to review Perry's case.

251. *catching some shut-eye:* Cullum, *Manhunt in Burma and Assam*, 18.

251. *thick Assamese fog:* Ibid.; Memo to Provost Marshal from Lt. Col. Harry E. Curtis, Jan. 21, 1945, National Archives at College Park, Md.

251. *eight-hour vacations:* Cullum, *Manhunt in Burma and Assam*, 19.

251. *coils of barbed wire:* Ibid., 21.

251. *were hardly impassable:* Ibid.

252. *deviate from that plan:* Ibid., 18.

252. *request without comment:* Ibid., 19.

252. *"original transmission":* Incoming classified message, Gen. Dan I. Sultan to Maj. Gen. M. C. Cramer (via Maj. Gen. James A. Ulio), Dec. 15, 1944, Clerk of Court, U.S. Army Judiciary, Falls Church, Va.

253. *he bluntly proclaimed:* Cullum, *Manhunt in Burma and Assam*, 19. According to an earlier version of this book, Cullum's source for the Dennis quote appears to have been Lieutenant Archibald Howell, who was also present at this meeting.

253. *on December 15, 1944:* Fred Espenak, "Six Millennium Catalog of Phases of the Moon,"

NASA Goddard Space Flight Center, http://sunearth.gsfc.nasa.gov/eclipse/phase/phase cat.html.

253. *the inmates' tents:* Cullum, *Manhunt in Burma and Assam*, 20.

253. *bite them in the ass:* Ibid., 20–21. In fairness, it should be stressed that Weaver was never definitively established as the source of Perry's wire cutters; this was Cullum's conclusion, based on a review of the official postescape report authored by Lieutenant Colonel Henry G. Thomas and Captain Arthur Rossett. Another indication of Weaver's probable involvement is that on January 8, 1945, in the thick of the postescape investigation, he was transferred from Ledo to a stockade in Bombay. His fate beyond that is unknown.

253. *checkerboard pattern:* Photographs of Ledo Stockade, private collection of Kathryn Cullum Lee.

253–54. *where he was working:* Cullum, *Manhunt in Burma and Assam*, 20.

254. *the stockade's edge:* Author's visit, Nov.–Dec. 2006.

THIRTEEN

257. *eight of his guards:* Earl Owen Cullum, *Manhunt in Burma and Assam* (Dallas: Self-published, 1993), 20–21. Dennis's assistant, Lieutenant Francis Mackin, also received a formal reprimand for negligence.

258. *849th Engineer Aviation Battalion:* Ibid., 22.

258. *"Not a bad life":* Ibid.

258–59. *"Sentenced to death . . . without delay":* "Wanted for Murder," *CBI Roundup*, Dec. 24, 1944. This clipping is from the private collection of Kathryn Cullum Lee.

259. *multitude of languages:* Cullum, *Manhunt in Burma and Assam*, 22.

259. *olive drab fatigues:* Herman Perry WANTED poster, private collection of Kathryn Cullum Lee.

260. *amid the tea plants:* Cullum, *Manhunt in Burma and Assam*, 22.

260. *bullet in their spines:* Ibid.

260. *unwitting roommate:* Bernard Frank interview, Mar. 2007.

261. *except inane chatter:* Cullum, *Manhunt in Burma and Assam*, 23.

261. *supplies to Perry:* Ibid.

261. *Perry's scent:* Ibid.

261. *posters on the Patkais:* Ibid.

261. *triumphant return:* Richard L. Johnston interview, Apr. 2006.

261. *tear them to shreds:* Celestine Perry Thompson interview, Mar. 2006. This anecdote was handed down by Ms. Thompson's late uncle, the Reverend Henry E. Johnson, who was Herman Perry's half-brother. As will be seen later in the story, the Reverend Johnson spent years researching what happened to his mother's second-eldest son.

261. *right before Christmas:* Outgoing classified message, Col. Robert M. Springer to Lt. Gen. Daniel I. Sultan, Dec. 18, 1944, Clerk of Court, U.S. Army Judiciary, Falls Church, Va.

262. *"written confessions":* Holdings of the Board of Review, *United States v. Pvt. Herman (NMI) Perry*, Dec. 27, 1944, 10. This document can be found alongside the other court-martial materials at the offices of the Clerk of Court, U.S. Army Judiciary, Falls Church, Va.

262. *eventual punishment:* Ibid.

262. *the legal adage goes:* The "fruit of the poisonous tree" doctrine stems from a 1920 Supreme Court case, *Silverthorne Lumber Co. v. United States*. Federal agents had illegally seized tax records from Silverthorne Lumber, and then photocopied them. The Supreme Court ruled that these copies were inadmissible at trial, establishing a precedent that derivatives of illegally obtained evidence should be considered likewise tainted.

262. *"illegal evidence":* Holdings of the Board of Review, *United States v. Pvt. Herman (NMI) Perry*.

263. *they wrote:* Ibid., 11.

263. *"voluntary manslaughter":* Ibid.

263. *the death sentence:* Ibid., 12.

263. *river's eastern bank:* William Boyd Sinclair, *Confusion Beyond Imagination: Book One* (Coeur d'Alene, Idaho: Joe F. Whitley, 1986), 254.

263. *were supposed to meet:* Ibid., 257.

264. *the American press:* Ibid.

264. *Assamese countryside:* Cullum, *Manhunt in Burma and Assam,* 23.

265. *another .45 soon enough:* Ibid.

265. *smiling on him:* Ibid.

266. *to the other side:* Ibid., 24.

266. *the Miri Hills:* These hills are named after the Miri tribe of Assam. Gentler than the Nagas—they did not hunt heads, preferring to collect Tibetan metal bells in lieu of skulls—the Miris were known for being unusually tall (males commonly exceeded sixty-eight inches in height, according to the British ethnologist Colonel E. T. Dalton) and for their chiefs' enthusiastic polygamy.

266. *another tribal beauty:* Roger Treat, "Gallows for a Jungle King," *Coronet,* Sept. 1945, 131; Bernard Frank interview.

266. *off with food and guns:* William Boyd Sinclair, *Confusion Beyond Imagination: Book Six* (Coeur d'Alene, Idaho: Joe F. Whitley, 1989), 65.

266. *"Never, ever":* Bernard Frank interview.

266. *the Jungle King:* Treat, "Gallows for a Jungle King," 130; e-mail interview with Tucker Hiatt, Jan. 2007.

267. *short of gravel:* Leslie Anders, *The Ledo Road* (Norman: University of Oklahoma Press, 1965), 213.

267. *the coming monsoons:* James L. Howard, ed., *1007th Engineer Special Service Battalion, Feb. 15, 1943–Jan. 11, 1946* (Lakewood, Colo.: Self-Published, 1992), 49.

267. *FROM INDIA TO CHINA:* Ted Price Collection, Military History Institute, Carlisle, Penn.

267. *MPs on motorcycles:* Sinclair, *Confusion Beyond Imagination: Book One,* 258–59.

267. *"never be completed":* Denton J. Brooks, "Brooks Tells of Entry into China with First Convoy on Stilwell Road," *Chicago Defender,* Feb. 10, 1945.

267. *according to Brooks:* Denton J. Brooks, "Ledo Road Battle Just Beginning, Writer Says," *Chicago Defender,* Apr. 21, 1945.

267. *selected for this mission:* Brooks, "Brooks Tells of Entry," *Chicago Defender.*

268. *at Mongyu, Burma:* Sinclair, *Confusion Beyond Imagination: Book One,* 261–63.

268. *the direction of China:* Ibid., 261.

268. *African American drivers:* Brooks, "Brooks Tells of Entry," *Chicago Defender.*

268. *total manpower:* Ibid.; Denton J. Brooks, "China Denies Bar on Negro Troops," *Chicago Defender,* Feb. 17, 1945. There were officially 372 men in the convoy. In addition to the nine black drivers, a tenth African American—T/5 Edgar Moore, an engineer—was invited along, too.

268. *two-thirds black:* Please see endnote in chapter 1 regarding this estimate.

268. *on the twenty-third:* Sinclair, *Confusion Beyond Imagination: Book One,* 263.

268. *"WHILE YOU'RE DRIVIN'":* Ibid., 219–20; Orville Strassburg interview, Mar. 2006. Most of these pinups were copies of Alberto Vargas's famed "Varga Girls."

269. *survived the onslaughts:* Ibid., 266; Ted Price Collection.

269. *bloodstained uniforms:* Theodore M. White, "Linked at Last," *Time,* Feb.5, 1945.

269. *566 miles to Kunming:* Ibid.

270. *"The Star-Spangled Banner":* Ibid.; Ted Price Collection.

270. *departed General Stilwell:* Sinclair, *Confusion Beyond Imagination: Book One,* 273.

270. *"[the road] and built it":* Barbara Tuchman, *Stilwell and the American Experience in China, 1911–1945* (New York: Macmillan, 1971), 511.

270. *cold weather existed:* Brooks, "China Denies Bar," *Chicago Defender.*

270. *to China's prosperity:* Sinclair, *Confusion Beyond Imagination: Book One,* 278–79.

270. *Vinegar Joe's legacy:* Even Barbara Tuchman, perhaps Stilwell's greatest defender, acknowledges the historical harm caused by Chiang's decision to rename the road. The Stilwell Road, she writes in her biography of the general, was "named as his monument and denounced as his folly."

271. *Lily Pons performed:* Sinclair, *Confusion Beyond Imagination: Book One,* 280–81; "China Denies Bar," *Chicago Defender.*

Theodore Roosevelt commanded the First U.S. Volunteer Cavalry Regiment, better known as the Rough Riders. The unit charged up nearby Kettle Hill before joining the main assault. They were given disproportionate accolades in the American press, thanks to Roosevelt's reputation as a historian, outdoorsman, and crimefighter; he had previously served as New York City's police commissioner.

285. *"over the age of ten"*: Stuart Creighton Miller, *Benevolent Assimilation: The American Conquest of the Philippines, 1899–1903* (New Haven, Conn.: Yale University Press, 1984), 220. The officer who gave this order, General Jacob Hurd Smith, was pilloried in the American press. The *New York Evening Journal* ran a cartoon depicting a row of emaciated, blindfolded children about to be dispatched by a firing squad; the caption read, "Criminals Because They Were Born Ten Years Before We Took the Philippines." In response to the public outcry, Smith was eventually court-martialed on a minor charge. He was found guilty and sentenced to be verbally reprimanded.

285. *"hunting all to pieces"*: Joseph Ryan, "The Saga of David Fagen: Black Rebel in the Philippine Insurrection," *Socialist Action*, June 1998.

285. *segregated U.S. Army*: "Soldiers in the Sun: The Philippine War," Presidio of San Francisco Web site, http://www.nps.gov/archive/prsf/history/buffalo_soldiers/philippine_war .htm. This chapter is part of an online history of the Buffalo Soldiers.

286. *"yuh white boys now!"*: Ryan, "The Saga of David Fagen," *Socialist Action*.

286. *"bonds that bind"*: Gail Lumet Buckley, *American Patriots: The Story of Blacks in the Military from the Revolution to Desert Storm* (New York: Random House, 2001), 158–59.

286. *Filipina wife*: Ryan, "The Saga of David Fagen," *Socialist Action*.

287. *"A colored Houdini . . . make him 'dance'"*: *Assam Police Gazette*, Feb. 1945, private collection of Kathryn Cullum Lee.

288. *six-foot-two Cullum*: Cullum, *Manhunt in Burma and Assam*, 27.

288. *sign of a trespasser*: Ibid., 26–27.

289. *well-trafficked Stilwell Road*: Ibid., 26.

289. *sickly frame*: Ibid., 27.

289. *stopped by for a chat*: Ibid., 28.

289. *in nearby Jaipur*: George R. Flamm, "Perry Manhunt," *Ex-CBI Roundup*, July 1953, 20–21.

290. *"we get the man now"*: Cullum, *Manhunt in Burma and Assam*, 28.

290. *tied to his wrist*: Ibid.

290. *rumored hideout*: Ibid.

290. *haze-shrouded Patkais*: Ibid.

290. *range if necessary*: Ibid.

291. *as not quite right*: Ibid., 28–29.

291. *"and asks for food"*: *Apastamba Dharma Sutra*, 8:2.

291. *distance or at night*: Cullum, *Manhunt in Burma and Assam*, 29.

291. *nights shy of full*: Fred Espenak, "Six Millennium Catalog of Phases of the Moon," NASA Goddard Space Flight Center, http:sunearth.gsfc.nasa.gov/eclipse/phase/phasecat.html.

292. *heavy with suspicion*: Postcapture photographs of Herman Perry, Mar. 1945, private collection of Kathryn Cullum Lee.

292. *his injured foot*: Bernard Frank interview, Mar. 2007. According to Frank, Perry would later state that he had been paranoid about being mauled by a tiger while on the run.

292. *two weeks earlier*: Cullum, *Manhunt in Burma and Assam*, 29; Sinclair, *Confusion Beyond Imagination: Book Six* (Coeur d'Alene, Idaho: Joe F. Whitley, 1989), 54. There remains considerable debate as to whether Perry lost his pistol, or had merely stashed it in the bushes in order to avoid frightening his Indian hosts. The fact that Perry attempted no further stickups after robbing Troxler and Toomer suggests to me that the former explanation is likely.

293. *pebbly streambed*: Cullum, *Manhunt in Burma and Assam*, 29.

293. *accident of birth*: Letter from Earl Owen Cullum to Rev. Henry E. Johnson, July 13 1994, private collection of Edna Wilson.

271. *foot on Chinese soil:* Brooks, "China Denies Bar," *Chicago Defen*
271. *insisted on the ban:* Gerald Astor, *The Jungle War: Mavericks, Mai the China-Burma-India Theater of WWII* (Hoboken, N.J.: John Wil
271. *pairs of leering eyes:* Nancy E. Brockbank, *The Context of Hero* Michigan University, 1998), 138.
271. *within forty-eight hours:* Brooks, "China Denies Bar," *Chicago D*
271. *originally from the South:* Enlistment records of Raymond To 32189387) and Otho Troxler (Army serial no. 32680808), National D.C. Toomer had been born in Georgia in 1916, Troxler in North
272. *at the timber camp:* Cullum, *Manhunt in Burma and Assam*, 24.
272. *within twenty-four hours:* Ibid.
272. *into the darkness:* Ibid.
273. *Major Earl Owen Cullum:* Ibid., 24–25.
273. *law enforcement:* Kathryn Cullum Lee interview, Apr. 2006.
274. *father's grocery store:* Letter from Earl Owen Cullum to his childre Aug. 8, 1988, private collection of Kathryn Cullum Lee. The Cotto known as Fair Park Stadium.
275. *"General McClellan's army":* Ibid.
275. *oversize ears:* Photograph of Earl Owen Cullum, c. 1945, private Cullum Lee.
275. *over the Patkais:* Cullum, *Manhunt in Burma and Assam*, 22.
275. *on January 11:* Ibid., 24.
275. *bring him in alive:* Ibid., 24–25.
275. *pinned down by gunfire:* Ibid.
276. *from their peers:* Ibid., 24.
276. *he could trust him:* Ibid., 25.
276. *hiding in their midst:* Ibid.
276. *them from doing so:* Ibid.
277. *get a move on:* Ibid.
277. *reset their trap:* Ibid.
278. *other side of the road:* Ibid.
278. *automatic setting:* Ibid.
278. *the heart to kill:* Ibid., 26.
278. *trampled vegetation:* Ibid., 25.
278. *would have to wait:* Ibid.
278. *on his right foot:* Ibid.
278. *Achilles tendon:* Photograph of Herman Perry's right foot, Mar. 194 of Kathryn Cullum Lee.
279. *in the wound:* Cullum, *Manhunt in Burma and Assam*, 25.

FOURTEEN

281. *color of their skin:* Earl Owen Cullum, *Manhunt in Burma and A* published, 1993), 26.
281. *betel-nut trees:* Ibid.
282. *battle of Myitkyina:* Joe Balak and Carl M. Hutsell, "CBI War Dog De bat," *Ex-CBI Roundup*, Mar. 1996, http://www.cbi-history.com/part_vi_
282. *as best he could:* Cullum, *Manhunt in Burma and Assam*, 26.
283. *"get away with it?":* Letter of Brig. Gen. Joseph A. Cranston to Maj. E Mar. 10, 1945, Clerk of Court, U.S. Army Judiciary, Falls Church, Va.
284. *the .45 behind:* Cullum, *Manhunt in Burma and Assam*, 26.
284. *pair from Asia:* Ibid., 24.
285. *San Juan Hill:* The most famous engagement of the Spanish-America of San Juan Hill, took place near Santiago, Cuba, on July 1, 1898.

294. *CONDEMNED ESCAPEE . . . FOR SAFEKEEPING*: Cullum, *Manhunt in Burma and Assam*, 30.

294. *grislier than dysentery*: Ibid.

294–95. *"No Sir! . . . our score sheet?"*: Letter of Cranston to Covell.

295. *"noose takes over"*: Ibid.

296. *"have reported him"*: Flamm, "Perry Manhunt," 21.

296. *the john and watched*: Sinclair, *Confusion Beyond Imagination: Book Six*, 57.

296. *"hang like a man"*: Ibid., 57–58.

296. *for security's sake*: Cullum, *Manhunt in Burma and Assam*, 33.

296. *riot in his honor*: Ibid.; Richard L. Johnston interview, Apr. 2006; Bernard Frank interview; Sinclair, *Confusion Beyond Imagination: Book Six*, 58.

296–97. *"IT IS IMPERATIVE . . . FOR CONFINEMENT"*: Cullum, *Manhunt in Burma and Assam*, 31.

297. *simply too great*: Ibid., 33.

297. *early morning chill*: Ibid.

297. *summarily shot*: Ibid.

297. *Patkais to the east*: Ibid.

297. *guards were black*: Richard L. Johnston interview; Sinclair, *Confusion Beyond Imagination: Book Six*, 58–59.

297. *odds of a riot*: Sinclair, *Confusion Beyond Imagination: Book Six*, 59.

297. *"the Hell will start"*: Cullum, *Manhunt in Burma and Assam*, 33.

298. *his brother Aaron*: Bernard Frank claims that Perry's last letter was addressed to his mother, "explaining to her just because I was colored, that's why they're hanging me." But I could not find evidence to corroborate this assertion.

298. *"Dear Brother . . . Dont answer"*: Roger Treat, "Gallows for a Jungle King," *Coronet*, Sept. 1945, 131–32. Unlike Perry's correspondence cited elsewhere in this book, the original of this letter has been lost. But Perry's sister, Edna Wilson, verified that the text cited in Treat's article is genuine. Richard L. Johnston also confirmed the substance of Perry's last letter, and the punctuation quirks—especially the dearth of periods and apostrophes—are hallmarks of Perry's writing style.

298. *a final cigarette*: Richard L. Johnston interview.

299. *slightly monstrous*: Cullum, *Manhunt in Burma and Assam*, 34.

299. *"gallows platform"*: Denton J. Brooks, "U.S. Soldier Hangs in India," *Chicago Defender*, Apr. 7, 1945.

300. *"the one who's going"*: Ibid.

300. *continued health*: Ibid.

300. *The hood went on*: Richard L. Johnston interview. There is an apocryphal story that Perry was still smoking when the hood went on, and that he chuckled, "Are you trying to burn me to death?"

300. *the jawbone's corner*: Ibid.; Sinclair, *Confusion Beyond Imagination: Book Six*, 59.

300. *gravity take over*: Sinclair, *Confusion Beyond Imagination: Book Six*, 59.

300. *The ladder was pulled*: Ibid., 62.

300. *legs went slack*: Bernard Frank interview.

300. *no breath*: Sinclair, *Confusion Beyond Imagination: Book Six*, 62.

301. *Perry's resting place*: Richard Mock Photograph Collection, Military History Institute, Carlisle, Penn. Mock captioned his set of Margherita cemetery pictures: "These pictures speak for themselves except for the one of Perry's Grave. This grave is on a plot away from all the others, because Perry was a deserter."

301. *still under review*: Edna Wilson interview, Sept. 2006.

301. *"his own misconduct"*: Battle Casualty Report for Herman Perry, Mar. 17, 1945, Clerk of Court, U.S. Army Judiciary, Falls Church, Va.

303. *never be seen again*: Richard L. Johnston interview; "Interview with Richard L. Johnston," Feb. 17, 1999, University of North Texas, Oral History Collection, Denton, Tex. I am deeply indebted to Johnston's wife of sixty-five years, Muriel, for assisting with this reporting.

FIFTEEN

305. *the coming monsoons:* William Boyd Sinclair, *Confusion Beyond Imagination: Book One* (Coeur d'Alene, Idaho: Joe F. Whitley, 1986), 283.

305. *"in the news again":* James L. Howard, ed., *1007th Engineer Special Service Battalion: February 15, 1943–January 11, 1946* (Lakewood, Colo.: Self-published, 1992), 49.

306. *Generalissimo yielded:* Denton J. Brooks, "China Gets Its First American Negro Troops," *Chicago Defender,* June 3, 1945.

306. *China during World War II:* Bennie J. McRae Jr., "858th Engineer Aviation Battalion," 858th Engineer Aviation Battalion Web site, http://www.coax.net/people/lwf/858.

306. *the Middle Kingdom:* Sinclair, *Confusion Beyond Imagination: Book One,* 283.

306. *"remarkable accomplishment":* Leslie Anders, *The Ledo Road* (Norman: University of Oklahoma Press, 1965), 213–14.

306. *"out of the way":* Sinclair, *Confusion Beyond Imagination: Book One,* 293.

306. *twelve thousand tons:* Anders, *The Ledo Road,* 235–36.

306. *down almost daily:* Sinclair, *Confusion Beyond Imagination: Book One,* 297.

306. *closer to fifteen:* Ibid., 285.

307. *"depredations by the Chinese":* Richard Selee officer's papers, Military History Institute, Carlisle, Penn. The Chinese were not the only ones in the drugs trade. According to William R. Peers, two American officers—one a captain, the other a major—became involved in opium running toward the end of the war. Peers also alleges that the unnamed pair buried a stash of arms near Moulmein in lower Burma, which they planned on selling to ethnic warlords. The two were court-martialed and convicted after the war, and sentenced to ten years apiece. "But it so happened that one of them came from a very influential family," Peers said in 1977. "There was enough political pressure put on Congress that Congress not only cancelled his sentence, so to speak, but they also gave him $20,000 in payment for all the rough treatment he had had." The connected man's coconspirator was given a similarly sweetheart deal.

307. *to southern China:* Anders, *The Ledo Road,* 236.

307. *defender of the Ledo Road:* Ibid., 236.

307. *should be abandoned:* Richard Selee officer's papers (entry dated June 30, 1945).

307. *dinner guest observed:* Ibid. (entry dated July 1, 1945).

307. *the Missouri River:* "Portraits and Profiles, Chief Engineer: 1775 to Present," U.S. Army Corps of Engineers, http://www.hq.usace.army.mil/history/coe.htm.

307. *"I love him":* Richard Selee officer's papers (entry dated July 10, 1945).

308. *such radical change:* Morris J. MacGregor Jr., *Integration of the Armed Forces 1940–1965* (Washington, D.C.: Center of Military History, 1985), 152–166.

308. *most of August:* Sinclair, *Confusion Beyond Imagination: Book One,* 295.

308. *from India and Burma:* Richard Selee officer's papers (entry dated Aug. 15, 1945).

309. *elsewhere for their spoils: Engineer Memoirs: Lieutenant General Walter K. Wilson, Jr.,* U.S. Army Corps of Engineers, May 1948, 101. This publication is part of an oral history series put together by the Office of the Chief of Engineers.

309. *worth of violence:* Author's visit, Nov.–Dec. 2006.

309. *"alien thoroughfare":* Sinclair, *Confusion Beyond Imagination: Book One,* 302–3.

309. *Christmas Eve 1945:* Ibid., 305.

309. *"civilian economy":* William Collins King, *Building for Victory: World War II in China, Burma, and India and the 1875th Engineer Aviation Battalion* (Lanham, Md.: Taylor Trade, 2004), 194. This page reprints a United Press article from Mar. 9, 1946, entitled "Stilwell Road Abandoned by U.S."

310. *"road is through forever":* David Richardson, "The Jungle's Victory," *The New Republic,* Feb. 10, 1947, 14.

310. *"Just 18 miles . . . churning Irrawaddy":* Ibid., 14–15.

310. *in today's dollars:* King, *Building for Victory,* 194.

310. *cost was impossible:* Anders, *The Ledo Road*, 234.

310. *$11.4 billion today:* Richardson, "The Jungle's Victory," 13.

310. *battle of Iwo Jima:* Anders, *The Ledo Road*, 235. The death toll breakdown in Anders's book, although the most detailed available, seems suspect. Based on the statements of doctors, nurses, and the soldiers themselves, Anders appears to have grossly underestimated the number of fatalities due to disease. He does not, for example, list any fatalities due to dysentery, a disease whose lethality was well known along the road. He also fails to make clear how many soldiers were part of the Ledo Area Command. I initially thought these 1,133 deaths were out of the universe of 15,000 engineers, which would make working the road more deadly than landing at Normandy on D Day. But the so-called Ledo Area Command probably refers to a figure closer to 50,000 soldiers, including Hump pilots based at Chabua and perhaps even Merrill's Marauders (though, again, this is not clear from Anders's accounting). However, it is safe to say that for an area of the war known for little actual combat, the death toll along the road was unusually high.

311. *expeditious manner:* Author's visit.

311. *the Pangsau Pass:* C. M. Buchanan, *Stilwell Road: Story of the Ledo Lifeline* (Calcutta: Office of Public Relations, USF in IBT, 1945), 44–45.

312. *Roosevelt himself promised:* Anders, *The Ledo Road*, 22.

312. *necessary for success: Engineer Memoirs: Lieutenant General Walter K. Wilson, Jr.*, 82.

313. *sky-high patriotism:* Nancy E. Brockbank, *The Context of Heroism* (Ypsilanti: Eastern Michigan University, 1998), 141. Interestingly, 52 percent of African American soldiers responded "very important," versus just 25 percent of white troops.

313. *"Can you blame them?":* Charles R. Rowley, ed., *Situation CBI: The Story of the 1880th Engineer Aviation Battalion in World War II, March 1943–December 1945* (New York: Ziff Davis, 1946), 179.

313. *over eighty thousand:* Kevin Graman, "Veterans Group Marks Final Meeting," *The Spokesman Review*, Aug. 28, 2005.

313. *closure in 2005:* Ibid.

314. *events for decades:* Muriel Johnston interview, Apr. 2007.

314. *"Socially, the Indians . . . is to live apart":* A. Z. Phizo, "Plebiscite Day Speech," May 16, 1951, http://www.northeastunlimited.com/facts/p/95.html.

315. *"force you to do that":* A. S. Shimray, *Let Freedom Ring: Story of Naga Nationalism* (New Delhi: Promilla & Co., 2005), 64.

315. *AUGUST 1947:* Neville Maxwell, *India and the Nagas: Minority Rights Group Report No. 17* (London: Minority Rights Group, 1973). This report is online at the NSCN-IM's Web site, http://www.nscnonline.org/.

315. *enforce tribal laws:* Shimray, *Let Freedom Ring*, 63.

315. *"Naga people arrived at":* Maxwell, *India and the Nagas*.

315. *"and unacceptable":* Ibid.

315. *insurgency ensued:* Ramachandra Guha: *Savaging the Civilized Verrier Elwin, His Tribals, and India* (New Delhi: Oxford University Press, 1999), 285.

315–16. *by the Americans:* Author's visit.

315. *India's mortal enemy:* Shimray, *Let Freedom Ring*, 74.

315. *"Mass arrests . . . part of the land":* Ibid., 70.

316. *closer to ten thousand:* Edna Fernandes, *Holy Warriors: A Journey into the Heart of Indian Fundamentalism* (London: Portobello Books, 2007), 191. I relied on an early galley of Fernandes's book, and the page numbering in the final version may be slightly different.

316. *capital at Kohima:* Shimray, *Let Freedom Ring*, 72–73.

316. *thousands or more:* There is tremendous debate regarding the size of the Naga population. The Nagas themselves typically claim a total population of nearly four million, with two million in Nagaland, a million in other Indian states, and a million in Burma. But the Indian government has said that there are only 1.2 million Nagas in India, and another one hundred thousand or so across the border in Burma. The truth, as is so often the case, is probably somewhere in the middle.

317. *torture and rape:* Institute for Conflict Management (Delhi), "National Socialist Council of Nagaland: Isak-Muivah," http://www.satp.org/satporgtp/countries/india/states/nagaland /terrorist_outfits/nscn_im.htm.

317. *"liberation movement":* Shimray, *Let Freedom Ring,* 161.

317. *"a tax to live":* Author's visit.

317. *a Christian minister:* Interview with Grace Collins, honorary ambassador of Nagalim, May 2006.

317. *compulsory treatment:* Charles Hack interview, Oct. 2006.

317. *"headhunters to soulhunters":* Grace Collins interview.

317. *decapitations in 1980:* Shimray, *Let Freedom Ring,* 159.

317. *for an earlier raid:* Janie Saul, *The Naga of Burma: Their Festivals, Customs and Way of Life* (Bangkok: Orchid Press, 2005), 188.

318. *influence in the Patkais:* Author's visit.

318. *kidnapping and extortion:* "15 dead as Myanmar cracks down on Indian rebels," *Times of India,* Jan. 29, 2007; author's visit.

318. *bombings and assassinations:* Institute for Conflict Management (Delhi), "United Liberation Front of Asom (ULFA): Terrorist Group of Assam," http://www.satp.org/satporgtp/ countries/india/states/assam/terrorist_outfits/ulfa.htm; author's visit.

318. *down in Nagaland:* Author's visit; Jamie Saul interview, Feb. 2006.

318. *Buddhism at gunpoint:* Naga International Support Center, "Naga History: Chronology of Events from NISC," Dec. 24, 2002, http://www.manipuronline.com/Manipur/December2002/ nagachronology2002.htm.

318. *slaves to the pipe:* Raul Goswami, "Opium in the Naga Hills," *The Atlantic Monthly,* Sept. 1, 1999; Jamie Saul interview.

318. *rolls of chicken wire:* Author's visit.

318–19. *"These graves . . . FOREVER MORE":* Ibid.

319. *the name's provenance:* Ibid.

319. *beneath a tree:* "Aaron Perry Held in Beating of Man, 65, On Northeast Corner," *The Washington Evening Star,* Aug. 23, 1953. It is unclear whether Aaron was passed out drunk, or suffering the effects of postconcussion syndrome related to his boxing career. Though his friends claimed the latter, the former explanation seems more plausible.

319. *Camp McClellan:* *The Washington Evening Star,* June 25, 1945.

319. *Billy Furrone:* BoxRec.com record for Aaron Perry, http://www.boxrec.com/boxer_display .php?boxer_id=009630.

319. *D.C.'s nightspots:* Edna Wilson interview, Sept. 2006.

320. *just a month before:* BoxRec.com record for Aaron Perry. Dubbed the Earl of Richmond after his hometown of Richmond, Calif., Turner was the top draw at the Oakland Auditorium during the early 1940s. But like a lot of boxers, he stayed in the fight game far too long; he didn't retire until 1954, after suffering nine consecutive defeats. Turner had an official career record of 54 wins, 37 losses, and 11 draws.

320. *Gales Street NE:* "Suit Asks Sale of Perry's Home," *The Washington Evening Star,* Aug. 6, 1951; Sales records for 1635 Gales Street NE, Washingtoniana Division, Martin Luther King Jr. Memorial Library, Washington, D.C.

320. *home-invasion robbery:* "Aaron Perry Bound Over on 2 Charges," *The Washington Post,* July 11, 1950.

320. *club off U Street:* "D.C. Boxer Perry Again Under Arrest," *The Washington Post,* Sept. 8, 1950. Roscoe Perry also had trouble with the law during this time period: in July 1949, he was sentenced to a prison term of between fifteen and forty-five months for his role in stealing $3,000 from a Giant Food Store.

320. *sustained while boxing:* "Boxer Perry Found Insane; Escapes Trial," *The Washington Post,* Oct. 24, 1950.

320. *eight months later:* "Cabbie Kicked, Ex-Pug Perry Lands in Jail," *The Washington Post,* Aug. 23, 1953. St. Elizabeth's had been the employer of Dr. John E. Lind, whom the cuckolded Robert I. Miller killed in 1944.

320. *assault, not homicide:* Ibid.; "Perry Guilty of Assault in Cabbie Death," *The Washington Post and Times Herald,* May 20, 1954.

321. *twenty-four-year sentence:* "Aaron Perry Jailed, Kin Held in Rape," *The Washington Post,* Apr. 13, 1957; "Boxer Perry Guilty of Rape," *The Washington Evening Star,* Mar. 23, 1957.

321. *Alcoholics Anonymous:* "Aaron Perry, Boxer, Ex-Treasury Engineer," *The Washington Star,* Dec. 30, 1980.

321. *he died of cancer:* Ibid. One of Aaron's three sons, Art Perry, gained some renown as a college basketball coach. In 1997, after one year spent coaching Delaware State to a 7-20 record, Art was hired by American University, which he had attended in the early 1970s. He was fired three years later, offering a refreshingly candid assessment of his failings to *The Washington Post:* "Obviously, I didn't win enough games."

321. *into Herman's case:* Celestine Perry Thompson interview, Mar. 2006.

321. *smelled a conspiracy:* "Johnson, Henry E." (Obituary) *The Times Union,* Nov. 28, 2003. In the late 1940s, Johnson briefly followed Aaron and Roscoe into boxing, at least on the amateur level. He fought in the prestigious Golden Gloves competition under the name Cubby Perry. Later, as an undergraduate at New York University, he excelled as a sprinter on the track team.

321. *over Herman's death:* Social Security Death Index for Flonnie B. Johnson, http://ssdi .rootsweb.com/.

321. *veterans of the Ledo Road:* Celestine Perry Thompson interview; Mahon East interview, Jun. 2006.

321. *hazy or inconsistent:* Mahon East interview. East recalled being contacted by one of Herman Perry's relatives—obviously Johnson—in the 1980s. East told Johnson that he remembered the shooting being caused by Cady physically kicking Perry "in the behind." He also thought that Perry had been sent back to the U.S. for punishment, rather than executed in Ledo.

321. *regale their grandkids:* As an example, the grandson of Orville Strassburg, one of the MPs who captured Perry in July 1944, asked to sit in on my interview of his grandfather. A history teacher outside Buffalo, he had never heard of Herman Perry prior to my con- tacting Strassburg.

322. *law firm in Ohio:* John C. Oberholtzer interview, May 2006.

322. *adventure with the world:* Earl Owen Cullum, "Dear Grand-Dad, What Did You Do in World War Two?" July 1992, 15, private collection of Kathryn Cullum Lee. This is a small, stapled booklet that Cullum created for his grandchildren.

322. *Bureau of Investigation:* Letter from Earl Owen Cullum to his children and grandchil- dren, Aug. 8, 1988, private collection of Kathryn Cullum Lee.

322. *J. Edgar Hoover:* Ibid.

322. *Watergate burglary:* Ibid.

323. *Texas at Arlington:* Ibid.

324. *Wraith of the Hills:* Earl Owen Cullum, "Wraith of the Hills: The Herman Perry Story," *CBIVA Sound-Off,* Spring 2000, 30.

324. *International News Service:* "Edward Hymoff Dies; Media Executive, 67," *The New York Times,* July 11, 1992.

324. *manager for NBC:* "Edward Hymoff, Was NBC Editor, Author and Policy Consultant, 68," *The Boston Globe,* July 11, 1992.

324. *Hollywood starlet:* Edward Hymoff, "The Army's Most Incredible Deserter," *Real: The Exciting Magazine,* Mar. 1956, 10–11. Other articles in this issue include "They Cut a Hole in My Heart," "Tragedy of a Boxing Champ: A Million Punches Drove Him Mad," and "The $64,000 Question for Commuters: Are Women Too Sexy for the Suburbs?"

324. *"renegade killer":* Edward Hymoff, "The Army Deserter Who Became King of the Jun- gle," *Impact: Magazine for Men,* May 1964, 19.

324. *in the 1950s:* Russ Parsons's eulogy for Henry "Hank" Burns Jr., Apr. 18, 2004, http://www .west-point.org/users/usma1955/20228/USMA/R/xBurns_H.htm. This online eulogy was in response to a request from Burns's son, Joseph Stillwell Burns, regarding the reasons for his father's departure from West Point.

325. *was never published:* E-mail from Joseph Stillwell Burns, Mar. 2006; Earl Owen Cullum, *Manhunt in Burma and Assam* (Dallas: Self-published, 1993), 2. I attempted to contact Burns's widow to obtain a copy of "Death on the Ledo Road," but she did not respond to my inquiries.

325. *"a 'softie' himself":* Cullum, *Manhunt in Burma and Assam*, 34.

325. *years after the fact:* William Boyd Sinclair, *Confusion Beyond Imagination: Book Six* (Coeur d'Alene, Idaho: Joe F. Whitley, 1989), 62.

325–26. *Dear Henry . . . Sincerely, Earl O. Cullum:* Letter from Earl Owen Cullum to Rev. Henry E. Johnson, July 13, 1994, private collection of Edna Wilson.

327. *"don't make it so":* Henry E. Johnson's copy of *Manhunt in Burma and Assam* (1993 ed.), private collection of Edna Wilson. This is a Xeroxed copy that Johnson sent to Wilson in 1994, along with a handwritten cover letter. A postscript to that letter asks, "Was Herman's girl name[d] ALMA?"

327. *passing away in 2003:* "Johnson, Henry E." (Obituary), *The Times Union*.

327. *the eastern seaboard:* I spoke with three of Johnson's children, who were well aware of their late father's longtime interest in Herman's case. The eldest of the trio claimed to have received several relevant documents during her father's convalescence; I was not given access to these documents. Judging from Johnson's notes in the margins of *Manhunt in Burma and Assam*, however, it does not appear that he had acquired anything beyond the court-martial transcript and standard Army communications related to the manhunt. He indicated, for example, that he never obtained Herman's sworn statements, nor any of the Ledo Stockade records detailing Herman's death row escape.

327. *cancer in 1994:* Kathryn Cullum Lee interview, Apr. 2006.

327. *serious auto accident:* Earl Owen Cullum, *Favorite Memories of a Bygone Century*, Mar. 23, 2000, private collection of Kathryn Cullum Lee.

328. *"the Exotic East":* Earl Owen Cullum, *Outstanding Arrests*, 1999 private collection of Kathryn Cullum Lee. This tract is addressed to Cullum's children and grandchildren, with a note that a copy is on file with the Dallas County Pioneer Association, a society "dedicated to preserving the history of Dallas County and those pioneers who settled the County before the year of 1880." As Cullum was fond of pointing out, his great-grandfather, Rev. Marcus Hiram Cullum, founded Dallas's Oak Lawn United Methodist Church in 1874.

328. *Celestine Perry Thompson:* Earl Owen Cullum, *The Herman Perry Case: 55 Years Later*, 2001, private collection of Kathryn Cullum Lee. This two-page tract is actually undated, but Cullum gives his age as eighty-eight, an indication that it was written several months after his November 2000 meeting with Thompson.

328. *authority on the case:* Ibid.

328. *about since childhood:* Ibid.; Kathryn Cullum Lee interview.

328. *to the Ledo Stockade:* Cullum, *The Herman Perry Case: 55 Years Later*.

329. *withered cheeks:* Celestine Perry Thompson interview.

329. *"[Herman's] life and death":* Cullum, *The Herman Perry Case: 55 Years Later*.

329. *smiles all around:* Photograph of Nov. 2000 meeting between Earl Owen Cullum and Celestine Perry Thompson, private collection of Celestine Perry Thompson.

329. *offer of forgiveness:* Celestine Perry Thompson interview.

329. *with marked pride:* Edna Wilson interview.

329. *executed soldiers:* Edna Wilson interview.

329. *sign of contempt:* Will Hoover, "Mysterious Schofield Plot Filled with Untold Stories," *The Honolulu Advertiser*, Apr. 22, 2002.

330. *nine-pound rock:* Ibid.

330. *in such company:* Edna Wilson interview.

330. *eventually, herself:* Kirk Wilson interview, Oct. 2007. Kirk graciously provided photographs of the disinterment process.

330. *and four grandchildren:* Edna Wilson interview.

330. *half-Naga son:* Author's visit.

331. *a knowing laugh:* Ibid.

INDEX

ABOUT THE AUTHOR

A contributing editor at *Wired* whose work appears regularly in *The New York Times* and *Slate,* Brendan I. Koerner was named one of *Columbia Journalism Review*'s Ten Young Writers on the Rise. Visit him at www.youthrobber.com.